W9-CBS-095

WOMEN IN THE UNITED STATES, 1830–1945

Women in the United States, 1830–1945

S. J. Kleinberg

Rutgers University Press
New Brunswick, New Jersey

First published in the United States 1999 by
RUTGERS UNIVERSITY PRESS
New Brunswick, New Jersey

First published in Great Britain 1999 by
MACMILLAN PRESS LTD
Houndmills, Basingstoke, Hampshire RG21 6XS
and London

This book is printed on paper suitable for recycling and
made from fully managed and sustained forest sources.

Library of Congress Cataloging-in-Publication Data
Kleinberg, S. J.
Women in the United States, 1830–1945 / S.J. Kleinberg.
p.   cm.
Includes bibliographical references.
ISBN 0–8135–2728–7 (cloth : alk. paper). — ISBN 0–8135–2729–5
(pbk. : alk. paper)
1. Women—United States—History—19th century.   2. Women—United
States—History—20th century.   I. Title.
HQ1418.K64   1999
305.4'0973—dc21   99–24885
                                                    CIP

Printed in Hong Kong

To Frances and Morris Kleinberg
with love

Table of Contents

List of Tables   x
Acknowledgements   xi

Introduction   1

Part I   Ante-Bellum America

1   Economic Activity in Ante-Bellum America   11
        Subsistence agriculture   12
        Urban and rural crafts and trades   15
        Commercial agriculture   19
        Slavery   21
        Industrialization   26
        Labor unrest   28

2   Family and Migration in the Era of Domesticity   34
        Demographic changes   35
        Domesticity defined   37
        Exceptions to domesticity as the dominant paradigm   41
        Race and domesticity   43
        Native American women   49
        The westward migration   51
        Domesticity in the West   54

3   Education and Culture in Ante-Bellum America   58
        The expansion of education   59
        Race, region, and education   65
        Higher education   67
        Women's art and writing   69
        The uses of literacy   70
        Slave narratives and African-American women's writing   75
        Literary protests over industrialization   77

4   Religion, Reform, and Politics in the Ante-Bellum Era   80
        The Second Great Awakening and women's activism   81
        Women in utopian communities   85
        Cultural and legal protest   87
        Women and abolitionism   88
        Women and politics   92
        Women in the Civil War   97

Part II   The Industrial Era

5   Women's Employment, 1865–1920   105
        The location of women's work   106
        Age, marital status, race, and employment   107
        The changing nature of women's employment   111
        Manual labor   114
        World War I and women's employment   118
        Labor unions and labor reform   119

6   Family, Migration, and Social Values in the Industrial Era   128
        The gendering of immigration   129
        Migration   133
        The family in the industrial era   139
        Motherhood and housekeeping   146

7   Education and Culture, 1865–1920   152
        Education   152
        Higher education and the professions   156
        Women as club members   162
        Women's cultural contributions   166
        Popular and high culture   170

8   Women and Reform in the Gilded Age and Progressive Era   176
        Temperance activism   178
        Rural women's activism   181
        Urban women's activism   184
        Progressive reform and the settlement house movement   188
        Civic rights   191

Part III From the Vote to World War II

9 Economic Activity during Boom, Bust, and War ... 207
  The differential labor market ... 207
  Female occupations in the 1920s and 1930s ... 209
  Racial and ethnic employment ... 212
  Labor unions and women ... 214
  The Great Depression ... 217
  Women and New Deal work programs ... 220
  The armed forces ... 226
  Women in the wartime labor force ... 228

10 Family and Migration, 1920–1945 ... 233
  The family in the inter-war years ... 234
  Housewifery, domestic technology, and domestic advice ... 237
  Changing gender roles in the 1920s and 1930s ... 242
  Migration in boom, bust, and wartime ... 244
  Married women's roles during the Depression ... 246
  Gender and assistance ... 248
  Families during World War II ... 250

11 Education and Culture, 1920–1945 ... 257
  Education ... 257
  Women's writing ... 263
  Fine arts ... 268
  Drama, music, and sports ... 268
  Radio ... 274
  Cinema ... 276

12 Reform and Politics, 1920–1945 ... 282
  The nature of women's political participation ... 283
  Gendered citizenship ... 287
  National Woman's Party and the Equal Rights
    Amendment ... 289
  Government reforms and the status of women ... 291
  Women, politics, and reform during the New Deal ... 296
  Women's war and its aftermath ... 304

Epilogue – The Feminine Mystique ... 309

Bibliography ... 317
Index ... 353

Tables

1.1	The occupations of free women, 1850	16
5.1	Proportion of women in the labor force, 1870–1920	105
5.2	Women's employment by age, 1890–1920	108
5.3	Percentage of women of each marital status in the labor force, 1890–1920	109
5.4	Racial groups in the labor force, 1900–1930	110
5.5	Percentage of women from each age and racial/nativity group in the labor force, 1900 and 1920	111
5.6	Women's non-agricultural employment, 1870–1920	112
9.1	Gainfully employed women by race, nativity, and marital status for women aged 15 and over	208
9.2	Occupational distribution of women workers, 1920–1940	211
9.3	Women's employment by race and occupation, 1930	213

Acknowledgements

One of the nicest aspects of writing a book is thanking the people who have helped one along the way. My first thanks are to Tony Badger who suggested this as a project and whose careful comments have guided the revisions. Members of the American Studies community in Britain have been encouraging and supportive. I am very grateful to Vivien Hart for her critique of an earlier draft of the manuscript. The annual conference of the British Association for American Studies has been a source of scholarly interchange and ideas and the opportunity to present papers has been most welcome.

My deepest intellectual debts in this project are to Anne Firor Scott and Gerda Lerner. These doyennes of women's history have established the highest standards of scholarship as they expanded historians' efforts to write women back into the past. Their researches have given historians an inclusive model for writing history, by race, class, gender, and region, and their books and articles have inspired a generation of women's historians.

Brunel University has supported this project in many ways, not least through reduced teaching loads and added research assistance. I have been especially fortunate to have the help of researchers Charlotte Keeble, Cheryl Hudson, and Dave Ryden, who always responded with alacrity to my requests to find yet another article or book. Cheryl helped cut the original manuscript down to size through ruthless suggestions about what to delete. Charlotte made valuable suggestions on the final draft. Dave's help with the index, bibliography, and internet is much appreciated. The office staff in the Department of American Studies and History at Brunel have been invaluable friends and allies over the years. My thanks to Janet MacPhail and Margaret Lester, whose unfailing good humor and common sense have sustained this project throughout the years.

Paul Jay has provided computer assistance through a series of technological disasters as one piece of hardware after another crashed around my desk. His ability to kickstart computers and transfer files kept this project going at times when a quill pen would have been a technological innovation.

No one writes a book without the aid – or at least the forbearance – of family and friends. My husband Nic Flemming has read drafts, given tactful advice, and kept the home fires burning throughout this undertaking as with all others. Kinnie and Peter have turned down all my offers to let them read a chapter, but have otherwise treated my long spells at my desk with remarkable tolerance. The neighbors at Sheets Heath have provided the most supportive community imaginable. They have pitched in and helped out through the various crises that seem to punctuate our lives.

My last thanks are to my parents, Frances and Morris Kleinberg, to whom this book is dedicated. They lived through some of the changes described here and illuminated the past through their own stories. My mother's queries about when the book was finally going to appear have kept me about my task. My thanks and gratitude are as immeasurable as the support I have received.

Introduction

The omission of women from most histories written before the 1970s denied women their past and presented a partial account of the forces which shaped American history. In *The Creation of Feminist Consciousness* Gerda Lerner observes that one can trace the study of women to "a significant and almost constant effort on the part of women to create Women's History from the 7th century AD forward." As Lerner notes, by the time people started to write history (a self-conscious record of the past), women were already significantly educationally disadvantaged. They were partners in making civilization, but very few were able to record or reflect upon it, and the chronicles of the past largely ignored women's contributions.

A few scholarly histories of women in the United States appeared in the early twentieth century, with pioneering works concentrating mostly on political activism and women's struggle against second-class citizenship. (See the Bibliography for full details.) In the 1960s and 1970s, the women's liberation movement and social history's inclusive, rather than elitist, approach to the past encouraged historians to question women's absence from the historical record. Initially concerned with female activism and political movements, the focus quickly expanded to the gendered dynamics of family, work, and welfare policy.

Women's history has gone from looking at the lives of notable women and their contributions to momentous events to an investigation of women's struggle for political, economic, and social rights, the complexities of their daily lives and life cycles, and the underlying experiences which encouraged female activism. Some recent historians have viewed women's history as a series of dichotomies which oppose family and work, private and public spheres, and women as equals or as having special characteristics. Such binary oppositions oversimplify women's existence since their lives partake of a range of attributes and carefully balanced choices rather than being confined to one extreme or the other. Other

1

histories analyze how women and society unravel the tensions between conflicting female roles and interpretations of appropriate behavior. Each generation of women resolves the conflicts in its own fashion, with social, economic, political, and cultural participation ebbing and flowing rather than progressing along a single path to some predestined goal.

Inserting women back into the historical record at every level in society changes our understanding of women's lives and our concept of the past by showing that women were active participants in most, if not all, events and processes. They had central roles in key historical events and transitions, including the industrial revolution, the temperance and anti-slavery movements, and the shaping of social welfare policy, to give but a few examples, rather than being bystanders on the sidelines of history. This book integrates women's economic, social, cultural, and political experiences by writing gender into American history, focusing on the industrial era when female roles changed and women collectively began to express and act publicly upon their beliefs.

Women's roles have been a source of controversy throughout civilization with a great deal of political, social, religious, and moral thought devoted to the place of women in society. Although important at the time, such debates and disagreements have frequently been overlooked by subsequent generations, while women's daily experiences come down to us through diaries preserved by chance, records kept about rather than by women (the US Census is an example of this type of documentation), or through organizational papers found in the backs of cupboards or library storerooms. Thankfully, libraries and archives now collect women's papers and organizational records so that the basic materials of the female past are preserved for posterity.

Even though they had to struggle to be heard or listened to, women took a vigorous part in political debates over slavery, suffrage, employment conditions, child labor, social welfare, temperance, education, the Civil War, the world wars, indeed, in virtually all aspects of American life. Their organized opinions and needs had an especially strong influence on welfare policy, albeit full citizenship rights came very slowly. Many contemporary historians have used female activism as the organizing framework for studying women's lives, although this tends to cast ordinary women into the shade of their more involved contemporaries, which is why it is so important to scrutinize the lives of women from different racial, ethnic, economic, and religious perspectives.

Historians frequently use wars and other dramatic events as demarcators in historical periodization. Whether such incidents affected women in the same way as men prompted Joan Kelly to ask whether the Renaissance was also a Renaissance for women? How differently do women and men perceive such forces and do they have the same impact upon both sexes? War is a case in point with historians commonly using military conflicts as dividing points in their studies of the past and focusing on the battlefields and international diplomacy. Yet, it is also possible to maintain that wars foment a crisis in gender relations by withdrawing men from the economy and the family and then to analyze how society puts itself back together. Linda Kerber's analysis of the American Revolution and the manipulation of republican motherhood in the late eighteenth century illuminates the influence of political perceptions on gender roles. LeeAnn Whites' study of the Civil War and Reconstruction in Augusta, Georgia, reveals how white southerners relied upon gender to prop up a society seemingly broken by war and to ensure the continuance of racial and sexual hierarchies.

The Civil War not only marked the conflict between North and South, but the events leading up to it and its consequences were also crucial to the redefinition of women's political roles and relations with the state. Women in the North had been directly involved in the issues which led to the Civil War, especially the anti-slavery crusade, but did not receive the vote or equal citizenship as a result. The Civil War encouraged female employment, as women supported families when male relations were fighting, died on the battlefield, or returned home disabled. Emancipation enabled some African-American women to withdraw their labor from the fields but their employment levels were far higher than whites'. The Civil War also made widows' employment a particular issue, and, by creating younger widows, increased their likelihood of working outside the home.

World War I, a shorter engagement with fewer casualties for the United States, had relatively little impact on American women. It facilitated public recognition of women as government employees, nurses, and streetcar conductors, but did not cause the same upheaval as in Europe. Winning the vote rather than the war had a lasting impact on women's lives, making 1920 the key dividing point for women in the early twentieth century. While Nancy Cott correctly points to the continuities in women's organizations before and after the vote, in "Across the Great Divide: Women in Politics Before and After 1920," it is also the case that women lost much of the organizing framework for political participation when they gained the vote. The chapters in this book on politics and reform examine women's efforts to speak out publicly on issues which concerned them, their struggle to obtain rights as citizens, and what happened to organized womanhood once women's suffrage had been written into the Constitution.

The significance of the Nineteenth Amendment granting women's suffrage was hotly debated at the time and continues to shape the study of women, although the vote affected some groups more than others. It took another four decades before African-American women in the South could vote in any numbers, and some western states barred Native Americans from voting until the 1940s. The consumer boom of the 1920s and the Great Depression of the 1930s demonstrate the ways in which economic, social, cultural and political events affected women's lives, but whether World War II was a turning point in American women's history, as William Chafe maintains, and led to the second feminist movement is a matter of debate and will be explored at the end of this book.

Women in the United States, 1830–1945 is intended as a general introduction to the history of women in industrializing America. It is both a history of women and a history of the United States and adheres to a chronology shaped by economic stages and political events, dividing the time span into three periods: 1830–1865, 1865–1920, and 1920–1945. These cover the years through the Civil War as the United States shifted from subsistence to commercial agriculture and industrialization; the period from the Civil War to 1920, when the United States became an urban, industrial nation, and the shorter span from 1920 to 1945 when white-collar work and mass entertainment became more important, especially to women. Throughout these transformations, gender – the roles imputed to the sexes – continued to define women's (and men's) lives. The parameters changed over time, but socially acceptable behavior still differed greatly for women and men. Indeed the post-World War II period actually witnessed a retrenchment in women's public roles as domesticity molded female activities to a greater extent than it had in the previous generation.

Viewing history from the standpoint of what matters to women means that much of the conventional history (the so-called Presidential synthesis) is taken for granted and omitted. The strategies behind various Civil War battles, the issues on which many elections were fought, or the controversies over the Bank of the United States form the staple of many history texts, but have little salience in this one. Many history books are concerned with which man got elected President and what happened during his administration. Where women are included (as they are increasingly), they are slotted into the existing chronology and framework or become a chapter in a history which mentions them occasionally.

Here the underlying concern is the female component of the grand forces shaping American life: the commercialization of agriculture, urbanization, industrialization, the demographic transition, immigration, slavery, and the westward movement. This book focuses on the part women played in the intersecting patterns of economics, social structure, religion, education, family life, politics, and reform movements; the organizations they constructed in the work place, church, and polity; their integration and their separation from economic, social, cultural, and political movements; and the enduring importance of gender in women's activities. It plots women's search for economic, social, and political equity and their responses to those grand forces in their novels, poems, diaries, magazines, songs, crafts, and popular culture.

In keeping with the diversity of women's lives, each part of the book has four chapters examining work, family, education and culture, and politics and reform, the main threads women wove together to form the fabric of their lives. Examining these constituents in their historical context illuminates the ways in which women's lives changed over time and how the grand forces interacted with the social construction of sex roles to define and alter women's position and opportunities. Women contributed to almost all literary movements, cultural activities, economic, social, and political issues of their day. While they did not make military strategy, have a say in the decision to go to war, or set public budgets in the years under examination here, they were involved in public and private events, even though their level of participation varied over time.

One of the issues facing historians of women is the complexity of factors molding women's lives. Race, ethnicity, class, and region interacted with gender to differentiate between groups of women. In a general work such as this one, complex patterns cannot always be fully explored, but I have tried to show how the forces considered here affected different groups of women. Some paradigms which have been accepted as basic in women's history, for example the cult of true womanhood propounded by Barbara Welter in 1966, applied only to a specific portion of American womanhood, in this case the white middle class. True womanhood had little salience to, among others, Native Americans, slaves, poor women, recent immigrants or rural dwellers. The history of these communities needs to be woven into a tapestry in which diversity enriches our understanding of the past, and explanatory models need to incorporate their experiences.

In many respects women's lives at the end of World War II bore little resemblance to those at the start of the industrial revolution. In 1830, most women's labor went unremunerated; by 1945, working for wages was commonplace, though still more prevalent among younger and poorer women and women of color than middle-class whites. The very definition of work had changed and with it the form and substance of women's place in the family economy. The chapters on economic activity explore the changing nature of those contributions, the shift to employment outside the home, the overwhelming impact of race, ethnicity, and marital status on the kind of work undertaken by women, and the strains between female domestic and economic activities. The chapters on family and migration treat this story from a household perspective, looking at demographic transitions including declining birth rates and migration, different concepts of women's work within the home, and attempts to reconcile the world of the household with other interests.

Few women had more than a smattering of education in the early nineteenth century and many had none, although educational standards began to rise, especially in the North. By the middle of the twentieth century, high school was the norm and college had become common, but again there were variations by race and class. Women's own sense of the importance and utility of education and the difficulties they encountered in obtaining schooling on the same basis as men are explored in the chapters on education and culture. The uphill fight to acquire professional education and to carve out careers in "male" fields continued for two centuries. Yet the importance of even basic literacy should not be underestimated. Literacy enabled women to communicate across great distances, to carry on political struggles, and to move into white-collar jobs with an aura of respectability which made them acceptable to the middle class. Many women chose literary or artistic careers despite the prejudices they frequently encountered; they were more successful as authors and actors than as directors or conductors.

Each of the chapters on politics and reform considers the context of female political and social activism and how women organized to express themselves on key issues. Efforts to achieve equality before the law followed on from other reform endeavors; for example the anti-slavery crusade made women much more aware of their own civic limitations. As the United States turned into a commercially based, industrial society in which all white men had the vote, the anomalous limitations on female property rights and political participation became apparent, at least to some women. Women's extra-household activities had been primarily limited to church in the early national period, but by the early twentieth century encompassed a rich variety of voluntary organizations such as the Red Cross, League of Women Voters, women's clubs, Young Women's Christian and Hebrew Associations, and many more. The struggles for the vote and full citizenship took on a life of their own in the late nineteenth and early twentieth centuries, while the full integration of women into political structures proceeded very slowly. Gender inflected everything women did in 1945 as well as in 1830, and debates raged continuously over their appropriate place in society.

Racism interacted with sexism to warp the lives of women of color. Particularly in the South, African Americans were second-class citizens, poorly served by government and prevented from participating in public life through intimidation. Native Americans endured the loss of their land and relegation to economically marginal areas. Mexican-, Chinese-, and Japanese-American women also encountered prejudices which limited the jobs they could get, their ability to vote, and own land. Race restricted access to better jobs, education, and public welfare, so that women of color were kept on the periphery of American society. Racial and gender politics inflected some of the most significant laws passed during the New Deal, for example the Social Security Act which shaped the federal government's role in welfare for generations, to the detriment of women, especially those clustered in domestic service and agriculture who were, not coincidentally, disproportionately from racial-ethnic minorities.

Each section of the book begins with an analysis of women's economic activities, whether through employment or unpaid labor, but it would be an oversimplification to assume that economic activities existed in isolation from other key variables such as race, religion, ethnicity, demographic status, and, above all, the social constructions of appropriate behavior for the sexes. This book demonstrates the extent to which gender has been and remains one of the dominant influences in American life and culture. Whatever the experience, be it slavery, immigration, the westward movement, Populism, industrialization, Progressivism, or the Great Depression, to select a few key phenomena, women shared it and shaped it, but from a perspective infused with cultural beliefs about appropriate female roles. These expectations changed over time and varied for different groups, but influenced all women's lives and activities even as women, acting upon their own concepts of gender roles, strongly shaped the society in which they lived.

PART I
Ante-Bellum America

1 Economic Activity in Ante-Bellum America

In 1830, the United States was a nation in transition, evolving into an urban, industrial society at an uneven pace. Agriculture dominated the economy, but subsistence and commercial farming coexisted with artisan and industrial manufacturing. While most people resided in rural areas, towns increased in size, and the population grew more diverse. Coupled with limitations on women's legal status, these economic and demographic transformations altered women's and men's understandings of work and of their place within the family and community. Economic development encouraged political and social reform movements which questioned gender roles and raised fundamental issues about slavery, religion, and the relationship of the individual to society. Yet women in the United States were a diverse group whose experiences were as much separated by particularities of race, class, ethnicity, and region as they were united by commonalities of gender, so this consideration of women in the ante-bellum era examines their divergent experiences within the framework of the economic changes which transformed life in the United States.

Between 1830 and 1865, gendered patterns of economic activity established the conditions in which a cult of domesticity flourished, especially for urban white middle-class women. The industrial revolution separated home and work place, making it more difficult for women to blend economic productivity with domestic responsibilities. By mid-century, affluent married women had resolved the difficulties of homemaking and income production in favor of domesticity, while poorer women combined the two through part-time labor and homework. The cult of domesticity justified this transition by ennobling motherhood and home management while relocating "work" to the public sphere. Most men and some single women worked in jobs outside the home, leading to sharp discontinuities between the sexes and women of different marital status. General trends dispersed unevenly across the regions, races, and ethnic

11

groups so that diversity characterized women's economic activities in ante-bellum America: European-American married women's duties narrowed to domestic commitments and emotional responsibility for the family, while Native and African-American women continued to be engaged in subsistence and commercial agriculture.

SUBSISTENCE AGRICULTURE

Women and men typically undertook separate tasks in subsistence economies, with varying amounts of overlap and interchange. The diverse cultures from which the United States derives allocated distinctive responsibilities to the sexes. Anthropologists credit Native American women with the domestication of corn about 5000 years ago in Mexico. From the Zuni of present-day New Mexico to the Iroquois of New York women grew the crops while men hunted and defended their territory. Yet the gender distinctions were not hard and fast; the sexes cooperated to clear land for planting, and some women participated in hunting, especially when the cornfields did not need intensive care.

About two-thirds of the more than 500 Native American tribes had matrilineal inheritance and descent patterns. They lived in matrilocal groups, where couples resided with the wife's family after marriage. Women in these tribes had charge of agriculture and derived status from their role in food production. Women controlled the seeds, the planting, harvesting, and food processing. They erected structures to protect the accumulated foodstuffs and made clay jars and reed baskets for storage.

The creation stories of many Native American groups acknowledged women's agricultural primacy. A woman, sometimes a grandmother like the Seminole's Corn Woman, brought corn, squash, and beans to her people. The Osage Indians, originally settled along the Mississippi, and later removed to Oklahoma, planted their corn in April, under the woman's or Planting Moon. According to the Acoma Indians, Tsichtinako (Thought Woman) taught two sisters to plant, pick, grind, and cook corn. These creation stories invest women's agricultural role with a sacred function and supernatural authority, confirming women's economic and political significance.

The Pueblo Indians of the arid Southwest associated corn with women and water (rain) with men, stressing the interdependence of the sexes. Grinding the corn in hollowed-out logs and stone metates (milling stones) women of the Apaches of the Southwest, Cherokee of the southern Appalachians, and Seminoles of Florida, prepared it for cooking. Control of the food supply gave women influence over the timing of male hunting, war, and peacemaking in addition to an advisory role in some tribal governments.

European conquest destroyed the economic foundations of Native American nations and by the 1830s, Native Americans along the eastern seaboard had been moved aside or decimated by diseases brought by Europeans. They tried to retain their farming practices despite incursions by European settlers who neither understood nor respected female-dominated agricultural systems. The federal government promised the Cherokees could keep their lands if they embraced European-style agriculture, but although the tribe agreed they were still forced along the Trail of Tears in 1838 to make way for land-hungry white settlers.

European Americans and Native Americans had divergent land ownership and agricultural patterns. European immigrants privileged male contributions, vesting land and property ownership in men and restricting married women's property rights. Should women own or inherit property, title passed automatically to their husbands. Even though white women made important labor contributions to the self-sufficient agricultural economy, the use of heavy implements and agricultural machinery devalued their labor as the nineteenth century progressed. Men farmed the staple crops, providing grain and fuel, while women processed the products and tended gardens and smaller animals.

In the early years of the nineteenth century, older traditions of communal labor still characterized much of the work undertaken by European-American women. They gathered nuts and berries, processed wool, husked corn, and quilted with groups of neighbors, exchanging their work with female family members, hired women, or neighbors. They shared tasks with men more rarely, helping to get the hay in or slaughter animals. Men worked with neighbors and hired help, monetizing their labor exchanges through the use of seasonal agricultural laborers at harvest time.

Gendered work patterns notwithstanding, farm women contributed significantly to the subsistence and near-market family economies of the early republic. In the transition period from subsistence to commercial agriculture and cottage to industrial production, economic activity remained centered in the home. Women supplied much of the food and clothing and brought in a cash income by marketing their butter, eggs, and cheese. Before the transportation revolution, women sold a wide range of processed agricultural products in nearby towns, even when it was difficult for men to haul their bulky agricultural commodities far, particularly in bad weather. "Butter belts" developed around large cities in the mid-Atlantic region in which women churned and sold millions of pounds of dairy products. Joan Jensen's study of the highly skilled butter makers of New York, Pennsylvania, New Jersey, and Maryland discovered they produced about $15 million in sales in 1840, making butter a lucrative cash crop for small and medium-sized farmers.

Women from diverse backgrounds, classes and races had a notable presence in the fluid market economies of many cities through the 1830s and 1840s. Enslaved African-American women carried on African traditions by growing vegetables, weaving baskets, and raising chickens. They used this food to supplement the meager rations provided by slave owners, also selling it in cities such as Savannah, where free and enslaved black women dominated the public market. Many white women also sold produce in the markets of northern and southern cities.

In the early national period women of all ages engaged in economically productive work. Young women served as apprentices to their mothers or other adult women, learning dairying, how to plant, weed, and harvest vegetables, care for chickens, spin, weave, and sew. Older women taught them to churn milk into butter and turn the curds into cheese. Together they processed the crops by salting, smoking, and drying meat and vegetables to sustain their families through the short, cold days and long nights of North American winters.

The women who devoted themselves to dairying had little time for other household activities, and they furnished employment to the young women of other households as dairymaids or general household helps. These busy women used the cash from their butter sales to buy the products of the nascent cloth manufacturing industry, proving a ready market for the linen and woolen cloth woven in small workshops and, by the 1830s, in large factories. Their growing reliance on manufactured commodities foreshadowed the shift from production to consumption which characterized American women's economic activities in the nineteenth century.

URBAN AND RURAL CRAFTS AND TRADES

Mercantile capitalism expanded rapidly in New England and the Mid-Atlantic region after 1800, frequently depending upon female labor. Merchants distributed raw materials for outworkers to process or make up in their own homes, relying upon a network of married women, unmarried daughters, and widows who combined subsistence agriculture and domestic responsibilities with cottage craft production. These women knitted stockings, gloves, and mittens; carded wool, flax, and cotton; spun these fibers and wove them into cloth; plaited straw into bonnets; made palm leaf hats; hand stitched shoe uppers; and sewed all manner of garments, trading the products of their hand labor for goods in local shops. The 12-year-old Betsey Metcalf's discovery of a method for braiding oat straw in 1798 sparked the straw hat and braid industry, which employed nearly 25 000 women and had an annual turnover of over $1.5 million by 1830. Young women devoted themselves primarily to their manufacturing tasks while older ones included them among the numerous occupations entailed in running a household. This divided women's economic activity by marital status and age, with payment for married women's work typically belonging to the family rather than to the individual female worker.

As part of a family economy women worked in their own time and had other resources upon which to rely. Since merchants and middlemen had little control over individual craftswomen, they expanded production by distributing raw materials across an ever-widening region. This drew more women into the market place and accustomed them to working for wages. Women clearly valued the opportunity to earn money through their craft labors, with many favoring cottage production over narrower domestic tasks, looking forward to the money or goods they produced.

Like rural women engaged in sporadic outwork production, urban women also worked to boost family incomes. Deteriorating economic circumstances and disparities in wealth even among native-born white women made employment a necessity for a growing number by the 1820s and 1830s. Women in smaller cities such as Petersburg, Virginia, kept gardens or a few pigs and chickens, marketing their surplus in the town, although this became increasingly difficult in larger cities. There, women turned to sewing, casual domestic labor, or boardinghouse keeping to earn money as cottage manufacturing opportunities declined. At mid-century as many as one-quarter of households took lodgers as a means of augmenting family income.

Urban women's occupational range narrowed as the nineteenth century progressed despite some women's efforts to monetize their domestic labors. At the start of the century, widows in Philadelphia, Boston, Baltimore, and Charleston were printers, shoemakers, engravers, and silversmiths, and sometimes blacksmiths, shipbuilders, or gunwrights. They were also street peddlers and shopkeepers, selling dress goods, provisions, dry goods, and liquor. In many cases widows took over the work done primarily by their late husbands, indicating great familiarity with the business. Such knowledge was possible when the workshop was in the home, but the separation of home and work place during the industrial revolution isolated women from the family business and made it difficult or impossible for them to continue it when widowed. The increased commercialization of the economy also marginalized women who had trouble obtaining credit or traveling long distances to conduct business.

Domestic service dominated the employment prospects for single women. Approximately three-fifths of white working women were domestic servants in 1850. Domestic service and sewing required no capital but capitalized on women's previous domestic and household experiences, making it accessible to older women who obtained jobs as mother substitutes in men's households. Widowers advertised for a household help with an "unsullied reputation" who would manage the "female concerns of country business." The list of jobs included "[raising] small stock, dairying, marketing, combing, carding, spin-

Table 1.1   The cccupations of free women, 1850

Occupation	Number	%
Domestic Service	330 000	58.3
Clothing	62 000	11.0
Cotton Textiles	59 000	10.4
Teaching	55 000	9.7
Shoes	33 000	5.8
Wool Textiles	19 000	3.4
Hats	8 000	1.4
Total	566 000	100.0

Source: Adapted from Helen L. Sumner, *History of Women in Industry in the United States* (Washington, DC, Government Printing Office, 1910).

ning, knitting, sewing pickling, preserving, etc." and occasionally instructing the daughters of the household in the domestic economy. In return the family promised to treat this "affable, cheerful, active individual with respect and esteem," and give her the encouragement due to such a character. She helped the family rather than served them.

"Help" before the supposedly egalitarian Age of Jackson encompassed a network of neighbors and relations and was part of the natural progression of growing up for native-born white women. Female adolescents either stayed at home or moved in with neighbors or relations to assist with diverse household tasks. They formed an extended family in which maiden aunt, spinster cousin, or fatherless younger sister assisted kinswomen to care for children, home, dairy, loom, and spindle. Rural families incorporated female labor into an informal work exchange, where one woman spun, another wove, and a third sewed the cloth into garments. Most women shared a set of republican values based upon a rhetoric of equality and politically responsible motherhood (republican motherhood) which promoted social equality. Where the servants were slaves or free women of color, however, their white employers regarded them as social inferiors who performed more onerous tasks.

While the older model of domestic help persisted on the frontier, a number of factors transformed help into service in the East. Greater choice (especially in industry and teaching) turned domestic service into a residual occupation undertaken by foreigners or women of color with few employment alternatives. Immigration and migration disrupted family patterns and left many women with little choice but to seek work which provided shelter. Between 1820 and 1845 about 20 000 Irish arrived annually on American shores. The Irish potato famine accelerated emigration with nearly half the 221 253 arrivals in 1851 being unskilled female laborers desperate to find jobs whether in kitchens or factories.

African-American women had even fewer economic opportunities than immigrants since employers valued only their domestic skills or day labor. They found it virtually impossible to purchase land in the South to farm; few industrialists would employ them except as unskilled workers in southern tobacco factories. As a result, free black women were over-represented amongst the ranks of domestic servants. The poverty of the African-American community meant that almost all the women had jobs, many working as laundresses or servants well into old age. Most married women in Philadelphia's long-established African-American community, for example, were servants or laundresses in the early nineteenth century.

As the semantic shift from "help" to "servant" implied, employers distanced themselves from domestic help in the second quarter of the nineteenth century because they no longer shared cultural, racial, and religious backgrounds. Protestant or European-American mistresses believed they had little common cultural ground with Irish Catholics or African Americans. Servant-employing families sought privacy and separation from these strangers inside their gates. Servants ate in the kitchen, slept in the attic, and wore uniforms to indicate subservient status.

By the mid-nineteenth century, between 15 and 30 percent of American urban households had servants. Unmarried women comprised the largest group of live-in domestics; married women preferred working on a casual basis as day workers or laundresses, picking up and delivering loads of washing or scrubbing clothes in different households, and so combining housewifery with wage earning.

Sewing at home was another relict from the earlier era of cottage production transformed by growing commercial pressures. Eighteenth-century women sewed clothes for family and neighbors but greater demand for inexpensive clothing gave rise to "slop work," ready-made work clothes for soldiers, sailors, and slaves in northern cities. Skilled male tailors cut the pieces from cloth which women sewed at home. A high tariff imposed by Congress in 1816 on imported clothing spurred manufacturers and middlemen to find more seamstresses to make baby clothes, pantaloons, work clothes, and shirts. They paid low wages to hold costs down in a competitive, price-sensitive market.

Low wages forced sewing women to toil late into the night for a pittance, unable to supplement their income by growing their own food as rural women did. Pittsburgh seamstresses in the 1830s earned as little as $12\frac{1}{2}$ cents per shirt; since even the fastest seamstress took an entire day to make a shirt by hand, few earned enough to live on. Printer and social reformer Mathew Carey concluded that the wages paid to "seamstresses, spoolers, spinners, shoe binders" were inadequate to pay rent, purchase food and clothing and had a deleterious effect "upon the happiness and morals, not merely of those females, but of their families, when they have any." The New York *Tribune* discovered sewing women earning less than $100 per year in 1853, at a time when a family of four needed about $600 per year for an adequate standard of living.

Slack trade and recessions forced down the rates per garment while desperate seamstresses undercut each other's prices to get work. Manufacturers reduced their own costs by requiring home sewers to supply their own thread, heating, and light, cutting into painfully small incomes. Frequent hard times forced seamstresses to rely upon charity to supplement earnings, leading female-run charities to provide sewing for indigent seamstresses or to give them food and alms. Charities focused particularly on women household heads, since few widows could earn enough with their needles to provide even the bare necessities. Such women sent their children to work and resorted to begging on the streets to make ends meet.

COMMERCIAL AGRICULTURE

By the 1830s, commercial agriculture had largely displaced subsistence farming in those areas accessible to markets, lessening free women's role in agrarian production while augmenting that of slave women. Transportation innovations facilitated shipping bulky agricultural commodities to distant ports and encouraged farmers to specialize in a single crop. Government land policies, including aggressive settlement of western lands, extension of slavery into the southern territories, and forced displacement of Native Americans, opened fertile land and fresh soil to white settlers while the growth of manufacturing, urbanization, and immigration promoted large-scale production as new and distant outlets opened up. The net effect of these changes was to undermine white women's economic activities while accentuating their family roles.

Two divergent forms of agriculture emerged, dependent respectively upon free and slave labor. In the North and West, farms worked by members of the immediate family relied upon improved agricultural technology and some hired help for their success. They specialized in wheat, corn, other grains, vegetables, livestock, and dairying. Commercial agriculture marginalized women who could not meet the rising volume of demand as they previously fitted dairying, egg-gathering, and market gardening into their other chores. Unable to obtain credit at banks (married women could not enter into contracts), few women could expand their agricultural operations by borrowing as men did. Farm women continued to sell their surplus, but as more male farmers near cities turned to dairy farming and market gardening they marginalized women's smaller enterprises. Rising incomes from male cash crops also contributed to the growing feeling that women should work for their family rather than for the market. Some Mid-Atlantic women became commercial butter makers, but they were notable exceptions.

The westward progression of cultivated land also altered women's contributions to the farm family. The diversified farmers in the Northeast found it difficult to compete against the larger, more fertile single crop farms of the Midwest. The center of wheat farming shifted to the Midwest by mid-century once the steel plow (invented in 1837) made it possible to break through the hard prairie sod efficiently. By the 1840s, wheat reapers enabled many farmers to harvest 10 to 12 acres a day. Mechanization (machines operated by men and bought on credit by them) devalued women's apparent economic role in the free farm economy because the care of draft animals, usage of heavy iron plows, and borrowing from the bank to buy more land and equipment tended to be men's province.

Public sentiment shifted away from praising female contributions to the farm economy and instead imposed a domestic framework upon rural women. Commentators criticized farmers for "permitting" their wives to undertake the hard physical labor of the dairy. One of the first female graduates of Oberlin College complained about farm women's arduous tasks in the dairy and at the churn in a letter to the *Ohio Cultivator* in 1848, while a male correspondent of the *Wool Grower and Stock Raiser* declared that no "intelligent man . . . can wish to make a perfect drudge of his wife or daughters" by demanding they milk or churn. The decline of domestic manufacturing and the growing penetration of the cash economy undermined female agricultural production and led women and men to value women's emotional place in the family circle more highly.

By the Civil War the ideal division of labor in the farm family economy mirrored that of urban dwellers: women looked after the family and men provided the economic sustenance. Women's butter and egg money, their non-monetized labor exchanges, and domestic manufacturing and food production constituted a smaller proportion of the family economy as men's crops became the basis of household income. Critics condemned white women's physical contributions to farm work as drudgery and generally regarded it with disdain. Both farm women and the correspondents of the farming press defined women's work on the farm as undertaken for love of their family not income. They downplayed their hard physical labor and disregarded their cash contributions to their families. Work, as Jeanne Boydston observes in her study of the ideology of labor in the early republic, became gendered, with the term referring to jobs undertaken for cash rather than within the household economy.

Despite the significance of women butter makers in the early national period and their important role in encouraging the commercialization of agriculture in the Mid-Atlantic states, few women made the transition to commercial farming. Their inability to raise capital or, if married, to own land, sign commercial papers, or obtain bank mortgages weighed against commercial agricultural production. The purchase of manufactured goods increasingly indicated family economic standing, devaluing items made by women at home and deepening the conceptual divide between women's labors of love and men's "work." Male employment outside the home defined a family's well-being, leaving women dependent upon their husband's income for social and economic status.

SLAVERY

Technological innovations such as the cotton gin encouraged the spread of cotton cultivation and accelerated the demand for low-cost slave labor. Like the northern textile, shoe, paper, and garment industries slavery incorporated women in large numbers into the work force. The slavocracy treated gender as a malleable category for the benefit of the white men who controlled the region's economy and society. Rather than decreasing women's direct economic contributions, southern and southwestern plantations placed a premium upon them, relying upon the labor of enslaved women no less than that of enslaved men. African-American women comprised approximately half the slave labor force, at a time when less than one-eighth of white women were economically active. Indeed, the productive and reproductive labor of women demonstrably increased slave holders' profit, since women not only worked in the fields but also procreated the labor force.

Plantations were a business run with little regard for the conventional gendered behavior thought desirable in the white world.

Sojourner Truth, a former slave from New York, attested to the dual burden of the bondswoman: production and reproduction. In 1851 she told the Ohio Woman's Rights Convention that she could plow, reap, chop, and mow as well as any man. Whether she also said she had borne 13 children and seen most of them sold into slavery is a matter of historical controversy, but many slave owners did use their bondswomen's fertility to augment their profits.

The vast majority (about 90 percent) of enslaved women toiled in the fields doing the same general tasks as men. Slave owners regarded both sexes as units of production from whom they exacted maximum labor contributions. For Truth and millions of slave women their sex afforded little or no protection from the vicissitudes of slavery, nor did it entitle them to the consideration genteel women received. Some masters treated women as three-quarter or half hands, expecting them to pick less cotton or tobacco than men, especially if they were heavily pregnant, had just given birth, or were nursing young babies. Certain tasks might be reserved for men, who tended to plow while women hoed, but this varied from plantation to plantation with no hard and fast divisions.

Slaves sometimes worked in family groups, as on a Virginia farm where men scythed and cradled the wheat while women raked and bound the sheaves. Boys and girls followed behind, stacking the sheaves. Families laboring like this protected those who could not keep pace. One ex-slave recalled that all the family would pitch in and help Momma who wasn't very strong. The man doing the cradling went no faster than the woman, usually his wife, who did the raking and binding, enabling her to keep up and protecting her from the slave owner's wrath.

Planters incorporated white society's sex/skill hierarchy into their gendered divisions of labor with bondsmen holding most of the skilled positions available to slaves. They, rather than women were the drivers, carpenters, blacksmiths, coopers, and masons. The acquisition of such skills meant bondsmen could earn a few pennies privately to supplement the meager rations and poor clothing allotted to them and their families. Yet the opportunities for advancement for either sex should not be exaggerated. Estimates vary, but it would seem that less than 15 percent of all male slaves were artisan or skilled workers and a lower proportion of bondswomen held skilled positions, mostly within the domestic sphere.

Where the slaves were organized into gangs, as on cotton plantations, women and men might work in the same gang, doing the same work. Early in the year women plowed, planted, hoed, and weeded the crop which they picked from July or August onwards. One worker set the pace while the white overseers and slave drivers ensured that all pickers kept to it. Some planters encouraged productivity by rewarding the slaves of either sex who picked the most cotton with extra rations, clothes, or a few coins. Picking cotton was not so bad, a former slave recollected, because they were used to it and received rewards such as a dress or a pair of shoes if they picked the most cotton.

When enslaved workers did not fulfill their quota or displeased their masters and mistresses, they encountered a wide variety of punishments, especially the lash. Some economic historians (notably Robert Fogel and Stanley Engerman in *Time on the Cross*) argue that historians of slavery exaggerate the prevalence of negative sanctions. Yet the testimony of ex-slaves and others indicates that bondswomen and men suffered grievously at the hands of slave owners and slave patrols ("paddyrollers"), since neither age, sex, nor state of health protected them from abuse. Former slaves described the beating of young children, pregnant women, and old people for diverse reasons including supposed disobedience, not doing the task assigned, or simply being physically unable to complete their heavy work load.

Sexual jealousy and the refusal of sexual advances might also result in the cruel treatment of bondswomen. Southern society valued sexual purity for white women, but refused similar protection to African Americans. The presence of slave children fathered by their masters attracted the ire of white women helpless to prevent their husbands' philandering. Former slave Patience Avery recalled that her mistress treated her cruelly because her father was white, depriving her of food and whipping her with a strap. Many slave women fought back, sometimes with consequences that included beatings or sale down river. They received little sympathy for their plight from white women who vented their jealousy and rage on them, as Harriet Jacobs testified in her *Incidents in the Life of a Slave Girl: Written by Herself* (1861). Yet African-American women also negotiated respect from plantation owners through their assertiveness (sometimes described by whites as being "sassy") or acting as a group to protect each other from the unwanted attentions of white men.

In addition to field labor, about 10 percent of bondswomen were cooks, seamstresses, laundresses, midwives, or house servants. Some were hired out, especially in the towns and cities, while others worked mostly or entirely on their home plantations. These specialized workers used their skills to benefit their own family and community where possible. The plantation cook might take food back to the quarters to augment the limited supplies doled out by the plantation mistress to slave families. Practices varied between plantations, with some white women maintaining a close watch on the household stores in order to prevent depredations by their underfed slaves, but on others the cook had more autonomy and managed food supplies as she saw fit.

House slaves got up before dawn to make up fires and cook breakfast for the white family. The cook on one plantation woke up very early, rushed frantically back and forth between her own children and the big house, trying to nurse her babies between cooking, doing laundry, and cleaning. Her day was an unremitting round of toil until she collapsed late at night into an exhausted sleep. On some plantations the cook also made breakfast for some or all slaves, with young children taking breakfast to slaves in the fields. Elsewhere bondswomen made breakfast, carrying it with them to eat in their short midday break.

Like cooks, midwives remained at work for very long hours, frequently providing the only medical care available to slaves, who rarely received formal medical treatment but were nursed within the community. Relying on herbal knowledge and traditional cures carried over from Africa, these women delivered babies, looked after the mothers, and tended the sick. A skilled midwife might be hired out to deliver babies on other plantations or for local white families, receiving a small gift or a few pennies while the slave owner received the fee.

Some white mistresses such as Mary Boykin Chesnut's mother-in-law looked after their slaves' well-being, doctoring slaves, tending newborn babies, and providing clothing. Mrs. Chesnut, senior, made clothes for slave infants so that each newcomer had, according to her daughter-in-law, an ample wardrobe. Some white women worked with their slaves, cutting out garments and sewing them together. Elsewhere slave women made their own clothes from cloth they wove or were given, although bondsmen usually had their garments provided already made up.

Few plantation mistresses were ladies of leisure; they directed and sometimes worked alongside their bondservants. They oversaw the food production and preservation, which was itself a considerable task given the numbers of people who needed to be fed throughout the year. The remoteness of many plantations from cities and markets meant that these households needed to be self-sufficient in most aspects of the household economy. Some slave mistresses believed themselves to be as enslaved as their bondspeople. Lucy Carter Minor wrote of Christmas: "What a slave a holiday makes of a mistress! Indeed, she is always a slave, but doubly and trebly so at such times." She looked after the health, clothing, food, and production of such disparate items as yeast, soap, lard, and cheese. While her work load was immeasurably lighter than that of slave women who undertook the tasks she supervised or rejected for herself, she nevertheless worked long and hard to ensure that all members of her household had basic necessities. She could also structure her working day so that periods of hard work alternated with resting or visiting friends and neighbors.

Despite slave mistresses' best efforts (or otherwise), few bondspeople had sufficient food, clothing, or household furnishings. Both enslaved women and men grew food, hunted, and fished in order to augment their meager diets. Evidence from Georgia in the early nineteenth century shows how important this could be. In a legacy of their African heritage, women on plantations near Savannah tended small plots of vegetables to feed their families and sold the surplus in local markets. Bondswomen might also gather firewood, carry it long distances to sell, and use this income to buy food, cloth, and other supplies which cost-conscious slave owners refused to give them.

Slavery for women meant exploitation of their bodies as workers and as reproducers of a captive labor force. Although the precise tasks might differ between plantations and in cities, one fact remained constant: slave women worked a double shift. They performed a full day's labor in the fields or big house, then returned to their cabins at night where they undertook the domestic chores of family life. They served their master's needs while maintaining a life for themselves and their families within an inhumane institution.

Slave owners compared the supposed security slavery provided to the labor force favorably to the economic uncertainty and sometimes dire poverty of industrial workers. The cotton textile industry, first in Britain, then in the United States, made slavery profitable through its high demand for raw materials. In so doing it encouraged slave owners to maximize the labor of all available workers including women and children. Many slave owners agreed with Thomas Jefferson's belief that slave women's "increase" was a significant factor in slavery's profitability, considering "a woman who brings a child every two years as more profitable than the best man on the farm." Northern industries also utilized women and children as inexpensive sources of labor. As industrialization progressed, many working-class families put their children to work in factories because parental income was insufficient to sustain an adequate standard of living.

INDUSTRIALIZATION

The American textile industry, largely dependent upon female labor, grew rapidly in the first decades of the nineteenth century, stimulated by embargoes on British imports during the American Revolution and the War of 1812. Transport improvements opened up the hinterland, which facilitated the free flow of labor, raw materials, and finished products upon which the American industrial revolution depended. Two other factors accelerated the spread of manufacturing in the United States: the development of the factory system of production in the cotton industry and the availability of an inexpensive labor force, including women and children.

Industrialization penetrated deepest in Massachusetts where one-third of all women aged 10–29 had industrial jobs by 1850. In the same year, the first national industrial census showed 225 922 women employed in factories with more than $500 annual turnover, nearly one-quarter of the manufacturing labor force. Most female industrial workers were single, widowed or living apart from their husbands; even by 1900, only 3 percent of married white women had jobs outside the home. The net effect of industrialization was to segregate home from work place and married from single women. Once economic activity became a full-time, extra-household employment, women had to choose between domestic occupations and wage earning. Many single, widowed, poor, immigrant, and African-American women had no choice but to work, but those married women who could afford to (largely urban, middle-class whites), opted for domesticity over jobs.

In 1812, approximately 500 men and 3500 women and children participated in commercial cloth manufacturing. Two years later,

Francis Cabot Lowell opened his cotton mill in Waltham, Massachusetts, bringing the mechanized carding, spinning, and weaving of cotton cloth under one roof. The factory system divided operations into their component parts, enabling untrained workers to tend machines while skilled workers undertook the more complicated tasks. The economies of scale and low-cost production rapidly displaced the domestic manufacture of cloth in the North. The success of industrial organization in textiles led to a sharp increase in the numbers employed from 12 000 in 1820, to 39 000 in 1831, and about 75 000 by 1860, and shifted manufacturing from the cottage to the factory.

Young women dominated the early textile labor force; as many as 85–95 percent of the operatives were women in the 1820s, with a small number of men holding supervisory and craft positions. The proportion of men employed by the industry rose after 1850, largely due to two factors according to one of the pioneering analysts of women's employment, Edith Abbott. Heavier machinery operating at great speeds made strength more important than dexterity. At the same time the labor supply altered as unskilled immigrant men desperate for jobs accepted the low wages and poorer working conditions proffered by mill owners striving to keep prices down and dividends up.

In order to attract a labor force, Lowell and his associates originally provided housing for them and carefully supervised their working and non-working hours. Attracted by the economic independence offered by employment outside the home and preferring mill work to domestic service, thousands of young women flocked to factories. The first generation of New England mill hands were socially diverse, coming from stony farms and middle-class backgrounds. Lucy Larcom entered the mill at the age of 11, propelled by the knowledge that her widowed mother could not readily support eight children by running a boardinghouse. By no means all of the new labor force came to the factory through economic distress. Hannah Borden, whose father was a large stockholder in the first cotton mill in Fall River, started work at the age of 14. Hannah learned to weave when she was 8 years old, indicative of the prevalence of domestic manufacturing at all levels of early nineteenth-century New England society. One of the leading weavers of her day, she taught other women to weave and worked on the finer grades of cloth in the mill.

Women in other industries also adapted domestic skills to manufacturing. By the 1810s and 1820s, trades like shoebinding became separated from the family manufacturing system. Workshops grew larger with factories attracting single women, although married women still did piece work in their own homes. Female workers and male factory owners interpreted the salient characteristics of home shoebinding very differently. Working at home and fitting stitching around domestic jobs, women acknowledged a fundamental reality of their lives: the need to combine domestic and income production without wholly neglecting one for the other. Manufacturers needed their labor but devalued it and paid little for it precisely because it differed from the male model of full-time wage earning separated from the domestic sphere.

This different vision set the stage for the cult of domesticity in which women (and men) valued the female presence at the hearth over that in the workshop, at least in part because women's waged labor paid so poorly. Low wages in domestic service depressed wage levels for all women. Employers did not need to pay well to attract female workers; they merely needed to exceed other poorly recompensed occupations or unpaid labor on the family farm. Employers also devalued female skills. Male tailors earned more than female stitchers; loom fixers made more than female weavers; and male cobblers received more per piece than female shoebinders. Thus work outside the home paid too poorly to lure many married women into the new work places given their domestic commitments, nor did these work places recognize women's dual responsibilities. As a result, married European-American women increasingly gave priority to the domestic sphere.

LABOR UNREST

Industrial unrest, much of it led by women, accompanied the first decades of manufacturing in the United States. Labor protests occurred among seamstresses working on their own and among textile workers toiling in groups. The seamstresses who sewed in isolation did not accept wage cuts passively; the first female-led strike occurred in New York in 1825. Seamstresses struck again in 1831, as the United Tailoresses Society called its 1600 sewing women away from their needles and onto the streets. Philadelphia, Boston, and Baltimore seamstresses downed tools in the 1830s in an attempt to increase their rates while seamstresses and tailors formed joint unions in the 1840s and 1850s in their quest for better pay. These efforts tended to be short-lived, but attracted widespread sympathy from reformers such as abolitionist Lucretia Mott who assisted Philadelphia's seamstresses and tailors to form a union which successfully fought for higher wages. The coming of the sewing machine in the 1850s and the division of work into tasks (sewing buttonholes rather than whole garments, for example) depressed wages in the garment trade, led to the sweated system of labor in the years after the Civil War, and markedly worsened seamstresses' working conditions.

Deteriorating circumstances also prompted collective action in the textile mills. At first, the factories seemed a means to achieve independence for young New England women since they received their wages directly instead of seeing them paid to their fathers. As Lucy Larcom noted in her reminiscences about her New England girlhood, initially the work left young mill workers time to read and play about the spindles. Harder economic times, increased competition, and the need to pay sufficient dividends to keep investors happy impelled manufacturers to economize on labor costs. Lower wages, speeded-up machinery, and restrictive labor practices contributed to worsening conditions in the textile mills, against which the female operatives protested.

Women joined male co-workers in marching out of the mills in Pawtucket, Rhode Island, in 1824, in one of the first joint strikes. Women protested on their own a few years later in Dover, New Hampshire, when they walked out over new company rules which fined those who arrived late or talked while they worked. Company threats to blacklist those who left their jobs without giving a fortnight's notice also angered the New Hampshire strikers. In what was to become a common pattern, the company fired the presumed ringleaders of the strike and kept its new rules.

A number of factors fostered female labor solidarity. The mill workers in the 1820s and 1830s were of much the same age, four-fifths being aged 15–30. Coming mostly from native-born white rural families, they shared a common background and frequently went into the mills because they had a relation or former neighbor who worked there and could ease their passage into a boardinghouse and a job. Women lived and worked with other women, numerically dominating the mills, with the few male overseers and young boys barely diluting the female atmosphere in the workrooms. The all-female environment of the boardinghouses gave them ample opportunity to discuss their situation at home and at work and reach a consensus over unreasonable wage cuts. The failure of spontaneous turnouts led to the organization of the Factory Girls' Association in Lowell in 1835. When the mill owners raised the fees for living in a company boardinghouse in 1836, about 1500 of the 2500 members walked out in protest.

The statement of "A Lowell Factory Girl" indicated growing resentment over the discrepancies in workers' and owners' standards of living. The mill owners required much harder work from their operatives in the 1840s than previously, cutting piece rates to force up productivity, while keeping their wage bills constant. Between 1842 and 1860, weavers' wages declined from $3.66 to $2.76 per week. The female operatives were particularly hard hit since male overseers and mill workers earned about twice as much as they did. Writing in the Fall River *Wampanoag and Operatives' Journal,* the "Factory Girl" queried why, if Lowell factories ran at a loss, did the owners not cut the fat salaries of their agents who rolled about the city in their carriages rather than making "the hard working female operatives" bear the burden.

Great disparities in wage levels pertained throughout the textile industry. In Maryland textile mills in the 1830s women earned about $1.81 per week compared with $3.87 for men, while in Virginia male wages averaged almost twice the female level. Similar disproportion characterized other manufacturing enterprises; women shoe workers in Lynn, Massachusetts, received about one-half to one-third what their male counterparts made, leading a *Voice of Industry* correspondent to ask in 1847, "what possible difference can it make to the employer whether he pays A or B one dollar for accomplishing a piece of work" as long as it is done "equally as well by the one as the other?" Women supported themselves and their families and needed an equal income. "It is folly to argue that labor performed by females is not in every respect done as well as by men; and there is no early reason why they should not receive as much." Despite this strong statement of economic equality by "Pro Bono", mill workers went on strike to maintain their own previous pay levels rather than for equal pay.

Under the leadership of Sarah Bagley, operatives formed the Lowell Female Labor Reform Association in 1845 to protest their rapidly deteriorating circumstances. Bagley belonged to one of the many self-improvement circles which proliferated in Lowell's boardinghouses in the 1840s. Her articles for the mill workers' journal, the *Lowell Offering*, railed against the assault on proud New England womanhood perpetrated by rapacious manufacturers who cut wages and speeded up the pace of labor. The Female Labor Reform Association submitted petitions to the Massachusetts legislature protesting against long hours and low wages. Bagley defended her public participation in the ten-hour movement by stating that "for the last half a century, it has been deemed a violation of woman's sphere to appear before the public as a speaker; but when our rights are trampled upon and we appeal in vain to legislators, what shall we do but appeal to the people?" Little came of this appeal, despite a petition numbering over 4500 signatures, although mill owners granted operatives an extra 15 minutes in which to eat their dinner during the summer when they worked from sunrise to sunset.

Women in other industries and cities also agitated for the ten-hour day but few tried to accomplish this through direct negotiation with their employers, who rarely bargained in good faith with female employees. Instead, they petitioned legislatures to establish fair and equitable working conditions. They compared their situation to that of slaves and protested that they lacked even the minimal safeguards which they believed the laws vouchsafed to bondspeople for support in old age. Industrial workers used these comparisons to argue for improved working conditions, but former slaves believed bondservice to be a far worse insult to the human condition. Harriet Jacobs declared in *Incidents in the Life of a Slave Girl* (1861) that: "there was no law forbidding [wage slaves] to learn to read and write; and if they helped each other in spelling out the Bible, they were in no danger of thirty-nine lashes . . . No master or overseer could come and take from him his wife, or his daughter." Industrial working conditions deteriorated, but workers still had the freedom to organize, change jobs, and decide at what age their children would go to work.

A new labor force displaced the militant native-born white textile operatives by mid-century as manufacturers hired immigrant workers, dividing the labor force by language and religion. Other changes also challenged labor solidarity. The introduction of sewing machines into shoemaking shifted production from the household to the factory and divided the work force into married women in the home and single women in the factory. The number of women working at home fell, as did their wages, while younger women recruited to factory labor on the new machines enjoyed better pay, but were also subject to factory discipline. As with the textile factories, workers protested the long day demanded in the shoe factories. The growing segregation between the work place and the home disadvantaged married women who wished to earn money and undermined female economic independence, leading to a family wage ideology in which men supported the family and women cared for the home.

The 1860 shoe workers' strike in Lynn, Massachusetts, illuminated the complex issues of gender, employment, and appropriate behavior for women when shoe workers struck over cuts in their wages. Insofar as they incorporated women into their strike activities, they did so "as moral agents and as family members" according to historian Mary Blewett. Female cordwainers in the factories organized their own parallel strike for higher wages, proposing an alliance with homeworkers, who were mostly married to male shoe workers. However, homeworkers feared their displacement by factory machine operatives, which made it difficult for them to join in common cause. They also worried that considering women's wages might imperil the main goal of the strike, namely, increasing men's wages and their families' standards of living.

Male strike leaders harped on this theme, trying to silence the women's demands. They called upon the women to "speak in a judicious and womanly manner." Ultimately the women strikers succumbed to the family wage ideology and supported a lower set of wage demands for women workers, assuming that men would support their wives and (to a lesser extent) their daughters. Married and single women perceived their interests to be distinct. Female homeworkers depended upon their husbands as primary breadwinners so their first allegiance was to them, not to the self-supporting women in the factories. Changes in the industry, notably the introduction of heavy machinery, also resulted in a declining proportion of women workers.

During the first half of the nineteenth century the United States shifted from self-sufficient agricultural production into commercial agriculture and industrial manufacturing. Many women's roles underwent revision as work came to mean labor outside the home, but for rural women, slaves, and the urban poor economic activity remained part of their daily lives. The work undertaken by women within the household came to be viewed as a labor of love rather than as "work," especially for the better off. Social changes accompanied these shifting definitions of productivity as women's role in the family altered. A growing number of single women took jobs outside the home, while fewer married women regarded the myriad tasks they performed within the household as contributing to the family's economic, rather than emotional, well-being.

The national income accounts omitted the value of goods and services produced by women within the home, reflecting the low regard in which such endeavors were held and ignoring their continued significance to family welfare. The ideology of domesticity also discounted women's economic contributions, yet even affluent women were rarely idle since they manufactured many items of food and clothing at home throughout the ante-bellum era. Nevertheless, female experiences grew more divergent as affluence permitted some women to withdraw at least partially from economic productivity into domesticity while other women, notably African and Native Americans, recent immigrants, and the poor, were increasingly enmeshed in an economy which relegated them to hard labor for low or no wages. A gulf emerged between the work performed for love in the home by married women and for remuneration by single women in the factories. Rural women's economic activities also polarized as fewer white women earned an income through domestic manufacturing and dairying, while African-American women toiled long hours for no pay in the fields and westward expansion threatened the Native American way of life. Thus industrialization and the commercialization of agriculture created separate spheres for some women, while subjecting others to hard labor for little or no recompense. The new economic order exacerbated inequalities and divisions but also led many women to reconsider their role in society.

2 Family and Migration in the Era of Domesticity

As women's economic functions altered, their roles in the family changed, with domesticity replacing domestic manufacturing as the central female role. Middle-class married white women in particular came to be associated with consumption, family care, and the private world of the home. Men, by contrast, moved outside the household to take waged employment and had less direct involvement with family matters. A specific set of economic and demographic circumstances gave rise to the mid-nineteenth-century cult of domesticity, accentuating female responsibility for home and family and male obligations for economic support. Domesticity and the separation of spheres turned the household into a haven from the increasing disorder of the urban, industrial world and sought to keep women within the home in order to protect them from the chaos and impurity of public life.

As explored in Chapter 1, the factory production of goods replaced household manufacturing, while the commercialization of agriculture lessened white, but not slave, women's agricultural labors. The growing prosperity of some urban dwellers and an increased supply of immigrant women servants to perform household chores freed some married women from domestic production. As the middle class prospered, these women redefined their social roles to accord with their altered economic functions, intensifying the emotional and nurturing aspects of family life over the production of goods. Affluent women and their cultural advisers claimed child-rearing and the home for their own, valuing precisely those functions that remained after manufacturing moved outside the home.

The heightened emphasis on domesticity, popularized by the growing number of women's magazines, invested women's daily tasks with a sacred dignity and importance. Household advisers informed women that "St. Paul knew what was best for women when he advised them to be domestic." By devoting time to one's children, investing in the emotional side of family life, and running the emerging family and household forms smoothly these women esteemed what they perceived as the core of female functions. Womanly weakness required their protection from the uncertainties of the volatile society which emerged in the second quarter of the nineteenth century, yet such weakness existed mainly among the native-born white middle class. Domesticity became the dominant paradigm for these women, but recent immigrants, frontier women, slaves, and other people of color did not share this model, either from cultural choice, economic necessity, or the imposition of others' values upon them.

Middle-class women's and men's spheres, previously intertwined on the family farm, now grew farther apart, particularly in the growing towns and cities. Republican motherhood, a term used by Linda Kerber to describe the role which emerged for women after the American Revolution, was a social solution to a political problem, namely how to inculcate loyalty to the new nation in an uncertain time when old hierarchies had been destroyed. Mothers were to educate citizens for the state, unlike in the cult of true womanhood in which women turned inward to the household for which they assumed an emotional responsibility. Motherhood became a vocation in the ante-bellum era, taking on new meaning as a sacred function to ensure the health and well-being of the family.

Celebrating the importance of motherhood and domesticity, women defined their roles as separate from the economic and political issues which dominated the popular discourse of the era. Despite this seeming distance from the public sphere, the cult of domesticity also subverted the separation of spheres because women increasingly sought to protect the home by attacking the problems which they perceived as threatening it: intemperance, immorality, poverty, and slavery. Ante-bellum women's education, cultural and reform activities are the subjects of the next two chapters; this one focuses on domesticity, family life, and the population changes which defined US women's lives in the years leading up to the Civil War.

DEMOGRAPHIC CHANGES

Urbanization, industrialization, migration, and immigration accentuated the diversity of American society. Between 1815 and 1865 some 5 million immigrants arrived in the United States, primarily from Ireland, the German states, and Scandinavia. Single women were particularly well represented among the Irish immigrants, while many Germans and Scandinavians emigrated in family groups. The newcomers congregated in cities, boosting the urban proportion of the population from 7 percent in 1820 to 20 percent by 1860. The new immigrants, especially the Irish, swelled the ranks of the urban poor, seeking employment in kitchens and factories. Desperate for jobs, they became the cheap labor upon which the cult of domesticity depended, taking low-paid jobs in textile and shoe factories and working in middle-class kitchens, giving family members, especially housewives, free time to devote to other activities.

Mothers devoted much of this "free" time to their children, since declining family sizes meant women could lavish more attention on each individual child. In the seventeenth century, families had as many as eight children. By the end of the eighteenth century, the average white woman had seven children, falling to between five and six children by 1850, with lower birth rates in the North where pressures on land were greater. Rising population densities acted as a brake upon the formation of new families and shortened the child-bearing period. At mid-century a new model of family life emerged, with greater emphasis on the welfare of individual members. Fertility declined because parents wished to develop individual children's characters and to invest more of their emotional and economic resources in them.

This demographic analysis does not consider industrialization as crucial in lowering the birth rate since birth rates fell in densely settled rural areas as well as in villages, small towns, and cities. The American birth control movement stressed women's health as the primary motivation for family limitation, with improved methods of contraception and wider dissemination of birth control information contributing to lower fertility levels. While not completely reliable, birth control enabled couples to limit family sizes and women to escape or lessen the impact of high fertility upon their health. Publications appearing from the 1830s onwards detailed methods of contraception to couples interested in controlling fertility with authorities such as "American Physician" advising readers that marital companionship would be improved by a smaller family and lessened "domestic drudgery."

The vulcanization of rubber in 1843 encouraged the middle and upper classes to use condoms. Diaphragms became available in the 1860s, although their usage remained restricted to the well-to-do until the twentieth century. Native-born white women practiced birth control to a much greater extent than immigrant women, with prosperous families more likely to restrict fertility than poorer ones. Techniques included *coitus interruptus*, abstinence, douching, and restricting intercourse during the woman's presumed fertile periods.

Women also relied upon abortions to restrict the number of children they had, using ergot and chemical preparations, knitting needles, midwives, and doctors to terminate pregnancies. Common law held that abortion before the fetus had "quickened" or moved inside the mother did not constitute a crime. Pregnancy terminations rose in the first half of the century from approximately one abortion for every 25 to 35 live births circa 1800 to about one for every five or six in the 1850s and 1860s, according to medical historian James Mohr. By 1860 some 20 states had made abortion illegal, although these laws were rarely enforced. The emphasis on female domesticity contributed to the negative attitudes towards abortion; women who terminated their pregnancies violated social norms by rejecting the motherhood now defined as their true vocation. Physicians also favored the criminalization of abortion as they asserted control over the birthing process and tried to curtail midwives' and informal practitioners' role in childbirth.

DOMESTICITY DEFINED

Domesticity depended upon a specific cluster of economic, cultural, and religious factors which coalesced for Protestant urban middle-class white women in the second quarter of the nineteenth century. Higher male incomes enabled affluent wives to withdraw from the production of goods inside and outside the home and turned their economic inactivity into a measure of male success. Families perceived this division of labor as benefiting all members, accepting ministers' and magazine editors' advice that mothers should have the paramount role in child-rearing. As living standards rose and birth rates declined, women devoted themselves more closely to their children's welfare and invested the economic surplus produced by their husbands in their children. Higher standards of cleanliness, warmer dwellings, and better nutrition contributed to child health and well-being.

Some demographers attribute women's heightened emotional

involvement in child rearing to declining infant death rates, believing that high death rates (especially in the seventeenth century) prevented parents from investing heavily in each individual child. A decline in stoicism and fatalism contributed toward this trend as the God of the Second Great Awakening (the religious revival in the late eighteenth and early nineteenth centuries) wore a more compassionate face than his Calvinist predecessor. Women's greater levels of literacy made it possible for them to record their anguish over children's deaths. Lydia Huntley Sigourney's 1836 poem, "'Twas But a Babe" depicts maternal devotion to her dying child:

> What know ye of her love
> Who patient watcheth, till the stars grow dim,
> Over her drooping infant, with an eye
> Bright as unchanging Hope of his repose?

Part of an outpouring of funerary sentiment, such verses betokened public acknowledgement of women's devotion to their children.

Sarah Josepha Hale, editor and author, celebrated the differences between women and men in her 1845 poem, "Empire of Woman," designating the "outward world" for men and reserving the holier empire of wife and motherhood for women. The proliferation of this type of domestic prose and fiction fostered what historian Barbara Welter described as the cult of true womanhood, a belief in the home as woman's natural place and the family as her paramount interest. The household became the middle-class woman's holy sphere; she lived through it and for it. Married women became their husbands' economic dependents, expecting family life to provide companionship, privacy, and a retreat from the commercial and industrial world. Women nurtured the members of their idealized haven, in Welter's phrase, "upholding the pillars of the temple, with her frail white hand," a phrase which limited true womanhood to genteel white women. Pious, pure, submissive, and domestic, they, rather than their husbands, had the responsibility of raising the future generation.

Propounded by women's magazines, the cult of true womanhood or domesticity idealized maternity and family life in periodicals aimed directly at mothers. When *Mother's Magazine*, edited by Abigail Whittlesey, first appeared in 1833, it inaugurated a long tradition of female editors advising their more domestic sisters on household and childcare. Instead of viewing children as personifications of original sin (as the Puritans had done), mothers' magazines followed the Enlightenment view of children as blank slates on which mothers inscribed the right message. Women's role in child-rearing assumed greater importance once fewer men worked along-side their children on the farm or family business. Statesman Daniel Webster, writing on the "The Influence of Woman" in *The Young Ladies' Reader* in 1851, adjured mothers to inculcate virtue in their children since fathers were too busy chasing the dollar. Thus proponents of true womanhood followed the educational precepts of their republican mothers, but detached maternity from the political context of their forebears.

Godey's Lady's Book, edited by Sarah Josepha Hale, informed its readers that "maternal instruction is the purest and safest means of opening the fountain of knowledge to the young mind." Like the editors of *Mother's Journal, Mother's Magazine*, and *Mother's Assistant*, Hale instructed women on their responsibility for children's salvation and well-being. Sisters Catharine Beecher and Harriet Beecher Stowe advised women to make training the human mind in its "impressionable period of childhood" their profession. Numerous maternal associations founded in northern states from the 1820s onwards attested to mothers' acceptance of their enhanced responsibility for child-rearing.

Maternal associations and magazines recognized and reinforced women's primacy in the raising of children as did the prevalence of widowed editors who combined child-rearing with literary ventures and naturally emphasized maternal responsibilities. Writing and editing were acceptable jobs for middle-class women and easier to blend with domesticity than teaching, the only other acceptable employment for genteel ante-bellum women. Sara Parton's character Ruth Hall, in her eponymous novel, tells her young daughter that "no happy woman ever writes." She wrote because financial hardship gave her no other way to keep a roof over her children's heads. When married women turned to their pens, as minister's wife Harriet Beecher Stowe did when her husband's salary proved insufficient, they sustained their families (and their husbands' egos) by glorifying the domestic sphere as women's proper domain.

Once it became less common for daughters to serve domestic apprenticeships on neighbors' farms, apostles of domesticity spread the new domestic order. The literary domestics divided the world into domestic and business spheres, with women firmly inhabiting the former, and provided rules and guidelines for well-bred women. Feminist abolitionist Lydia Maria Child penned the *American Frugal Housewife* in 1829 to guide women in economical household management. She believed that women needed instruction in the domestic arts because their education did "not usually point the female heart to its only true resting-place," the home.

Housewifery itself altered as technological innovations and industrialization modified earlier domestic routines. By the 1840s, Philadelphia, Boston, Cincinnati, and Manhattan had installed water mains and gas pipes. Domestic advisers taught housewives how to take best advantage of cooking, heating, and lighting innovations. Catharine Beecher's 1843 *Treatise on Domestic Economy* included a section on cooking over an open hearth with an iron pot. By the time she and her sister published *The American Women's Home, or Principles in Domestic Science* in 1869 they expected their readers to have cast iron stoves and to need assistance in managing them to best advantage.

The new technology made complex cooking possible; utensils became more elaborate and multiplied in number. Cooking itself took on a new meaning once meals with many dishes replaced the simple stews and one-pot dishes of an earlier era. Instead of merely fuelling hungry people, meal preparation symbolized women's care for their families. In the 1850s recipe books and magazines published detailed instructions for cakes, cookies, and desserts, encouraging elaborate domesticity among emerging middle-class families, and investing meals with emotional significance. Cooking symbolized maternal devotion to Beecher and Stowe who urged women to undertake it themselves rather than delegate it to hired help.

While mid-century housewives were by no means idle and even wealthy women led busy lives, the increased employment of domestic servants facilitated complicated household routines. Increasingly, affluent women delegated scrubbing, washing, and cleaning to servants while retaining supervisory roles. Domesticity still occupied much of women's days as standards of cleanliness rose and household furnishings became more elaborate; voluminous draperies trapped the dust of the cities and towns as did the ornately carved furniture popular with Victorian Americans. Even closed stoves required more tending than the open fires they replaced. They needed to be filled, riddled, emptied, blacked, and nurtured into performing their allotted task of heating irons, boiling water, frying, and baking.

Their temperamental nature and tendency to spew wood ash or coal dust over kitchen and cook increased the cleaning required.

The apostles of domesticity sought to reconcile the inequality of women in the home with the supposed equality of men outside it, while advising women that the home was their only proper sphere. Catharine Beecher conjectured that domesticity would reduce conflict in a tempestuous and troubled society since: "by carefully dividing the duties of man from those of woman . . . the great work of society may be the better carried on." Women's work was as significant as men's but completely separate; it facilitated the working of society but remained apart from it.

The commercial production of cloth, the purchase of meat rather than the killing and curing of animals, and the enhanced availability of household items turned women from producers to consumers. For some women, the growing commercialization and industrialization of American society subverted rather than accentuated female domestic roles and enabled them to pursue other interests. Abolitionist Sarah Grimké noted the altered nature of women's work in her *Letters on Equality* (1838): "When all manufactures were domestic, then the domestic function might well consume all the time of a very ableheaded woman. But nowadays . . . when so much of a woman's work is done by the butcher and the baker, by the tailor, and the cook, and the gas-maker . . . you see how much of a woman's time is left for other functions." The industrial revolution facilitated the cult of domesticity but also gave women time to pursue public concerns such as Grimké's anti-slavery crusade.

EXCEPTIONS TO DOMESTICITY AS THE DOMINANT PARADIGM

Not all women, then, conformed to the emerging domestic norm. Lydia Maria Child, the influential author, abolitionist, and reformer born in Massachusetts in 1802, protested the double standard embodied in the cult of true womanhood, although she accepted domesticity as women's proper sphere. Her *Letters from New York*, written in the early 1840s, refute the ideals of submissive purity and piety applied to women alone, remarking that the world would be a better place if supposedly female virtues permeated men's behavior and double standards ceased.

Would it not be an improvement for men also to be scrupulously pure in manners, conversation and life? Books addressed to young married people abound with advice to the wife to control her temper, and never to utter wearisome complaints, or vexatious words when the husband comes home fretful and unreasonable from his out-of-door conflicts with the world. Would not the advice be as excellent and appropriate, if the husband were advised to conquer his fretfulness, and forbear his complaints, in consideration of his wife's ill-health, fatiguing cares, and the thousand disheartening influences of domestic routine?

Despite Child's protests and those of women's rights advocates, society laid the responsibility for domestic happiness at the woman's door.

While some women rejected the cult of true womanhood's double standards, race and poverty kept others outside the paradigm of domesticity. Poorer families could not dispense with women's productive labor because a relative decline in working-class financial circumstances, especially among the unskilled, necessitated high levels of female economic activity. The dominant culture also denied the sacredness of the home and its domestic virtues to slaves who remained trapped in an abusive pattern of agricultural labor. Domesticity likewise had little or no meaning for the Native and Mexican Americans who attempted to follow the ways of their ancestors despite the incursions of European Americans. Rural women also experienced less separation of spheres since they continued to produce some of the goods that their families consumed and to contribute their labor on the farm.

Poverty and irregular income meant lower standards of living and consumption for urban working-class women who could not afford new household technologies. Poor women did less and simpler cooking, lacking the resources to make the economies of scale recommended by the household advisers in this era. Their lives were a "ceaseless round of scraping, scrimping, borrowing, and scavenging" according to historian Christine Stansell. Instead of the intricate furnishings of middle-class households, rag rugs and a few sticks of furniture sufficed in overcrowded and unwholesome dwellings. High population densities led to lower standards of living, poorer sanitation, and ill health for city women and their families.

Working-class women had to carry buckets of water indoors, frequently up flights of steps, making housework more arduous in teeming cities where human and animal wastes contaminated water supplies. This endangered health as epidemic diseases swept through the poorer districts. Women and children scavenged for necessities; even firewood was harder to find as cities grew, so they frequently had to purchase a few sticks in order to cook their food or heat their homes. Some resorted to pawning clothes, pots, and bedding to buy food. They lived their lives outside the precepts of domesticity proclaimed by its middle-class proponents. More affluent members of the working class, who had a steady male income upon which to rely, acquired some comforts, but even their homes suffered in times of economic turmoil and unemployment which grew more prevalent as the nineteenth century progressed.

RACE AND DOMESTICITY

The cult of domesticity hardly applied to enslaved African-American women nor did it benefit the approximately 6 percent of blacks who were free. Slavery denied African-American women the things genteel white women most prized, including time to be with their children and be the major influence in their lives. White women used religion as a basis for asserting their moral vision of the world, but slave owners tried to channel African-American women's piety for their own purposes. They refused them the right to practice religion freely, although many slaves held surreptitious evening meetings. One former slave recalled they were only allowed to attend the "white folks' church" and his master didn't even like that because he worried his slaves would learn too much. Other whites permitted slaves to worship since white preachers told them to be good to their masters. They ignored these injunctions and sang, prayed, and served God in their own way.

Sexual terrorism was part of the institution of slavery; many slave owners rejected slave women's purity. They manipulated slave fertility, arranged marriages, and, not infrequently, raped bondswomen. Former slaves' narratives indicate a significant level of miscegenation; about 5 percent mentioned having a white father. While a few bondswomen may have had loving relationships with white men, slave narratives indicate a strong element of compulsion. White men defined all African-American women as available and took those they wanted, sometimes in front of their children or husbands. Minnie Folkes, born into slavery, told a Federal Writers' Project interviewer that an overseer beat her mother with a horsewhip many times for refusing his advances. Virginia Hayes Shepherd described the treatment of a slave on a neighboring plantation: Old Master Gaskins "made demands on Diana just the same as if she had been his wife." She repulsed him repeatedly so he "put her in a cart, and took her to Norfolk and put her on the auction block." Other women or the husbands who tried to protect them endured beatings and abuse. Masters impregnated their slaves themselves or encouraged their sons to do so. A former slave in Virginia explained, "if you was a slave and had a good looking daughter, she was taken from you. They would put her in the big house where the young masters could have the run of her." Such practices asserted white control over African-American women and denied them the purity so prized in white women.

Southern courts declared the rape of a slave was not a crime if perpetrated by a white. Only in 1860, did Mississippi define the sexual assault by an African-American man on a female slave under the age of 12 as unlawful. Thus African-American women had no protection in law, although some fought back against their attackers. White women rarely challenged their husband's behavior, even if they disapproved, while a successful defense of virtue by a bondswoman could result in her being sold away from her own family.

Slave owners demanded submissiveness from their bondspeople regardless of their sex, but the character of that submissiveness differed from that required of northern or even southern white women. Proponents of domesticity wanted women to be submissive for the sake of family peace and to reduce contention in the home. The submissiveness of slavery had little to do with relations inside the slave cabins and everything to do with the control people in the big house exercised over those in the quarters. Slaves were expected to work the hours demanded and were beaten if owners thought they were slacking or not sufficiently subservient.

Slave masters controlled aspects of slave personal life in ways unthinkable in white society; they were, in effect, a third party to social relationships in the quarters. Slaves had to ask their owners' permission to marry. Even though such marriages had no legal validity and were no protection against separation through the sale of one spouse, they still played a crucial role in plantation life. Slave owners relied upon bondswomen to reproduce their labor force, encouraging them to have children and selling those who remained barren. They ensured that slave women augmented their families by forcing them to take husbands, regardless of the woman's wishes. Some provided wedding celebrations, made a formal ceremony of joining the couple, or watched them jump over a broomstick, a common plantation marriage rite.

Yet even slavery was not a monolithic institution: the treatment of women during pregnancy, childbirth, and child-rearing varied greatly. Owners might instruct overseers to be "kind and indulgent" to pregnant women and not force them to undertake "any service or hardship" that would injure the child. Slave women, as historian Deborah Gray White suggests, understood their usefulness to their owners in this regard. Some masters gave the mothers of large families Saturdays off while others reduced their servitude in the fields, especially during pregnancy. Yet infant mortality was high among slaves and many slave children were seriously underweight, indicating that slave mothers continued to carry heavy work loads well into pregnancy and that slave nutrition was poor. Even in the last weeks of pregnancy, bondswomen picked at least three-quarters as much cotton as other slaves.

The employment of slave women under the gang labor system of the cotton plantations limited the amount of weight put on during pregnancy and imperiled their babies' health. By denying these women the protection afforded to white women of lighter or no work in the last trimester of pregnancy, slave owners put the value of the present crop to be picked above the long-term gain from a larger labor force. They believed slave women were less delicate and needed less careful attention during pregnancy than white women.

Slave women's experience of family life differed from that of white women in other ways. Although they started having children at a younger age they did not do so at the earliest age possible. Despite pressure from owners to be fruitful and multiply the average bondswoman had her first child at the age of 19 or 20. The delay of two to three years between the age of menarche and first pregnancy suggests a conscious attempt to postpone childbearing, while the relatively high proportion of childlessness (perhaps as high as 15–20 percent among slaves compared with about 4 percent of white women) indicates poor health and possibly a reluctance to bring children into the horrors of slave life.

After childbirth many plantation masters permitted new mothers three weeks in which to recover before reassigning them to the fields. Englishwoman Frances Kemble, married to the owner of rice and cotton plantations on Georgia's Sea Islands, described the anguish experienced by these women in her *Journal*. A number of pregnant slaves begged her to intercede with her husband to modify the sentence "which condemns them to resume their labor of hoeing in the fields three weeks after their confinement." While Kemble could not interfere with their work, the slaves hoped she would use her influence to obtain a longer respite from field labor after childbirth.

These women suffered high rates of infant mortality as hard physical labor reduced their milk supplies and they seldom nursed their babies on demand. Instead they fed them hurriedly before they went to the fields in the morning, and young children brought the babies out to them for nursing during the day. Some bondswomen kept their babies with them while they hoed and picked and a few managed to nurse and work at the same time by carrying the baby in a cloth sling so it could suck while the mother picked cotton.

Slave owners did not suspend their normal harsh treatment of bondswomen who did not pick enough cotton, rice, or tobacco, who did not spin their quota, or who otherwise fell short in their productivity while pregnant or nursing. Medical historian Todd Savitt believes that planters regarded "pregnancy as almost holy." While some did, former slaves recounted how planters would whip pregnant or nursing mothers "so that blood and milk flew mingled from their breasts." Historian Jacqueline Jones posits that "the pregnant woman represented the sexuality of the slave community in general, and that of her husband and herself in particular; she thus symbolized a life in the quarters carried on apart from white interference." Whipping expectant mothers punished the entire slave community for its very existence and attempts to survive under a sadistic and brutal regime.

Slaves employed various strategies to compensate for the evils of slavery. Their African heritage of co-residence in kinship groups (one spouse joined the other's compound, the children resided with their mother and the kin group bore much of the responsibility for childcare) helped slaves cope with the strains slavery placed on the family. Fictive or adopted kin solaced younger and older slaves alike; older men and women addressed as uncle and aunt provided emotional support for children and young adults sold away from their own parents. When Martha King was sold at the age of 5 with her grandmother, aunt, and uncle, her Uncle Henry looked after her, and she resided with members of her extended family in the slave quarters. Former slaves' narratives frequently referred to the role of grandparents or extended family in bringing them up. Thus the West African pattern of extensive kin involvement in child-rearing helped to sustain families during slavery.

Bondspeople reinforced family networks through child naming patterns. Male children frequently bore their father's name and daughters were sometimes called after aunts or grandmothers but rarely had their mother's name. This pattern reflected a harsh reality: fathers were more likely to be separated from their children than mothers. Although historians dispute the exact proportion of families broken apart by selling a member, the forcible severing of family ties was a dreadful possibility for all bondspeople. The majority of slaves grew up with both parents present, but individual experiences varied considerably. Robert Fogel and Stanley Engerman calculated that one in every eleven marriages between slaves ended through the sale of one or both partners. Herbert Gutman places the estimate at about one in six. Naming sons after their fathers helped bind the family together symbolically, even when slavery broke it apart.

The custom of marrying men from other plantations exacerbated marital separation. Since West African traditions prohibited marriage between first cousins, slaves on smaller plantations and farms sought partners "abroad," outside the extended family network. Wives and husbands in such marriages saw each other at weekends, but the sale of husband or wife might sever even this tie. Ministers commonly accepted that a partner's removal farther away than 30 miles constituted divorce because husbands could not walk this distance and back between Saturday at sundown and Monday at sunrise, which was the time slave owners permitted their bondspeople to visit kin on distant plantations.

Once married, slave women tried to create a comfortable domestic environment for themselves and their families, sacrificing sleep and leisure for domestic chores. They held quilting parties and made clothes for their families and did most or all of the domestic work in their cabins, cooking, cleaning, and washing. Even men living on other plantations would bring their dirty washing to their wives for laundering. Bondswomen grew additional food for their families on garden plots, raised chickens and occasionally pigs, and saved up

feathers or gathered moss to stuff mattresses. In all this they followed older customs of self-sufficiency and tried to compensate for
the inadequacies of their rations.

Domestic work done for their own family took on special significance since they were working for themselves then, as one former
slave recalled. Prompted by harsh necessity, bondswomen's self-sufficiency remained a source of pride and wonder to their descendants,
as did men's work providing for their families. Bondsmen made furniture from planks and logs. Men and some women fished and hunted, using their skills to provide meat for their families who would
otherwise have had little protein.

On most, but not all, plantations women cooked for their families.
According to folklorist Charles Joyner, food spiced with the memories of the "African culinary grammar . . . became one of the symbols
of group identity in the slave community." Many slave narratives
mention maternal exhaustion and the poor quality of food given to
bondspeople. They got suet and a slice of bread for breakfast and for
dinner they ate ash cake baked on the blade of a hoe. Extra rations
given out at Christmas, the foodstuffs slaves grew in the evenings or
on Sundays, and women's cooking and men's hunting skills sustained slaves through harsh times and cruel treatment. Slave women
were, "self-reliant, self-determined survivalists" to use historian
Brenda E. Stevenson's description, employing their agricultural,
cooking, and nurturing skills to succor their families and communities.

Some historians cast these domestic roles into exact images of
white society, believing bondswomen sustained their husband's masculinity through their domestic labors. Eugene Genovese claims that
men's work corn shucking, hunting, and fishing strengthened their
role as provider. Nor did women, in this view, resent cooking and
quilting rather than shucking corn, since they supported male authority and the gendered division of labor. Still, slave women and men
both provided added food and comfort for their families.

Deborah Gray White believes slave families were egalitarian
because the partners had complementary roles with neither holding
economic power over the other. As bell hooks indicates, African
women had traditionally performed agricultural labor, but as they
assimilated white American values they came to believe field work
degraded women. After emancipation, wrote Alabama plantation
owner Henry Watson, "the women say that they never mean to do

anymore outdoor work, that white men support their wives; and they mean that their husbands shall support them." This desire to spend more time caring for their children and providing domestic comforts for their families was a compensation for the abuses of slavery, but it does not mean that African-American women accepted the stereotyped passivity of the cult of true womanhood. Their heritage and their experiences engendered strong working partnerships, while practices such as abroad marriages contributed to independence within relationships.

After freedom, the number of African-American women working in the fields dropped as they attempted to redress the imbalance between caring for their families and economic production. White land owners adopted sharecropping as a way of forcing entire freed families to labor, while poverty did not permit former slaves to withdraw from productive work altogether. Since most African-American women lived in rural areas and combined some work on the farm with domestic and family-oriented labors, few could subscribe to the cult of true womanhood even if they wanted to.

NATIVE AMERICAN WOMEN

The cult of true womanhood also had little relevance for Native American women who valued interdependence in social and economic relations. The Pueblo Indians of the Southwest marked these relations through the exchange of gifts between the generations as well as between the partners. Prospective marriage partners exchanged equal amounts of wealth, indicating each partner's parity of importance. While many couples remained together for life, others parted through the simple expedient of one party living elsewhere. In this settled agricultural society, older men and women had great prestige, controlling social well-being and ownership of the household, respectively. According to historian Ramon Gutiérrez, Pueblo households were "preeminently a female domain of love and ritual" in which men moved in with their wives' families, respecting them, and laboring for the good of the household.

The Native Americans on the Great Plains who followed the buffalo using dogs as pack animals prized stamina in both sexes since both women and men needed to keep pace with travois. Men who could no longer march with the group as it traveled donned their best hunting clothes and went out with a war-party "just to find a chance to get killed while fighting." When a woman grew too old to sustain the long drives, her family set up a lodge, provided her with meat and firewood and left her to die. According to Pretty Shield, whose grandmother told her of the time before the white people came to the Northern Plains, her people had no choice: "They could not pack old women on their backs, and dogs could not drag them." Once they obtained horses, they could travel farther and pull heavier loads, enabling older men and women to stay with their families as they traveled.

Native American society celebrated both sexes' coming of age with elaborate puberty rites. Among the Apaches, these ceremonies honored the spirit White Painted Woman, who controlled fertility. The celebration consisted of eight phases, each marking a girl's entrance into womanhood, her role in the continuation of the tribe, and her useful and fertile life to come. The Piutes of the Great Plains placed the young woman under the care of two older friends; they spent 25 days together, living in a teepee, according to Sarah Winnemucca Hopkins, gathering firewood, fasting from meat, and going through additional "labors which are thought to be strengthening." After this period, young women could marry, which they usually did in their late teens. Other tribes placed young women under the special protection of their grandmothers who instructed them in womanly matters.

Courtship proceeded directly between the couple in some groups while in others the prospective husband approached the young woman's parents, giving them presents. Relations between the marriage partners had an egalitarian base. After a Piute woman gave birth her husband did the household work for 25 days. There was strong social pressure upon men to be careful of their wives' health and to look after their children. Mothers fed their children for an extended period; the Kickapoo children of what became Illinois were still partially breast-fed at the age of 4 or 5. Some Native Americans practiced multiple marriages or serial monogamy. Among the Crow of the Great Plains, for example, a husband might marry his wife's unmarried sisters if their relatives believed he could take good care of them.

The coming of the white people disrupted many Native American customs as westward expansion displaced Native Americans under brutal conditions. Before the Civil War western tribes managed to retain their traditional patterns of gender relations and behavior, although eastern tribes had been decimated and pushed off their lands, and some southwestern ones had suffered the loss of traditional ways through contact with the Spanish religious and military conquerors. The European migration provided opportunities for the newcomers at the cost of impoverishing Native people and destroying their distinctive way of life.

THE WESTWARD MIGRATION

Soldiers, trappers, missionaries, and miners comprised the majority of the first whites to move west, followed closely by farmers, ranchers, their families, teachers, prostitutes, and others seeking opportunities, health, and a fresh start. Some women went for the adventure, employment, or to find husbands; others, most notably African-American bondswomen, had no choice. The move to the cotton and rice frontier wrenched slaves from all contact with their families since illiterate slaves could not write to distant kin. Native-born whites predominated amongst the migrants, but there were also Germans, Scandinavians, and other northwest Europeans settling on the frontier before the Civil War.

The sex ratio in the West varied with the stage of settlement, with initial male predominance giving way amongst white migrants as the economy diversified and more women and families arrived. In the Midwest in 1820, there were 111.6 men for every 100 women, compared with 103.3 men per 100 women in the United States as a whole. By 1860, the sex ratio had fallen slightly to 108.9. As whites flooded west to find gold and other precious metals, the sex ratio in the Mountain and Pacific territories and states skyrocketed to 280.9 men per 100 women in 1850 but fell to 214.2 in 1860 and 159.8 in 1870.

Early historians of the frontier, notably Frederick Jackson Turner, regarded it as a land of opportunity for men, but ignored women's presence. Even when historians noticed female migrants they assumed them to be reluctant venturers, based largely on white women's letters describing their loneliness and longing for their families. Dee Brown, author of one of the first histories of western women, depicted them as unwilling pioneers dutifully following their husbands west. Clearly some women resented leaving their kinfolk behind, as Julie Roy Jeffrey's study of frontier women indicates, yet others migrated in family groups or to areas where other family members had settled. John Mack Faragher's analysis of the first settlers of Sugar Creek, Illinois, documents a large number of extended family networks created by migration. About half the families on the Overland Trail traveled in groups containing relatives. In 1850, about two-fifths of the households in Oregon had relations nearby, indicating the extent to which migration encompassed the extended family.

It is difficult to quantify the decision-making process which led an individual or a family to uproot from a settled existence and trek into the unknown. Given the patriarchal cast of American society, one might conclude that men made the decisions and women followed them. Laura Ingalls Wilder, the author of *The Little House on the Prairie* books about her family's experiences on the frontier, concluded that "Ma did follow Pa wherever he went, but Pa never went anywhere that Ma wouldn't follow." In many families, women's opinion about migration had a significant role in the decision to go or not. Undoubtedly some husbands wanted to go but their wives objected so the family stayed put. Because these non-pioneers did not travel west, their successful campaigns to remain in the East do not figure in migration history.

Women's cooperation was essential to the migration process since the preparatory work required active participation by female family members. As the distances to be crossed lengthened with the colonization of the far West in the 1840s and 1850s, women had to prepare for a journey of four to six months duration. They wove the cloth to cover the wagon and sewed the heavy canvas pieces together by hand. They grew, pickled, preserved, salted, and dried sufficient food to last the entire trek. They made several sets of clothes for each family member and ensured a sufficient supply of bedding, soap, candles, and other necessities. It is possible that an unwilling woman might undertake such arduous work, but most joined their husbands in a sense of common cause.

Some women would travel just so far, but no farther. Women headed a disproportionate number of families on the mining frontier. They traveled with their husbands or followed after them, but mining was a transient and dangerous occupation. One woman, speaking no doubt for many, told the husband who announced he wanted to relocate to "move on if you have to, but I've dragged two boys and a houseful of furniture just as far as I'm going to." She enumerated the places they had lived. "First it was Ohio, then Michigan, then the Peninsula, then Minnesota, Michigan again, then Denver, Weaver, and Creede . . ." and declared "right here I'm going to stay." Single and newly married women found it easier than married women with families to uproot and move. Not surprisingly the entire process was far more complicated for women with children to look after.

Life on the Overland Trail followed gendered divisions of labor; men mostly drove the oxen and mended wagons while women cooked, washed, and cared for children. Women rose early in order to stoke up the fire for cooking, they milked the cows and churned the butter. But women and men shared some jobs; men occasionally cooked and might even wash. Helen Carpenter's memoir of her 1857 trip across the Plains in an ox wagon described "an old gentleman farmer" who made the fire, got out the pots and kettles and food-stuffs while "mother makes the bread and coffee." Women with less obliging husbands found themselves doing domestic chores at the end of a hard day's journey; they even washed and mended clothes and gathered wood or buffalo chips for fuel on precious rest days.

As transport improved, more women made at least part of the westward journey by train, a less arduous form of transport than cov-ered wagon. Reformers Amelia and Dexter Bloomer from Seneca Falls, NY, purchased an interest in the *Western Home Visitor* in 1853. Mrs. Bloomer announced she would accompany her husband to Mount Vernon, Ohio, taking the temperance paper, the *Lily*, with her, notifying readers that "as a true and faithful wife" she felt "bound to say in the language of Ruth 'where thou goest, I will go.'" The opportunity to improve her newspaper outweighed her sorrow at "sundering the many ties that bind us to home and friends in our native state." Two years later the Bloomers removed to Council Bluffs, Iowa, where Mrs. Bloomer could no longer edit the *Lily* owing to Council Bluff's limited links to the outside world (it took another decade for the railroad to reach it), yet she still wrote and maintained her interest in temperance, suffrage, and women's proper-ty rights.

Other women migrated west with a sense of mission to convert Native Americans to Christianity or construct a utopian world. The first white woman to cross the Rocky Mountains, Narcissa Whitman, accompanied her missionary doctor husband in his work in Oregon in 1836. Like the Mormon women who trekked west, sometimes pushing handcarts, in order to avoid persecution and establish a theocratically based society free from gentile pressure, these women saw themselves as an integral part of western settlement, not as reluctant pioneers.

DOMESTICITY IN THE WEST

Once women arrived at their final destination, they faced the challenges of establishing a new home, a new life, and a new community. Subsistence farming required hard work from all family members in the initial phases of settlement. Faced with primitive living conditions, frontier families had to be resourceful. Sod houses and log cabins were the norm since sawn timber had to wait for the establishment of lumber mills or railroad links. Agnes Miner's account of her Colorado childhood in the 1860s describes how the family constructed its floor: her mother sewed burlap sacks together and made a carpet which her father tacked down with homemade pins. The family fashioned three beds on top of this floor by building an enclosure from logs, filling it with hay, and placing feather beds brought from Pennsylvania on top. When they moved two years later Agnes helped her father construct a fireplace and a cellar.

Settlers created homes by cutting the sod into building blocks with plows or spades, first placing doors and window-frames, then building up the sod walls around them, and forming the roof from whatever materials were available. Straw, corn stalks, or willow boughs laid over the rafters were carefully topped with sod turves to keep the soil from crumbling and the rain from dribbling through. When time permitted settlers made up a rough plaster from sand and clay to cover the internal walls. In *Chronicles of Comanche County*, Oklahoma, Elva Page Lewis described keeping house in a primitive dwelling as "a chore, but one never knew what might fall from the roof to vary the routine." Other pioneers lived in tents, even through the cold winters, until they could construct more permanent homes. Eveline M. Alexander, the wife of a cavalry officer, found that everything in her tent on the Arkansas frontier had been arranged "most comfortably." The tent was lined with blue army blankets, which kept out the glare of the sun and protected her from dampness. She even had a buffalo skin carpet.

Since all the furnishings had to be transported from the East or constructed on the spot, it was years before western homes reached the same level of decoration and comfort as eastern dwellings. A few women hauled pianos across the prairies, while others made do with a cook stove, sink, or smaller items. Amelia Bloomer set up housekeeping in Council Bluffs, Iowa, with an old table, two wooden chairs, a bed made on the floor, three trunks, an old-fashioned cook stove, and a few dishes. Women returned to domestic manufacturing to remedy the deficiencies of frontier life, using handcrafted items to furnish their dwellings comfortably, sewing scraps of cloth into rugs and quilts, saving chicken feathers to stuff pillows and comforters, and sewing the family's clothes.

Economic and demographic conditions undermined the cult of true womanhood in the West where women lived far from markets and shops. The unbalanced sex ratio contributed to a demand for sexual services, especially on the mining frontier. Prostitutes existed outside the constraints of true womanhood; indeed, they violated every tenet of it since by definition they were neither pure nor submissive to just one man. Few had homes of their own; instead they had bedrooms in brothels or inhabited one-room "cribs" in the red light district. Churches excluded them and even when they had children it was difficult to raise them since zealous child welfare advocates tried to place them in the county poor farm or orphanages. Many sporting women boarded their children with relatives or foster families to avoid losing contact with them completely.

Western prostitutes came from varied ethnic origins. Businessmen brought young Mexican women to California to service miners and other unattached men. Native American women were also subjected to prostitution for the benefit of miners in the 1850s, according to the San Francisco *Home Missionary*. A high proportion of the early female Chinese immigrants to the United States who had been indentured or sold by their parents in China were forced into prostitution. Judy Yung's history of Chinese women in America estimates that 85 percent of the Chinese women in San Francisco in 1860 were prostitutes who assented to contracts they could not read. They endured physical and mental abuse, although some managed to escape to rescue homes established by missionaries.

Did the cult of true womanhood pervade frontier women's lives? It certainly had little applicability to Native American women or those of Mexican and Chinese descent, while bondswomen in Texas and Arkansas did field work almost exclusively. True womanhood seemed irrelevant to many country women immersed in wresting a living from the land. Pioneer women, Julie Roy Jeffrey notes in *Frontier Women*, had an economic importance which eastern women had lost. There was some blurring of the boundaries between men's and women's work, although most tasks were assigned to one gender or the other. However, the nature of western life meant that women had to take on men's work when they traveled to distant mining claims or ranches. Mormon women, for example, assumed responsibility for supporting their families when their husbands undertook missionary work.

In the West as in the East, only middle-class urban women could refrain from economic production. Elizabeth Jameson believes that western women accepted some of the ideals expressed by the cult of true womanhood, but only affluent city dwellers could totally fulfill these precepts, and not all migrant women wished for a wholly domesticated existence. Amelia Bloomer might have moved with her husband beyond the reach of the railroad, but she remained true to her suffragist and temperance principles. She continued to lecture on women's rights and to organize suffrage and temperance societies. Like many other migrants she became actively involved in establishing networks of women devoted to civic improvement and the integration of women into their society. Female activism in the West across a broad variety of activities including suffrage indicates that true womanhood had less of a grip than in the East.

Recent immigrants, frontier women, slaves, and other women of color did not necessarily share the middle-class model of domesticity and separation of spheres, either from cultural choice, economic necessity, or the imposition of others' values upon them. The family forms which emerged in the ante-bellum era depended on the interaction between economic, demographic and cultural practices. The movement of manufacturing outside the home, the switch from production to consumption and the increased number of domestic servants, when combined with lower birth and death rates, enabled affluent women to devote greater attention to each child and to infuse domesticity with moral responsibility for the family.

In the increasingly heterogeneous society of ante-bellum America many women still divided their attention between economic productivity and family life and had little time to devote to their children. Such complicated patterns indicate that a purely domestic focus characterized relatively few mid-nineteenth-century families. The cult of domesticity simultaneously empowered and restricted those women whose economic and cultural circumstances permitted their withdrawal from household manufacturing, waged or agricultural labor, and elevated motherhood and domesticity to crucial importance in the emotional life of the family while rejecting political involvement and wage earning for married women. Although the new socio-cultural norms applied to a narrow sector of the female population, they nevertheless established the terms of the debate over women's roles in the United States before the Civil War.

3 Education and Culture in Ante-Bellum America

Writing in 1790, playwright and essayist Judith Sargent Murray inquired whether it was "reasonable that a candidate for immortality, for the joys of heaven, an intelligent being, who is to spend an eternity in contemplating the works of Deity, should at present be so degraded as to be allowed no other ideas, than those which are suggested by the mechanism of a pudding or sewing the seams of a garment?" Her questions echoed the growing sentiment favoring greater public education, especially for girls, who had lower levels of literacy than their brothers, were less likely to go to school, studied a more limited curriculum, and had fewer opportunities for advanced education.

The surging levels of education and literacy in the post-Revolutionary era had important consequences for women, opening up employment opportunities, facilitating communication over greater distances, and permitting them to record their feelings and ideas for public and private consumption. Women's new-found literacy enabled them to write magazines and books, teach school, and enter the professions in growing numbers, and so altered their place in American intellectual and cultural life. The arguments in favor of expanding female education reflected the political and commercial needs of the new nation as well as female aspirations, varying with region and race so that northern and western women had the highest levels of education, while few women of color received any formal education in this era.

Women participated in the public cultural life primarily through their writing, although some developed careers in painting, sculpture, acting or singing. Women's artistic and craft activities took place mostly in the home where female creativity and skill could make the difference between four bare walls, rough furnishings, and ill-fitting clothing and an attractive domestic environment with paintings, decorative fittings, and warm linen and garments. Especially in remote

areas or where money was scare, female craft work melded adorn-
ment with practicality in complex quilts, embroidery, tatting, and
knitting. This creative work received little public recognition in ante-
bellum America, nevertheless it was an important part of women's
social and domestic culture, treasured by families who handed quilts
and samplers down the generations.

THE EXPANSION OF EDUCATION

Public schooling for girls expanded in the late eighteenth and early
nineteenth century especially in the North where it built upon earlier
traditions valuing literacy for religious purposes. In 1647, the
Massachusetts General Court sought to keep "Old Deluder Satan" at
bay by requiring townships to open schools to teach children to read
the Bible. A number of girls in the northern colonies also went to
dame schools run by women in their own homes which combined
childminding and inculcation of the 3Rs, but fewer girls than boys
received any formal education. Girls' book learning typically ended
once they reached the age of 10 or 12, whereas some boys went on to
academies or college.

The daughters of elite families sometimes shared their brothers'
private college preparatory tutoring. Judith Sargent studied along
with her brother under the aegis of the Reverend John Rogers in mid-
eighteenth-century Gloucester, Massachusetts. Young Judith thus
received tuition in Greek, Latin, and mathematics while her brother
prepared for further studies at Harvard and continued teaching her
when he came home for the holidays from his college.

Most girls (and boys, too) did not share this privileged access to
education, prompting charitably minded women to establish free
schools for poor children such as Anne Parrish's Charity School for
Poor Girls which opened in Philadelphia in 1796. Since most cities
still charged tuition fees, pauper schools provided the only access to
education for poor children. Even quite large cities such as Boston
had few free schools for children of either sex in their early years,
while publicly supported academies (for children over the age of 12
or 14) were only for boys until the 1820s.

As long as parents had to purchase education for their children,
they tended to favor sons over daughters; by the end of the colonial
era, about four-fifths of white male New Englanders could sign their

names, compared with about two-fifths of white women. Pressure to increase female educational opportunities in the postcolonial era came from several interrelated sources. The Revolution challenged existing hierarchies, replacing inherited position with patriotic citizenship. Politicians and social theorists worried how to disseminate the new political morality in a society bereft of its traditional moorings. The rush to found public schools testified to the importance attached to learning in the new republic. The constitutions of northern states such as Massachusetts and Pennsylvania required towns to provide free or low-cost public schooling. Especially in rural areas such schools educated boys and girls separately, with older boys having classes in the winter taught by men, while girls and very young boys attended school in the summer and were taught by women.

Proponents of female education based their arguments on two distinct lines of reasoning. Judith Sargent Murray contended that women and men started life equally and had equal souls. Boys received book learning while girls had to be content with domesticity which subsequently disadvantaged them, especially if they had to earn their own living. In contrast, Benjamin Rush and other proponents of republican motherhood favored female education because it would make women better mothers and inculcators of patriotism and morality.

Republican motherhood channeled women's political contribution through maternity. As fathers increasingly worked outside the home, mothers had direct supervision of both sons and daughters. They educated both sexes at home in their early years, transmitting republican values to sons and daughters alike. Republican motherhood also foreshadowed decreased public acknowledgement of female economic productivity. During the Revolution women shouldered responsibility for domestic arrangements, household management, and childcare in addition to securing the family's living. Abigail Adams, wife of the second President of the United States, achieved notable success with her agricultural ventures during John's long absences on Continental Congress business. Other women found the combination of economic and domestic responsibilities daunting and gladly jettisoned the economic role after peace arrived. Once their husbands devoted themselves to the business of building a prosperous republic these women preferred to be educators of children rather than producers of goods. Their education, as fostered by proponents of republican motherhood, typically was limited to the household arts and other subjects which would suit them for their family vocation.

Yet not all educators and social commentators viewed women's education through the prism of family life. Echoing Enlightenment sentiments, Sarah Pierce emphasized that students at her female academy in Lichfield, Connecticut, in the 1790s were "rational beings" who deserved "the discipline of the mind" as much as men. Unusually for her generation, Pierce had been educated with the specific intention that she would open a school with her older sister. The curriculum at Lichfield Academy featured history, geography, mathematics, and language skills but included needlework and painting. Pierce's influence extended through her pupils Catharine Beecher and Harriet Beecher (Stowe) to shape female education and sentiments throughout the ante-bellum era.

Sarah Pierce's contemporary Judith Sargent Murray (1751–1820) similarly advocated educating women for their own good, since she herself combined writing poems, magazine articles, plays, and novels with raising a family. Her widely read essays propounded the importance of a well-rounded education for women. The protagonist of her *Gleaner* articles, 16-year-old Margaretta, knew needlework, English, French, could reckon her accounts, "had skimmed the surface of astronomy and natural philosophy," and studied history and the poets. She could sketch a landscape, make patterns for her dresses, dance, and play the piano. She exemplified scholastic accomplishments without descending into vainglory or artifice, according to Murray.

Written under the pen name Constantia, Murray's *Essay on the Equality of the Sexes* (1790) endorsed female education for its own sake, arguing that boys and girls began life with the same abilities, but society limited females to a smaller sphere. Opportunities provided to one sex were denied the other, so women experienced "a mortifying consciousness of inferiority, which embitters every enjoyment." Writing at the same time as Mary Wollstonecraft, the English advocate of improved female education, Murray believed it unfair that: "one is exalted, and the other depressed . . . the sister must be wholly domesticated, while the brother is led by the hand through all the flowery paths of science." Like Wollstonecraft, Murray believed schooling should suit females to earn a living in an increasingly commercial and business-oriented world.

Changing religious beliefs also encouraged female education.

Direct conversion experiences characterized the Second Great Awakening, a religious revival among American Protestants from the 1790s to the 1820s, which appealed particularly to women attracted by a Christ depicted as sacrificing and suffering for humanity. Evangelical Protestants emphasized individual responsibility and the value of each person's soul and, as with their Puritan forebears, considered that education had an important role in enabling people to experience God's word directly. Southern abolitionist Sarah Grimké believed academic study would strengthen women's self-respect, character, and dignity and help in the battles against sexism and slavery. Grimké complained that men translated and interpreted the Bible in their own favor. When women "were admitted to the honor of studying Greek and Hebrew" they would produce a different and less restrictive reading of the Bible which would enhance women's standing.

As the cult of true womanhood elevated the social significance of women's activities in the home, girls' schooling took on greater importance. Responsible now for inculcating republican virtues and running the home with little or no assistance from their husbands, they needed more knowledge to carry out their duties. Teacher Emma Willard's "Address to the Public" (1819) indicated that national prosperity depended "on the character of its citizens. The character of these will be formed by their mothers" so state legislatures had an obligation to provide schools for "the females, who are to be their mothers, while it is yet with them a season of improvement." The author of "Female Instruction" (probably magazine editor Sarah Josepha Hale) echoed these sentiments in 1845, asserting that: "the tone of *family education* and of society needs to be raised. This can never be done till greater value is set on the cultivated female intellect."

The cult of true womanhood thus fostered young women's intellectual development as part of their maternal vocation. Female education was crucial to family well-being once men took jobs outside the home, according to pioneering family historian Arthur C. Calhoun, who felt that "the rush of the new country left the men no time to be fathers, they were away all day and children came to be left entirely in the care of their mothers." Lydia Maria Child recognized the social and economic importance of educating women in her widely read *Mother's Book* (1831) in which she declared that the safety and prosperity of the nation depended on mothers' "intelligence and discretion." As a result female education expanded rapidly between 1830 and 1850, especially at the elementary level, where boys and girls attended on an equal basis. Once again the North led the expansion of public education; over half the children in New York State were in school at mid-century and in 1852, Massachusetts passed the first compulsory school attendance law, applying it equally to girls and boys.

Coeducation had its disadvantages as some school masters tyrannized and frightened their new female pupils. Lucy Larcom wrote of her grammar school in the 1830s that the tall gaunt master "used to stalk across the school-room, right over the desk-tops, to find out if there was any mischief going on." This man had a "fearful leather strap, which was sometimes used even upon the shrinking palm of a little girl." Louisa May Alcott's *Little Women* (1868) depicted the terror girls felt at school masters' harsh treatment. Amy described one of her school friends as "*parrylized* with fright" when dragged by her ear to the recitation platform and made to stand for half an hour holding her slate with a naughty picture on it. Unlike the cozy dame schools of the colonial era, these new educational institutions were serious places in which discipline was as important as reading and writing.

Private single-sex schools proliferated alongside coeducational ones in the early nineteenth century as many women turned to teaching as a livelihood and to disseminate their hard-won knowledge. Emma Willard, a passionate believer in women's education, opened her Middlebury Female Seminary in 1814 to help support her family, offering a curriculum which included science and classics and favoring women teachers who provided role models along with a well-balanced academic tutelage. Willard appealed to the New York State legislature to spend public funds on girls' schools, stressing their destiny as mothers and inculcators of republican virtues. Although New York rejected the Willard Plan in 1819, it attracted attention to the cause of female education.

In 1821, the Troy, NY, city fathers assisted Willard in opening the Troy Female Seminary with a liberal arts curriculum which reflected affluent New Yorkers' aspirations for their daughters. Willard's rigorous academic program became the model for over 200 similar academies. Almira Phelps, Willard's sister, taught at Troy Seminary and later opened Patapsco Female Institute in Baltimore, Maryland, at a time when there were few public schools in the South. In 1823,

Catharine Beecher established the Hartford Female Seminary, successfully appealing to elite women to raise funds for buildings and teachers' salaries. New York City and Boston established tax-funded high schools for girls in 1826 with other cities following their lead in the 1840s and 1850s.

Support for female learning, though widespread, was not universal. The General Association of Congregational Ministers opposed Mary Lyon's attempts to raise funds for her academy at Mount Holyoke, Massachusetts. Instead she solicited contributions from moderately situated families seeking to advance their daughters' opportunities. Women gave generously to the cause and enabled Mount Holyoke Seminary to open in 1837 with three permanent buildings. Lyon hoped to train women for useful work in society rather than to be ornaments to it and, imbued with notions of self-sacrifice, many graduates became missionaries and teachers. Their eagerness to serve and sense of vocation may have contributed to their acceptance of low salaries as well as to school boards' willingness to hire them.

Indeed, female teachers were highly cost-effective. Catharine Beecher linked the advancement of education to an inexpensive labor force. She appealed to Congress for funds to train women teachers in the 1850s, arguing that universal education would only happen if it were cheap. Unmarried women could afford to work for half the salary paid to men, according to Beecher, since they had only themselves to support. Beecher did not consider that married women would want or need to work outside the home. Her belief that women did not need comparable wages with men, of course, did not take account of the many women who were the sole support of their families, either as daughters or widowed mothers, but it firmly established female educators as cheap labor.

The second advantage of women teachers was their supposed vocation for teaching as a natural extension of the female role. Emma Willard believed "nature designated our sex for the care of children," but envisaging teaching as a vocation, rather than an occupation, meant it did not warrant a decent salary. The low wages paid to women staff subsidized the rapid expansion of education as school boards hired them to instruct the expanding school population. At the outbreak of the Civil War, about one-quarter of all teachers were women; by 1870, half were. Women soon dominated the teaching profession at the lower ranks: they accounted for four-fifths of all

Massachusetts teachers by 1860 and some medium-sized cities such as Utica, New York, employed only female teachers by mid-century.

RACE, REGION, AND EDUCATION

There were dramatic regional and racial variations in the spread of education in the 1850s. Three-quarters of the white school age population attended classes in the North, compared with less than one-third in the South. Low population densities contributed to the poor educational facilities for white southerners while the fear of slave revolts led southern states to prohibit the education of African Americans by the 1830s. Even northern states provided little or no public schooling for them.

Motivated by abolitionist sentiments and a desire to expand opportunities, some African-American and white women tried to overcome public reluctance to educate black children. The first school to accept African-American children opened in 1793 when ex-slave Catherine Ferguson established her School for the Poor in New York City, teaching European- and African-American children together. The Pennsylvania Committee for Improving the Condition of Free Blacks founded its school in the same year with an African-American woman teacher. Unlike white schools of the early national era which were largely single sex, most schools educating black children taught both sexes together, perhaps because of the relatively small numbers in northern cities.

Most northern states segregated their educational facilities so that even cities with large black populations such as Philadelphia had separate schools. This led prominent African-American citizens including Robert Bridges Forten, father of Charlotte Forten, to educate their daughters at home or in private academies because they did not want their daughters to experience the humiliation of segregated schooling. In order to overcome the hostility of many whites towards black females seeking to further their knowledge, a number of African-American women such as Charlotte Forten's Aunt Margaretta opened their own schools.

African-American children living in border states had varying degrees of access to private and public instruction. Cincinnati, across the Ohio River from the slave state, Kentucky, barred African Americans from public institutions. In 1832, evangelical Protestant abolitionists of both races opened a school in Cincinnati's black district where three New York women taught African-American women and children in day, night, and Sunday Schools. As abolitionists, their struggle for the education of African Americans originated in their evangelical mission to further the cause of freedom.

African-American education expanded in single-race settings in some border states. The Oblate Sisters of Providence in Baltimore, a French-speaking black sisterhood, began St Frances Academy for African-American girls in 1829. For many years it was one of a handful of secondary schools open to black females. The Oblate nuns challenged racial and gender hierarchies as they expanded opportunities for their pupils. The bishop of Baltimore opposed their efforts, believing that the sisters and their students should be domestic servants. Such schools were pioneering ventures at a time when public education in the South was still rudimentary. Although Maryland passed a general school law in 1826, it contained a local option clause; only Baltimore opened public schools under its provisions and there was no statewide school system until after the Civil War.

Farther to the south, African Americans struggled to educate each other, frequently in secret schools. In 1819, Julian Froumountaine, a black woman originally from Santo Domingo, began a school for African Americans in Savannah, Georgia. She continued her educational efforts secretly in the 1830s after Georgia made it illegal to instruct them. Similar clandestine schools operated in other southern cities and occasionally on plantations. Some African-American women learned to read and write as slaves, taught by their masters' children.

The struggle to educate black women encountered strong opposition even where legal. Quaker Prudence Crandall tried to overcome the racial prejudices which inhibited the education of African Americans in the North. She admitted the daughters of local black farmers to her private academy in Canterbury, Connecticut, in 1833, provoking a storm of opposition and the wholesale withdrawal of white children from the school. "Determined if possible . . . to benefit the people of color," as she wrote to abolitionist William Lloyd Garrison, Crandall re-opened her school as a "High school for young colored Ladies and Misses." Canterbury selectmen retaliated by forbidding the education of African Americans from outside the state. When Crandall continued to teach, local merchants refused to supply provisions, the town fathers imprisoned her, townspeople poisoned the school well, and someone set fire to the school. A few years later, Bronson Alcott (Louisa May's father) had to close his Boston academy after protests over the admission of an African-American girl. While African Americans were educated separately, if at all, because of racial prejudice, Roman Catholic sisterhoods opened girls' schools throughout the United States in order to avoid Protestant religious indoctrination in public schools. The first American order of teaching nuns, the Sisters of Charity, founded by Catholic convert Elizabeth Seaton in 1809, ran both schools and hospitals. Mother Seaton wrote one of her supporters in 1810 that "her Blessed bishop" was fond of her establishment, and the clergy supported it through their prayers. Other congregations met hostility from clergy who doubted the validity of educating girls. A priest in Kentucky commanded the Dominican sisterhood there to disband because it persisted in its "foolish experiment" of operating a girls' school. The sisters persevered in the cause of female education although the diocese sold some of their land and withheld the sacrament from them. Nevertheless, the acceptance accorded to Mother Seaton by the Church fathers typified the growing endorsement of universal education (at least in the North and for whites) and a belief that literate girls would be better mothers.

HIGHER EDUCATION

Even after schools opened their doors to girls in large numbers, young women had relatively few opportunities to pursue higher education. Female seminaries and academies provided secondary schooling but did not grant undergraduate degrees until later in the century. Oberlin College admitted women in 1838, initially to a separate women's course. A number of other institutions allowed women to attend classes but not to enroll formally. Public tertiary education remained largely closed to women until after the Civil War. The few exceptions occurred in the West; the University of Iowa accepted four women out of a total of 89 students when it opened in 1855. The University of Wisconsin also allowed female students to register for a collegiate program in 1863, although the college president attempted to segregate them into a separate female faculty with less rigorous courses.

Because so few women's academies received public money,

women who wanted advanced education had to pay for it themselves, frequently laboring in factories or as teachers to defray their costs. Abolitionist Lucy Stone's father paid for her brothers' education, but refused to fund hers, so she taught school to cover the tuition fees at Oberlin College. Women flocked to the early Normal schools to prepare themselves for careers as teachers, especially once the rapid expansion of school systems in the West accentuated demand. Organizations such as the National Board of Popular Education in Hartford, Connecticut, prepared female teachers and missionaries for the western territories in the 1840s.

Other professional occupations and training schools were much less receptive to female entry; prejudice impeded women's progress in medicine throughout the nineteenth century. Harriot Hunt had worked as a self-taught doctor for more than 20 years in Boston before she attempted to matriculate at Harvard in order to improve her knowledge of physiology and anatomy. The President and Fellows of Harvard College informed her in 1845 that it was "inexpedient" to consider her request, fearing that a female would distract male students. Hunt finally received permission to attend lectures in 1850 but not to get a degree. Her fellow students protested that her attendance imperiled their self-respect since no woman of true delicacy, they complained, would listen to medical topics in the company of men. They were not "opposed to allowing woman her rights, but do protest against her appearing in places where her presence is calculated to destroy our respect for the modesty and delicacy of her sex."

Elizabeth Blackwell experienced similar obstacles in her efforts to become a doctor; many medical colleges rejected her application before Geneva College admitted her in 1847. Blackwell's own family supported her aspirations, but could not finance them, so like Lucy Stone she taught school to raise funds. These difficulties led to the founding of female medical colleges in the 1850s, easing access to the medical profession for a small number of women. Most female medics trained and practiced in single-sex institutions where they enjoyed the support of their sisters in medicine and their patients.

Even if women managed to get a medical education they met extreme hostility from doctors when they attempted to practice their profession; no hospital would permit Elizabeth Blackwell to use its facilities. She opened the New York Infirmary for Women and Children in 1857 with her sister Emily and Dr. Marie E. Zakrzewska, a graduate from Western Reserve. Even fewer women trained as physicians in the South, although many southern women practiced medicine informally in their families and communities, sometimes as granny-midwives. Almost none had the credentials which were becoming necessary for the public practice of medicine although female herbalists and healers remained sought after in rural areas into the twentieth century. Despite the expansion of women's education in this era, gendered conventions restricted the uses to which women could put their knowledge and frequently limited their efforts to quasi-domestic occupations.

WOMEN'S ART AND WRITING

A growing number of women used their hard-won literacy to record their thoughts and feelings, made significant contributions to popular literature and intellectual life, and sometimes subverted restrictive norms. Cultural historian Ann Douglas maintains that American culture became feminized during this era as women increasingly dominated the cultural market place and comprised about four-fifths of the reading public. Men turned their attention to business, leaving their wives and daughters to look after the non-commercial affairs of the home, church, culture, and charity. Other historians, including Kathleen D. McCarthy, counter that women's influence remained peripheral to (at least) certain aesthetic forms, especially the fine arts.

A few women obtained space in art galleries and museums, but many institutions simply refused to hang their pictures on their walls. McCarthy concludes that, "Art was a public and commercial enterprise, and in the ante-bellum period women had no place in such ventures," yet there were a handful of exceptions. Anne Whitney sculpted the abolitionist statue, *Africa*, while Vinnie Ream undertook busts of Abraham Lincoln, Thaddeus Stevens, General Custer, and Horace Greeley. Some women achieved success as actors and singers, but even in the world of entertainment, they could be marginalized and stigmatized, as were the "dance-hall girls" of the West. In a society which debated whether women should appear in public without a chaperone, the stage and concert hall had a limited attraction to supposedly respectable females.

Women reconciled their artistic endeavors with motherhood

through domestic crafts, especially quilting. Quilts symbolized frugality, reusing scraps of cloth to provide warmth in poorly heated houses and cabins, and allowed their makers to express their creativity in a way suited to their domestic and work lives, in patches and small pieces. Quilting reflected the segmented nature of many women's lives: they had little time to themselves and pieced quilts over many months in the snatches of time between doing other tasks. Women incorporated a wide range of designs and patterns in their quilting. African Americans drew upon techniques and color schemes common in West Africa; British Americans transposed patterns following the Revolution, turning Queen Charlotte's Crown into Indian Spring; and Native American quilts incorporated striking geometric designs from blankets and rugs. Before the destruction of the buffalo on the Northern Plains, Native American women decorated the rugs and blankets they made from buffalo skins, revealing the ubiquitous urge to combine beauty with function.

Elaine Showalter describes quilting as a metaphor for a female aesthetic, for sisterhood, and the politics of feminist survival. Each woman pieced her own quilt individually, then a group sewed the completed quilt top to its backing fabric. Frances Trollope wrote in *Domestic Manners of the Americans* (1832): "when the external composition of one of these is completed, it is usual to call together their neighbors and friends to witness, and assist at the quilting, which is the completion of this elaborate work." These quilting bees gave women opportunities to exchange news, ideas, and gossip and sometimes had a political dimension. Women's rights advocate Susan B. Anthony delivered her first speech on women's suffrage at a quilting bee. Quilting reflected the constraints upon women's lives as well as the beauty they brought to their homes and families, frugally turning small pieces of material into warm coverings, deploying their artistry in the service of their families.

THE USES OF LITERACY

The spread of literacy in the early nineteenth century resulted in an entirely new audience for the printed word since common schooling meant many more women and poor people could read. New technology decreased the cost and difficulty of publishing when machine printing presses replaced the heavy wooden presses of the colonial era. Advances in printing and engraving technology improved visual appeal; illustrations became relatively inexpensive to incorporate into newspapers and magazines; and improved transport facilitated the diffusion of illustrated magazines across the nation. A few women entered the printing trades as printers, but many more undertook careers as writers and editors. Literate women trying to make sense of lives so different from their mothers' constituted an expanding female audience, hungry for advice, information, and amusement.

Women carved a significant place for themselves in the burgeoning popular literary culture from the 1820s onwards through their editorship of magazines focused mainly upon the world of the home. Titles including *Mother's Magazine and Family Monitor, The Mother, Mother's Assistant, Mother's Monthly Journal,* and *Mother at Home and Household Magazine* signaled the importance of maternity and preached a limited sphere of activities for women, concentrating on domestic management, fashion, and personal relationships. They supported and propounded the cult of domesticity, simultaneously reinforcing women's importance and containing them within the home by depicting women as subordinate to their husbands even though crucial to the well-regulated household.

Books such as Eliza Farrar's *The Young Lady's Friend* (1836) preached the virtues of domesticity and elevated it to a vocation, for according to Farrar, "if a woman does not know how the various work of a house should be done, she might as well know nothing, for that is her express vocation." It mattered not how much learning or "how many accomplishments she may have, if she is wanting in that which is to fit her for her peculiar calling." Yet, while housework was woman's "express vocation," it should be done efficiently with any spare time to be dedicated to self-improvement, according to the popular literature of the day.

More than 100 magazine titles for women appeared between the 1820s and 1860s. Some addressed specific and narrow constituencies, while others sold tens of thousands of copies. One of the largest and most influential was *Godey's Lady's Book* edited by Sarah Josepha Hale, who embodied the dilemmas of the cult of domesticity and its potential to expand women's spheres. She believed that women's "empire is purer, more excellent and spiritual" than the "public duties of government," but she also supported female intellectual development. Invited in 1837 to edit the *Lady's Book* published by Louis Antoine Godey, she built it up from a circulation of 10 000 to 150 000 by 1860.

Literary domestics such as Hale lauded the cult of domesticity, at least for other women, expressing an ambiguous attitude toward women's place. Hale wrote in 1828 that it was "far more praiseworthy" for a woman "to make a happy home for her husband and children . . . than to make a book," though, of course, she dedicated herself to a literary career. Journalist Cornelia Walker edited the *Boston Transcript,* a newspaper founded by her late brother, from 1842 until 1847, advocating advanced education for women, but opposing female suffrage. Many literary domestics found it difficult to reconcile their own activities outside the home with the ideology of the era; they regarded domesticity as women's true vocation, but abandoned it for financial or intellectual reasons.

Godey's Lady's Book published the distinguished authors of its day along with fashion plates, household hints, recipes, and songs. It took a conventional view of women's place in the world, neither supporting women's suffrage nor acknowledging the social and political turmoil of the era. Yet Hale, a widowed mother of five children, believed every woman "should be qualified by some accomplishment which she may teach, or some art or profession she can follow, to support herself creditably, should the necessity occur," which led her to support female doctors, charity workers, and missionaries.

If Sarah Hale represented the domestic pole of women's quest for education and self-fulfillment in ante-bellum America, Margaret Fuller (1810–50) epitomized the egalitarian antithesis. Superficially, Hale and Fuller had much in common: they wrote prolifically, favored better education for women, and edited influential magazines, yet there were major differences in their visions of how women ought to live their lives. Born into a prominent New England family, Fuller received her education at home and at a boarding school where she perceived her interests and intellect to be a world apart from her fellow students. She rebelled against prevailing assumptions of women's intellectual inferiority and confinement to marriages which totally submerged them. She condemned the basis of marriage as practiced in the 1830s and 1840s, stating that "the very fault of marriage, and of the present relation between the sexes [is] that the woman does belong to the man, instead of forming a whole with him." Fuller believed it was a "vulgar error that love, *a* love to woman is her whole existence."

One of the leading intellectuals of her day, Fuller nevertheless believed that "some duties come first, – to parents, brothers, and sister." Fuller experienced the tensions between family and career, even though not married. She managed her parent's home when nine pregnancies, two infant deaths, and the care of an emotionally disturbed son wore out her mother's strength. Amid these complications, she devoted her spare time to self-improvement and writing, educating her younger siblings at home, and trying to generate an income. Fuller observed other women engaging in the leading issues of the day, which encouraged her to speak, write, and teach at a time when many disdained such activities by women. Her contemporaries Susan B. Anthony and Elizabeth Cady Stanton believed her to be a great influence over other women, while the questions she raised in her writing stimulated discussion over women's roles in ante-bellum society.

The Transcendentalist notion that people became godlike by developing their intellectual and spiritual potential bolstered Fuller's resolve to write and speak out. Transcendentalists extended their acceptance of the integrity of the individual to encompass African Americans and women, believing that all souls were equal on earth as well as in Heaven. Like the Unitarians (which many of them were) they rejected predestination and a vengeful God. They considered it possible to have perfection on earth, a view that gave rise to many utopian movements in this era, including abolitionism and women's rights.

After teaching school, studying, and undertaking responsibility for her mother and siblings, Fuller wearied of trying to catch her education in snatches. She wished to encourage other women to study and assert their intellectual capacities and so began a series of Conversations, informal classes with small groups of like-minded women in 1839. Fuller hoped to raise women's self-esteem by developing their minds and sense of responsibility, while the money earned from these Conversations enabled her to devote her energies to other projects, including the editorship of the Transcendentalist journal, *The Dial*.

Fuller edited this influential periodical for two years, maintaining close control over the content. She subsequently enlarged one of her essays, *The Great Lawsuit: Man vs. Men, Woman vs. Women* to book length in 1845, basing *Woman in the Nineteenth Century* upon the premise that all souls are equal. Fuller explored women's awareness of their own limitations and their similarity to slaves. Prefiguring an argument used in the Declaration of Sentiments of the Seneca Falls Women's Rights Convention in 1848, Fuller believed the phrase, "all men are born free and equal" should apply to women, African and Native Americans. She reasoned that "there is no purely masculine man, no purely feminine woman," an idea which disquieted many even within the Transcendentalist movement.

Like Judith Sargent Murray 50 years earlier, Fuller challenged the narrow intellectual compass granted to women. *Woman in the Nineteenth Century* was a polemical statement which defined and extended women's rights and made a persuasive case for female independence based upon self-awareness. Woman needed to "lay aside all thought, such as she habitually cherishes, of being taught and led by men." She should be educated for her own sake since "too much is said of women being better educated, that they may become better companions and mothers for men." Women had to battle for independence based upon education and self-help and reject the customs of inequality so common in her day. She declared that women should take any job they wanted whether as sea captains, gardeners, or builders while still believing that many would still choose to be mothers who delighted "to make the nest soft and warm . . . Nature would take care of that." Women who wished to undertake unusual careers should not be limited by others' domesticity since "*all* need not be constrained to employments, for which *some* are unfit," an argument which undermined the cult of true womanhood through individual choice.

Male Transcendentalists had complex and sometimes contradictory attitudes towards literary women. Ralph Waldo Emerson believed women should be educated and develop their intellects, but his commitment was limited since he wished women to demonstrate their attainments in "passive non-competitive ways." He believed that women should not be creative in themselves but should do "all by inspiring man to do all." Emerson's friend Nathaniel Hawthorne made his preference for passive women abundantly clear in *The Scarlet Letter*. His writing hinted at a dichotomy in female roles but preferred true womanhood to real independence of mind and spirit. He viewed female intellectuals as dark ladies with mysterious powers over men, sexual beings whose antitheses were the fair, faint, and passive heroines of his work. Many male authors probably felt, like Nathaniel Hawthorne, that women should embody the cult of true womanhood in their submissive acceptance of domesticity; in contrast, female authors such as Fuller challenged these constraints.

SLAVE NARRATIVES AND AFRICAN-AMERICAN WOMEN'S WRITING

While Fuller drew analogies between the situation of (white) women and slaves, former slaves and free African-American women employed autobiographical forms to challenge contemporary racial and gender conventions. They deployed the tool of literacy to reflect upon and influence key social and political issues, contesting the narrow range of roles permitted to them. *The Life and Religious Experience of Jarena Lee, A Colored Lady,* published in Philadelphia in 1836, used a popular form of writing, the conversion narrative, to testify to its author's spiritual development and legitimacy as a preacher of the gospel. By styling herself a "Colored Lady" Lee placed herself on an equal footing with whites and made her own Christian witness an example for people of both races and sexes. Her work grew out of the Second Great Awakening in which women's religious spirit sometimes led them to challenge the gender conventions of the day, in this case to minister as well as to testify.

Slave narratives authored by women asserted their physical and emotional integrity and desire to define and shape their lives and, as with white women's writing, supported authors who had limited career alternatives. Revealing the gendered and racial discrimination endured by African-American women, these authors struggled against racism and sexism to convince audiences that black women could write their own stories. Harriet Jacobs's autobiographical slave narrative indicted slavery, exposed its cruelty, and condemned its special abuse of women as sexual objects. The title of Jacobs's narrative, *Incidents in the Life of a Slave Girl: Written by Herself* (1861), accentuates the personal and autobiographical nature of her account. Jacobs asked the "virtuous reader" to feel pity for the slave who "shuddered at the sound of [her master's] footsteps, and trembled within hearing of his voice."

Incidents interweaves the narrative of Linda Brent's life with a direct condemnation of slavery as Jacobs appealed to white women immersed in the cult of true womanhood to accept that slave women also had a right to their purity of body and devotion to their children.

Jacobs exposes the brutality of slavery, the tyranny of patriarchy, and the fears which led white women to collude in the oppression of black women and children. Simultaneously, she condemns the hypocrisy of southern women like Mrs. Flint who did not have the "strength to superintend her household affairs; but her nerves were so strong, that she could sit in her easy chair and see a woman whipped, till the blood trickled from every stroke of the lash."

Jacobs depicted a community of African-American mothers and surrogate mothers who supported each other's attempts to achieve freedom, sometimes at great risk to themselves. Linda Brent's grandmother hid her for many years and looked after her children when she finally escaped, encouraging her "never to yield. She said if I persevered I might, perhaps, gain the freedom of my children; and even if I perished doing it, that was better than to leave them to groan under the same persecutions that had blighted my own life." Jacobs strongly contrasts loyalty to other slaves with the abysmal behavior of Mrs. Flint, who shared Grandmother's milk with Aunt Nancy but worked her milk sister so hard that she could not have children of her own.

Harriet E. Wilson's sentimental novel, *Our Nig: or, Sketches from the Life of a Free Black, in a Two-Story White House, North. Showing That Slavery's Shadow Falls Even There* (1859), was the first African-American woman's novel. It sympathetically portrays the marriage between a black man and a white woman and attacks northern racism rather than slavery. The villains in *Our Nig* are white women, not slave holders, so that by exposing racism Wilson may have alienated some of her potential audience. Ironically she also presaged the split in the feminist-abolitionist movement which took place a decade later.

Although men authored most of the narratives published by exslaves, the few female ones articulate the peculiar traumas of being simultaneously woman and slave. Both *Our Nig* and *Incidents in the Life of a Slave Girl* incorporated "a particularly black and female politicization of domestic ideology," comments Claudia Tate in her analysis of nineteenth-century African-American women's writings. Wilson condemns racism as an attack on black domesticity, while Jacobs declares that "slavery is terrible for men; but it is far more terrible for women." Both works lament the attacks upon motherhood, domesticity, and family life inherent in the racist, slave society of the nineteenth century.

Mid-nineteenth-century women's novels characteristically framed their plots in domestic terms and made domesticity the dominant paradigm for interpreting the American experience. Harriet Beecher Stowe responded to the Fugitive Slave Law which permitted runaway slaves to be shipped back from freedom to their former owners with her 1852 novel, *Uncle Tom's Cabin,* attacking slavery for its violation of slave family life. By using the all-pervasive rhetoric of motherhood and sentimental domesticity, Stowe bridges the racial divide which existed even among abolitionists and imbues her African-American characters with contemporary virtues including piety and maternal love. The sentimentalized Christianity of the mid-nineteenth century found its expression in the Christ-like Uncle Tom and the suffering of innocent little Eva. Stowe's writing exemplified her sister Catharine's advice to women to exert influence through "the domestic and social circle" but had an impact that transcended the household.

Stowe demonstrated the entanglement of family life with economic matters and called for female virtues to be applied to the most contentious national problem of the day when she depicted slavery as an immoral attack on the integrity of the family, with many innocent victims of both races. Like Harriet Jacobs, Stowe gave substance to abstract political debates and helped bring about the Civil War. One contemporary southern critic described her as a "termagant virago and a foul mouthed hag who had left the retirement proper to her sex and could therefore hardly expect deference." Stowe and Jacobs overtly challenged gendered conventions of behavior, notwithstanding the domestic focus of their work, by speaking and writing on this inflammatory topic.

LITERARY PROTESTS OVER INDUSTRIALIZATION

The cult of domesticity also framed cultural discourses for the white working class with factory workers incorporating pious domestic imagery into their writings. The *Lowell Offering* published by mill workers in the early 1840s sought to prove their respectability and culture to a sceptical and not always sympathetic world. An outgrowth of the mill operatives' self-improvement clubs and modeled on contemporary popular periodicals, the *Lowell Offering* contained poems, articles, and letters written by factory operatives. Widely imitated in mill towns across New England, this industrial working women's paper encouraged mill workers to express themselves in print but followed the conventional formulae of the era. They eschewed controversial topics; as one declared, "the paper will be free from a party spirit and nothing will be admitted to its columns with a view to establishing any particular opinion." The *Lowell Offering* depended upon the factory owners for its support and took particular care not to offend them.

Editor Harriet Farley strenuously defended her fellow workers' rational motives. Responding to Orestes Brownson's accusations in 1840 that work in the mills morally contaminated female operatives, Farley claimed that the women worked "to get money, as much of it and as fast as we can . . ." The wages drew "worthy, virtuous, intelligent and well-educated girls to Lowell." It would be odd indeed, "if in money-loving New England, one of the most lucrative female employments should be rejected because it is toilsome, or because some people are prejudiced against" women's work outside the home.

Critics of the *Lowell Offering* pointed out that it rarely contained great literature and certainly much of the poetry tended toward the doggerel. The editorials defended working women's rights to decent wages and shorter working hours in general terms, but they also preached the importance of respectability and gentility to operatives whose working life had grown more oppressive. Growing militancy among the hard-pressed textile labor force and suspicions that the *Offering* had become "a mouthpiece of the corporations," according to leader of the ten-hour movement Sarah Bagley, led to its demise in 1845.

The *Lowell Offering's* brief existence encouraged other women to write about their working conditions in less saccharine terms for newspapers in New York and New England. Numerous operatives' magazines attacked the bosses and censured the increasingly abusive conditions in the mills. The *Wampanoag and Operatives' Journal*, published in Fall River in the 1840s, attested to female operatives' literacy and militancy. Periodicals such as *The Factory Girl* (established in 1842) defended factory women's right to organize and carried articles critical of the corporations, but as the New England textile industry came to be dominated by foreign-born workers in the 1850s, these journals ceased publication.

Southern industry received less written criticism from its workers since far fewer factory hands there could read or write. Unlike the operatives of the North, southerners depended upon middle-class spokespersons to defend them. Rebecca Harding Davis's powerful novella *Life in the Iron Mills* (1861) protested the abuse of factory hands in a naturalistic urban hell blighted by industry. First published by *Atlantic Monthly*, it tells the story of a hunchbacked cotton operative and the artistically talented iron puddler who pities, but does not love her. Davis denounces the cruelty of the ruling classes by depicting a mill owner who shirked responsibility for his workers' lives: "I wash my hands of all social problems, slavery, caste, white or black. My duty to my operatives has a narrow limit – pay-hour on Saturday night."

When Deborah steals money to help Hugh, they are both imprisoned. Hugh dies of consumption, but a Quaker woman prison visitor rescues Deborah, who pleads with her to get Hugh buried in open ground rather than in the town graveyard where he would smother "under t'mud and ash." The Quaker community redeems and cares for Deborah through "sunshine, and fresh air, and slow, patient Christ-love." Rescued from the mills, Deborah looks to "hills higher and purer than these on which she lives" for hope and redemption in an explicit rejection of urban life and factory labor. The dark satanic mills of *Life in the Iron Mills* contrast bleakly with the idealized depiction in the *Lowell Offering* and reflected the deteriorating conditions endured by mill workers as owners sought to increase productivity and lower wages.

Marrying late in life, Rebecca Harding confronted the dilemma so common for other women: how to reconcile the demands of home and family with the desire to write. While the cult of true womanhood sanctified female emotional and domestic concerns, a number of women rejected these as their sole or primary focus. They questioned women's place inside and outside the home and their part in the upheavals racking the nation. Education not only gave some women careers, it led them to agitate on behalf of slaves, to question women's status, and to protest against the inadequacies of ante-bellum philanthropic, religious, and utopian movements. Literacy, the ability to communicate over long distances and beyond one's immediate circle of family and friends, and a desire to use their education propelled women into social and political activism in the second quarter of the nineteenth century.

4 Religion, Reform, and Politics in the Ante-Bellum Era

The United States had become a less hierarchical and more egalitarian nation by the 1820s, at least for white men, for whom status increasingly derived from their occupation rather than birth. Yet declining levels of deference meant affluent women lost privileges deriving from their class. Once politics included all white men, the ability of elite women to sway events through family connections lessened. The industrial revolution resulted in married women having fewer responsibilities for economic production within the home and more for its emotional and moral well-being. Many sought a public voice based on rights rather than influence, especially in areas which affected home life. In this period, religious and political activism were strongly intertwined, as Protestant piety encouraged women to speak out on issues as diverse as temperance and slavery.

Tensions over gender roles in a highly volatile society led some women to embrace the social order; others wished to reform parts of it or rejected it totally by joining utopian communities. Numerous women expanded their public activities in the conventional settings of church societies and religious meetings, sometimes moving onto radical abolitionism or suffrage, and frequently combining an interest in several reform movements simultaneously. Moreover, women's response to the problems of their era indicates an awareness of the world beyond the household which the cult of true womanhood, if as pervasive a paradigm as supposed by some historians, would have precluded. Passive femininity might be an ideal, but as the lives of tens of thousands of female Sunday School, reform, benevolent, abolitionist, and temperance society members attested, such strictures impeded but did not prevent women's growing social and political engagement.

THE SECOND GREAT AWAKENING AND WOMEN'S ACTIVISM

Much of women's participation in public matters can be traced to the Second Great Awakening in which faith replaced doctrine as the wellspring of religious participation. Revivalist meetings urged sinners to show repentance through actions as well as words. The new religious order gave meaning and structure to the lives of newcomers to the capitalist commercial ethos while the emphasis on emotional conversion experiences made religion more accessible to those excluded from the learned ministry, especially women. Membership in Protestant churches doubled in this era, with women and young people comprising the majority of converts as men devoted themselves to business affairs.

The American God changed from a patriarchal, authoritarian figure to a maternal, emotional one. The expanding Baptist and Methodist denominations took religion to the people through revivals and benevolent activities. Women now comprised the majority of church congregations and actively sought new socio-religious functions. Minister and social reformer Theodore Parker observed that rich men built factories which exacted sweated labor from the poor, while their wives and daughters set out to "heal the sick and teach the ignorant, whom their fathers, their husbands, their lovers have made sick, oppressed and ignorant." Some ministers preached female submissiveness, but the conversion experience and attendance at prayer meetings led women to take their own moral feelings seriously. They formed separate organizations to evangelize, sew clothes for poor people, and raise funds for their benefit. Women taught Sunday School and established missions to the poor, bringing them into sometimes controversial contact with the larger world.

The Sunday School movement flourished in the 1830s and 1840s, supported by women who amalgamated their maternal and pious attributes. Revivals inspired the women of the social elite to establish Sunday schools for poor children, especially in the North, but even southern women such as Anne Clay of Georgia ran Sunday Schools for slave children. Elsewhere, Sunday Schools and missionary societies appeased elite anxieties over the widening economic gulf between the classes. Conversion of poor children, it was hoped, would reach their irreligious parents, win souls, and ensure stability by preaching deference and resignation to one's fate.

In the early 1800s, female benevolent societies helped the poor and spread awareness of the problems women encountered in earning a living and raising a family. Female reformers interjected women's domestic and moral concerns into public discussions about poverty and reform. As more women demonstrated their piety and social standing through charity work they became the nation's moral conscience. An early account of Boston's female elite recalled "a lady hardly thinks her life complete, unless she is directly aiding in some work of reform or charity." At a time when support for the poor consumed 20 to 25 percent of city budgets, female benevolence augmented public funds and occupied genteel women as friendly visitors to poor families.

Church women's guilds, mothers' missions, and sewing societies stitched clothes for the poor, furnished employment for working women (usually as seamstresses or servants), and distributed food, clothing, and money to the "deserving" poor in cities and towns. These organizations cared primarily for poor women and children, particularly widows and orphans, who were considered deserving because they had not caused their own poverty through unregenerate behavior. In 1803, the Mariners' Family Asylum was established for the aged wives, widows, and daughters of seamen on Staten Island, NY, and a widows' shelter opened in Baltimore in 1811. Sectarian provision became increasingly common at this time. The Widows' Society of Bethlehem (Pennsylvania) founded by the Moravian Brethren Church in 1770 was one of the first church-run widows' homes. By the 1830s and 1840s women of various races, religions, and ethnic groups founded charities, homes, and welfare societies for group members. Free African-American women established one of the early female benevolent organizations in the United States, the Female Benevolent Society of St. Thomas, in Philadelphia in 1793. Protestant women across the nation developed orphan asylums in the 1830s and 1840s; at the same time nuns opened orphanages and schools for Roman Catholic children.

Dorothea Dix's career indicates the far reaching consequences of female-led reform and the progressive nature of their involvement in reform activities. Religious convictions moved Dix, a former school teacher, to conduct a Sunday School class for women at a Massachusetts prison where she discovered insane women shackled to walls and sharing cells with criminals. In the early 1840s she investigated conditions in insane asylums and prisons first in

Massachusetts and subsequently in mid-western and southern states, where her memorials and appearances before state legislatures led to widespread improvements in the care of the insane. Grass roots female moral reform societies supported these innovations, pressuring state legislatures into hiring women to look after female inmates. In turn, state governments recognized women's role in caring for the distressed by appointing them to positions of responsibility in newly built institutions, usually in charge of women and child inmates.

The formal conduct of women's organizations and their diverse concerns testify to female engagement with contemporary issues. Although many female benevolent societies limited their assistance to their own sex or to children, and preferred to assist the worthy poor (temperate, deferential, and native born), some confronted indelicate matters in a way previously thought unsuitable for respectable ladies by working among prostitutes and opening homes for unwed mothers. The New York Female Moral Reform Society inaugurated its Magdalene Home in 1838, with similar societies founding rescue homes in other cities in the 1840s.

Female reformers fought against the sexual double standard at mid-century. The New York Female Moral Reform Society appealed to the state legislature in 1848 to protect women from predatory males by making seduction a criminal offense. Its crusading journal, *Advocate of Moral Reform,* declared that *"virtues* like vices *know no distinction of sex.*" As more women became aware of the social and economic barriers to female employment, the female reform movement shifted from moral to social betterment by offering employment to poor women who had few well-paid employment options apart from prostitution. Male reformers made this transition more slowly, if at all, as attested by the Whig politicians and their successors who criminalized female sexual behavior while ignoring men's conduct in seducing or patronizing prostitutes.

The temperance movement similarly expressed women's concern over double standards. In the popular mind of the 1820s and 1830s it was men who drank to excess and women and children who suffered the consequent poverty and abuse. Temperance reformer Mary C. Vaughan depicted the woes of the "drunkard's wife" who shrank under her husband's blows, her earnings "transferred to the rum-seller's ill-gotten hoard" while her "ragged, fireless, poor, starving children" shivered about her. Seen as the victims of men's lack of restraint, such women deserved public protection from liquor and other excesses.

Nativism and class differentiation also played a part in a temperance movement which reflected class, ethnic, and gender tensions as cultures clashed in the urban maelstrom. Alcohol consumption rose sharply in the 1820s and 1830s, prompting strong middle-class native-born white reactions against the drinking habits of city dwellers, especially Irish and German immigrants. By the mid-1830s the American Temperance Society's 5000 branches had about a million members, and rallies against drinking took place in many cities, attacking the saloons which were workingmen's refuge, informal club house, and union hall.

Paralleling other improvement movements, women formed separate temperance societies when mixed organizations relegated them to the sidelines. Temperance reformer Amelia Bloomer wrote that women attended meetings and listened to eloquent men, but did not speak themselves, instead they raised money to support temperance lecturers and met in each other's homes to discuss the problem. Susan B. Anthony initiated a Daughters of Temperance chapter in Albany, NY, when the newly organized Sons of Temperance excluded women. Daughters of Temperance worker Mary C. Vaughan told its New York conference in 1852 that women as well as men could work for reform without neglecting their families. To her mind there was no reform "in which woman can act better or more appropriately than temperance." Women had a responsibility to look after the morals of society and care for the less fortunate, making temperance a female vocation.

Some women used the temperance struggle to ensure their husbands met their family obligations. In an era when new forms of industry threatened artisan working conditions, working-class advocates of temperance connected restraint with the fulfillment of male breadwinning responsibilities. Female factory workers supported abstinence because money spent in the tavern could not be used to feed the family. The Martha Washingtons were the female counterparts of the male artisan-based Washington Temperance groups which flourished in the early 1840s. Martha Washington societies assisted the families of those who signed the abstinence pledge by sewing clothes for them and supplying bedding, furniture, and cash. Like their middle-class sisters, the working-class Martha Washington societies brought domestic concerns into the public domain in order to protect family well-being.

Religiously inspired temperance reformers believed alcohol constituted a grave threat to peace and happiness. Amelia Bloomer, editor of the temperance and reform newspaper *The Lily,* wielded her pen to suppress drink. She threw "aside the modest retirement which so much becomes her sex" because intemperance made a woman's "home desolate and beggared her offspring." Both the Martha Washingtons and genteel temperance advocates believed that temperance reform defended the home. Their associations publicly indicated an activist mentality and a desire to communicate their views beyond their immediate neighborhood, frequently led them into other reform activities, and made them conscious of the limitations their society placed upon women.

WOMEN IN UTOPIAN COMMUNITIES

The perfectionist spirit of the age inspired numerous women and men to reject conventional society in favor of innovative living and worship arrangements. Religious sects experimented with new economic and social practices, altering relations between the sexes or developing communal economies. The most long-lasting religious community of this era, the Church of Jesus Christ of Latter Day Saints (Mormons), attracted many female converts, invested female roles with real importance, but restricted them to traditional spheres. Their relief societies provided social welfare in the wilderness, giving women opportunities to do "what was pleasing in the sight of heaven." These societies were part of the church structure rather than challenges to the patriarchal hierarchy.

Mormon marital customs set them apart once Joseph Smith sanctioned plural marriages in the late 1830s, possibly to provide partners for the many women attracted to the Latter Day Saints. Like other unconventional marriage arrangements, polygamy attracted extreme hostility, influencing Mormons to migrate west, first to Nauvoo, Illinois, then to the Salt Lake Basin. While no more than 10–20 percent of Mormons actually entered into plural marriages, gentiles regarded them with horror. Mormon women had mixed feelings. For some rural women, plural marriage provided companionship and shared child-rearing; for others it was a trial to be borne for the sake of eternity.

Other utopian communities challenged conventional gender roles or marital practices. Ann Lee's Shaker followers believed she embodied Christ's spirit in female form. Growing from a membership of 1000 at the beginning of the nineteenth century, it achieved 6000 members at mid-century, but virtually disappeared by 1900. The Shakers set up separate communities to protect themselves from the tainted world of non-believers. They segregated the sexes while establishing equality between them and glorifying manual labor. They believed they were the first community to "disenthrall women from the condition of vassalage," and secured women "just and equal rights with men" as demanded by God and Nature.

Shaker celibacy provided women with a refuge from unsuitable marriages. Most converts were women between the ages of 20 and 45 who had been married or were seeking a means of support outside marriage. Contact between the sexes took place in formal groups, never individually. Shakers divided tasks along traditional gender lines, but regarded all labor as consecrated to God, fusing temporal and spiritual values. Although women retained housewifely roles and looked after a specific brother's clothing and room, these were minor activities rather than the focus of their day. Women's work in the dairies, cheese and butter making, seed rooms, and craft workshops sustained their communities, while their spiritual lives incorporated Ann Lee's belief that the godhead contained male and female elements.

Scotswoman Frances Wright's Neshoba Colony in Tennessee, founded in 1825, also advocated equality between the sexes. She hoped to emancipate slaves gradually, supported complete equality for the sexes, liberal divorce laws, and married women's property rights. Wright wrote that "the mind has no sex but what habit and education give it" and opposed marriage as denying women's independence. The slave members of Neshoba opposed her unconventional child-rearing arrangements which separated children from their parents in order to educate them. Rejecting marriage and organized religion, and favoring racial amalgamation, the community failed when its financial backers withdrew their assistance following charges of "free love."

Appalled by the toll that frequent pregnancies took of his wife, in 1847 John Humphrey Noyes founded the Oneida Community which had a complex marriage system, avoided sexual exclusivity, and promoted voluntary motherhood. Women and men worked together, shared domestic work, used birth control (*coitus reservatus*) to avoid pregnancy and enhance female pleasure, and raised children communally. They wished to attract women and upheld their claim to equal rights within the community. Their marital practices were widely attacked, and they abandoned the complex marriage system in favor of more conventional arrangements in 1879. Of all the utopian communities, only the Mormons survived into the twentieth century in any number, and they, like the Oneidans, accepted public sentiment regarding marriage structure.

CULTURAL AND LEGAL PROTEST

Amelia Bloomer's career indicates how intertwined female reform activities became: she advocated women's rights, dress reform, and public activism for women. Like many women's rights supporters, she moved between various ante-bellum reform movements, using the experience gained in one campaign to help fight another. In 1852, her temperance newspaper carried patterns for "Turkish pantaloons," nicknamed Bloomers after her. Bloomers enjoyed a brief vogue, but campaigners stopped wearing them because of the ridicule they encountered. Elizabeth Cady Stanton sadly recorded "such is the tyranny of custom, that to escape constant observation, criticism, ridicule, persecution, [and] mobs, one after another went back to the old slavery and sacrificed freedom to repose." Stanton mourned the loss of the practical Bloomer costume which would have made it easier for her to climb upstairs holding a lantern and carrying a baby without tripping. They continued to be worn in the West and presaged the more comfortable, active clothing for women which became popular at the turn of the century.

Bloomer believed that her newspaper was the first devoted "to the interests of woman" and the first to be owned, edited, and published by one. Elizabeth Cady Stanton, who lived in Seneca Falls, wrote a column for *The Lily* under the sobriquet "Sunflower." Her increasingly vigorous articles on temperance, literary subjects, childcare, and theories of education incorporated women's rights, under which banner she advocated the repeal of "unjust laws relating to married women." Other women carved out careers in newspaper work, notably Jane Swisshelm, who first published her *Saturday Visiter* [sic] in Pittsburgh in 1848. Laws governing married women's property hampered her efforts to run an independent enterprise, prompting her to editorialize in favor of improved rights for women. Married women's property rights received widespread attention in the 1830s–1840s when state laws grappled with changed attitudes towards debtor–creditor relations. As the United States developed a commercial and industrial economy, legislatures conceded the right of married women first to inherited property and later to earnings. They wished to protect the family in case the husband's business ventures went bankrupt or his debts exceeded his assets. Ernestine Rose, a Jewish immigrant to New York, campaigned vigorously for married women's property rights in the 1830s, as did New Yorkers Elizabeth Cady Stanton and Pauline Wright Davis. An 1839 Mississippi statute declared that a wife's slaves did not constitute her husband's property in cases of debt disputes, the first state law establishing separate ownership. New York recognized married women's rights to inherit property but not to their earnings or property they had purchased. The governor of Pennsylvania credited Jane Swisshelm's *Saturday Visiter* editorials with influencing property legislation in that state, demonstrating how women's awareness of limitations imposed upon them in one area politicized them in others.

New York women fought for the right to their wages in the 1850s. Filled with indignation at women's unfair legal treatment Stanton presented a petition of 10 000 signatures favoring full property rights for married women to the state legislature. Her argument struck at the heart of all gender-based legislation. "We ask for all that you have asked for yourselves in the progress of your development . . . simply on the ground that the rights of every human being are the same and identical." She wanted the vote, full property and inheritance rights, custody of children, and an end to feudal attitudes towards women by calling for them to be viewed as individuals with rights rather than in terms of their family status.

WOMEN AND ABOLITIONISM

Many women's rights advocates moved between various ante-bellum reform movements, first participating in the temperance movement and then speaking out against slavery. White southerners, Sarah and

Angelina Grimké, joined evangelical and Quaker women such as Lucretia Mott and Lucy Stone, and leading African-American reformers including Sojourner Truth, Margaretta, Charlotte and Sarah Forten, and Maria W. Stewart to oppose slavery. Angelina Grimké, like many white female abolitionists, sought a church affiliation which reflected her world view. Quaker religious tenets, especially their strong belief in the equality of all souls, furnished a distinctive basis for female activism which set them apart from the world of separate spheres and domesticity. Instead, they relied upon their Inner Light to show them the correct way and led some (though not the majority) to accept African Americans and women of all races as equals in the meeting house and in anti-slavery agitation.

In 1832 one of the first American women to speak out against slavery, initially to all-female and later to mixed audiences in Boston, Maria W. Stewart implored the Boston Afric-American Female Intelligence Society: "Daughters of Africa, awake! Arise! Distinguish yourselves." She deplored the prejudice that restricted her sisters and brothers to domestic service and unskilled labor. Imbued with evangelical Christian spirit, she urged the sons of Africa to form temperance societies and save money for their children's education. Her farewell address to her friends in Boston admonished her "brethren and friends" not to be surprised that God raises up "your own females to strive, by their example, both in public and private, to assist those who are endeavoring to stop the strong current of prejudice that flows so profusely against us at present."

Over the 30-year span of vigorous female participation in the anti-slavery movement, women's concerns became public concerns as they asserted their right to speak out in defense of their homes and the rights of those who could not easily defend themselves. Because the law (and much of society) treated women as a form of property, some women readily sympathized with that other form of property, slaves. Elizabeth Cady Stanton believed that a woman is "more fully identified with the slave than man can possibly be, for she can take the subjective view . . . For while the man is born to do whatever he can, for the woman and the Negro there is no such privilege." Yet female participation in the abolitionist movement revealed serious disagreements about the means to accomplish the common goal. Many male campaigners opposed female membership in their organizations or wished women to be confined to auxiliary societies. As with other moral reform movements men accepted women's participation, but expected them to restrict themselves to fund-raising and the periphery of the movement.

Anti-slavery women also disagreed over the form female participation should take. Sarah and Angelina Grimké's 1837 public speaking tour on behalf of abolition shocked many when they turned from female audiences to "promiscuous" or mixed groups. This antagonized conservative clergy, already lukewarm supporters of immediate emancipation and hostile to women who "travel about from place to place as lecturers, teachers, and guides to public sentiment." The Pastoral Letter of the Massachusetts Congregationalist Clergy issued in 1837 did not mention the Grimké sisters by name when it thundered "if the vine, whose strength and beauty is to lean upon the trellis-work and half conceal its clusters, thinks to assume the independence and the overshadowing nature of the elm, it will not only cease to bear fruit, but fall in shame and dishonor into the dust." Women who took up cudgels on behalf of the slave unsexed themselves, imperiled childbearing, and entered into a world of things "which ought not to be named." The Massachusetts clergy believed no respectable woman should know about the sexual abuses of bondswomen which Harriet Beecher Stowe and Harriet Jacobs later used to attack slavery.

Influential educator, author, and reformer Catharine Beecher rejected her former student Angelina Grimké's appeal for help in mobilizing women against slavery. Beecher's *Essay on Slavery and Abolitionism* indicated that a woman might "seek the aid of co-operation and combination among her own sex, to assist her in her appropriate offices of piety, charity, maternal and domestic duty" but should not engage in party conflict. This conservative vision acknowledged women's right to have opinions but expected them to influence men to end slavery rather than thrust themselves into the public sphere.

Beecher's beliefs did not deter the Grimké sisters. Angelina became the first woman to appear before an American state legislature when she presented an anti-slavery petition with 20 000 signatures to the Massachusetts state legislature. Sarah responded to Congregational clergy's attack by rejecting "influence" in favor of "rights." Angelina's *Letters to Catharine E. Beecher in Reply to an Essay on Slavery and Abolitionism* (1838) repudiated the "regulation of duty by the mere circumstance of sex" as she jettisoned double standards in matters of morality and conscience.

The formation of all-female societies enabled women to campaign more actively. African-American women formed anti-slavery societies in Salem and Rochester in 1832. A year later Maria Weston Chapman and her sisters inaugurated the Boston Female Anti-slavery Society, initially an auxiliary to the New England Anti-slavery Society. When the American Anti-slavery Society in Philadelphia barred women from voting or signing their declaration of sentiments and purposes, Quaker Lucretia Mott and African-American women including Charlotte, Margaretta, and Sarah Forten and Sarah and Grace Douglass established the Female Anti-slavery Society. By 1837, there were over 1000 anti-slavery societies in the United States, 77 comprised solely of women. These female activists held their first National Female Anti-slavery Convention in that year, with 81 delegates drawn from 12 states. Women chaired the meeting since, as Sarah and Angelina Grimké wrote to Theodore Weld, "the Boston and Philadelphia women were so well versed in business" that they did not need his authority on the platform.

Some female abolitionist societies had members of both races, but others marginalized or refused to accept black women. Even those societies which enrolled African-American women frequently condescended to them. For example, Susan Paul, a Boston abolitionist, was sent to the 1837 Anti-slavery Convention in New York because Boston's white female abolitionists considered her "a favorable specimen of the colored race." Yet the hostile reception accorded Maria W. Stewart in Boston a few years earlier suggested racial as well as gendered tensions within the abolitionist movement.

Appeals to women to "know their place" and unwillingness to treat African Americans as equals within anti-slavery societies had little impact upon the courageous couriers on the Underground Railroad and those who sheltered them on the dangerous trek to freedom. Harriet Tubman, born into slavery in Maryland c.1821, fled slavery in her late twenties. With extraordinary daring she repeatedly journeyed south to rescue an estimated 200–300 slaves despite a $40 000 reward offered by Maryland planters for her capture. During the Civil War she further demonstrated her bravery by serving as a battlefield nurse and spy for the Union.

Campaigning on behalf of abolition politicized women in the 1840s and 1850s and undermined the separation of spheres in which men's concerns were outside the home and women's within it. The anti-slavery crusade encapsulated the dilemmas faced by women who wished to have a public voice since both women and men disputed the extent to which women should air their concerns in public. Yet their strength of feeling, its religious and moral base, and growing disquiet about the contradictions between the nation's ideals and the practice of slavery sustained many female abolitionists and encouraged them to breach the genteel public–private divide.

WOMEN AND POLITICS

Increased female autonomy in the Victorian family helped provide a basis for women's activism. The social purity, temperance, and civic reform movements were based upon women's desire to insulate the home from negative external influences. Historian Daniel Scott Smith concludes that women's "larger arena of activity was not so much an alternative to the woman-as-wife-and-mother as an extension of the progress made within the family itself." The family furnished a refuge for women and made even their more radical demands, such as the vote, reasonable devices to protect the home.

The same economic and religious forces which gave rise to reform movements encouraged female participation in mass political parties. The Whig Party emerged from the evangelical Protestant denominations that favored temperance, female benevolent activities and abolitionism. To the dismay of older Protestant groups and Roman Catholics these denominations attempted to use the power of government to foist their moral convictions upon the nation. Whigs coupled the emerging cult of domesticity with mass political participation to invest public issues with domestic concerns and encouraged a female presence at rallies, fund-raising suppers, and parades. This subverted the separation of private and public space by merging their interests and participants. Yet even Whigs favoring women's political involvement wanted influence and calming voices rather than equality. Other parties recognized female energies, initially at the symbolic level and then by their presence, so that by mid-century women had achieved a modicum of political integration, even though they still played minor roles.

The fact that the women's rights movement began and attracted its greatest successes in the northern part of the United States has led many historians to correlate feminism with abolitionism. Indeed, the early women's rights movement drew its strongest supporters from a cluster of northeastern and midwestern female temperance and abolitionist activists. Southern urban and small town women had a rich associational life, but evangelical piety rarely convinced them to favor abolitionism or feminism. Like northern women, they engaged in benevolent and temperance activities and raised money for missionary causes, but they differed in their pro-slavery stance and reluctance to extend women's legal rights. There were fewer objections to them speaking out because their voices supported rather than challenged the dominant southern ideology.

By the 1840s abolitionism became the defining radical issue in American politics, engaging many women, regardless of the supposed dichotomy between public and private spheres. While not all abolitionists became feminists (regardless of sex) and not all feminists were abolitionists, numerous women became politically aware as a result of their participation in this great movement. Jean Fagin Yellin suggests that abolitionist women appropriated words and images "from evangelical anti-slavery discourse to structure a feminist discourse." Yet the connection drawn between abolitionism and feminism is neither simple nor direct. Women moved from abolitionism to feminism, but many female abolitionists opposed women's rights or were indifferent to separate, gender-based organizations. Lydia Maria Child, author of *An Appeal in Favor of That Class of Americans Called Africans,* wrote to Lucretia Mott that she never "entered very earnestly into the plan of female conventions and societies. They always seemed to me like half a pair of scissors." Radical thinker Frances Wright favored emancipation, but criticized the women's rights movement as irrelevant to working-class and slave women. Some feminists were indifferent to the plight of the slave or hostile to African-American civil rights.

While it was not the sole impetus behind women's rights, organized activism for women in the United States owed much to abolitionism, which offered a model for waging a radical struggle and turning it into a social movement. The chronology of the American women's rights struggle shows isolated glimmerings that predate abolitionism. As early as 1647, Mistress Margaret Brent, the executrix of Lord Calvert's estate in Maryland, petitioned the legislature for the right to vote. Abolitionism, along with benevolent reform, temperance crusades, and trade union organizing helped shift the arguments from individual pleas to mass action by gathering women together in groups.

The quest for women's rights emphasized individual worth, accountability, and ability to achieve, values similar to the commercial ideology that flourished in the Age of Jackson. When women encountered limits on their ability to effect their goals they began to oppose restrictive gender roles. Hostility to female public speaking by conservative abolitionists at the 1840 World Anti-slavery Convention in London troubled activist Elizabeth Cady Stanton who wrote "it was really pitiful to hear narrow-minded bigots, pretending to be teachers and leaders of men, so cruelly remanding their own mothers, with the rest of womankind, to absolute subjection to the ordinary masculine type of humanity."

The World Anti-slavery Convention convenors originally welcomed all "friends of the Slave" to its meeting, but rejected "promiscuous female representation." It relegated Stanton, Mott and other female delegates to the balcony, precluding their speaking or voting. Some American delegates argued strongly for women's participation. Charles Remond, an African American from New England, remained true to the "kind and generous" support he received from the Bangor Female Anti-slavery Society, the Portland Sewing Circle, and the Newport Young Ladies Juvenile Anti-slavery Society which paid his travel costs. Along with radical white abolitionist William Lloyd Garrison he took a seat in the gallery to which female delegates had been banished. Henry Stanton, Elizabeth Cady's newly wedded husband, voted against seating women because he felt women's rights alienated support from the abolitionist cause.

Female activists believed this incident sparked the women's rights movement. Carrie Chapman Catt and Nettie Rogers Shuler wrote in *Inner Story of the Suffrage Movement* that the rejection of properly accredited delegates because they were women opened their eyes to injustice in all spheres. The rebuff based solely upon sex rankled even as Stanton raised her young family and religious and reform obligations diverted Mott. Eight years later, Stanton and Mott issued an invitation to women and men to come to Seneca Falls to consider women's status, announcing a two-day meeting; the first day was exclusively for women, while the general public could attend on the second. Some 300 women and men came to Seneca Falls at a week's notice "to discuss the social, civil, and religious condition and rights of women."

Stanton and Mott used the Declaration of Independence to express their principles, adapting its language to women's situation. They drew upon America's revolutionary tradition and reflected the radical sentiment sweeping through Europe in the late 1840s by framing their arguments in terms of human rights. The Declaration of Sentiments declared it self-evident that "all men and women are created equal," enumerating the ways in which men behaved tyrannically toward women, depriving them of property rights, child custody in event of death or divorce, most "profitable employments," and voting rights.

The Declaration rejected domesticity and separate spheres as the basis for women's rights by demanding equal access to professions, public platforms, and citizenship for both sexes. It deplored gendered standards of behavior, resolving that "the same amount of virtue, delicacy, and refinement of behavior that is required of woman in the social state, should also be required of man, and the same transgressions should be visited with equal severity on both man and woman." Seneca Falls delegates made equality and equity rather than difference the platform for their movement.

The self-selected delegates to Seneca Falls were relatively young (average age 35 for women and 39 for men), mostly middle class, involved in other reform activities, including abolitionism and temperance, with a Whig-Republican orientation. There was a preponderance of Quakers, which partially explains the emphasis on equality rather than separate spheres as the underpinning for women's rights. Even at this early stage there were divisions within the movement. Quaker participants such as Lucretia Mott insisted that women and men had the same potential for morality and moral failings, while others believed that women's moral superiority entitled them to greater participation in public life.

The Seneca Falls delegates reacted against giving the vote to "the most ignorant and degraded men – both natives and foreigners" while denying women the "inalienable right to the elective franchise." Yet the Convention accepted suffrage for women by a narrow margin after prolonged debate. Frederick Douglass, ex-slave, reformer, and newspaper editor, argued vigorously in its favor, persuading some participants, but others were reluctant to conflate women's rights with those of African Americans.

The Seneca Falls Convention and Declaration of Sentiments attracted mixed responses. Most newspapers ridiculed it, with the exception of Douglass's *North Star* which editorialized strongly in favor of women's rights. The example of Seneca Falls was widely emulated. Two weeks later, another convention was held in Rochester which broadened the debate by considering the economic wrongs of Rochester's seamstresses who earned a pittance sewing 14–15 hours a day.

There were no African-American women at Seneca Falls, but they also fought for equal moral standing within the reform movement. Black women's first official proposal for equality came at the 1848 National Convention of Colored Freedmen in Cleveland. Their request for voting and speaking rights at this meeting encountered opposition, but eventually passed. African-American women achieved better success at the local level than at national conferences, which continued to sideline them into flower arranging and moral reform rather than incorporating them into the main business of the meetings.

As the issues of women's rights and anti-slavery became entangled, women and men from both races disagreed on how to achieve their ends. Sojourner Truth attempted to speak to the Women's Rights Convention in Akron, Ohio, in 1851. Some delegates objected to being identified with abolitionists, but Truth attacked the notion that all women were privileged or delicate. "I have as much muscle as any man, and can do as much work as any man. I have plowed and reaped and husked and chopped and mowed, and can any man do more than that?" She identified herself as being in favor of women's rights because men would oppress women regardless of race.

Other supporters of abolitionism and women's rights felt the issues needed to be kept separate. Frederick Douglass, one of the most ardent male supporters of feminism, told the Rochester Ladies' Anti-slavery Society in 1855 that he did not object to women sitting on committees with men, but opposed the American Anti-slavery Society being "rent asunder by a side issue." Like many abolitionists Douglass believed "the battle of Woman's Rights should be fought on its own ground." Slavery and women's rights were separate issues; merging them endangered the fight for freedom.

Women of both races continued their struggle in the 1850s to advance women's legal and social standing. They met and sent memorials and petitions to their state legislatures favoring women's suffrage. Much of the agitation focused on the legal discrimination against married women. Ernestine Rose connected married women's property rights and married women as a species of property in her speech to the 1851 Worcester Woman's Rights Convention. She denounced the legal system which punished theft of a pair of boots with six month's imprisonment, but merely reprimanded the man who committed assault and battery upon his wife. Such arguments made little headway in this era, indicating the extent to which all women were still viewed as property and their mistreatment as a matter of private rather than public concern. The women's movement achieved some successes in the 1850s as more states recognized married women's rights to own property, but despite the pleas of some feminists, women continued to be viewed in terms of their family status rather than as individuals.

WOMEN IN THE CIVIL WAR

As an agent for the American Anti-slavery Society Lucy Stone expected "to plead not for the slave only, but for suffering humanity everywhere. *Especially do I mean to labor for the elevation of my sex.*" The Civil War and its aftermath led to divergent interpretations about how to elevate the female sex when the rights of different segments of suffering humanity seemingly conflicted. Fratricidal war ended the argument over slavery, but placed the debate over women's status on hold. The last women's rights convention took place in Albany, New York, in February 1861. Ironically the war to free the slave intensified many women's and children's vulnerability; women scrambled to support their families, and almshouse numbers increased as war widows and orphans floundered in the chaotic economic climate.

Women took up the reins of economic management throughout the nation. With men away at war, white women shouldered much of the burden of feeding the Confederacy, managing plantations and sometimes working in the fields when able-bodied men either fought or were conscripted as laborers. Previously leisured ladies turned their hands to gardening, making clothes, and caring for livestock. The war reduced poor families to subsistence levels as women struggled to plow, plant, harvest, pay taxes, and redeem mortgages. Farm women petitioned state governors for assistance, asking for husbands to be sent home to sow or harvest crops.

Most African-American women remained enslaved until the last year of the war, since whites withheld information about freedom, sometimes even after the war ended, according to reminiscences of ex-slaves. Bondswomen frequently had to make up the work of slave men conscripted as non-combatants by the Confederate Army. The chaos of wartime facilitated flight into Union-held territory, but the Union Army did not always welcome female contrabands (escaped slaves). There were few jobs which women encumbered with children could undertake, although they occasionally washed and cooked for the soldiers. Families slowed down the march and were sometimes abandoned or ill-treated. Plantation owners fleeing beyond the fighting treated bondswomen and children callously. They took their most valuable male slaves, leaving women and children behind. Further dislocation ensued as ex-slaves traveled in search of former partners, children, and parents.

African-American women contributed to the Union war effort in myriad ways. Susie King Taylor, brought up in freedom in Savannah, Georgia, moved to the Sea Islands with her family during the war, first teaching small children, then enlisting as a nurse and laundress with the First South Carolina Volunteers, a black regiment. Charlotte Forten and other northern African-American women journeyed south to educate freedmen and women. Nearly half the black teachers in Charleston's schools were women, although some of them had only the rudiments of literacy themselves. Northern African-American women also established relief societies such as the Ladies' Contraband Relief Society which helped support former slaves who fled for safety to Washington.

Women across the Union and the Confederacy built upon their associational experiences to found over 7000 aid societies. These ranged from handfuls of women sewing and rolling bandages in small towns and rural districts to large-scale societies in major cities. Just weeks after Confederate troops fired on Fort Sumter, 3000 women came to a meeting called by Dr. Elizabeth Blackwell in New York City to establish a relief association to raise funds for the war effort, equip hospitals, and train nurses. Women comprised half of the New York Central Relief Association's management committee and had a crucial role in its fund-raising efforts. In other cities female activists encountered resistance from men who, according to Mary Ashton Livermore of Chicago, "barely tolerated" the idea of female involvement. Nevertheless, Chicago's Sanitary Commission Fair raised about $100 000. Disparate people made donations, including contrabands anxious to help the cause of freedom. Sarah Edwards Henshaw's memoir of the Northwestern Sanitary

Commission recorded gifts of potatoes from young farm women, socks mothers knitted for sons, and a homespun sheet woven by an ex-slave.

The Civil War justifiably boosted women's confidence in their abilities and place in public life. Northern women raised $50 000 000 for the Sanitary Commission and while the South did not have a centrally organized relief system, women's groups held bake sales and bazaars, collecting large sums of money and goods in kind. In one month in 1862, an Alabama women's group took in hundreds of shirts and undergarments, boxes of hospital stores, foodstuffs, and some money. An account of South Carolina women's place in the Confederacy enumerated "519 shirts, 267 pairs of drawers, 189 pairs of socks, 179 pairs of pants, 23 pairs of shoes, 37 blankets and comforters, handkerchiefs, and scarves" as one group's contribution to the quartermaster's stores.

A number of women sought more direct involvement in the war effort as spies and informers. Mary Chesnut's diary entries for 1861 recorded that women smuggled "all manner of things . . . under the huge hoop skirts" as they traveled over the border from Washington to Richmond. Rumors about female spies were rife; women feigned insanity or eccentricity to carry out their clandestine missions. Elizabeth Van Lew used this ruse in Richmond as she gathered information to pass to General Grant. Rose O'Neal Greenhow gathered snippets of information from her political contacts in Washington to assist the Confederacy in planning their battle strategies. Subsequently arrested and kept under armed guard, she spent a year in a federal prison. On her release she journeyed to Richmond, where Confederate president Jefferson Davis told her, "but for you there would have been no Battle of Bull Run." She later carried official papers from Davis to Paris on board a blockade runner.

Although not always welcomed by military authorities women volunteered as nurses. The Army appointed Dorothea Dix Superintendent of Women Nurses over Dr. Elizabeth Blackwell because she presented less of a threat to the male medical establishment, which had little use for women physicians. Dix insisted that her nurses be plain women over the age of 30 to allay suspicions about propriety and respectability. Southerner Sally Tompkins established a hospital in Richmond to care for the injured, later receiving a captain's commission from Jefferson Davis. The southern authorities slowly accepted women nurses, initially relying upon dedicated volunteers, but eventually paying wages to nurses and hospital matrons.

Most women who nursed did so in hospitals, but a few tended the wounded on the battlefields. "Mother" Mary Ann Bickerdyke, a widowed nurse in her forties, journeyed from her home in Galesburg, Illinois, to care for the wounded and dying, first in Cairo, Illinois, and then with General Grant's army on its march through Tennessee. Mother Bickerdyke overhauled army field hospital conditions, instituted a sanitary regime, and fed patients with nutritious food. In 1862, the Northwest Sanitary Commission appointed her as their "agent in the field" to distribute food and medical supplies. Her impatience with military authorities led her to snap, "on the authority of Lord God Almighty: have you anything that outranks that?" to an army surgeon who queried her authority. Mother Bickerdyke made a number of speaking and fund-raising tours on behalf of the Sanitary Commission, gathering contributions to feed the wounded, whose appalling diets impeded their recovery.

Some women opposed the war effort. The Draft Law of 1863 required all northern white men between the ages of 20 and 45 to undertake military service but permitted them to hire substitutes or pay $300 to be exempted. The law inflamed racial and class tensions, especially in New York City where recent Irish immigrants competed against African Americans for housing and employment at the bottom of the economic hierarchy. Resentment at turning the war into "a poor man's fight" prompted largely Irish mobs of both sexes to attack African Americans, shops, saloons, and houses. The six-day riot resulted in the arrest and jailing of hundreds of women and men for their savage attacks on people and property. Provoked by food shortages and rising prices, poor women in other cities participated in bread riots in 1863 and 1864.

Women from the abolitionist reforming tradition responded much more positively to the war because they supported its goals and were less economically threatened. Soon after Abraham Lincoln's election, Elizabeth Cady Stanton, Susan B. Anthony, and Lucretia Mott, among others, embarked upon a speaking tour in New York State urging "Immediate and Unconditional Abolition." Following the Emancipation Proclamation freeing slaves in the Confederacy, Charles Sumner introduced a constitutional amendment abolishing slavery. Fearful that it would not obtain the necessary two-thirds majority, Henry B. Stanton (Elizabeth's husband) wrote to Susan B.

Anthony suggesting that she mobilize popular sentiment in support. In calling a meeting in New York City of "The Loyal Women of the Nation" in May 1863, Anthony and Stanton combined "woman's legitimate work" with the "settlement of this final problem of self-government." Despite opposition to linking abolitionist and women's rights sentiments with the war effort, the persuasive rhetoric of Anthony, Stanton, Lucy Stone, Angelina Grimké Weld, and Ernestine Rose led to resolutions of support for the government. The New York meeting also promised to gather signatures on a petition supporting the Thirteenth Amendment. Over the next two years, the National Women's Loyal League campaign garnered 400 000 signatures, involving thousands of women across the North and giving them another significant experience of organizing to achieve a common purpose.

While the Civil War ended slavery, it did little to resolve the tensions between political involvement, reform aspirations, and domestic roles for women. Emancipation and the awful carnage on the battlefields pitched large numbers of women into a labor market characterized by racial and gendered biases. Religious and reform movements gave some women experience in organizing outside the home, while the war brought home to most the importance of politics to their own daily lives. Women took part in events outside their immediate domestic frame to an extent which had no parallel, not even during the American Revolution. In many ways, women's revolution came during the ante-bellum era as they asserted the legitimacy of their public voice across a broad spectrum of issues. An increasing number agreed with Margaret Fuller that women's supposed weaknesses should not hinder their political participation, but all but the most ardent female reformers still placed familial obligations first.

The commercial and industrial revolutions, the heightened individualism of the ante-bellum era, and the war itself all expanded the scope of women's roles and interests at the same time that they polarized male and female roles by withdrawing men from the home. Women simultaneously became more important in the household and concerned about the relationship between the public and private spheres. As women sought to reconcile their spiritual and reformist concerns in the temperance and anti-slavery struggles with contemporary understandings of women's place, they encountered a maze of legal and social restrictions which led a growing number to place women's issues, including suffrage and legal equality, upon the political agenda.

By the time of the Civil War a number of American women asked no less and no more than that they should be treated as individuals with equal rights rather than as property. For some, such as African-American women who had been literally enslaved, this quest had particular meaning. Still mostly constrained by domestic responsibilities, many American women used them as a springboard for legitimizing their involvement in a variety of crusades including better female education, social and moral reform, abolition, and women's rights. There was much greater acceptance of the female presence in schools and benevolent societies than in party politics or even the abolitionist movement. As the war absorbed the nation's energies there was still little consensus about whether women would be treated as citizens on the same basis as men.

PART II

The Industrial Era

5 Women's Employment, 1865–1920

Between 1865 and 1920 a steady transformation occurred in employment patterns as more women entered the labor market, stayed at work longer, and moved into white-collar occupations. Nevertheless, women's economic experiences remained distinct from men's, subject to gendered limitations, and determined by demographic characteristics to a much greater extent than men's. Class, race, ethnicity, and locality explained the sort of work a man might do, but not whether he worked at all. The Census believed that men worked "as a matter of course" for the greater part of their lives, yet in 1900 economic activity was "far from being customary, and in the well-to-do classes of society is exceptional" for women. In 1840, about 10 percent of free women held jobs, climbing to 15 percent in 1870 (when all African-American women would have been included in the totals for the first time) and to 24 percent by 1920. Marital status was crucial in determining whether a woman worked for pay, although class, race, age, and ethnicity all had an influence. Labor force participation rates were highest for African-American women, but even their employment levels decreased after marriage.

As the economy diversified and paper qualifications became more important the proportion of gainfully occupied women increased. Professional occupations and white-collar work lured middle-class and married women into the labor market, and more young working-class women stayed in school to obtain the education needed for

Table 5.1 Proportion of women in the labor force, ages 16 and over, 1870–1920

	1870	1880	1890	1900	1910	1920
Women Employed (%)	14.8	16.0	19.0	20.6	24.0	24.2

Source: US Department of Commerce, Bureau of the Census, *Comparative Occupation Statistics for the United States, 1870–1940* (Washington, DC, Government Printing Office, 1943), 91–2, 99.

white-collar jobs. Prevailing stereotypes kept wages low for almost all women, despite the rising educational levels of the female labor force and their battles for better wages and working conditions.

THE LOCATION OF WOMEN'S WORK

Women's presence in the labor force varied with the nature of the local economy as well as demographic factors: segregated employment patterns marginalized female workers in some cities but offered great scope in others. In 1880, the proportion of gainfully employed urban women ranged from 11 to 40 percent, depending on which activities dominated the local economy, and differentiated women's laboring experience from men's, whose employment levels showed little variation.

Cities dominated by heavy industry or in the newly settled West had few non-domestic jobs for women and tended to attract only the poorest women into the labor market. At the other extreme, textile cities such as Lowell, Fall River, and Manchester had 30 to 40 percent of women working, almost exclusively in the mills. By 1920, the tide of female economic activity rose as the US developed a national economy. The proportion of women in the labor market increased in all localities with less variation between cities; 26 to 50 percent of women in urban centers with more than 100 000 inhabitants had jobs.

Even so, some areas remained distinctive. Southern urban and rural districts had high proportions of female employment as post-Civil War poverty meant many white and even more black women worked. Immediately after emancipation, African-American women tried to devote themselves to their families by withdrawing from field labor, but poverty and pressure from white land owners forced them into the fields at least part time. Economic historians Roger L. Ransom and Richard Sutch estimate that after emancipation the working week of African-American men fell by about one-fifth as they chose increased leisure (including hunting and growing subsistence food crops) over, literally, working like slaves. Women's and children's work week decreased by about two-fifths, as mothers now took time out of the fields to care for their families (including growing food crops, cooking, and making clothes) and children spent some time in school. These figures are suggestive rather than definitive, but indicate an African-American investment in family life to an extent deplored by white land owners. Nevertheless, African-American women had higher levels of employment and a narrower range of occupations than other racial groups, with two-fifths holding jobs in 1880 and 1920, almost all in agriculture or domestic service.

Definitions of what constituted economic activity for women were culturally determined and changed during this era. The 1910 Census encouraged enumerators to include women, requiring them to ask rather than assume whether a woman had an occupation. Different instructions in 1920 led to a serious undercount of women workers, especially in rural areas where enumerators recorded "no occupation" for women working "only occasionally or only a short time each day at outdoor farm or garden work, or in caring for livestock or poultry," which described the blend of farm and domestic responsibilities characteristic of rural women.

Using this definition, few Native American women "worked" since, herded onto reservations, they engaged in subsistence agriculture which enumerators ignored. Asian women, though few in number, tended to live in western cities and towns where about one-fifth had jobs. The Census did not enumerate Hispanic women's employment experience separately in this era. Definitions of employment, then, reflect the views of the enumerators, but by 1920 almost all women experienced a period of economic activity, even if its length and type fluctuated with age, marital status, and race.

AGE, MARITAL STATUS, RACE, AND EMPLOYMENT

Regardless of where they lived, women's employment status fluctuated greatly with age, unlike men's. Males entered the labor force earlier and stayed in it throughout most of their adult lives, although the proportion of men over 65 who worked decreased from two-thirds to three-fifths between 1900 and 1920. Most women left gainful employment when they married, typically by the age of 25. Mandatory school attendance laws, especially in the North, curtailed the number of very young workers of both sexes by 1920, but male and female employment patterns remained distinctive. The proportion of economically active women aged 15–24 rose by nearly one-third between 1890 and 1920; that of 25–44 year olds

Table 5.2   Women's employment by age, 1890–1920

Ages	1890 (%)	1900 (%)	1920 (%)
10–15	10.0	10.2	5.6
15–24	29.0	31.6	37.6
25–44	15.6	18.1	22.4
45–64	12.6	11.4	17.1
65+	8.3	9.1	8.8

Source: US Department of Commerce, Bureau of the Census, *Statistics of Women at Work* (Washington, DC, Government Printing Office, 1907), 11–14. US Department of Commerce, Bureau of the Census, *Women in Gainful Occupations, 1870–1920*, by Joseph Hill (Washington, DC, Government Printing Office, 1929), 67.

increased by over two-fifths, and for 45–64 year olds by three-tenths, yet men were still much more likely to be in the labor force, especially over the age of 65 where female employment remained static.

Between 1870 and 1920, gainful employment became the norm for single women of all races and featured more prominently for married, widowed, and divorced women, especially African Americans. The proportion of married women with jobs doubled between 1900 and 1910. This increase partially reflected the more inclusive enumeration of their labors, but even with the more restrictive definitions of work employed by the 1920 Census, married women's employment remained elevated. While most women left the labor market at marriage, a growing proportion either worked throughout their marriage or returned to the labor market at some point, prompted by financial necessity or a desire to use their education and training. Rising levels of married women's employment coincided with the sharp decline in child labor; since many families needed more than one income to survive, mothers substituted for children in the labor force. Like the married women in the shoe factories in Lynn and the immigrant garment workers of New York, these women combined childcare with gainful employment inside or outside the home, leaving the labor force only when their children were old enough to work.

African-American women stayed in the labor force after marriage to a much greater extent than white women. In 1900, about 3 percent

Table 5.3   Percentage of women of each marital status in the labor force, 1890–1920

	Single or unknown (%)	Married (%)	Widowed and divorced (%)	Total (%)
1890	40.5	4.6	29.9	18.9
1900	43.5	5.6	32.5	20.6
1910	51.1	10.7	34.1	25.4
1920	46.4*	9.0	*	23.7

*The Census aggregated single, widowed, and women of unknown marital status into the single or unknown category in 1920.

Source: US Department of Commerce, Bureau of the Census, Fifteenth Census, 1930, *Population: General Report on Occupations*, vol. V (Washington, DC, Government Printing Office, 1933), 272.

of white and 26 percent of black married women had jobs. By 1930, the proportions rose to 9 and 33 percent, respectively. The overall employment of widows increased slightly in the early twentieth century, with large discrepancies also occurring between the races. In 1900, three times as many African-American widows had jobs, falling to about twice as many by 1930. The rising proportion of working white widows suggests that the state widows' pensions instituted in the 1910s and 1920s had relatively little impact on their employment. Changes in domestic service also facilitated widows' employment; once day work replaced live-in service, widowed and married women found it easier to combine employment and domestic responsibilities instead of sending their children to live with relatives or in orphanages.

The discrepancies between African-American and white women's employment were greatest for older women. The gap narrowed slightly as more native-born white women entered gainful employment in the early twentieth century, but older black women were still much more likely to have jobs. Young foreign-born women and those with parents born abroad also had very high rates of employment in 1900 and 1920, although employment levels for those over 25 resembled those of native-born whites. These generalizations, of course, obscure the variations between different ethnic groups. For example, French Canadian immigrants to New England textile towns had much higher levels of employment than, say, the Italian women of

Table 5.4   Racial groups in the labor force, 1900–1930

	1900[a]		1930[b]	
	Wives (%)	Widows (%)	Wives (%)	Widows (%)
Native white	3.0	27.1	9.3	31.9
Foreign white	3.6	20.7	8.5	21.1
African American	26.0	67.0	33.3	65.0
Average	5.6	31.5	11.7	34.4

[a] Includes women 16 years of age and older.
[b] Includes women 15 years of age and older.

Sources: *Statistics of Women at Work*, 1900, 14. 1930 Census, *Population*, vol. V, 275.

Pittsburgh or Buffalo who tended to stay out of the labor force, especially after marriage.

The experiences of Caroline Lake Quiner Ingalls, Laura Ingalls Wilder, and Rose Wilder Lane illustrate the transformation in women's work between 1860 and 1920 and the impact of location, age, and generation on female economic activity. Laura's mother taught school for one term in the 1860s before marrying a fur trapper and farmer. The family made its own food, clothes, furniture, and houses, with Caroline doing most of the domestic work, assisted by Laura and her sisters. Most of the family income came from Pa's furs, carpentering, and farming. Caroline did not count as part of the labor force, although her rural labors were certainly productive ones and the family could not have survived without them.

The family expected Laura to earn an income, moving so that she could attend school in the autumn and spring. Laura started teaching at 15 and married at 19. She left the labor force, but continued to toil, feeding farm workers, mending clothes, breaking sod, milking cows, and making cheese and butter. She also did a day's sewing in town when she could get it in order to contribute badly needed cash to her struggling family. This occasional work did not place her in the Census's gainfully employed column, although it enabled the family to buy a farm after their homesteading venture in Dakota Territory failed. After the family settled on a farm in the Ozarks, Laura wrote the stories which brought her fame, combining writing with housekeeping and the numerous activities of a farm wife. Her daughter grew up on the farm in the 1890s, went to school, moved to

Table 5.5   Percentage of women from each age and racial/nativity group in labor force, 1900 and 1920

Age	Native parents 1900 (%)	Native parents 1920 (%)	Foreign parents 1900 (%)	Foreign parents 1920 (%)	Foreign born 1900 (%)	Foreign born 1920 (%)	African American 1900 (%)	African American 1920 (%)
16–20	20.8	25.0	40.0	45.2	56.8	52.0	49.6	38.0
21–24	21.3	32.5	37.8	48.8	41.5	37.7	45.6	45.0
25–44	12.9	18.4	19.5	24.6	16.6	18.6	41.7	45.2
45+	10.5	12.4	11.9	15.6	9.7	11.8	38.8	41.8
Total	14.6	19.7	25.4	29.0	19.1	18.8	43.2	43.1

Sources: see Table 5.4.

San Francisco and became a noted journalist. Of the three generations, only she remained in the labor force continuously after marriage and unambiguously qualified as "working."

The experience of these three generations of native-born white women set them apart from their foreign-born and immigrant-stock counterparts, especially those who lived in cities. In 1900, about one-fifth of young native-born white women with native-born parents had jobs; by 1920, that proportion climbed to one-fourth for 16–20 year olds and one-third for 21–24 year olds. While lower than for first or second generation women (those born abroad or with foreign parents) it shows that gainful employment grew more acceptable and commonplace for younger white women. The vast majority still left the labor force after marriage, but even this pattern began to break down after World War I.

THE CHANGING NATURE OF WOMEN'S EMPLOYMENT

Changes in who worked resulted from changes in the type of work available and women's eagerness to advance up the occupational hierarchy through education. In 1870, six out of every ten working women were servants while almost none (less than one in a hundred) held clerical, secretarial, or sales positions, and 6 percent had professional occupations. The white-collar boom created employment for women as secretaries, stenographers, bookkeepers, telephone operators, and clerks. Employers preferred women workers for repetitive service positions, believing them to be more polite to the customers,

Table 5.6   Women's non-agricultural employment, 1870–1920

	Servants (%)	Clerical (%)	Factory workers (%)	Professionals (%)	All others[a] (%)
1870	60.7	0.8	17.6	6.4	14.6
1880	47.3	1.9	20.9	8.5	21.4
1890	40.3	5.3	20.3	9.5	24.6
1900	33.0	9.1	22.3	10.0	25.7
1910	25.5	14.8	23.1	11.6	25.0
1920	18.2	25.6	23.8	13.3	19.1

[a] Seven-tenths of this category consisted of (in descending order) laundresses, dress-makers, telephone operators, boardinghouse keepers, and retail dealers.

Source: *Women in Gainful Occupations 1870–1920*, 45.

easier to control than young men, and cheaper to employ. By 1920, over one-quarter of all women held clerical posts and nearly one-seventh had professional situations.

While education helped white women to escape from domestic service and factory jobs into genteel white-collar positions, racial and ethnic segregation segmented the female labor force. Few foreign-born, but many more second generation and native-born women wore white blouses; in contrast African-American women experienced a narrow range of occupations throughout this era. Even black female high school graduates found shops and offices closed to them, except in the few businesses run by African Americans. Virtually all those in southern cities were domestics as were most of those in the North.

Less than 1 percent of non-white women had clerical jobs in 1890 or 1920, while only 3 percent held professional posts, mainly as teachers in segregated schools. There were several hundred African-American nurses who graduated from training programs in segregated hospitals, but other nursing and medical schools routinely denied entrance to women of color. White-run hospitals, the Army and the Red Cross refused to employ trained nurses with dark skins throughout World War I.

Few women moved up corporate hierarchies in this era, although some exceptional women carved out business careers, especially in beauty and health care products. Lydia Estes Pinkham began distributing her home-made Vegetable Compound in 1875. Concocted from herbs and roots, and highly (18 percent) alcoholic, it sold widely as a remedy for female complaints. Her company's Department of Advice received thousands of letters from women reluctant to discuss female problems with male doctors. She advised them on matters of hygiene, diet, exercise, and reproduction. By the time of her death in 1883, the company had sold about $300 000 worth of patent medicines.

Beauty product entrepreneur Harriet Hubbard Ayer pioneered the technique of getting celebrity endorsements, featuring actress Lillie Langtry in her facial cream advertisements. Sarah Breedlove (Madame C. J.) Walker developed a hair care process for African-American women which facilitated combing and styling hair. She created opportunities for other African-American women in her factories and sales force, opening a trade where African-American saleswomen could earn decent wages. Walker told the National Negro Business League convention in 1912 that she came from southern cotton fields, worked her way from the washtub to the kitchen and then began making specialized hair care products. When she died in 1919, she was reputed to be a millionaire and one of the wealthiest self-made businesswomen in the United States.

Madame Walker prospered in business by engaging in what would today be labeled niche marketing. Likewise, former slave Mary Prout founded the Grand United Order of St Luke in Baltimore in 1867 to provide medical and burial insurance for African Americans. Maggie Lena Walker, a former teacher from Richmond, later established a Juvenile Department and Council of Matrons within the Independent Order of St. Luke. She opened the St. Luke's Penny Saving Bank in 1902, becoming America's first female bank president. St. Luke's bank lent money to African-American businesses that white-owned banks regularly refused to service.

Such self-made businesswomen were exceptional even though many women capitalized on their education to establish careers; by 1920 women constituted nearly half (47 percent) of the professional workers in the United States. However, they were much more narrowly distributed across the professions than men; 70 percent of female professionals taught school or gave music lessons, while another 14 percent were trained nurses. The next largest category (5 percent) consisted of semi-professional pursuits, mostly keepers of charitable institutions and religious, charity and welfare workers. Thus almost nine out of every ten women professionals came from just three occupational groups. There were no more than a handful of female lawyers, architects, engineers, ministers, dentists, or veterinarians.

Even when they managed to enter the professions women encountered extreme discrimination. They were encouraged to become nurses and positively discouraged from becoming doctors or practicing medicine. Less than 10 percent of all hospitals hired women as doctors or would accept their patients in 1920. Despite such hostility, Dr. Alice Hamilton pioneered a new branch of medicine concerned with industrial health and safety. Other strong-minded women, including Jane Addams and Lillian Wald, opened settlement houses in cities across the United States, where genteel women (and a few men) worked in poor neighborhoods to improve education, housing, and health. The settlement houses and their network of female reformers shaped social welfare policies throughout the first decades of the twentieth century, giving employment to educated women with a vocation and insight into the lives of densely packed urban neighborhoods.

MANUAL LABOR

The expansion of white-collar employment for women occurred at the expense of domestic and manual labor. By 1920, less than two in ten working women held domestic posts. In 1870, most northern domestic servants were white women, usually immigrants or of immigrant stock; by the 1920s, African Americans had begun to take the jobs whites left behind. At the turn of the century over half of all employed Irish women were domestics as were many Scandinavian immigrants in the Midwest, although Italian and Jewish women tended to reject domestic service for factory or industrial homework which had less stigma attached to it. The average domestic worker received between $2 and $5 per week at the end of the nineteenth century compared with about $5 or $6 garnered by factory workers who had to pay their own room and board. The wages paid to black domestic servants were considerably lower, as were their factory earnings in those few industries which employed them.

Industrial jobs grew in importance as an employment for white women in the late nineteenth and early twentieth centuries. In 1870, 18 percent of all women workers worked in factories, rising to 24 percent by 1920. Most of these women worked in semi-skilled or unskilled positions, with little chance of occupational advancement, tending machines which ran at ever faster speeds, working long hours, frequently in unsanitary and unsavory conditions. Most female shoe workers after the Civil War operated machines in factories in contrast to their mothers who bound shoes at home. The introduction of the McKay stitcher in 1850 mechanized and de-skilled the industry, opening more jobs to women. In 1870, about 5 percent of shoe workers were women, by 1920, 36 percent were. Shoe working paid better wages than the textile factories, but female shoemakers still averaged only 60 percent of male earnings, a proportion little changed from the middle of the nineteenth century. Given the paucity of alternative occupations for women, employers persistently discriminated against them, knowing they could not earn more elsewhere.

Women dominated the textile labor force; six out of every ten cotton mill workers in 1880 were women, as were over half of all textile mill operatives in 1900. By 1920, women's share of the textile labor force had fallen slightly as manufacturers moved production to low-wage southern states, where men could be hired cheaply once declining agricultural profits forced them to look for other types of work. Southern mill owners also employed large numbers of children which depressed wages and deprived children of the education which might have enabled them to get better jobs.

Employers established a sexual division of labor which reserved the more "skilled" jobs for men and relegated women to supposedly less skilled, lower paying occupations. Some women, especially the weavers, had highly skilled jobs, however because such positions as loom fixer, foreman, or overseer were closed to them, women had few opportunities to move up the mill hierarchy. Even in those rare instances where women and men performed the same tasks, men received higher pay. An 1890 Bureau of Labor study of 150 000 workers located only 800 men and women doing similar work and three-quarters of these men received higher wages.

Southern industrial establishments reinforced racial and gender hierarchies. One or two mills hired African-American women to work on cheap goods, but almost all southern textile workers were native-born whites from rural backgrounds. Mill owners preferred to employ entire families, paying children 25–50 cents a day (in the 1880s) while adult women earned 50–80 cents. While these wages were low, they exceeded those paid to African Americans in tobacco factories. Tobacco companies used black men and women to undertake jobs similar to those performed by slaves before emancipation; women stripped the leaf from the stem in a highly labor-intensive process while the men did the heaviest, hottest labor.

Industrial homework emerged as an adjunct to the manufacturing process in many industries. Ante-bellum women intermingled domestic and productive responsibilities, but by the end of the nineteenth century, home production became synonymous with tenement sweatshops where workers labored in family groups to maximize output and income. Industrial homework enabled women from patriarchal cultures which restricted their mobility outside the home to work under the watchful eyes of their husbands, parents, or other relations. Most homeworkers in the early twentieth century were foreign born (or of foreign parentage) with young children, although a significant number were over the age of 50. They tended to have larger than average families, suggesting that homework attracted those who could not leave the home for domestic or cultural reasons.

Industrial homework encompassed a broad variety of occupations and industries in the Gilded Age and Progressive Era. Mexican women in Texas shelled pecans and embroidered clothing; white women in the Appalachian mountains made bedspreads and appliquéd quilts; coal miners' wives in Western Pennsylvania sewed jeans and overalls while Japanese women in Los Angeles stitched handkerchiefs. Bohemian women rolled cigars in New York City and their Italian and Jewish women neighbors made paper flowers and clothing. Rural African-American women in Kentucky combined sewing shirts for the Army during World War I with farming. In all cases, the blending of homework and childcare enabled women to earn while looking after their children.

Social surveyors in 1907 concluded: "in the tenement shops there is less emphasis on speed and more laxity as to hours, but there are counterbalancing disadvantages of frequent night work, congested workrooms, and unsanitary as well as unventilated buildings." Subjected to time and motion studies to extract maximum labor, factory women worked long hours at limited tasks under close supervision, sometimes under appalling conditions. The tragedy at the Triangle Shirtwaist Company in 1911 occurred because the owners of the New York City clothing factory refused workers' demands for fire escapes and unlocked doors. Afraid that seamstresses would sneak breaks from the intolerable pace of the machines, the company locked them in: 146 women burned or jumped to their deaths in the fire.

Hazardous working conditions came in many forms. Low wages, competition for jobs, and unscrupulous employers made female workers vulnerable to sexual advances from male supervisors. Some women received higher pay for making "concessions" to their employers or were allowed to keep their jobs. Ona in Upton Sinclair's *The Jungle* acceded to the boss's demands because he threatened to fire her: "He told me he would – we would all of us lose our places. We could never get anything to do here again. He meant it – he would have ruined us." Foremen routinely dismissed women who resisted their sexual advances or protested against sexual harassment.

Social purity campaigners believed that higher wages for women would preserve their virtue. The Illinois Woman's Alliance complained that inadequate sanitary conditions in the workplace threatened "womanly purity." Notwithstanding the Census's exclusion of prostitution from its published tables, enumerators described sexual service workers in the manuscript schedules as sporting women, cigar store keepers, residents or boarders in brothels. Women turned to prostitution because low wages made it difficult to make ends meet in more respectable employments. About two-fifths of New York City's prostitutes at mid-century had previously been domestics or seamstresses. The Commissioner of Labor's 1889 survey of prostitutes in eastern and midwestern cities concluded they came from working-class backgrounds, a finding echoed by later surveys. Pittsburgh's Morals Efficiency Commission in 1913 discovered that women had a broad range of blue-collar jobs, but none came from the comfortable classes.

Unlike most female occupations, prostitution drew from all ethnic and racial groups. Southern cities had segregated brothels, while a number of northern ones had racially integrated houses. African-American, Japanese, Mexican, and Chinese women were over-represented in the ranks of sporting women, since they had even fewer employment opportunities than white women. Until the curtailment of immigration from China there was a considerable trade in women indentured to brothels serving the Chinese community, while unscrupulous employment agencies attempted to lure African-

American and "greenhorn" (recent immigrant) women to brothels in northern cities.

For many women prostitution was an economically rational occupation since they earned about five times more than other working women, although it was a hazardous occupation, with pimps, venereal disease, unwanted pregnancies, violent clients, and the police posing threats. Most cities had a spectrum of brothels, ranging from 50-cent houses which served immigrant and unskilled workers to $1- and $2-houses for clerks and skilled workers, and fancy establishments for businessmen. Two sisters opened the Everleigh Club in 1900 to cater for the urban elite who enjoyed its art gallery, ballroom and music room as well as the favors of prostitutes who charged $25–$50 per visit. Madame Lulu White, who described herself as "the handsomest octoroon in America" ran a fancy house which contained "the most costly oil paintings in the southern country" according to her advertisement in a guide to prostitution in New Orleans at the turn of the century.

WORLD WAR I AND WOMEN'S EMPLOYMENT

Prostitution flourished in most cities until a coalition of urban reformers and military authorities succeeded in clamping down on it during World War I. The war gave women the chance to shift from lower paying service jobs into occupations vacated by men drafted into the army. The new jobs had their own status hierarchies and were filled accordingly by white, educated women (white-collar work, especially with government), white, less educated women (factory operatives), and African-American women (recruited directly into the unskilled factory positions for the first time). Wartime employment heralded new opportunities for African-American women in northern cities although educated African-American women still experienced great difficulty in obtaining jobs that suited their qualifications.

Like other women in wartime, these new industrial workers moved in search of work. American women undertook battlefield nursing and ambulance driving in Europe, while many more served their country by making armaments and uniforms, driving streetcars, and working in offices. Such opportunities had a dramatic impact on where women worked. In 1920, many of the gainfully employed women in Washington, DC, were newly arrived war workers who stayed in the nation's capital after the conflict ended. Nearly half the women in the District worked outside the home in 1920, a significant increase over the already large contingent (two-fifths) employed in 1910. Indeed, the nation's capital had the single greatest concentration of female employees in 1920, outdistancing the textile manufacturing cities of Lowell and Fall River for the first time. This signaled the future of women's employment in the white-collar sector and government service, rather than in textiles, the clothing trades, shoe manufacturing, or, especially, domestic service. Although American participation in the war was shortlived, women were used during the conflict, as they would be again in World War II, as a reserve army of labor to be granted access to more desirable and better paying jobs, if only for a short period. The briefness of American engagement in the war meant that many women were fired from their new jobs only a short time after obtaining them.

LABOR UNIONS AND LABOR REFORM

The decades between the Civil War and World War I were a period of labor unrest. Investigations into the condition of working women and legislation to curtail abuses of factory workers signaled unease over the growing numbers of women workers and the unfair return they received for their toils. For all the hostility to women by male trade unionists, and despite structural obstacles to building a career rather than just having a job, female militancy flared during this era as women protested against deteriorating working conditions, low pay, and unsteady employment. Many industries had rush seasons or rush days when employees toiled ceaselessly only to be un- or underemployed for other parts of the year or days of the week. Laundry workers, for example, put in especially long days on Friday since the finished goods needed to be returned to their owners by the weekend. Rather than hire more workers or fire up the boilers on Saturdays, owners squeezed more work out of existing employees. The drive to keep costs down resulted in poor working conditions and precarious incomes in this and other female occupations.

Female workers in some industries actively fought their low wages, being "sufficiently schooled in the arts of organization to form effective trade unions of their own," according to John B.

Andrews and W.P.D. Bliss's *History of Women in the Trade Unions* (1911). In 1864, the collar workers of Troy, NY, went on strike for higher wages, appealing to their employers' sense of justice to raise wages in line with wartime inflation. Female Collar Laundry Union (CLU) members struck again in 1869, and provided a core of militancy in Troy for strikes in the 1870s and 1880s. They formed the Joan of Arc Assembly of the Knights of Labor in 1886, with skilled laundry workers, especially starchers, being most active. Male trade unionists supported the CLU, but employers cooperated to defeat the strikers when male iron puddlers and female laundry workers struck simultaneously. The laundry owners locked out the collar workers, ending the strike and leading to the disappearance of the Joan of Arc Assembly.

Women in other cities and industries also organized to improve their status. Female cigar makers formed their own union in 1864, the Ladies' Cigar Makers' Union, based in Providence, RI. Augusta Lewis founded the Women's Typographical Union in 1868, becoming the first woman elected to a national union office when she became corresponding secretary of the International Typographical Union in 1870. The Daughters of St. Crispin, a trade organization of shoe workers, was a national female union, founded in 1869 as a parallel organization to the male Knights of St. Crispin, and although it disappeared during the depression of the 1870s, its former members incorporated their organizing knowledge into later union activities.

In 1875, women walked out of Fall River's mills protesting wage cuts. Despite their militancy and support from male workers, the strike ended in defeat after eight months when the mill owners blacklisted the ringleaders and virtually starved other workers into submission. Women in Lawrence, Massachusetts, Pacific Mill struck in 1882 over a 20 percent cut in wages, a 20 percent speed-up in production, and a switch from day to piece-rates. This was as much a protest over their unequal position in the mills as over the wage cuts, and female ring spinners and weavers received little support from male trade unionists who thought they should be at home, not debasing men's skills and undercutting their position in the mills. The strike failed after four months as the mills entered their annual summer slow period and women left Lawrence to search for work elsewhere.

Employers set different segments of the working class against each other, used women as strikebreakers and machinery operators and exploited ethnic tensions to divide the labor force. At the same time, national unions tended to be lukewarm supporters of female organizing activities because they regarded women as competition for skilled jobs. Even astute organizers such as Susan B. Anthony, founder of the Working Women's Association, found it difficult to steer a clear course between the rights of women as workers and the sensibilities of male trade unionists. Anthony sought work for women printers during a strike in 1869, believing they had a right to gainful employment. This split the Working Women's Association as working-class women withdrew because of its strikebreaking activities and the middle-class emphasis on suffrage.

Yet some unions did support women's organizing efforts. The Cigar Makers' International Union's national convention declared that "no local union shall permit the rejection of an applicant for membership on account of sex or system of working." The Knights of Labor supported equal pay for equal work in a resolution passed in 1878. Active in the 1870s and 1880s, the Knights had female "master workmen," assigning Elizabeth Flynn Rodgers to that post in 1881. In that same year it accepted Mary Stirling as the first female delegate to its national convention. It had a committee which collected statistics on women's work, appointed in 1885 on the motion of Mary Hanafin, a saleswoman and delegate from Philadelphia. This committee discovered women members averaged $5 per week for a ten-hour day, except in the shoe trade which was "more lucrative." When the Knights peaked in the mid-1880s, they had 50 000 female members, about 10 percent of the total membership. They also had over 100 all-female local assemblies, accepted African-American members, and actively recruited unskilled workers and immigrants.

The skilled workers of the American Federation of Labor (AFL), which replaced the Knights as the largest national union in the 1890s, exhibited less sympathy for female, unskilled male, immigrant, or African-American workers, all of whom it regarded as potential competition. Although the AFL hired several female general organizers, including the redoubtable Mary Kenney O'Sullivan in 1892, and favored equal pay for equal work, it did not accept that women had a legitimate place in the labor market. Equal pay was a ploy to oust women from the work place since it made women less attractive employees to cost-conscious employers. The AFL recruited few female members, so that by 1900 only 2 percent of all trade unionists were women.

Many working-class women were involved in (male) trade union affairs as members' wives. They believed that men should be the family breadwinners and earn a wage large enough to sustain the family. Women took an active part in the miners' strikes at Cripple Creek between 1894 and 1904. Largely dependent upon their husbands' wages for survival, they supported a strong union presence as a means of improving their families' standards of living.

Most skilled workers supported the family wage ideology, wanting men to be paid enough to keep their women and children out of the labor force. As economic dependents they would no longer need to compete with legitimate (male) breadwinners. They associated women with the machines introduced by employers to undercut skilled workers' hegemony over key production processes. The *Labor Leader* coupled de-skilling with the use of women and child wage earners with drastic consequences: "Boy labor, girl labor, and woman labor are reducing the wages of manhood labor, and thus tending to destroy family discipline, endanger morals, and reduce the standard of living."

A decade later a trade union leader writing in *The American Federationist* asserted that the demand for female labor sprang neither from philanthropy nor the milk of human kindness. It was an attack, "aimed at the family circle. . . threatening the land, the community, the home." Female labor did nothing less than imperil the sanctity of the home as "mother, sister, and daughter" replaced "the father, the brother, and the son" in the labor force. Both in 1893 and in 1914, AFL annual conventions passed resolutions opposing the presence of women in the labor force, particularly that of married women who had husbands to support them.

Despite male trade unionists' ambivalence and hostility, women struck repeatedly during the Gilded Age and Progressive Era. There were over 6000 strikes in these years, with particular activism among the New York and Chicago garment workers and the New England mills. During the mass strike of the shirtwaist workers in 1909 young clothing worker Clara Lemlich lost patience with the interminable speeches, declaring: "I am a working girl, and one of those who are on strike against intolerable conditions. I am tired of listening to speakers who talk in general terms. What we are here for is to decide whether or not we shall strike. I offer a resolution that a general strike be declared – now!" The shared culture of many of the textile workers, mostly Russian Jewish immigrants, facilitated labor organizing, as did the birth of new-style labor organizations. The International Ladies' Garment Workers' Union emerged from this strike as the leading labor organization in the garment industry, with a majority of female members but a male-dominated leadership. It organized unskilled as well as skilled workers, which differentiated it from older style unions open only to craftsmen.

Other labor organizations, including the Industrial Workers of the World (IWW) and the Women's Trade Union League (WTUL), also supported women's organization. Formed in 1903 the WTUL was a coalition of female middle-class reformers and working-class, frequently immigrant, laborers which promoted cross-class cooperation, agitated for improved working conditions, and assisted striking women. It supported protective legislation since women workers seemed unable to improve conditions in the work place through conventional forms of labor activism.

Skilled male workers and middle-class reformers of both sexes agreed that women needed protection in the work place and that married women should devote themselves to their families. Labor investigations censured industrial homework as a threat to family life. Florence Kelley, an investigator for the National Consumers' League in 1910, condemned the homework system which forced women to neglect their homes and children while laboring under "the twofold strain of home maker and wage earner." Reformers complained that sweated labor (and indeed married women's working outside the home) violated the gender norms while placing an intolerable burden on the women who attempted to fulfill two conflicting roles. Other investigations such as the massive 1911 *Report on the Condition of Woman and Child Wage Earners* documented women's deplorable working conditions.

The IWW supported direct action through strikes, justifiably fearing state intervention in labor relations since the police powers of the state had frequently been turned against employees. Events in Lawrence, Massachusetts, demonstrated that supposedly benign protective legislation could harm women workers. State labor legislation lowered the number of hours women and children could work, which prompted mill owners to reduce wages. The IWW supported the ensuing 1912 strike of textile workers in Lawrence which began when a group of Polish women in the Everett Mill left their looms to protest pay cuts. These unskilled women relied upon community networks and support from the IWW in their successful strike.

The presence of large numbers of young single women in the garment industry unions indicates that this age/gender group could be organized, despite their presumed lack of interest in combination. The poverty of working women, however, and the significance of their wages to poor families, impeded organizing among women workers. So did the sectors of the labor force in which they operated. Domestic servants, three-fifths of gainfully employed women in 1870 and one-third in 1900, found it particularly difficult to organize. There are scattered examples of them doing so after the Civil War and later, but the personal nature of domestic employment made it difficult to sustain union activities. Nevertheless, black washerwomen and domestics struck in Jackson, Mississippi (1866), Galveston, Texas (1871), and Atlanta (1881) in support of higher wages.

By 1920, when nearly a quarter of all women workers held factory jobs, trade union activity among women grew more pronounced. The militancy of textile and clothing industries raised the proportion of female labor union members from its nadir in 1910 (about 1.5 percent) to 6.6 percent, although female unionization still lagged behind men's. One-fifth of male workers belonged to a union and 92 percent of all union members were male. About half of all female trade unionists were in the clothing trades, one-fourth were in the printing trades, and the rest were scattered across other industrial establishments. Female activism in the garment industry improved conditions for some workers, but increasingly reformers and state governments turned to protective legislation, substituting paternalism (or maternalism in the case of female reformers) for bargaining between women and their employers.

Some of the impetus for protective legislation came from within the (male) working class itself. In 1879, Adolph Strasser, president of the Cigar Makers' International Union declared in the *Cigar Makers' Journal* that it was impossible to drive women out of the trade, but laws could restrict their numbers: "No girls under 18 should be employed more than eight hours per day; all overwork should be prohibited; white married women should be kept out of factories at least six weeks before and six weeks after confinement." Other trade unionists echoed these sentiments, although their opinions were sometimes rooted in a desire to improve working conditions rather than to eliminate female competition. At the Knights of Labor General Assembly in 1888 Leonora Barry recommended a state factory inspection system, child labor laws, and the abolition of the sweating system in order to protect "the mothers to whom a nation must look for her strength of manhood and womanhood in future generations."

Commissioners of labor, independent investigators, and social reformers documented deteriorating working conditions in the late nineteenth and early twentieth centuries. In 1884, Carroll D. Wright, head of the Massachusetts Bureau of Statistics of Labor and later US Commissioner of Labor, described women's work in the clothing trades as a "tax on the strength" of the nation. The National Consumers' League, Women's Trade Union League, state boards of labor, settlement houses, and social reformers conducted investigations into the conditions of gainfully employed women after 1900 and found them shockingly abusive.

These reform organizations coalesced around a program of protective legislation, wages and hours laws, and the regulation of women's and children's employment. They feared for the welfare of a nation beset (as they saw it) by diversity, poor working and housing conditions, and new immigrant groups who needed to be acculturated to American ways. While skilled male workers could bargain for themselves over most issues, reformers believed women and children needed protection from their own poverty, rapacious employers, and misfortunes over which they had no control.

States attempted to overcome the abuses of industrial workers through two mechanisms. One was to rely upon their widely accepted public health and welfare provisions to regulate undesirable situations concerning workers' health and disease prevention in tenement factories. The other was to appeal to a "higher good." States regulated access to the labor market and working conditions for women and children after a series of court decisions rejected the public health argument as a means of limiting all workers' hours.

Courts deemed freedom of contract sacrosanct for men, but barely applicable to women, and excluded children altogether. States repeatedly attempted to restrict female occupations. A California law forbade women's employment in premises selling alcoholic beverages. Although they were voided in 1881, Ohio and Washington courts sustained similarly restrictive statutes on the grounds that female moral integrity might be impaired and that women's health was particularly susceptible to injury from certain industrial processes. Massachusetts prohibited night work for women in 1890. Several years later Pennsylvania limited women to a 60-hour working week, stating "Adult females are a class as distinct as minors, separated by natural conditions from all other laborers, and are so constituted as to be unable to endure physical exertion and exposure to the extent and degree that is not harmful to adult workers." In this context, "adult workers" clearly meant male adults, the legitimate labor force.

In 1908, the Supreme Court sanctioned a highly gendered interpretation of legitimacy in the labor force, emphasizing women's physical weaknesses and needs for protection, while accepting that sex- and age-based regulation of the labor force was a legitimate exercise of state power. *Muller vs. Oregon* distinguished women from other workers. "Woman's physical structure and the performance of maternal functions place her at a disadvantage in the struggle for subsistence." Woman was "in a class by herself," the Supreme Court observed, so that: "legislation designed for her protection may be sustained, even when like legislation is not necessary for men and could not be sustained." The Court believed that women looked to men for protection. "Her physical structure and a proper discharge of her maternal functions – having in view not merely her own health, but the well-being of the race – justify legislation to protect her from the greed as well as the passion of man."

The Supreme Court ruled that "sex is a valid basis for classification." Female biology took precedence over rights of contract, enshrined in Court decisions for male workers only. The Court agreed with a 1900 AFL columnist that "female labor should be limited so as not to injure the motherhood and family life of a nation." By accepting protective legislation for women (and children) but not for men, the Supreme Court incorporated a highly gendered view of women's capabilities and rights. Biology was destiny and foreclosed job opportunities and citizenship rights.

Social reformers, concerned to improve the truly appalling working conditions under which many women workers toiled, believed protective legislation would succeed where union organizing had failed. The legislation they proposed and the Court accepted had a narrow scope. These statutes invariably excluded domestics and farm workers who had even longer working days than industrial workers. When the Supreme Court upheld protective legislation it referred to "the well-being of the race," by which it meant the white race, the industrial workers of America, rather than darker skinned peoples who formed a growing segment of household and farm workers.

As more women entered the labor force, the state defined women in terms of their functions as mothers, or potential mothers. This chapter began by positing that marital status was the best predictor of female labor force participation in this era. When the growth in numbers of women workers outside the home seemed to threaten the home itself, or what it symbolized – motherhood and domesticity – the state moved in to ensure that women would regard home and family as their primary interests, whether they wanted to or not. Many states barred married women from public employment such as teaching. Women's share of the labor force increased, but the state rejected the employment of married (white) women, preferring them in the home as caretakers of the next generation rather than in the labor force competing on an equal basis with men.

State labor legislation treated women as incompetents incapable of acting in their own best interests. As more women attended school the basis on which they worked altered: they stayed in the labor force longer, branched into white-collar occupations, and worked after marriage in greater numbers. Despite these changes, the perceptions of women as workers gave primacy to their gender, family status, and race rather than their abilities or wishes. White women succeeded in moving into new areas of employment where literacy was important, but much of the work was routine paper processing. In those areas in which female working might conflict with men's vested interests they encountered fierce opposition, whether in the professions or in the factories. The areas of the labor force into which women were channeled changed in the decades between the Civil War and 1920, but gender stereotyping of women's employment remained entrenched, despite many women's efforts to make the labor market their own.

6 Family, Migration, and Social Values in the Industrial Era

The family of the industrial era was the battlefield where matters of gender were resolved and cultural contacts were mediated at a time of great demographic change. Urbanization and westward expansion proceeded simultaneously, the South and Northeast lost population to western and north central states, and immigration accelerated after 1900, with women participating in these upheavals sometimes as prime movers and at other times as reluctant venturers. This demographic and economic turmoil prompted the state and other external agencies to intervene increasingly in family life in an attempt to bring all sectors of the population into conformity with reformers' and lawmakers' views about appropriate gender and age relations. They regarded the white middle-class urban model of wage-earning father, home-making mother, and dependent children as the ideal family, yet the discrepancies between ethnic and racial groups over women's individual interests and those of the family continued to characterize population trends in this era.

By 1920, the household itself had contracted to the nuclear family with fewer working-class and middle-class homes containing boarders or extended family, although these had been commonplace earlier. The family became an isolated unit of consumption which stressed maternal devotion to its interests, yet many women believed social and political issues affected the household and therefore were part of their domestic concerns. Schemes to aid the widowed mothers of young children and to combat violence between partners or generations expressed reforming women's anxieties over the state of the family, the belief that women should not work because of their family status, and an increased willingness to use the mechanisms of the state to safeguard family members.

There were numerous tensions between women and their families. Mothers were expected to devote themselves entirely to their household, even though a growing number had jobs outside the home.

Immigrant families transported their own norms to the United States, with traditions of mutual obligations resulting in generational conflict as the second generation struggled to mediate between their parents' collective strategies and the more individualistic American society. Racial and ethnic groups varied in the way they deployed female labor, heightening tensions over whose version of family life would prevail. Sex ratios (the number of men per 100 women) also impinged upon women's ability or desire to conform to native-born white cultural norms, as groups with high sex ratios (mostly immigrants) might encourage early marriage while in those with lower ones (especially African Americans where there were 99 men for every 100 women) women might have trouble finding a partner. Despite the dominant norms, then, particular demographic circumstances and customs influenced female roles inside and outside the family.

THE GENDERING OF IMMIGRATION

Immigration accelerated rapidly in the early twentieth century; the majority of immigrants came from southern, central, and eastern Europe, with significant numbers arriving from Scandinavia, Canada, and Mexico. From the Civil War until the turn of the century nearly 400 000 immigrants entered the United States each year, two-fifths of them women. Immigration peaked between 1903 and 1914, when between 800 000 and one million people arrived annually, although the proportion of women declined to about one-third. Many women immigrated by themselves, primarily to New York, Massachusetts, Pennsylvania, and Illinois, which had the greatest number of foreign-born inhabitants. A study of Pennsylvania's industrial districts indicated that two-fifths of the immigrant working women had journeyed alone and that three-fifths were under 18 when they got to the United States.

As with earlier generations of immigrants, the new arrivals experienced a simultaneous push out of the old country and a pull to the new one. Hundreds of thousands of Russian Jews, Italians, and Poles took advantage of cheap steerage fares to escape oppression and poverty. In 1916, a young Russian Jewish immigrant described her fears of being massacred by the same gentiles who murdered her aunt and uncle. So strong were her worries that she emigrated on her own, expecting no help from anyone, and determined to make her way to a place without pogroms.

Chain migration played a significant role in many other women's entry into the United States. A St. Vincent de Paul Society survey in 1897 found that friends or relations met almost all Irish female arrivals in Boston. Pauline Newman, who started work at the age of 8 and later became an organizer for the International Ladies' Garment Workers' Union, emphasized the lure of the New World and the role of the family in facilitating emigration: "America was known to foreigners as the land where you'd get rich." Her brother emigrated first, sending for each sister in turn in a process of linked migration replicated by tens of thousands of families.

There were great variations in the sex ratios of immigrants from different nationalities, with northern Europe and the Americas being the most balanced, and southern Europe and Asia having far more men than women. Canadians averaged about 52 female immigrants for every 48 men who crossed the border, while Mexicans had a different pattern, with around 57 men migrating for every 43 women. Northwestern Europe closely resembled the Canadian profile, whereas 60 Italian men came for every 40 women who settled in the United States. Before the 1924 immigration restriction act severely curtailed numbers, Russia, Poland, and other central and eastern European nations fell between the two groups with about 55 male emigrants to every 45 women. The destination of these immigrant groups varied widely: Mexicans remained primarily in the Southwest, Canadians in the Northeast, and Europeans moved in a well-defined belt from the Northeast to the Midwest.

Few Chinese women emigrated to the United States in the years before the Chinese Exclusion Act of 1882 limited immigration to merchants and their wives. Chinese venturers to the United States rarely came as part of a family group, resulting in a highly unbalanced sex ratio, ranging from 19 men for every woman in 1860, to 27 to 1 in 1890. The extreme disparity prompted labor contractors and Chinese secret societies to import thousands of Chinese women as prostitutes, a number of them sold into this occupation by their families. In San Francisco in 1870, for example, seven out of every ten Chinese women worked in brothels, mostly as contract laborers. Some women married to escape prostitution, while a few (50–80 a year) fled to the Chinese Mission Home, run by Protestant female missionaries. Prostitution declined in the first decades of the twentieth century as reform campaigns inveighed against the practice and sex ratios eventually evened up.

Only a handful of Japanese women lived in the United States at the turn of century, mostly in Hawaii and California. A few joined their husbands as contract laborers in the 1890s, but the majority emigrated as picture brides, selected by men's relatives in Japan. Typically 10–15 years younger than their husbands, they joined them as working partners in the fields and shops, or as domestic servants, seamstresses, or cannery workers. Several factors restricted the number of Japanese women in the United States. After the Gentlemen's Agreement of 1907 Japan no longer issued passports to laborers and, responding to white Americans' objections to the picture-bride practice, stopped giving such women passports in 1921. California legislators agitated against the supposedly barbarous practice of picture brides as an election ploy, playing upon California fears of Japanese land owning (forbidden under the Alien Land Law of 1913). By restricting the emigration of Japanese women, these legislators hoped to curtail the growth of the Japanese population and prevent the conversion of the Japanese population from aliens without rights to citizens.

Female immigrants found jobs and housing through a variety of channels. Boston's Travelers' Aid Society agents met incoming steamers, directed women to temporary accommodation if they arrived on their own or if no one met them at the pier, and assisted them to locate respectable work. The Immigrants' Protective League of Chicago looked after women arriving in that city. New York's *Hevra Hachnosas Orchim* (Hebrew Sheltering Society, 1890), Hebrew Immigrant Aid Society (1902), Pan-Hellenic Union, Italian Immigrant Aid Society, Polish National Alliance, and other ethnic aid societies smoothed women's passage from the ship to the shop.

Most women who came to America expected to work either inside or outside the home since immigrants' desperate poverty required the economic activity of all family members. Seven out of ten single foreign-born women in the United States at the turn of the century had jobs, with the proportion being highest amongst the recent immigrant groups. The largest single occupation for these women was domestic service, followed closely by factory labor, although location, ethnic customs, and preferences influenced the job taken. Agents from the New England textile mills recruited impoverished farm families from Quebec, promising company housing if they would put the entire family in the mill. Italian women worked in the garment industry with other Italians or at occupations which they could pursue in family groups, making artificial flowers, hand-finishing or embroidering garments. During the summers, many took their children with them to pick and process crops, as they had done in Italy. Jewish women were concentrated in the garment industry, especially in the crowded tenement districts of the Lower East Side of New York City, while Polish and Slavic women in eastern and midwestern cities undertook unskilled factory labor, and Mexican immigrants clustered in needle work, food processing, and agriculture.

Hampered by language barriers and fearful of people from outside their ethnic or religious group, most immigrant women remained immersed in a world of co-religionists or fellow-country people. Ethnic communities established their own organizations for sociability, protection, and solidarity. These provided comfort for newcomers, although they might also insulate them from wider society. Ethnic newspapers (58 in Massachusetts alone) reinforced group solidarity while advising newcomers how to handle unfamiliar situations. A Russian shopworker wrote to New York City's *Jewish Daily Forward* in 1907 inquiring what to do about the foreman in Vineland, New Jersey, who set low wages, "insults and reviles the workers" and worst of all, "allows himself to 'have fun' with some of the working girls" even though he was married with several children. This young woman needed her job to help support her family of eight, but she "didn't want to accept the foreman's vulgar advances." The *Forward* advised her to bring the situation out in the open because in a small town, "it shouldn't be difficult to have him thrown out of the shop and for her to get her job back." Whether she succeeded or not, her letter indicates young female immigrants' vulnerability to exploitation and their determination to resist it.

The values of the new world challenged those held by immigrants and sometimes impeded their objectives. American individualism ran counter to immigrants' collective strategy for survival and advancement which fostered mutual obligations between family members. Anzia Yezierska, a Russian Jewish immigrant, captured these dilemmas in her stories of immigrant life on New York City's Lower East Side. She experienced the strains between the older generation's desire to control their children's behavior and paychecks and the younger one's wish for freedom and assimilation. In one of her *Hungry Heart* stories the daughter spent 50 cents of her wages on a toothbrush, towel, and bar of soap for herself. Her mother lamented "Mashah had no heart, no feelings, that millionaire things willed themselves in her empty head, while the rest of us were wearing out our brains for only a bite [to eat] in the mouth." To Mashah her own toothbrush symbolized Americanization and assimilation; her mother regarded it as an act of selfishness that deprived the entire family of her contribution to its welfare.

The conflict between ambition and immigrant circumstances loomed large in Yezierska's stories as she depicted the clash between the collectivist immigrant and individualistic American cultures. Many female immigrant servants experienced a sharp contrast between the luxurious living standards of well-to-do Americans and their own modest backgrounds. The Slovak immigrant maid who worked for people who had "four people in twelve rooms" came from a neighborhood where, according to Thomas Bell's *Out of this Furnace*, eleven people crowded into four rooms. Cleaning gave her insight into living standards in her new country but emphasized the gap between the native and foreign born.

Immigrants wanted the comfort and affluence of the native born, but they came at a high price, either in dislocation from one's own culture or through long hours working at low pay. Relatively few married immigrant women held jobs outside the home (about 3 percent in 1900), but a sizeable proportion worked within family groups in the garment industry and other sweated trades or took in boarders, and thus combined domestic responsibilities with economic activity, even if Census enumerators did not place them in the employed category. In doing this, they enhanced their family's economic standing while still upholding traditional values.

MIGRATION

Mobility accelerated after the Civil War under the terms of the 1862 Homestead Act which promised 160 acres of land to settlers who would live on it for five years, planting crops and trees. The new western women's history pioneered by Joan Jensen, Susan Armitage, and Elizabeth Jameson, among others, has done much to correct the impression left by historian Frederick Jackson Turner and his acolytes that trappers, miners, cowboys and soldiers settled the West by themselves. Between 1860 and 1920 the western population increased fifteen-fold, while the sex ratio declined from 214 men for every 100 women to 115. The West remained the most male-dominated region of the United States, followed by the north central and southern states, but women also saw it as a land of opportunity.

Female migration to the West thus constituted an important part of that region's demography in the late nineteenth and early twentieth centuries. First by the Overland Trail, later by railroad, women and men searched for land, mineral wealth, riches, and a new start. A number of women stayed in the frontier towns, housekeeping with their husbands or working as teachers, domestics, prostitutes, and clerks. Others continued their journey by horse and wagon away from settled districts to prove homestead claims. The first years on homesteads tested women's skills to the fullest since homestead families were still economic units where work roles could overlap and women's contributions resembled those of previous generations of rural women.

The near-subsistence economies of many rural western families in the late nineteenth century resulted in lower levels of female employment outside the home. In 1900, about 15 percent of women over the age of 16 living in the Rocky Mountain and Western North Central states were economically active, compared with 28 percent of New England and Southern South Atlantic women. Western native-born white women had lower levels of employment than immigrant, African or Mexican Americans. Definitions of "work" are important here: few Native American women had jobs in the sense of paid wage labor and the Census simply excluded their subsistence agricultural activities from its definitions of work outside the home.

Female homesteaders were particularly prevalent in eastern Colorado and western Nebraska, where they comprised between 5 and 33 percent of those filing claims. Married women could not file for separate farm homesteads from their husbands, although in the early twentieth century Congress amended the homestead legislation, permitting women to retain farms or ranches after marriage. The Homestead Act required settlers to live on the land for at least six months of the year, build a house, and cultivate at least 10 acres in order to acquire title to their 160 "free" acres. This posed a serious dilemma for poor families since part of the family had to stay on the land while the rest earned a living, resulting in the wife and children trying to farm while the husband worked in town.

Children of both sexes contributed valuable labor since rigid gender roles were simply impractical in families struggling to farm with limited resources. Willa Cather's novel of immigrant farmers in Nebraska, *O, Pioneers!*, describes Alexandra Bergson as competent and in charge from an early age: "Before Alexandra was twelve years old she had begun to be a help" to her father. Many western daughters went beyond conventional gender stereotypes as they roped, branded, and herded stock or plowed, sowed, and reaped.

Eastern agricultural practices were unsuited to the harsh winters and drought-ridden summers of the Great Plains; it took years for incomers to discover appropriate farming and ranching techniques. In the meantime they froze, their crops dried up, and prairie fires burned them off their claims. Over two-fifths of the homestead claims in Nebraska failed, prompting farmers to try their luck elsewhere in the West – or go back East. Many New Mexico settlers sold up to return to Texas or Oklahoma because the grazing was so poor in dry areas and markets were too far away.

The pioneer woman's skills sustained newly settled families. Women carried small household items somewhere in their wagons, including "plates, cups, frying pan, coffee pot, wash basin, water pail, picket ropes and pegs," and chickens in their coop. They made and remade their homes, softening the difficult pioneering process with their domestic skills. Almost all grew and preserved their own vegetables. Lightweight, dense women's crops such as eggs, butter, cheese or lard contributed significant amounts of cash to these households, being less bulky than men's corn or wheat, easier to transport, and plentiful before the main crop was harvested. Migrant women learned from Mexican and Native Americans how to exploit local conditions to produce edible and saleable crops as they adjusted to the new landscape.

These homestead claims occurred at the expense of the existing Mexican and Native American inhabitants whom the Army subdued and displaced. Battles such as Little Big Horn in 1876 attest to Native Americans' continued refusal to be dispossessed, but even after many had been forcibly removed to reservations, they defended traditional ways. Merial A. Dorchester, a special agent in the Indian School Service, noted in her report to the Commissioner of Indian affairs: "It is a truism that in order to reach any heathen people the mothers and homes must be interested first. It is also just as much a truism . . . that the Indians as a whole are still pagan, and the women most conservatively pagan of all . . . The mothers keep up the old superstitions and laugh down modern ideas and customs." The missionaries and Indian agents attempted to convert and assimilate Native American women to European-American values, ignoring the complex gender systems of many Indian groups in which women had significant economic and political roles.

Decimation of the Native American way of life took many forms as did their resistance to white incursions. White hunters slaughtered the buffalo, depriving the Plains' Indians of their basic subsistence. Once they were stopped from following the buffalo, their land was more readily available to the railroads and white farmers. The Dawes Act of 1887 divided Native American land into private farms, undermining traditional collective agricultural practices, and further imposing patriarchal European nuclear family models. In the 1880s, missionaries and the Bureau of Indian Affairs objected to Osage marriage ceremonies celebrated with foot and horse races, exchanges of gifts, and feasting, trying to substitute Christianity for supposedly pagan rituals. Native Americans in other parts of the West came under similar pressure to abandon their traditional agricultural and hunting practices and to vest land ownership in men rather than through the matrilineal line.

Cultural conflicts accompanied the rising number of Mexicans moving into the Southwest. The original inhabitants of this region lost their land when territorial and state governments imposed land taxes and complex laws. Following the Mexican Revolution of 1910 and the growing industrial opportunities of the developing Southwest more Mexicans moved northwards. In 1900, there were 100 000 Mexicans living in the United States, but by 1930 this had grown to 1.5 million.

As families reconstituted themselves in southwestern cities, Mexican women became the targets for "Americanization" workers who adopted as their motto "go after the women." Americanization programs focused upon mothers, using them to mold their children's behavior in accordance with white, Protestant values. Alfred White, an Americanization teacher, wrote in 1923: "the greatest good is to be obtained by starting the home off right. The children of these foreigners are the advantages to America, not the naturalized foreigners. These are never 100% Americans, but the second generation may be. 'Go after the women' and you may save the second generation for America." The California Commission of Immigration and Housing compiled a *Primer for Foreign Speaking Women* (1918) which detailed ideal family roles for Americanized foreign women, channeling them into domesticity and urging them to use traditional domestic skills in the lower strata of the labor market. Cultures clashed as the conquerors tried to overturn traditional gender patterns of land ownership, working, and family relationships in order to "save" the newcomers from their own traditions.

The search for improved opportunities sparked the African-American migration out of the South, which began as a trickle after emancipation and turned into a flood in the 1910s and 1920s. The Southern Homestead Act of 1866 (repealed in 1876) allocated public land in Alabama, Arkansas, Florida, and Mississippi to ex-slaves. Assisted by the Freedmen's Bureau, about 4000 families settled on these lands, mostly in Florida. Conditions deteriorated badly for African Americans at the end of Reconstruction as whites used violence and intimidation in an attempt to force social, political, and economic subservience. Some African Americans fled the South altogether, like the Exodusters who moved in family groups to Kansas between 1879 and 1881. About 20 000 former slaves settled successfully in Kansas and Nebraska, while others moved farther west, founding all-black farming communities in Oklahoma, Texas, and Colorado.

The remorseless tide of legalized racism in the South and growing economic opportunities in the North contributed to increased mobility for African Americans, eventuating in the great migration to cities after 1910. Some mobility also stemmed from the efforts to reunite kin separated during slavery. Families persevered for decades to find relatives previously sold to other parts of the South during slavery times. A former slave from Virginia recalled his family got word of their "granny working on a sugar and cotton farm in New Orleans" and kept looking until he found her. Forty years after the Civil War, African-American newspapers still carried notices from former slaves trying to locate long-lost relations.

Approximately nine-tenths of African Americans lived in the South before 1900. About 10 percent owned land while many more were sharecroppers, farming in return for a portion of the crop. Women formed a crucial part of the southern cotton labor force, since more hands in the field meant larger acreage could be tended. Women combined domestic and economic labors, frequently exhausted by toiling 12 hours in the field and doing domestic tasks late at night. Southern white land owners used sharecropping (letting land on shares rather than for cash), threats, and violence to ensure African-American women and children farmed. It is clear from the shorter hours in the field worked by African-American women after emancipation that black families tried to resist these demands, but the sharecropping system cheated illiterate farmers of their profits, forced them to buy goods at inflated store prices, and prevented them from branching into other crops or keeping domestic animals. These factors pushed women into agricultural labor. Black families resisted these abuses by changing crop tenancies frequently in search of better land and landlords. Each December, once the shares had been reckoned up, about one-third of African-American tenants changed farms, usually staying near networks of relatives who helped out in field and cabin.

In 1880, African Americans had a much higher proportion of rural dwellers than whites; 87 percent lived in the countryside, compared with 72 percent of whites, and 78 percent of "others" (the Census aggregated Chinese, Japanese, Mexican, and Native Americans together, obliterating the variations between the groups and making it difficult to differentiate within this category). The tendency for whites to move to the cities accelerated after the Civil War; by 1900, four-tenths resided in cities as did two-tenths of blacks. In 1920, more than half the white population were urban dwellers compared with one-third of blacks, with the greatest growth occurring in the North and West.

Intertwined economic and demographic factors accounted for the preponderance of European- and African-American women in cities. Single women had an increasingly marginal place in the economy of agricultural communities, with African-American women enduring both restricted opportunities and racially inflected sexual harassment. Cities offered a greater range of employment opportunities and higher wages. Widows had an urban bias which was more pronounced among African Americans; 10 percent of rural women were widows, compared with 12 percent of urban white and 18 percent of urban African-American women. Although most African-American women had worked the land during their marriages, few white land owners would negotiate crop tenancies with them, impelling them toward cities where domestic service paid more, especially in the North.

Falling cotton prices, the legal acceptance of southern racism in Supreme Court decisions such as *Plessy vs. Ferguson* (1896), and the disenfranchisement of black men by southern states accelerated urban and northward migration. In 1910, 300 000 African Americans left the South, but the World War I-inspired exodus dwarfed even this figure. Employment opportunities burgeoned as the conflict drew men out of the economy and curtailed the supply of European immigrants. Nearly a million African Americans journeyed north during the war. Although it is not possible to determine exactly how many men and women migrated, the convergence in the proportion of African-American urban dwellers of each sex substantiates the initial male bias of the great migration. In 1910, 26.2 percent of black men lived in cities compared with 28.5 percent of black women; by 1920, these proportions rose to 33.4 and 34.7 percent, respectively.

Migration out of the South offered different advantages to each sex. For African-American men it meant suffrage and a broader set of occupations, especially in heavy industry which needed a steady supply of laborers to shovel coal, bash metal, and toil in construction gangs. African-American women experienced little occupational mobility, but had greater social freedom. They formed vigorous church and social organizations and had access to better education for their children. They were also less vulnerable to the disrespect routinely meted out to black women in the South.

THE FAMILY IN THE INDUSTRIAL ERA

Both the structure and functions of the family changed during the industrial era as prosperity and women's aspirations restricted households to two generations with no strangers present. The mean age at marriage fell in this era from 22 to 21 years for women and from 26 to 24.6 years for men, although not all groups had an equal likelihood of marrying. Men outnumbered women in most racial and ethnic groups, but high military mortality rates, especially in the South, meant many native-born white women contemplated spinsterhood in the years immediately after the Civil War. The African-American population had more women than men from 1840 onwards, making it more difficult to marry or find a new partner should the initial union break up.

Declining fecundity meant that the entire shape of family life changed within living memory, and with it, how women cared for their families (investing more intensely in each remaining child), whether they were economically active inside or outside the home and, possibly, their growing interest in political and social issues. Birth rates decreased at varying rates, with African-American and immigrant fertility remaining higher than native-born white. In 1860, the average native-born white woman had 5 children. By 1890, this had fallen to 4 children and by 1920, to 3 or less. Italian, French Canadian, and Polish women had especially large families, normally 7 or more children each at the turn of the century, while Irish and German families were somewhat smaller, with about 5 children.

The last generation of African-American bondswomen averaged 7 children. Their daughters, born in the decade after slavery ended, had about 4.6 children, while their granddaughters (born between 1895 and 1904) had only 2.9. Class, as well as race and ethnicity, influenced fertility levels as women from higher socio-economic groups tended to have lower birth rates than poorer women. Businessmen's wives who had completed their families by 1910 bore an average of 3.6 children, compared with 4.0 for skilled workers' partners, and 4.8 for farm women.

Falling birth rates provoked concern that the "white" race would be swamped by higher African-American and immigrant birth rates. States attempted to regulate sexuality by outlawing birth control devices and abortion. New York made contraception illegal in 1868, emulated by other states, and in 1873, the federal government enacted legislation banning "Obscene Literature and Articles of Immoral Use" from the post. Cities and states also began to criminalize prostitution in the 1870s and 1880s, trying to curtail brothels as a "trap for young men and boys," in the words of Pittsburgh's chief of public safety. New York's Society for the Suppression of Vice, Pittsburgh's Morals Efficiency Commission, and various western branches of the Women's Christian Temperance Union all pressed to prohibit prostitution and abortions, leading desperate women to terminate pregnancies under dangerous circumstances.

Women still tried to regulate their fertility despite these laws. Although the proportion of women having intercourse before marriage rose after 1890, most women having abortions were married and trying to control family size. The use of contraception spread throughout the social scale as Margaret Sanger and others opened birth control clinics in the early twentieth century. Inspired by nursing a married woman who died from a botched abortion after trying to limit her family's size, Sanger wished to make contraception as available to poor women as to the better off and to improve the quality of women's relationships.

As life expectancies lengthened and family sizes fell, women wanted kind, considerate partners who provided well and grew more willing to divorce men who did not fulfill their expectations. The rise of organizations opposed to family violence indicates altered perceptions of the marital relationship and women's role within it; women were no longer seen as men's property to be used or abused as the husband saw fit. The number of divorces accelerated in the 1870s and 1880s and continued to climb through 1920, giving the United States the highest divorce rate in the world. In 1860 there were 1.2 divorces for every 1000 marriages, 4 divorces per 1000 marriages by 1900, and nearly 8 by 1920.

Men had greater custody rights, although a growing emphasis on maternal importance in child development meant that judges began to favor mothers' claims. At the turn of the century only nine states granted the sexes the same rights over their children in cases of death or divorce, nevertheless many judges preferred women as the custodial parent when the child was of "tender years." New Jersey and California judges in the late nineteenth and early twentieth centuries granted custody to women in a majority of cases. As a Philadelphia court decreed in 1881: "We do not look upon the wife and the children as mere servants to the husband and father, and as therefore held, subject to his will." Such decisions recognized the individual rights of women and children.

Women initiated about two-thirds of all divorce proceedings in the Progressive Era, according to William O'Neill, because their strength and self-assurance led them to be intolerant of bad marriages and confident they could survive on their own. As the companionate model of marriage filtered through society in the early twentieth century, women desired friendship and sexual satisfaction from their mates and rejected husbands who did not meet their emotional needs or did not fulfill their financial obligations. The testimony given at divorce hearings in Baltimore in the 1890s illustrates the cross-currents of troubled marriages. Ella Stroemer brought suit against her husband Max, an ex-soldier, on grounds of adultery and cruel treatment, claiming he beat her and ran around with other women. She supported herself as a seamstress and believed she was better off on her own.

Women testified before the court about the difficulties they perceived with their marriages, principally nonsupport and desertion. Mary Cook Schulteis, a Catholic, supported four children by washing and ironing after her husband abandoned her. She claimed that he abused her physically and emotionally, struck her, and ran around with other women. Married in the African Methodist Episcopal Church in 1909, Bertha Bowen echoed these complaints, stating that her husband abandoned her just months after their baby's birth. Although she was "a loving and faithful wife," her husband was always drunk, disagreeable, and did not support her. In common with most women who divorced their husbands, she complained about his financial and emotional nonsupport.

Men sued their wives for disregarding their wifely obligations. The Census Bureau's study of divorce between 1867 and 1906 indicated that about four-fifths of the male petitioners felt their wives were not properly submissive, did not fulfill their female duties, or tried to assert their autonomy. As petitioner Edward Turk complained to the Baltimore court, his wife "would not explain to me her whereabouts." Other men protested that their wives failed to perform their duties. Conversely women defended themselves and their relations in divorce cases by citing their wifely devotion and conformity to the domestic ideal.

Violence between partners surfaced over and over again in divorce proceedings as women rejected abusive relationships. Divorcing wives in the 1880s and 1890s accused their husbands of physical and mental cruelty with increasing frequency. While marital rape was not illegal, judges accepted sexual cruelty as valid grounds for divorce, sustaining women's rising expectations of the marital relationship. Violent behavior did not accord well with the companionate marriage and sentimentalized views of the family idealized by Victorians. Women also sued violent husbands in the civil and criminal courts, especially in magistrates' and aldermanic courts. In a number of divorce cases the husband accused his wife of cruelty but, in the public forum of the lower courts, rarely accused her of physical maltreatment.

Legislatures and reform organizations also became more involved in the regulation of family matters, asserting public interest in such relationships, and eventually regulating relations between parents and children as well as husbands and wives. In 1641 the Massachusetts Bay Colony prohibited men from beating their wives, except in self-defense, and later banned overly severe correction of children. Prosecutions were rare, usually against a husband for mal-treating his wife. There was no further legislative mention of family violence until Tennessee outlawed wife beating in 1850. Courts and legislatures curtailed absolute parental power over children, declaring that parental authority should not be exercised merely for parental profit, "but for the advantage of the child," according to the Philadelphia Court of Quarter Sessions in 1881. This helped establish a climate of individualism which distinguished children's rights and needs from those of their parents.

A series of overlapping campaigns in the late nineteenth century thrust issues of family violence into the public arena. The Women's Christian Temperance Union believed the mistreatment of women and children stemmed from alcohol abuse and persuaded some state legislatures to make a partner's drunkenness grounds for divorce. At the same time, the male and female elites of many large cities campaigned against cruelty to animals and children. Between 1875 and 1900 some 300 Societies for the Prevention of Cruelty to Children (SPCC) were founded, principally in urban areas. These organizations focused primarily upon child neglect, but sometimes intervened in cases of physical assaults upon women. Depending upon individual state legislation, anti-cruelty societies either assumed some of the police powers of the state or brought cases to the attention of local authorities.

Different forms of mistreatment frequently intertwined, complicating the action which could be taken. In a typical case in 1889, the Western Pennsylvania Humane Society discovered that a laborer who was almost continually drunk had neglected and abused his wife and two children. After taking the children home to her parents, the wife stated that her husband threatened to kill them all and "gave her a shameful beating." The society's agent advised her to bring charges for assault and battery since he had no power to intervene between spouses, only between parents and children.

Humane societies virtually defined abuse as a problem of foreign or lower-class values. Linda Gordon's study of the Massachusetts SPCC found charity workers manipulated their clients' lives to ensure conformity to prevailing middle-class norms with gender-status violations and drinking attracting particular opprobrium. They castigated men who drank their wages for neglecting their role as breadwinners as well as contravening the temperance predilections of these societies. Mothers who "gadded about," drank, or did not keep their home tidy also transgressed gender norms. These organizations favored the family wage model with a breadwinning father, housekeeping mother, and dependent children which the poverty of many working-class families made difficult to emulate.

Child protection agencies aimed to change the family's behavior rather than reform society. They typically blamed the mother for the dysfunctionality, because it was her job to care for the family. As the twentieth century progressed a growing emphasis on family reconciliation, counseling, and social work support for distressed families led to fewer prosecutions for family violence and greater efforts to keep households together, even in the presence of wife or child abuse. Female reformers also worked actively to change the laws regarding child labor and to establish federal protection of children through the Children's Bureau, established in 1912 by the federal government to promote child welfare.

Popular depictions of family violence portrayed it as a problem of drunken, working-class men. D. W. Griffith's 1919 movie, *Broken Blossoms*, epitomized this belief. Dealing in archetypes and stereotypes like many silent films, *Blossoms* depicts a brutal father shamefully mistreating his delicate daughter, and finally beating her to death in a drunken rage. Poverty, alcohol, and sexual innuendo furnish a highly charged condemnation of poor families. Significantly there was no mother present to protect Lillian Gish's innocent character from her brutal boxer father, reinforcing stereotypes about men's child-rearing incompetence.

The model of family relations favored by prosperous Americans also demonstrated an increasing preference for domestic privacy which social welfare agencies incorporated into their policies. While the affluent in the nineteenth century had complex household structures with boarders, relatives, and servants, by the twentieth century they rejected nonmembers. Their homes relegated servants to top floor attics, behind baize doors, or made no provision at all for live-in help. The absolute number of servants increased, but the proportion residing with employers fell sharply. By 1920, few middle-class families had full-time domestic help so that married women had greater responsibility for domesticity and childcare. They used new forms of household technology to replace the work previously done by servants, while relying upon an occasional cleaning lady to do the most arduous jobs.

Well-to-do married women no longer wanted or needed to look

after boarders to augment family income as this era progressed. Complex households peaked between 1880 and 1900, being more common in cities than rural areas and more favored by some groups than others. Immigrant and African-American families particularly served as a stepping stone for newly arrived relations and also offered housing to unrelated people from the same country or district. In 1880, both middle- and working-class families took in lodgers, but by 1900, only poorer women supplemented family incomes through this form of domestic work. In some areas over half the laboring households contained lodgers, but few affluent families did. Studies of immigrant and working-class family life in such disparate cities as New York, Johnstown, Fall River, Baltimore, and Buffalo discovered immigrant and African-American women typically taking one or two lodgers, sometimes more. Childless couples, recent arrivals in the city, families with young children, and widow-headed households were the most likely to have boarders at the turn of the century.

Boardinghouse keeping fell into disfavor for several reasons after 1900. Social reformers strongly opposed the practice, believing it diverted maternal attention and left women "neither the time nor the patience for wise discipline." Few states or charities would grant financial assistance to widows who had unrelated male boarders. By 1920, few widows and fewer wives still looked after boarders. About 4 percent of native born white and immigrant widows had lodgers compared with 12 percent of African-American widows. The racial disparity indicated the poverty of urban black women. Boarding also protected women, with newly arrived African-American women turning to those who had been longer in the city for a place to live, companionship, and employment advice.

Middle-class families also grew more reluctant to house members of their extended families, even though working-class families continued to take in their relations at least through the period when immigration and migration were greatest. In the 1880s, about one-tenth of the urban population lived in extended families, but fewer did so by 1920, although taking in a widowed mother remained common. Smaller and simpler households increased the "empty nest" phase of women's existence. In the colonial and early national era, women rarely survived the marriage of their youngest child by more than a few years. By 1900, the youngest child married while her mother was in her early to mid-50s and could expect to live another decade, mostly as a widow with no children at home. This demographic transition helps explain the rising concern for older women and widows at the turn of the century and their growing tendency to live out their days as dependents in a daughter's home.

MOTHERHOOD AND HOUSEKEEPING

Although women became increasingly involved in political and social matters outside the home, their roles as mothers and housekeepers were crucial to that participation and to many (if not most) women's perceptions of what mattered most in their lives. In the *American Woman's Home* published in 1869, Catharine Beecher and Harriet Beecher Stowe turned housewifery and motherhood into vocations, in a tradition carried on by Progressive Era domestic efficiency experts, home economists, and organizations such as the National Congress of Mothers (founded in 1897). The National Congress of Mothers (NCM) began with Alice McLellan Birney's post-partum musings: "How can the mothers be educated and the *nation* made to reflect the supreme importance of the child?" The NCM wished to "carry the mother-love and mother-thought into all that concerns or touches childhood in Home, School, Church, State or Legislation." In so doing, it recognized mothers as the primary parent and made this the basis for its legislative and social programs. It epitomized what Molly Ladd-Taylor has described as sentimental maternalism, a desire to preserve traditional gender roles while improving child welfare and professionalizing motherhood.

Motherhood and housekeeping were, of course, central to the domestic ideologies of most Americans. The African-American novelist Amelia Johnson wrote in *The Hazeley Family* (1894) that it was a woman's duty to make her home "pleasant and comfortable." She differentiated housework (sweeping, dusting, and cooking) from homework, "brightening and making it cheery by both word and deed, shedding a healthful and inspiring influence, so that those around us may be the better for our presence." These desires combined with the need to work for racial uplift led to the founding of the National Association of Colored Women in 1896. The NACW's motto, "Lifting as We Climb," encompassed a broad spectrum of political and welfare issues, including kindergartens to assist working mothers, anti-lynching campaigns, and child welfare. Women of all races shared the perception that mothers were the pivotal force in creating a happy family, but African-American women connected child welfare to the racial politics of the day.

In this era men became increasingly remote from their families. They no longer worked with their children alongside them. Their long hours of labor outside the home meant they might "go for weeks without seeing [their children] except in their cribs" according to one analyst of men's work in 1907. A midwestern working-class woman echoed this sentiment two decades later when she told a social investigator into family life: "my man is so tired when he comes home from work that he just lies down and rests and never plays with the children." Under such conditions, or when fathers left home to find work, women had the primary or sole responsibility for child raising.

Public policy reinforced the importance of motherhood through the provision of pensions for widowed mothers with dependent children. These pensions, granted by many states in the second decade of the twentieth century, gave widows a small sum of money to enable them to stay at home to care for their children. Pensions indicated widespread sentiment against previous methods of family support, including the taking of boarders, the employment of young children, or the breaking up of widowed families so that the mother could take a live-in job as a domestic servant while the children either stayed with relatives or were sent to an orphanage. The sums allocated were usually too small to support a family, but the principle behind the legislation was that mothers should focus their entire attention upon home and family.

The emphasis on childhood as the formative period for economic productivity and political responsibility led many people to support this aid to young children channeled through their mothers. Mothers' pensions were part of the surge of child-centered activism which produced compulsory education legislation, laws regulating and attempting to abolish child labor in factories, shops, and offices, the Children's Bureau, and child health measures such as the Sheppard–Towner Act of 1921 which offered matching grants to states which established child health clinics. State legislatures enacting pensions in the 1910s regarded them as an "integral part of the legislative machinery for child conservation." Pension advocates were "not concerned with the mother of the children as an individual" but submerged widows' welfare with that of their children. Widowed mothers received support for the service they rendered to the state by raising children in a moral, wholesome environment. Conversely, if they did not conform to certain behavioral norms (including sexual abstinence and temperance) they were shorn of their pensions.

Only certain women and children received assistance in any case. Few pensions went to women of color, partly because the pension movement began in the North and Midwest, where there were relatively few women of color until after World War I, but primarily because the childhoods to be conserved were those of white children. Southern states gave virtually no subvention to African-American widows, while southwestern ones discriminated against Native and Mexican Americans. Less than 3 percent of pensions went to women of color in the 1910s and 1920s. Never-married mothers or those who gave birth outside wedlock rarely obtained benefits. Widows received over four-fifths of all pensions with the rest going to women with incapacitated, incarcerated, or institutionalized spouses. Few divorced mothers or those with children born out of wedlock received help.

Even social commentators who questioned women's political and economic status accepted the importance of women's maternal and domestic roles. The novels and stories of Charlotte Perkins Gilman contained scathing attacks on the constraints placed upon women in the name of motherhood (for example "The Yellow Wallpaper"). She also wrote "the baby is the founder of the home. If the good of the baby requires the persistent, unremitting care of the mother in the home, then indeed she must remain there." While the purpose of the home and motherhood was to care for the young, Gilman observed that the number of occupations a woman practiced as cook, sewer and mender of clothes, and nurse limited the time she could spend with her children. She proposed to resolve these competing demands by collectivizing housework through the use of central kitchens and laundries.

Christine Frederick, a leading efficiency expert, had a different solution to the inefficiency of private housekeeping, using her position as household editor of the *Ladies' Home Journal* and her studies of household management to turn housewifery from an amateur art into a professional science. Frederick urged the 92 percent of American women who had no domestic servants in 1910 to take the opportunity to manage the home according to their "own highest standards of thrift, efficiency, sanitation, and family happiness."

Frederick belonged to the growing home economics movement, a term dating from 1899, when a small group of women (and one man) including Ellen Swallow Richards, met in Lake Placid, New York, to found an organization dedicated to turning housewifery from a craft skill into a scientific discipline.

Home economists believed women needed to become intelligent consumers in order to fulfill their housewifely roles. Sharing the progressive belief in science and efficiency, they condemned the craft aspect of housekeeping in favor of carefully articulated principles for all aspects of domestic work. Helen Campbell, who trained as an economist and investigated women's work outside the home, voiced scientific contempt for the "rude and primitive" approach many women took to their daily tasks. "Even the intelligent housekeeper," she noted in 1899, "still talks about 'luck with her sponge cake!' There is no such word in science, and to make sponge cake is a scientific process." Home economists believed that women needed to be taught how to cook and do housework properly, in accordance with scientific principles. This devalued knowledge passed down between the generations at the same time that it recognized that housekeeping changed with new appliances and materials.

Technological innovations proliferated at the turn of the century, especially in cities and suburbs, and eased some of the burden of housework. Affluent households acquired labor-saving and health-improving sanitary appliances in this era, making housekeeping more acceptable to middle-class women. In 1893, less than 10 percent of all households in Baltimore, Chicago or New York had bathrooms. Families with incomes over $500 per year at this time (artisan or white-collar households) were much more likely to have such conveniences. Tenement house families in New York City in 1905 made do with water closets in the yard, although they did have a cold water tap in the kitchen. One in ten unskilled wage-earning households in Washington, DC, had a bathroom with a flush toilet or hot and cold running water.

Dramatic differences appeared between urban and rural housekeeping methods in the industrial era. Few rural or poor families benefited from piped water or indoor plumbing until after World War I. In 1900 almost all working-class and farm women baked their families' bread, as did about three-fifths of middle-class housewives. By 1920 homemade bread appeared in few urban households, regardless of class, while most rural women still baked bread several times a week and continued older customs of preserving, bottling, and pickling their produce. Indeed, rural families produced over two-thirds of the food they consumed, compared with just 2 percent of home-produced food among city dwellers. Rural women were thus far more involved with food production than their city sisters, although they had fewer labor-saving devices to assist them.

By 1920 shifting patterns of technological innovation, the commercial manufacture of clothing, household articles, and food, and especially, declining birth rates, led many to rethink women's place in society. Female roles in the family had developed from republican motherhood to true womanhood at mid-century, and now entered the social motherhood phase, in which women gave birth to fewer children, looked after them more intensively, and expanded their maternal horizons to embrace a wide range of social and political issues. Domesticity remained central to married women's roles, but their expectations of marriage changed, with more rejecting husbands who did not live up to their economic or social ideals. The proportion of married women who took jobs outside the home started to rise, but most concentrated on the seemingly irreducible core of women's roles, namely motherhood and household management.

For single women, motherhood had, obviously, less salience as a defining issue. Their family role increasingly became that of wage earning, as it did for women of color and a growing number of married women. The public sector used many mechanisms to acknowledge the centrality of women's role in the family, including custody and testamentary rights and mothers' pensions, as it sought to propagate a version of motherhood which depended upon a male wage earner, ignored women's economic activity, and submerged ethnic, cultural, and class variations in a single vision of family life. Women's organizations also lobbied for motherhood's importance through the WCTU, National Congress of Mothers, and National Association of Colored Women. Social reformers hoped to manipulate motherhood in order to raise better citizens and tolerated few variations from their norms. Increasing numbers of cookbooks, home economists, Americanization classes, and agricultural extension agents instructed women how to operate new technology and look after their children, all the time reiterating the importance of domesticity to women's lives.

Presaging complaints about mandatory domesticity which surfaced again in the 1950s and 1960s, Carol Kennicott, a doctor's wife in

Sinclair Lewis's *Main Street* (1920), felt smothered by domesticity. She was, in Lewis's characterization, "a woman with a working brain and no work." To resolve this dilemma many women turned to literary and reform clubs, seeking to use their education, even as they looked outward beyond the household.

7 Education and Culture, 1865–1920

In 1860, the *Saturday Review* flatly stated "the great argument against the existence of this equality of intellect in women is that it does not exist." Despite such negative attitudes, the reappraisal of social and cultural norms which accompanied the end of slavery and the transition to an urban industrial nation prompted a reevaluation of women's roles, especially in education. Some people argued that academic study would prevent women from marrying or being mothers, but female educational levels increased in all sections of the nation and among all social groups. In an era which required credentials for the practice of teaching, medicine, and law, study through high school and university became the prerequisite for many occupations. Women of the Gilded Age and Progressive Era believed obtaining these credentials would overcome the obstacles to employment and community standing their foremothers encountered. At the same time, higher literacy rates and growing population densities encouraged female authors and the formation of women's literary, social and reform clubs.

EDUCATION

The aftermath of the Civil War and massive immigration from diverse nations led many to hope education would unify the nation and assimilate the foreign born. State after state passed legislation requiring children to attend primary school. Mandatory attendance laws drew no distinctions between the sexes, so by 1900 education became the norm for almost all white children up to the age of 12 or 14, especially in the North and West and the educational gap between the sexes decreased. In 1870, 53 percent of white females between the ages of 5 and 19 were in school compared with 56 percent of white males. By 1920, 66 percent of both sexes were in school, although, as will be discussed below, men continued to outnumber women in higher education. This meant that the average white woman born in the late nineteenth century completed eight years of school, rising to nine years for those born at the beginning of the twentieth century.

The South lagged behind the North in literacy because these states devoted relatively little money to education before the Civil War. Post-bellum constitutions provided for public school systems, while the need to rebuild the economy fostered a reliance upon education as the cornerstone of the New South. Southern women had an important role in expanding women's education in the South as elsewhere and pressed state legislatures to establish normal schools to train teachers. Ironically the first state to establish a women's college was also the last to make school attendance compulsory. Mississippi opened its State Industrial Institute and College for women in 1884, but only implemented compulsory education in 1918.

High school and college education broadened in this era to women's benefit. In 1870, there were 200 high schools in the United States; by 1920 every city and most towns had a secondary school with half of all American youth attending. Although men dominated college enrollments women outnumbered them among high school graduates by 1890. The growing availability of public secondary schools enabled poorer girls in all sections of the country to get an education, frequently with a vocational orientation. Young women and their families perceived the advantages of training for business and professional occupations. A growing number of female high school students took practical courses in typing, stenography, book-keeping, and business practice to help them get a job. Philadelphia's Commercial High School for Girls had over 900 pupils in 1908, while half the students at the Boston Girls' High School were in the Commercial Department. St. Louis, Washington, and Pittsburgh, among other cities, also had commercial high schools or large business departments in their schools.

Class, race, and ethnicity influenced attendance patterns throughout this era. The daughters of recent immigrants were more likely than their native-born white counterparts to have jobs rather than go to school, especially after the age of 12 or 14. Many foreign-born parents were wary of potential religious or cultural biases in public schools and sent their daughters to parochial schools which incorporated appropriate theological perspectives. Religion figured especially in advanced training for women. Nearly half the "institutions for the superior instruction of females" in the 1870s had a minister or nun at the helm. At the turn of the century, many large cities with complex ethnic patterns had at least one-quarter of their pupils in parochial schools. Nationwide in 1920, Catholic schools accounted for about 8 percent of all school children.

The length of time a child spent in school correlated directly with social class, so that children from wealthier families had higher educational levels than those from less affluent backgrounds. Some poor parents sacrificed their daughters' education for the sake of the domestic help or income they could provide and withdrew them from school. Yet, as Sara Burstall, Headmistress of the Manchester (England) High School for Girls, noted in 1908, "many parents of the poorest class make heroic efforts and sacrifices to let their children, especially their girls, go through a high school course." As many as three-fifths of all high school pupils in the larger cities in the early twentieth century came from immigrant families, indicating the effort foreign-born parents made to educate their children.

American public schools had a dual purpose, to teach and to inculcate values. The large American flag flying from the roof or a pole in the school grounds emphasized the institutional intention to make good citizens as well as learned ones. Schools also had a gendered curriculum, teaching domestic arts to the girls and mechanical ones to the boys, preparing them "for the rights and duties of citizenship," according to one early twentieth-century educational analyst, while channeling the sexes into their gender-appropriate roles.

Ethnic minority women encountered difficulties in obtaining and utilizing schooling. In 1870, only one out of ten non-white females aged 5–19 was enrolled in school, climbing to about one in three by 1900 and to over half by 1920. Poor educational provision meant that African-American women born just after the Civil War completed about three years of schooling and six years by the turn of the century. Many tax-supported institutions barred women of color while others channeled them into the domestic arts. Despite paltry public expenditure on African-American education, especially in the South where local authorities spent 10 cents on black schools for every dollar devoted to whites, literacy levels rose from about 10 percent at the close of the Civil War, to 70 percent by 1920.

Education served as a passport out of the field and the kitchen for some African-American women who taught in the segregated school systems to pass on their hard-won knowledge. Of all African-

American women workers in 1910, 1 percent had teaching posts, although there were few high schools or teacher training colleges open to them. In 1917 only 64 southern public high schools accepted African Americans, prompting the foundation of over 200 private secondary schools. There were 3 black colleges and 15 institutions offering some college-level work in the region.

Much of the post-primary education, such as that offered at Hampton and Tuskegee Institutes, focused on agricultural and mechanical arts, although many of Hampton's early graduates became teachers. While all students undertook field work in order to learn the value of physical labor, female students also studied cooking and sewing so they could pass these skills on once they became teachers. Urban African-American colleges had a more academic approach. Supported by the federal government, Howard University opened in 1867, offering a liberal arts education for African Americans. Unusually for a co-educational institution, Howard had women faculty members from its inception. Even though many women students in the 1870s and 1880s were in its teacher training programs, some matriculated in medicine, law, pharmacy, and dentistry.

Private religious and secular schools trained many African-American women as teachers, some of whom, like Lucy Craft Laney, went on to found their own educational establishments. Born in 1854 to ex-slaves who purchased their freedom, Laney attended a missionary-funded high school in Macon, Georgia, and graduated from Atlanta University. She taught in Georgia's segregated public schools then opened a school in a church basement in Augusta. Sustained by gifts from Presbyterian women benefactors, the Haines Normal and Industrial Institute was one of the few teacher training institutions for African Americans in the South. In the 1890s, the Haines Institute opened a kindergarten and nurses' training program.

As part of its assimilation efforts, the federal government sponsored education programs for Native Americans. The founder of the Carlisle Indian Boarding School wanted to "kill the Indian and save the man," reflecting the widespread belief that depriving Native Americans of their culture would force them to accept white people's values. Although most girls and boys who attended government boarding schools subsequently returned to their families, they received an education designed to alienate them from tribal values. Boarding schools had the unintended effect of bringing together

Native Americans from different tribes and fostering a pan-Indian consciousness. A few exceptional Native American women obtained higher education. Susan La Flesche, daughter of an Omaha tribal leader, attended mission and government schools and Hampton Institute. The Women's National Indian Association sponsored her medical training and she subsequently returned to Nebraska as a medical missionary, providing health care for a widely dispersed population and founding a hospital.

Educators from racial minority groups lamented racial and gender double standards in the schools. Oberlin College graduate and principal of the Washington, DC, black high school from 1901 to 1906, Anna Julia Cooper advocated "not the boys less, but the girls more." Believing that the advancement of her race required an educated female population she railed against those forces within both black and white communities which impeded formal study by black women. Educational access did expand between 1865 and 1920, but on a racially segregated basis with women of color enjoying fewer opportunities than whites.

HIGHER EDUCATION AND THE PROFESSIONS

Women of all races had to fight hard for access to advanced education. In 1858 the Michigan Board of Regents refused a woman's application, claiming it needed more time to consider the issue. The University of Iowa admitted women in that year, while Wisconsin took female students on its normal school course in 1863. The University of Michigan finally accepted women in 1870 when only two-fifths of the 582 colleges and universities in the United States admitted women. By 1890, the number of institutions of higher education had doubled and over three-fifths accepted female applicants. At the beginning of the twentieth century almost all publicly funded institutions of higher education took women, albeit many demanded higher entry qualifications from them to keep their numbers down, a practice that continued well past the middle of the twentieth century.

Numerous state universities diverted women to teacher training or home economics and worried that too many women students would undermine an institution's appeal to men. Military academies and institutions modeled upon them, such as Texas A & M and the Citadel, barred women until 1960s equal opportunities legislation prised their doors open. Some southern states maintained women's colleges, and a number of private colleges, including Harvard, Tufts, and Columbia, opened "sister" institutions which accommodated women's demands for education in separate and unequal facilities.

Opponents of women's higher education used biological and sociological arguments. The author of *Sex in Education* (1873) believed study diverted blood from the reproductive organs and nervous system and would undermine women's health and ability to reproduce. The first generations of college-educated women formed strong female friendships, had lower marriage rates, and fewer children than their contemporaries. Women's colleges founded in the 1870s and 1880s perceived their mission as educating women without undermining their health, childbearing proclivities, or femininity, introducing rigorous intellectual programs but also acting in *loco parentis* and regulating their students' social behavior.

Many women attended normal schools or colleges in order to become teachers, and their dominance in the teaching profession increased in the late nineteenth and early twentieth centuries. In 1870, women comprised 61 percent of all teachers, rising steadily to 86 percent by 1920. Women's place in the classroom seemed assured since school boards felt they could pay them meager wages, yet advancement in colleges and universities came more slowly, especially at the higher degree and faculty level. In this same 50-year span, the proportion of undergraduate degrees awarded to women doubled, from 15 to 31 percent; their proportion of masters' or second professional degrees rose from 19 percent (in 1900) to 30 percent in 1920, and female doctorates increased from 6 to 15 percent.

Many higher educational institutions discriminated against female faculty on the basis of their looks or marital status, and married women were routinely refused appointment or promotion. One of the first female graduates from Howard University, Lucy Ella Moten, was appointed to head the Miner Normal School in 1883 over the trustees' objection that she was too pretty to be authoritative. Even some women's colleges refused to hire women who had married, assuming that they would place their "self-elected home duties" before their academic work. Nevertheless, the proportion of female academics rose in these years, although it stayed significantly below that of teachers. In 1870, about 12 percent of university teachers were women, rising to 26 percent by 1920.

Medical schools and law colleges routinely and persistently discriminated against women through the imposition of quotas. Harvard even turned down a donation of $10 000 in 1878 rather than admit females into its medical school. Such widespread discrimination meant that at the turn of the century women comprised a small fraction of medical school entrants and were concentrated in women-only medical colleges. Paradoxically, their admission to formerly all-male medical schools in the early twentieth century had the unintended consequence of reducing opportunities since it resulted in the closure of some female medical colleges. In the 1880s and 1890s women comprised about 10 percent of medical students, but the proportion declined to about 5 percent after the turn of the century.

Sara Tew Mayo's career demonstrated the importance of women's medical schools and the continued barriers women professionals encountered. Barred by Tulane University's medical school because of her sex, she obtained a medical degree from the Woman's Medical College of Pennsylvania in 1898. When New Orleans hospitals blocked access to their facilities, she founded the New Orleans Hospital and Dispensary for Women and Children with a small group of similarly trained women. Although Dr. Marie Mergler placed near the top of the examination for appointment as physician to the Cook County Insane Asylum, the trustees refused to employ her because she was a woman. She subsequently became an assistant surgeon at the Woman's Hospital of Chicago, taught at her alma mater, and headed a hospital for women and children. Even though these physicians found their way blocked by prejudice against women doctors, they managed to use their skills to teach and treat other women.

Women achieved greater success in the allied medical field of nursing. Inspired by the experiences of female nurses during the Civil War and by Florence Nightingale's nursing school at St. Thomas's Hospital (London), hospital-based training schools for nurses began in the United States. Dr. Susan Dimock opened the first American nurses' training school at the New England Hospital for Women and Children in 1873. By 1880, there were 15 nurses' training programs, mostly attached to hospitals. These hospital training schools taught sanitation, medicine, and patient care, striving to differentiate nursing science from the care women routinely gave their families and neighbors. As the number of hospitals increased in the 1880s and 1890s, so did the demand for nursing staff and nurse education programs. By 1900, 432 hospitals offered training for nurses and in 1920, 1700 schools produced 15 000 graduate nurses.

Doctors and hospital administrators expected nurses to be obedient and deferential, which prompted many to leave hospital nursing for the more lucrative, if less stable, world of private duty nursing. Nurses also used their skills to initiate health care for the poor in the crowded districts of American cities. Settlement houses opened clinics while visiting nurses went into people's homes to nurse and educate the public about health matters. In 1893, Lillian Wald founded the Nurses' Settlement (subsequently known as the Henry Street Settlement), inaugurating the field of public health nursing. She was also instrumental in the founding of the Children's Bureau by the federal government in 1912.

As the number of doctors swelled and competition grew within the medical profession, doctors tried to regularize, regulate, and monopolize medical services, encouraging female nurses under their control but trying to eliminate independent midwives. In the early twentieth century articles in medical and popular journals attacked "the midwifery problem" and the supposed health consequences of using uncredentialed female practitioners instead of obstetricians. Some northern states made midwifery illegal while southern ones registered and trained midwives in infant health care techniques. The doctors' and health reformers' campaign against midwives used racial and ethnic stereotypes to ridicule female birth practitioners, complaining about "Rat Pie Among the Black Midwives" or that immigrant midwives brought "filthy customs and practices" with them.

The medicalization of the birthing process did not necessarily improve maternal or infant health. A 1913 comparison between midwife- and doctor-delivered babies in New York City reported that midwives had better success in preventing stillbirths and infections. They also cared for the mother and family during and after birth, easing the new mother into her maternal role. Even so, most states regulated midwives out of existence in response to public health arguments and the vigorous campaigning by doctors who wished to monopolize childbirth for their own, if not their patients', advantage.

As the situation of midwives made clear, local and national authorities could outlaw or straitjacket female activities. Legislatures and the courts made it difficult or impossible for women to practice certain occupations, regardless of their level of education. Law illustrates the resistance to female efforts to participate fully in burgeoning professions. Some women studied law informally in the years before the Civil War, reading their father's or brother's law books, but none obtained a formal legal education until 1869 when St. Louis University law school admitted women. A few large private and state universities accepted women in the 1880s and 1890s, but the commonplace attitude among law school professors that "women did not have the mentality for law" hampered their progress.

Nevertheless a small number of women carved out legal careers for themselves or used the law as a springboard to other occupations. Myra Bradwell began her study of law with her husband and went on to publish and edit the *Chicago Legal News*. Illinois refused to accept her into the bar even though she passed the bar exam. She sued, only to be told by the Illinois Supreme Court: "God designed the sexes to occupy different spheres of action, and that it belonged to men to make, apply, and execute the laws." The Supreme Court upheld the right of each state to regulate entrance into the professions on grounds of its choosing. Thus while Iowa admitted women to the bar in 1869, and the Supreme Court permitted lawyer Belva Lockwood to argue cases before it in 1879, other jurisdictions barred women from practicing law until much later in the century. Although no state formally prohibited female lawyers by the end of this era, women comprised only 1.4 percent of lawyers in 1920.

Not all women who qualified as lawyers practiced their profession. Social investigators Crystal Eastman and Florence Kelley deployed their legal training in the service of progressive reform movements. The first woman admitted to the Kentucky bar in 1894, Sophonisba Breckinridge, quickly discovered that prejudice kept clients away. She moved to Chicago to study for a PhD, later taking an advanced degree at University of Chicago's Law School. Subsequently Breckinridge resided at the Hull House settlement and taught one of the first social work courses at the Chicago School of Civics and Philanthropy. Her investigations into delinquency and truancy drew on her experiences as a settlement resident, city health inspector, and professor of social work.

Many educated women turned to settlement house work, residing in the teeming urban districts as "good neighbors" and becoming "spearheads for reform" (to use Allen F. Davis's evocative phrase) in the fight against bad housing, unsanitary conditions, and poverty. Initially most of the settlement house workers were amateurs and volunteers, drawn to helping the poor, but with few formal qualifications for the work. Social work, as a profession, reflected the desire of a growing number of practitioners to distinguish themselves from charity-based "do-gooders," through the scientific and systematic investigation of the problems and circumstances of the poor.

By the turn of the century, paid workers supplemented and eventually supplanted volunteer philanthropists. Like charity workers themselves, over half the social workers in the United States were women, increasingly educated in social work methods. Training courses opened at the Chicago School of Civics and Philanthropy, the Boston School for Social Workers, and the Western Reserve School of Applied Social Sciences in the early 1900s gradually replaced the charity summer schools which had first appeared in the 1890s. Social workers such as Mary Richmond wished to diagnosis social ills by reference to the personal problems of their clients and to put into place action plans which would enable them to overcome these difficulties. In a highly critical speech to the National Conference on Charities and Correction in 1915 Abraham Flexner underscored the ambiguous nature of social work as a profession, observing that social workers were not autonomous professionals but mediated between other professions such as medicine, law, and education. The anxieties provoked by Flexner led social workers to strive for scientific rigor in diagnosis and treatment of social problems.

Like social work, librarianship had been demeaned as a "semiprofession," meaning that demands for professional entrance qualifications did not prevent unqualified individuals from undertaking it. Librarians tried to overcome this by establishing the American Library Association in 1874 and developing university courses in librarianship by the turn of the century, but literacy and a love of books remained the vital professional qualifications for many years. The number of libraries increased dramatically in the last decades of the nineteenth century. As with schools, the desire to keep costs down while providing a mass service meant library trustees welcomed (low-waged) female librarians to look after women and children, the primary public library clientele.

Eight out of every ten librarians were women in 1910 (rising to nine out of ten by 1930), yet they rarely penetrated the higher echelons of library service. Large libraries preferred to hire men, especially as head librarians. Not until 1918 when Linda Eastman became head of Cleveland Public Library did a woman finally lead a metropolitan library system. In mixed-sex professions where women might form the bulk of the labor force they rarely had executive positions, especially in large or prestigious institutions. In this librarians resembled both teachers and social workers, where men dominated the upper ranks and women had few opportunities for advancement.

Women led the development of one professional field above all others: home economics. Ellen Swallow Richards, a chemistry graduate of the Massachusetts Institute of Technology (1873), started the field of "sanitary chemistry." Convinced that the home was the center of society, Richards worried about poor city housing and domestic conditions. She established a school of housekeeping at the Woman's Educational and Industrial Union in Boston in 1899 which subsequently became the Department of Home Economics at Simmons College. A series of conferences at Lake Placid, New York, led by Richards and Marion Talbot (head of the University of Chicago Department of Household Administration), on "the betterment of the home" resulted in the formation of the American Home Economics Association in 1908. The Negro Rural School Fund (established in 1907 by wealthy Quaker Anna Jeanes) taught home economics – gardening, cooking, laundering, nutrition, homemaking and sewing – to girls and their mothers. Home economics thus became the female equivalent of industrial education for young men, gender-appropriate and frequently with a limited horizon.

WOMEN AS CLUB MEMBERS

The late nineteenth-century club women's movement rested upon the twin pillars of female literacy and activism. Female organizational activities encompassed women of all classes, races, and ethnic groups, empowered by a growing belief in the legitimacy of gender-based concerns and women's special contributions to solving the problems of their era. Such organizations were not necessarily feminist, using Linda Gordon's definition, since they neither criticized masculine supremacy, nor believed that gender characteristics were mutable. Instead, these groups accepted what they believed to be the differences between the sexes and used them as the basis for sociability and social action.

Working "girls'" clubs, temperance societies, religious and ethnic organizations, and literary and social associations all indicated women's desire for female company and a growing belief that they could and should unite to improve themselves and society. Women's clubs had their roots in ante-bellum female organizations including missionary, anti-slavery, and temperance societies. They differed crucially from earlier movements in their more general outlook, interest in cultural matters, and broad reaching improvement programs.

The first general women's clubs sprang up after the Civil War. Angry at being excluded from the New York Press Club's luncheon honoring Charles Dickens in 1868, Jane Croly and other female journalists founded Sorosis, dedicated to making "the female sex helpful to each other and actively benevolent in the world." In the same year, professional women in Boston established the New England Woman's Club, a social club which developed a reforming agenda. A generation later women were still agitating for admission to male-dominated professional organizations. In 1908, the National Press Club barred females, leading to the formation in 1919 of the Women's National Press Club. The creation of women-only organizations thus had a defensive character as well as serving their needs for solidarity and professional reinforcement.

As the number of clubs proliferated they established national umbrella organizations. In 1882, alumnae from the new women's colleges formed the Association of Collegiate Alumnae, merging with the Western Association of Collegiate Alumnae in 1889. Female college graduates from the southern states formed a similar association in 1903, with all branches uniting in 1921 as the American Association of University Women, dedicated to advancing the educational status of women and offering female college graduates a cultural focus. Other clubs followed a similar pattern of networking across great geographical distances. The General Federation of Women's Clubs (GFWC) held its first national organizing meeting in 1888, with 61 delegates from as far apart as New England, Louisiana, and California. In 1893 it had 100 000 members and 500 affiliated societies. By World War I, one million women belonged to GFWC affiliates while 190 000 belonged to the National Congress of Mothers.

Local branches of the GFWC met regularly to discuss literature, read members' work, and enjoy the conviviality that came from meeting like-minded individuals. Such clubs particularly appealed to high school and college-educated women who wished to advance their reading and discussion of literature when they worked outside the home, married, and had children. They also became a focal point for social activism as women reinforced each other's concerns, publicly expressed their views, and acted upon them. The National

Consumers' League, the Chicago Civic Club, Women's Municipal Leagues of Boston and New York, and San Francisco's Century Club campaigned for better municipal facilities, crèches, housing improvements, kindergartens, and improved public health care. Their activism had a specifically female orientation but, containing a higher proportion of single and professional women than the Parent–Teachers' Association or National Congress of Mothers, they campaigned on a broader range of progressive issues.

Even though white women reformers referred to the "woman movement," there were many women's movements in the Progressive Era. While they were aware of the problems of immigrants, poor families, and schooling, ethnic and cultural prejudices blinkered many of these groups. They rejected African-American women who wanted to join or work alongside their organizations, exhibiting a social conservatism which belied their reforming zeal. The Board of Lady Managers of the Columbia Exposition in Chicago in 1893 appealed to women's groups from across the nation and overseas to send delegates to the Exposition in order to demonstrate women's achievements, yet it rebuffed applications from several African-American women's clubs, underscoring the lack of common purpose among women's groups.

African-American women's self-education efforts continued those begun in the ante-bellum era by free black women. Cities with relatively large, educated, and affluent African-American populations had active female reform organizations which coalesced into regional and national networks by the 1880s and 1890s. Their many clubs and societies combined encouragement for female African-American authors with social betterment programs within the African-American community. Secular, women-only groups raised funds for orphanages, old age homes, charities, and community defense.

In 1892, the teachers who comprised the female elite of the Washington, DC, black community formed the Colored Woman's League while their sisters in Boston, New York, and other large cities formed similar organizations. Stung by white club women's refusal to countenance their presence at the Chicago World's Fair in 1893, ostensibly because they were local rather than national groups, the African-American women's movement united as the National Federation of Afro-American Women (NFAAW) in 1895, and joined forces in 1896 with the National League of Colored Women to become the National Association of Colored Women (NACW) under the leadership of Mary Church Terrell, an educator and the first black woman to serve on the District of Columbia Board of Education. Although fractured by regional rivalries, the NACW promoted reform and self-help endeavors in many cities and incorporated a "womanist" perspective (in Alice Walker's memorable term), working for and with other women.

Working women's organizations sprang up in the last quarter of the nineteenth century as factory workers united to form "Working Girls' Clubs" and urban churches sponsored Girls' Friendly Societies for young working women. Social welfare worker Grace Dodge and 12 New York City factory workers established the New York City Working Girls' Club in 1884. Although an outgrowth of Dodge's Sunday School Class, the club moved beyond religious teaching to include education and vocational training. As with their more affluent sisters, working women's organizations banded together to form an Association of Working Girls' Societies, with branches in the Northeast and Midwest. The clubs offered a variety of classes, maintained residences for working women, and had well-attended lecture series covering social and personal topics.

Other laboring women established ethnic and beneficial societies to protect their members and provide friendly contact in the growing cities. In the early twentieth century the Ladies' Catholic Benevolent Association, Polish Women's Alliance, Caledonian Ladies' Aid Society and similar ethno-religious organizations attested to the strong organizational alliances developing among immigrant women. Many women's ethnic associations also had national and sometimes international memberships. Jewish women formed the National Council of Jewish Women in 1893. Hadassah, the women's Zionist organization, began in 1912, after Henrietta Szold's trip to Palestine. An activist within the Jewish community, Szold believed that Jewish women should promote Jewish institutions and enterprises in the Holy Land. Hadassah campaigned for Zionist teaching in Jewish summer camps and schools and raised money to support Jewish welfare activities in Palestine. This organization gave women a focus for cultural and political activities and provided a base for women within the synagogues and larger Jewish community. As in other gender-based class or ethnic societies, female organizational talents furthered the aims of their group and thrust women's issues into the public arena. Such societies denoted common perspectives and interests, using gender as a basis for activism since women were largely excluded by men from their groups and saw themselves as having distinctive talents to contribute to society.

WOMEN'S CULTURAL CONTRIBUTIONS

The growing number of women readers and the literary club women's movement contained an eager audience for female authors. Louisa May Alcott, Emily Dickinson, Willa Cather, Charlotte Perkins Gilman, Sarah Orne Jewett, Kate Chopin, Frances Ellen Watkins Harper, and Edith Wharton achieved national and international standing in this era. Although female authors encountered prejudice in their search for audiences they transcended the limitations of gender more easily than other women professionals because the entry criteria (literacy and imagination) were as available to women as men and spread to diverse racial and ethnic groups in this era.

Writing offered particular opportunities to women because it could be combined with domesticity at a time when most middle-class women eschewed leaving the home to work. The romantic image of motherhood, dangling an infant on one knee while balancing writing tablets on the other, encouraged many women to put pen to paper. Popular literature's sentimental nature provided topics from women's own experience or fantasies. Female readers responded avidly to the domestic focus of much women's writing with schoolgirls eagerly reading Louisa May Alcott's *Little Women* series while their mothers enjoyed Cather, Gilman, and Chopin. Women also pored over the advice columns in the newspapers and magazines which instructed them on home and family management, rapidly developing domestic technologies, and new modes of behavior.

Women's writing underwent a transition in this era, from a concentration on the domestic to an exploration of new forms, styles, and topics which went far beyond the household. *Little Women* (1868) stands out as both a challenge to domesticity and an acceptance of it, reflecting Louisa May Alcott's upbringing and realization of the importance of domesticity as a source of comfort and well-being. She described a female domain of sisterhood, benevolence, and good intentions and a feminized world where men figured peripherally, if at all. The male absence from the March household incorporated both the Civil War experience and men's growing immersion in commercial and industrial endeavors distant from the family hearth.

Despite seeming conformity to contemporary social norms regarding the importance of domesticity, Alcott subverts notions of female dependence. Her heroines, especially Jo March, might best be described as "plucky," embodying the best of male and female characteristics. Jo was the "man of the family" while her father served as a chaplain with the Union forces, and retained her tomboyish attitudes even after his return. By not marrying Jo to Laurie, the rich boy next door, Alcott indicated that marriage was not "the only end and aim of a woman's life" even though she believed in the centrality of domesticity and a carefully managed home. *Little Women* affirmed the female experience, posited female virtues as the cornerstones of a happy life, and indicated that women could combine fulfilling careers with marriage.

Given Alcott's upbringing in the most heavily industrialized state of the nation where textile mills offered plentiful employment to women, it is ironic that she ignored factory labor in her depiction of the March girls' attempts to earn money. The world of the home was so important that women rarely moved beyond it, even if employed. Alcott's heroines, including Christie Devon in *Work* (1873), obtained a series of domestic and quasi-domestic employments while eschewing the textile mills that dominated Massachusetts employment opportunities for poor young women, especially immigrants.

Other female authors reflected upon similar themes, but from distinctive vantage points. Emily Dickinson (1830–86) was Alcott's contemporary, though few read her poetry during her lifetime. Having been rejected in an early effort to publish her work in its highly original form, Dickinson subsequently showed her poems only to a few trusted confidants and remained unpublished until 1890. For reasons which remain unclear, Dickinson became a recluse, pouring her emotions and perceptions into poetry which pondered domesticity, nature, religion, and relationships. These were commonplace topics for female authors and poets, but her construction was unique, far in advance of contemporary techniques. Dickinson accepted domesticity but never married, finding fulfillment through her poetry. Her poetry revealed an "anxiety of gender" as Vivian R. Pollak labels it, seeking resolution of the crises of sexuality, social isolation, and family relationships through enigmatic verse.

Some women writers at the turn of the century transcended narrowly defined gender interests and rejected domesticity as the core of female existence. Proletarian fiction, the ethnic press, and newspapers provided a forum for working-class and immigrant women to explore economic, social, and political issues which affected them closely. Theresa Malkiel, a Russian Jewish immigrant, wrote her *Diary of a Shirtwaist Striker* to expose the appalling employment conditions under which Jewish and Italian women garment workers toiled and which led them to strike repeatedly between 1900 and 1920. The *Diary*'s narrator cast off double standards in pay and personal relations, becoming a new woman who delayed her wedding until the boss agreed to settle the strike on the workers' terms. Declaring her loyalty to the women with whom she struck, she expected her husband to meet her on an equal basis.

Willa Cather, Kate Chopin, and Sarah Orne Jewett rooted their stories in the West, South, and Northeast, respectively, but were more than mere local colorists, as they were sometimes condemned. They employed their particular settings to illuminate various aspects of the new woman, marking her transition from preordained domesticity to individuality. Cather's reflections on nature and the pioneering experience entranced readers across the nation. Her heroines relished their part in making the prairies their own, undertook the male role of farmer and breadwinner with equal ease, and projected a vision of western women as active creators of a more egalitarian society. As Elaine Showalter has observed, Cather and other authors in this era put their "literary ambitions before domestic duties," which differentiated them from women writers of the ante-bellum era, whose domestic crises punctuated their writing.

African-American women's writing altered from a redemptive and sentimental belief in the power of marriage, domesticity, and hard work after the Civil War and Reconstruction to a bleaker vision of racial injustice by the end of the century, indicative of their disillusion with persistent racism and legal restrictions. Frances Ellen Watkins Harper, Anna Julia Cooper, and Pauline E. Hopkins used literacy to further their career ambitions, social justice, and ethnic pride. Hopkins (1859–1930) attended Boston Girls' High School, wrote and performed with the Colored Troubadours, and co-founded *The Colored American Magazine*. Her work emphasized the tragic consequences of persistent racism and the racism and sexism she encountered curtailed her literary career. Cooper, a feminist educator, published *A Voice from the South by a Black Woman of the South* in 1892, exploring the complex situation in which southern black women found themselves. Harper (1825–1911) wrote prolifically, achieving international recognition as a journalist, novelist and poet. A conductor on the Underground Railroad before the Civil War, Harper believed education and domesticity would facilitate racial and gender betterment. Her heroines work outside the home after making egalitarian marriages, dedicating themselves to racial uplift and social justice.

Harper's *Iola LeRoy: or, Shadows Uplifted* (1892), a novel of "morality, race loyalty, and uplift," contained a coded reference to another African-American writer and reformer, Ida B. Wells-Barnett, who sometimes used Iola as a pseudonym. Wells-Barnett encountered discrimination in many forms, including eviction from a "ladies' car" on the Chesapeake and Ohio Railroad in 1884. When the Tennessee State Supreme Court ruled against her, she felt "utterly discouraged," but continued to battle against discrimination. She worked as a newspaper reporter and editor in Memphis where her courageous documentation of the horrible crime of lynching, *A Red Record: Tabulated Statistics and Alleged Causes of Lynchings in the United States, 1892–1893–1894*, incurred death threats and attacks. The ensuing controversy and the aspersions cast upon African-American women's virtue and character prompted the formation of the National Association of Colored Women several years later.

While Harper, Wells-Barnett, and Cooper, among others, challenged the racial hegemonies of their world, many white writers accepted them as given. Kate Chopin's stories incorporated the deep racial divides of her native Louisiana even as she confronted the constricted roles available to women. *The Awakening* (1899) rarely named individual African Americans, labeling them "the Octoroon" or "the Negress," but contested contemporary gender conventions by seemingly endorsing extra-marital sex and female flight from domestic responsibility. Her protagonist seeks fulfillment by exploring her own sexuality rather than devoting herself to her children or husband and commits the ultimate solipsism, escaping wife- and motherhood through suicide. In rejecting a domestic solution, Chopin turned her back on the literary domesticity that dominated earlier women's writing.

Charlotte Perkins Gilman also cast domesticity aside in some of her writing and questioned conventional gender roles. "The Yellow

Wallpaper" (1892) condemns the treatment meted out to women suffering from post-partum depression, namely a rest cure which deprived them of all non-domestic interests. Literary critic Elaine Hedges draws a connection between *The Awakening* and "The Yellow Wallpaper," finding it symptomatic of *fin de siècle* America that both works ended with their heroines' self-destruction. Gilman's later work, notably *Women and Economics* and *The Home,* challenged the relegation of women to unalloyed domesticity, repudiating the gendered basis for female activities and activism. She believed that "the home, in its ceaseless and inexorable demands," stopped women from developing their talents. Collective kitchens, cleaning services, and crèches would emancipate women from the household and permit them to participate in the affairs of the world outside the home, based on ability and interest rather than gender.

Edith Wharton's novels moved decisively beyond domesticity and separate spheres as the source of female strength. Wharton had a cosmopolitan upbringing, living in Europe as a child and educating herself largely through her father's extensive library. Her novels contrasted genteel "old New York" with the modern commercial and manufacturing center, exploring the ways in which individuals resolve their place in society. Wharton's characters rebuked class and gender stereotypes for the shackles they imposed upon individuals and thus rejected domesticity as the sole aim of women's lives.

POPULAR AND HIGH CULTURE

Women's place in American culture expanded from literature and journalism to include acting and the cinema, although their standing in the fine arts remained equivocal. After the turn of the century, female investigators for muckraking magazines such as *McClure's* examined and condemned the workings of American business. Ida Tarbell, who contributed to the *Chautaquan* and *Scribner's* magazines, probed the workings of the Standard Oil trust for *McClure's.* Along with other leading magazine writers she initiated the muckraking style of investigative reporting which featured largely in progressive reformers' attack on unrestrained corporate power, but did not support suffrage.

As a consumption-oriented culture came to dominate the market place, magazine writers and editors urged women to use up-to-date domestic technologies and incorporate new values and behaviors into their household routines. The *Ladies' Home Journal (LHJ)*, founded by Edward Bok in 1889, regarded the home as a civilizing force within American society. Women implanted ideas in men's minds which they implemented in the "outer world." Yet *LHJ* advised women to be active, educated, and not to smother their children. Its pages included the tips and hints that have been the staple of women's magazines ever since. It also carried many pages of advertising which urged women to buy their family's love through mouthwashes, laundry powders, and fancy cooking, further enmeshing women in the cult of consumption.

Consumer culture blossomed in the late nineteenth century as producers and retailers turned to new methods of attracting customers. Commercial artist Jessie Wilcox Smith's illustrations for *Ladies' Home Journal, Scribner's, Harper's* and *Good Housekeeping* lent a soft, romantic feeling to selling soap and other household products. Such ads encouraged consumption of basic commodities by identifying them with emotional requirements and promoting new "needs" in the minds of consumers. Advertising budgets expanded greatly at the end of the nineteenth century, tripling pre-Civil War levels by the 1880s and reaching $95 million by 1900. Much of this advertising was directed at women, training them to buy what their mothers made.

Department stores contained a wide variety of products under a single roof, but they also offered a fantasy land of goods and services designed to augment sales and win customer loyalty. These urban institutions differed from their rural counterparts (the general store) by targeting female shoppers directly, advertising in local newspapers to attract customers, and displaying wares for easier selection. As women's domestic workload decreased, household advisers like Christine Frederick adjured them to become "trained consumers" and manage purchases efficiently. Popular women's magazines reinforced this message for middle- and upper-class women who had discretionary incomes that could be spent on impulse purchases. Economist Thorstein Veblen recognized this new order in 1899 when he described women's role as that of conspicuous consumption, displaying their husbands' wealth through their apparel. Shopping replaced household manufacturing as a major component of women's work, while retailers, manufacturers, and advertising agencies all spread the message that it was a pleasurable social activity.

Advertisers targeted female consumers directly since they controlled most spending decisions for household items, making them valuable customers.

Efficiency in housework became increasingly important when the supply of domestic servants decreased and affluent women undertook more or most housekeeping tasks. Articles on appliances and advertisements for processed food and cleaning products stressed saving time in order to undertake other, more pleasurable activities. Two Ivory Soap ads highlighted this transition in graphic form. In the first, dating from the turn of the century, a maid in mobcap and long apron scrubs the carpet on her hands and knees with a solution made from Ivory Soap Paste. In 1916, Procter & Gamble advertised its soap with a middle-class mother instructing her teenage daughter from a booklet entitled "Unusual Uses of Ivory Soap." These two magazine advertisements and the editorial content which surrounded them demonstrated the selling of housework to the middle classes, but other articles such as "How 25 Clever Girls Made Money" indicated that the new journals stretched women's horizons beyond the home as well.

Manufactured forms of pleasure replaced more homespun pastimes in the late nineteenth century. Urbanization, increased free time, and the declining physical effort required to run a home facilitated participation in commercial leisure activities. As more women worked outside the domestic sphere, they had long but definite working hours and set periods of time when they were not at work. While servants had half a day off a week if they were lucky, factory and office workers had shorter working days and weeks. As a result, they could go to the cinema or dance hall in the evening or at the weekends, a treat rarely available to the live-in servant.

Physical activity became a fashionable diversion as women cycled, played tennis and golf, and skated, wearing loose-fitting clothing appropriate for active life. College women played baseball, basketball, and other team sports. Charles Dana Gibson's "Gibson Girl," featured in *Life* magazine in the 1890s, epitomized the new woman who moved beyond the confines of the previous era's corsets and restrictive dress. The *Ladies' Home Journal* also recommended a new sporting look to its readers in features depicting female recreation, even though magazine articles adjured young women to let men win in order to be popular.

New forms of entertainment monetized leisure time activities.

Women attended the legitimate theatre, music halls, and vaudeville in large numbers, watching stars such as Lillian Russell who earned a phenomenal $1250 per performance at the height of her career. Women enjoyed amusement parks, nickelodeons, and, increasingly, the cinema. These commercialized amusements embodied American culture to the daughters of immigrants and other urban newcomers, who affirmed their individuality by partaking of social activities beyond parental control. Coney Island, Kenneywood, Luna Park and the countless amusement parks which sprang up in urban centers at the turn of the century all attested to city dwellers' desire for thrills and fun.

From the first movies shown as accompaniments to vaudeville in the 1890s, motion pictures proved incredibly popular across ethnic, class, racial, age, and gender divisions. The kinetoscopes in the penny arcades initially attracted a male audience, but the nickelodeons appealed to both sexes. Their modest price (5 cents) brought them within reach of even poor city dwellers and enabled the entire family to go together. Early film plot lines derived from older forms, frequently mimicking vaudeville or popular melodramas. While Majorie Rosen argues that the age of cinema coincided with, and hastened, the age of the modern woman, Kathy Preiss observes that most films upheld the patriarchal order and emphasized personal pleasure over "reformers' schemes and feminist utopias."

Hollywood's modern woman incorporated many of the basic characteristics of an earlier view of feminine roles. Women were vamps, virgins, or mothers in old-fashioned dresses. Few films showed any awareness of the complexities of women's roles or the political upheavals of the day. Instead, constrained by a format which emphasized the visual over the verbal, silent movies dealt in readily recognizable icons rather than complex political debates or carefully nuanced characters. Action rather than intellect ruled the silver screen. Chase scenes abounded, with women sometimes taking an active part. Early serials such as the *Perils of Pauline* (1914) featured a spirited heroine who resourcefully solved her own problems.

Some actresses and a few female screenwriters and directors managed to take charge of their own careers in the early days of Hollywood. Lois Weber, the first successful female director, was one of the few directors of either sex to tackle controversial topics such as birth control. Frances Marion wrote scenarios and scripts prolifically. Mary Pickford negotiated high salaries, even though she never made the transition from innocent to adult on-screen. In 1919, she founded United Artists along with D. W. Griffith, Douglas Fairbanks, and Charlie Chaplin to control the artistic content of their movies. Other women, including Theda Bara, played *femme fatale* roles: dangerous women draped in an aura of sensuality, who wore cosmetics and clinging gowns. Movies demonstrated the benefits of consumer culture, presented romance as a staple theme, and brought glamour into the lives of millions of women who went to the pictures every week.

Women enjoyed great acclaim as writers and actresses but still met with less success in the fine arts, especially painting. The French Académie Royale rejected Mary Cassatt's paintings though two of her murals hung in the Woman's Building at the 1892 World's Fair. Georgia O'Keeffe achieved her first one-woman show in 1917, but she was very much the exception. Many women painted and drew, but few received the patronage needed to sustain an artistic career. Women were patrons of the arts, founding museums and galleries, but few female artists received space in these public facilities.

Some women obtained sculpture commissions and others turned craft work into fine art. Potter Maria Montoya Martinez's black on black pottery attracted critical acclaim, while many Native American women turned their basketry and pottery into small-scale commercial ventures. Maria Longworth Nichols Storer founded Rookwood pottery in 1880, winning a gold medal at the 1889 Paris Exposition for her art pottery decorated with rich glazes. Edmondia Lewis, daughter of a Chippewa mother and African-American father, attended Oberlin College, then journeyed to Boston where she worked on abolitionist and Native American themes. Her statue of Hagar in the Wilderness manifested the "strong sympathy" she felt for "all women who have struggled and suffered."

By the close of this era, women had demonstrated how wrong the *Saturday Review*'s writer had been to belittle their intellect in 1860. They achieved recognition for their writing and their place in education was assured, even if they had not obtained parity in higher education. Yet, education also channeled women into a narrow range of acceptable roles. Women became deans of women, not deans of faculties. Their presence in colleges and universities tended to be at small private or religious schools rather than large research universities, and while women dominated the ranks of school teachers, few achieved managerial posts.

Domesticity, while less important than earlier, nevertheless framed most women's lives. Female authors were an accepted part of the literary scene, but their place in the other arts was less secure. Even the glamorous new medium of the movies offered few and gender-stereotyped places for women in front of the camera and almost no place behind the scenes. Female professionals succeeded best in those occupations which seemed most closely allied to the home and traditional female roles, such as teaching and nursing, but had greater trouble finding acceptance in medicine and law, which were perceived as authoritative and public.

Women's education engendered social and political activism and many women deployed their communication and networking skills to advance female legal and political standing. Moving away from the parental home to attend college helped women to see themselves as separate from their families and they developed strong female networks based upon common interests. The club woman movement, women's ethnic and religious societies, and female professional organizations derived from women's consciousness of their separate interests as well as men's rejection of their participation in their organizations. More women gained credentials which enabled them to participate in the world outside the home, but gender still constrained their schooling and cultural contributions, with most positions of leadership and authority reserved for men. Nevertheless, rising levels of female education and a growing awareness of social problems encouraged women's involvement in a broad spectrum of non-domestic activities, even if these were sometimes rationalized in terms of their maternal roles.

8 Women and Reform in the Gilded Age and Progressive Era

The Civil War contributed to the redefinition of women's political roles and relations with the state. Women gained in moral authority as they raised funds for the relief of the Confederate and Union armies, sewed clothes, and nursed the wounded. After the war, higher levels of widowhood, economic distress, and an awareness of their own contributions to society meant women could not, and in many cases, did not wish to return to their pre-war roles. Instead they redefined their civic responsibilities building upon their wartime experiences, in order to overcome what they perceived as political obstacles to their equal incorporation into public life. In the aftermath of the war it became clear that the quest for suffrage would not flourish if allied to other causes but had to stand or fall on its own merits. The crusade waxed and waned as its rationale shifted from a state by state quest for equality between the sexes to an expedient means to accomplish other items on the maternal-political agenda, finally succeeding as a federal amendment in 1920.

Female reform and welfare activities went through a number of stages. Immediately after the war women established charities as temporary measures for the worthy poor, Civil War veterans, and their families. They drew upon their wartime experiences as organizers, fundraisers, and carers in order to remember the dead and assist the living. Other groups of women assumed that social ills stemmed from intemperate behavior and attempted to reform individuals through restrictions upon the consumption of alcohol. As the Gilded Age and Progressive Era wore on a growing number of American women perceived the need for collective rather than individual answers to the nation's problems. The seriousness of the depressions of the 1870s and 1890s convinced female reformers that the business cycle and structural economic issues rather than individual failings contributed to the widespread immiseration they observed. This, in turn, led to greater concern over children's welfare and education, the reshaping of laws and civic institutions during the Progressive Era, and ultimately to a renewed battle for women's suffrage as a means of solving these problems.

The Civil War had disrupted families throughout the nation and created an ethos of social motherhood in which women provided for society as a whole services they had previously tendered individually to their families. In the process they created a public role that extended their maternal and domestic functions to the entire nation. The vast numbers of wounded men, young widows, and orphans in Union and Confederate populations accentuated anxieties over the family and encouraged women to nurture society, or certain parts of it, as well as their own biological kin. Northern and southern women had sacrificed their male relatives and family life in order to defend or defy the Union, but their divergent attitudes toward the conflict itself influenced the levels and type of post-war activism. Many northern women had agitated for abolition and regarded the cause as their own, unlike southern women, who were more isolated and less politically involved. Northern women continued their political commitment after the war, while white southern women remained enmeshed in a race-gender hierarchy which discouraged reformist political activities.

Social motherhood in the South had a more conservative and segregated approach as the women of the former Confederacy formed themselves into societies to remember the past by tending graves (a service to mothers too distant to put flowers on their sons' tombstones), constructed memorials to the fallen, and ran homes for Confederate widows and wounded veterans. White southern women reconstructed themselves as depoliticized presences, shrinking from the public gaze as they wrapped their activities in the cloak of motherhood. Even when they undertook such public functions as building war memorials and arranging ceremonies to honor the Confederate dead, they regarded themselves as public mothers defending their families, based on the "politics of domestic loss," to use LeeAnn Whites' description. They sought not independence but family reconciliation and healing through memorializing the dead and caring for the living. Their organizations excluded African-American women and thus reinforced the divisive racial politics of the post-bellum South. African-American women formed their own self-help societies, but were largely excluded from the civic enterprises of the New South.

Northern social motherhood took different forms, with a more overtly political cast, but also made family concerns into public issues by attempting to use the power of the state to implement temperance, municipal, maternal and child health, child custody, and social welfare reforms. Female participation in public life ranged across many issues, including racial discrimination, charity, settlement houses, rural reform, and married women's property rights, as well as suffrage. The latter made scant progress after the Civil War as an issue of gender equality, while succeeding in the twentieth century as a means for women to act upon their maternalist agenda and as a thank-offering for their participation in yet another war.

Not all women shared an activist political perspective in which they tried to assert a greater public role. White southern women questioned both the desirability and the feasibility of female independence, according to historian Drew Gilpin Faust, because their wartime experiences of poverty, conquest, and shattered families convinced them that such independence carried intolerable burdens. A number of northern reformers also had serious reservations about how women would be incorporated into the public world. Catharine Beecher advocated an expanded role for women both inside and outside the home but rejected female voting because she believed it violated the natural order, would introduce chaos into the home, and would expose women to the sort of corruption widely associated with nineteenth-century politics. In an "Address to the Christian Women of America" in 1871 she appealed to women to influence their families and so bring about a more moral nation. Female activism in this era attempted to do that despite disagreements over how it should be accomplished.

TEMPERANCE ACTIVISM

One of the most inclusive maternal-political campaigns was to safeguard the family by restricting alcohol consumption. Female temperance crusaders believed men's drinking threatened the sanctity of the family and the home. They also worried about assimilating immigrants whose cultural and religious backgrounds condoned drinking, initially Irish and German Catholics, but later southern and eastern Europeans. Temperance was a way of asserting cultural hegemony in a rapidly changing world. The Women's Christian Temperance Union

(WCTU), founded in 1874, had its roots in the small towns and cities of the Midwest, and appealed primarily to evangelical Protestants.

Women's temperance organizations attracted into public life those who did not (at least initially) consider themselves to be women's rights advocates. The WCTU provided a socially conservative alternative to the more radical suffrage movement although it eventually endorsed women's suffrage as a means of obtaining its primary goal, banning the sale and consumption of alcoholic beverages. Many rural and small town branches of the WCTU preached to the converted (members of their own churches) and approached outreach activities warily, constrained by their own acceptance of gender conventions. The first president, Annie Wittenmyer, wanted to limit the WCTU to temperance activism while younger members, including Frances Willard who took over the presidency from Wittenmyer in 1879, advocated suffrage and general reforms. Restrictive notions of female propriety prompted local chapters to narrower and less aggressive approaches. Members pledged abstention from alcohol and the employment of "all proper means to discourage the use of and traffic in the same." They refused to engage in work among miners or railroad men as "inexpedient," that is, unladylike, and probably futile.

The WCTU's social and moral respectability encouraged rapid growth. It expanded from its base in the Midwest to encompass 27 000 members in 24 states five years after founding. Membership trebled by the mid-1880s and reached 168 000 by the turn of the century. By 1920 it had about 800 000 members, making it one of the largest women's organizations in the United States, exceeded only by the General Federation of Women's Clubs. By stressing social purity and family life, while still supporting suffrage, it avoided the radical image that beset suffrage groups.

As a women-only organization the WCTU encouraged female activism, political mobilization, and leadership skills. Frances Willard believed that if men were allowed to join the WCTU, "women would not develop so rapidly or become so self-respecting." Since women held all the leadership positions, they acquired self-confidence and a belief in their own abilities which they employed on behalf of temperance and other socio-political causes. The WCTU used moral persuasion to induce state legislators to pass prohibition or local options laws in the 1880s and 1890s, at a time when the women's suffrage movement was in abeyance or achieving little real progress. It successfully lobbied state legislatures to mandate temperance instruction in the schools and persuaded some states to control the liquor trade through Sunday trading laws. The WCTU also worked for the passage of pure food and drug legislation as a means of removing alcohol and opium from pharmaceutical products.

Despite WCTU efforts, the consumption of alcohol rose after the turn of the century, prompting a new wave of concern. Some reformers took a direct approach to flagrant violations of their moral codes. Carrie Nation, whose first husband had been an alcoholic, smashed bottles in turn-of-the-century saloons. On a more sustained and organized basis, the Anti-Saloon League lobbied strongly for prohibition. It was particularly strong in the South where it drew upon the temperance doctrines of evangelical churches and the flagrant racism of Jim Crow voters to persuade five states to enact prohibition statutes as "one more weapon in the arsenal of white racism," according to historian Ross Evans Paulson.

Although the WCTU had some African-American and immigrant members, they were in separate branches. Novelist and journalist Frances W. E. Harper served as superintendent of the Colored Section of the Philadelphia and Pennsylvania WCTUs in the 1870s and 1880s. She believed the racism she encountered was a relic of the dead past which true Christianity would eradicate. Cross-race organizing in the North usually took the form of separate branches or "colored unions" to which white branches extended modest financial assistance. For African-American women in the South the WCTU was a vehicle of racial uplift, enabling women to organize in accordance with their religious precepts. Southern white WCTUs attempted to organize "colored" branches under white leadership, while at the same time disfranchising African-American locals in 1900 as the rising tide of racism engulfed interracial cooperation.

Rural states with small Catholic populations passed prohibition legislation, while urban states with large numbers of immigrants kept the "Drys" at bay. Congress eventually passed a national prohibition amendment in 1918, which the states ratified rapidly. It did so in the context of a national wartime emergency with fears of food shortages and the perceived need to control workers both on the production line and in the army camps. Prohibition as it entered the Constitution thus had less to do with social purity (as advocated by the WCTU) and more to do with social control over potentially disruptive elements during a period of great upheaval.

RURAL WOMEN'S ACTIVISM

Rural women, especially in the West, campaigned actively in defense of farmers and country dwellers as well as for prohibition and women's rights. From the 1860s onwards, they joined various rural organizations, including the Patrons of Husbandry (the Grange), the Farmers' Alliance, and the Populists, because they were part of a family business suffering under a new economic order. An emerging national and international agricultural system disadvantaged small and medium-sized farmers when competition drove down the prices they received for their crops, the need to reach distant markets put them at the mercy of railroads, and the cost of borrowing for seed, farm machinery, and fertilizer left them indebted to the banks.

Organized in the late 1860s and concentrated in the Missouri River Valley, the Grange provided for equal participation by both sexes in recognition of the continuing importance of women to rural family economies and communities. Women had the right to vote and run for office and comprised a significant proportion of the Grange's 750 000 members by the mid-1870s. They participated fully in Grange matters through speaking tours, writing for the *Grange Visitor* and other rural papers, and lobbying in state and local forums for fairer treatment for small farmers. Because women were an integral part of the Grange movement, it was particularly receptive to their needs and developed buying cooperatives which purchased household as well as agricultural items. It used its political power to fight against margarine manufacturers whose product undermined one of the bases of the rural economy, women's butter manufacturing.

The Grange's political influence quickly waned as railroad operators, bankers, and grain silo operators fought back through the courts and state legislatures. In the late 1880s and 1890s, the Farmers' Alliance concentrated in the South and the Great Plains defended rural interests along similar lines to the Grange. Like the Grange, the Farmers' Alliance had a large number of female members in both black and white branches. Farm women were particularly outspoken members of the Texas Alliance as they urged women to "work for change because they had a direct interest in economic reform," according to rural historian Joan Jensen, who observes that this was especially radical since southern women had no tradition of public speaking.

Female members of the Farmers' Alliance included Sarah Emery, who traveled extensively in the Midwest speaking out on rural interests, temperance, and women's suffrage, and Mary Lease who lectured on rural and women's issues. Women addressed meetings, wrote, and voted on an equal basis with men in the Alliance and the Populist Party, but these organizations were less supportive of women's rights than the Grange movement had been, possibly because the successor organizations had a large southern membership and began to fight a national political crusade. Where the Grange had been an economic and social movement, the Farmers' Alliance and the Populist Party gave primacy to the economic issues which faced rural Americans, since repeated economic crises made railroad, monetary, and land reform seem essential to the farmers' cause.

Despite the shift in emphasis, women worked actively for the Populist and Alliance movements. Luna Kellie and her husband, a Nebraska farmer, turned to politics when they realized that the costs of transport and credit doomed them and their 11 children to a marginal existence. Kellie made a rousing speech at her first Farmers' Alliance meeting. "Stand Up for Nebraska" she urged her listeners, who elected her secretary of the Nebraska Alliance. Kellie did not support William Jennings Bryan's presidential candidacy, fearing he would compromise farmers' interests, and eventually lost interest in politics, although she remained active in the Alliance movement until its demise at the turn of the century.

Mary Elizabeth Lease, one of the Populist Party's most famous orators, reputedly told a gathering of Kansas farmers to "raise less corn and more hell" as a means of bettering their lot. She made innumerable speeches for the Populist Party, but, like Kellie, withdrew from the party when William Jennings Bryan ran for President of the United States. Many female Populists distrusted party politics and the failure of the rural movement to achieve significant change disillusioned them. Kellie, for example, never voted. Her memoirs concluded "nothing is likely to be done to benefit the farming class in my lifetime. So I busy myself with my garden and chickens and have given up all hope of making the world any better."

Like the Grange, the Populists encountered virulent opposition from business interests, especially in the South where politicians disfranchised poor white men though poll taxes introduced in the 1890s, used violence to prevent African-American men from voting, and strenuously opposed women's suffrage as a threat to both their social and political hegemony. Once the Farmers' Alliance became enmeshed in national politics through the Populist Party, women's issues disappeared from sight. Urban–rural tensions did not dissolve with the defeat of the Populist Party in the 1896 election, but rural matters received a more sympathetic hearing after Theodore Roosevelt became US President. Having been a farmer and a rancher he appreciated rural problems and established the Country Life Commission in 1907 to strengthen agricultural communities.

The progressive agricultural experts of the Country Life Movement believed farms should be managed on sound business principles in order to become more efficient enterprises. They regarded rural women as overburdened and felt that the solution to their problems rested with lifting rural standards of living generally. Roosevelt himself emphasized that rural women were mothers, "whose primary function it is to bear and rear a sufficient number of healthy children [otherwise] she is not entitled to our regard." In the pages of *Good Housekeeping* magazine Charlotte Perkins Gilman queried how the Country Life Commissioners, all men, could know about farm women's problems or propose sensitive solutions for them. The establishment of the US Department of Agriculture Extension Service in 1914 was in keeping with the male agronomist view of rural life; it had separate programs for farmers and farm wives and did not recognize rural women's economic activity as part of the farm economy.

Rural Native American women, not enmeshed in commercial farming, played little part in the Populist movement, although they had a significant role in tribal activism. Sarah Winnemucca served as a guide for the United States Army and spoke on behalf of Native Americans to Interior Secretary Carl Schurz and President Rutherford B. Hayes in 1880. Supported by sympathetic white reformers she conducted a lecture tour, sold her own book, *Life Among the Piutes,* and circulated a petition requesting land grants for the Piutes, which they eventually received in 1884. Other women active on behalf of Native Americans included Amelia Stone Quinton and Mary Lucinda Bonney, who collected signatures on a petition to Congress, asking it to honor previous treaties with Native Americans. In 1883, they launched the Women's National Indian Association (WNIA), which sought to "hasten . . . their civilization, Christianization, and enfranchisement," indicating their missionary agenda and cultural objectives. The WNIA campaigned for land grants, which the Dawes Act (1887) facilitated, sometimes with disastrous consequences as tribal lands could be sold by individuals rather than belonging to the community. It also provided funds for Native Americans to obtain higher education and professional training and improved health and education on the reservations.

URBAN WOMEN'S ACTIVISM

Building upon the knowledge and networks established in the Civil War, urban women sought to resolve the civic and moral dilemmas of the post-war period. They became important social activists in charity, municipal reform, and settlement house movements. Coupled with rising educational levels, these activities shifted the acceptable paradigms of female behavior by transferring women's domestic agenda to the political arena, paving the way for progressive reform and, by the early twentieth century, making suffrage into a tool to accomplish social motherhood and, as such, less of a challenge to accepted gender conventions.

Women participated in male-dominated charitable and reform organizations but increasingly established separate societies with their own agendas, interjecting women's domestic and family-centered concerns into social welfare movements. A network of mainly middle-class women organized reform societies, benevolent groups, and welfare organizations in this period, marking women as an autonomous political force and contributing to the growing politicization of American women. By the end of the nineteenth century, women had moved on from the benevolence which characterized charity at the beginning of the century to social reform at mid-century, Civil War patriotism, and to charitable and welfare work reflective of their class, race, ethnic, and gender positions by 1900.

The post-Civil War period divides into three distinct periods: the first lasting until the 1880s, in which genteel ladies organized the outdoor relief of their cities in response to the depression of 1873–9 which belied the widespread assumption that personal failings caused poverty. From the late 1880s onwards female reformers took paid jobs in charities and welfare organizations and made their homes in the tenement house districts as settlement house workers. In the third stage, progressive reformers lobbied at all levels of government to place women's welfare concerns on the public agenda.

The growing disparity in wealth accompanying industrialization alarmed many affluent citizens. They wished to assist and reform poorer people, whose behavior sometimes frightened them, especially as the number of beggars increased during the depressions which racked the late nineteenth century. From the 1870s onwards, people wishing to systematize charity and make it more efficient joined "improvement of the poor" groups, frequently under the Charity Organization Society or Associated Charities' banners. Many of the women who set up these societies had been active in Civil War fundraising efforts and drew upon the expertise they had gained during the conflict. They tried to overcome the geographical, ethnic, and economic distances between the classes by becoming "friendly" visitors. These volunteers gave advice to the poor in their own homes along with cash and gifts in kind, but they only assisted those who met their criteria: piety, sobriety, and deference being key characteristics.

Once assistance became a privilege gained by being acceptable to private charities rather than a right one had by virtue of need, the possibilities for manipulating the behavior of the poor increased. By the 1870s, few cities gave the poor cash, referring them to private charities, and only offering a bed at the workhouse or county poor farm as a last resort. Consequently women, who ran most of the private charities, had an increasingly important role in the social welfare of American cities. They asserted a maternalist perspective, transforming the public discourse by making domesticity and motherhood public concerns.

Many cities and states appointed women members to their boards of charities in the 1870s and 1880s in recognition of their legitimate place in welfare matters. Josephine Shaw Lowell, a leading member of the New York Charities Aid Association and first female member of the State Board of Charities, led the attack on public relief, believing it took money out of the pockets of the provident and gave it to the feckless. In her view relief was an evil, even when necessary, because it undermined "energy, independence, industry, and self-reliance." In fact, the Charity Organization Society (COS) movement gave money to the poor, but only after intensive investigation of potential recipients.

As cities expanded the middle and working classes lived at greater distances from each other. Separated by ethnicity and geography from the poor, the affluent organizers of charity felt the need to investigate the personal circumstances of those they assisted. The friendly visitor constituted a friend, an adviser, and a role model. Genuine concern for the less fortunate motivated most friendly visitors, but they also wished to ensure that the money they raised was not spent profligately or taken under false pretences.

The scientific charity movement differentiated between types of poor people, separating them into the worthy and unworthy. Widows and orphans, by and large, fitted into the worthy poor category, but still needed investigation. Insisting on the morality of the poor, even widows, was not entirely new. The New York Society for the Relief of Poor Widows with Small Children struck some off their relief rolls in the 1790s for drinking, begging, and promiscuity. Nevertheless, the scientific charity movement subjected the lives of the needy to increasing levels of scrutiny and intervention. It aided only those who conformed to conventional family models since assisting nonconformists might encourage deviance and lead others astray.

The elite women who comprised the various charity boards favored the white, native-born, and English-speaking over other groups. Strong self-help societies led by the foreign-born and women of color rendered similar assistance to members of their own groups. Most immigrant groups ran secular or religious institutions catering for the young, old, and destitute of their communities. The nuns of various Roman Catholic orders established orphanages, old age homes, and charitable services on an ethnic as well as a religious basis. There were German Catholic orphanages and old people's homes and French Canadian children's homes while African-American nuns operated homes for black orphans and elderly in some southern cities. Protestant churches ran many of the homes in both black and white communities, leading to a racially, religiously, and ethnically segregated provision for the young, old, and poor.

After 1900 paid social workers supplanted friendly visitors, developing treatment plans, and trying to systematize the provision of assistance. They advocated rehabilitation of individuals or families, but did not necessarily challenge structural problems such as the unequal distribution of wealth. Mary Richmond, general secretary of the Baltimore and Philadelphia Charity Organization Societies and later director of the Russell Sage Foundation's Charity Organization Department, established the "case work" approach to social welfare.

She favored the abolition of child labor and improved public health regulation, but opposed the use of tax dollars to support poor families. She campaigned against widows' or mothers' pensions, which gave cash to mothers to stay at home to look after their children rather than put them in orphanages. The use of tax money to provide entitlements based upon status ran counter to the COS approach based on individual investigation and the curtailment of public charity.

Mothers' pensions offered public recognition of the social, economic, and political importance of motherhood and the jobs women did in the home. They were cheaper than orphanages, where many poor parents placed their children while they worked. Pension advocates believed that paying mothers a small cash sum would enable them to stay at home to look after their children. Widows' children would no longer have to leave school prematurely in order to find work and contribute to their family's support. These pensions incorporated gendered social thinking into law, providing public assistance to widowed women to stay at home, while ignoring the plight of widowers with young children, who continued to rely upon orphanages or the extended family for childcare.

Despite organized charity's persistent opposition, the pension movement grew from nothing to a tidal wave in the 1910s. By 1920, almost all northern and western, and some southern states had enacted pension legislation, providing assistance to deserving mothers (widows, and the wives of the insane or incapacitated, but not divorced or unmarried mothers) with children under the age of 14. The trade union movement, newspaper chains, popular periodicals, the National Congress of Mothers, suffragists, fraternal societies, and the Women's Christian Temperance Union supported this legislation. The pension movement asserted the social importance of (legitimate) motherhood to society, recognizing that educating children and assisting poor families benefited the nation as a whole. It also provided for the close supervision of pensioned widows to ensure their behavior conformed to social norms.

While legislatures quickly passed pension legislation, they did not appropriate sufficient funds to help all who qualified. No more than one-third of the eligible mothers and children received assistance, and there were serious racial distortions in the distribution patterns. Mexican-, African-, and Native American widows and their children were much less likely than white women to receive assistance, partly because they tended to live in rural areas where pension levels were lower in any case, but also because racially prejudiced social service departments ignored their claims. Social motherhood thus had a racial dimension which gave some groups a greater claim upon public assistance than others.

PROGRESSIVE REFORM AND THE SETTLEMENT HOUSE MOVEMENT

Along with their male colleagues, the women of the Progressive Era believed that the powers of the state should be used to improve living and working conditions. They favored efficient government, opposed civic corruption, and were wary of big business. Most regarded the vote as an essential tool in the creation of a more just society. Unlike the previous generation of reformers and social welfare activists, progressive women typically had higher education and jobs. Less tolerant of restrictive gender conventions, these women established female networks, especially through the settlement house movement, to work for social betterment.

The settlement house movement was a distinctively female contribution to reform and social welfare in the United States. Over half of all settlement house residents were women. Some stayed a few years before moving on to other careers, while others, such as Jane Addams, stayed a lifetime. Although the idea of the settlement house originated in England, Catharine Beecher had earlier advocated a prototype of settlement houses where "several ladies" would live in poor urban areas in order to care for orphans, the old, ill, and sinful.

Stanton Coit initiated the first Neighborhood Guild under the sponsorship of the Ethical Culture Society in New York City in 1886, modeled upon Toynbee Hall in London, where he had briefly been a resident after receiving his doctorate in Germany. Several years later, the College Settlement, operated by alumnae from leading women's colleges, opened its doors on the Lower East Side. In 1889, Jane Addams and Ellen Gates Starr, graduates of Rockford College, Illinois, launched Hull House in the heart of Chicago's diverse immigrant district, believing they could benefit as much as the poorer people among whom they settled. College graduates would give something back to society, while poorer people would have the opportunity to further their education, recreation, and knowledge of culture.

The settlement would participate in the neighborhood's social life and interpret democracy in social terms, according to Addams.

There were over 400 settlements by 1910, mostly in the immigrant districts of large cities. Approximately two-fifths of these settlements had religious connections, typically Methodist, Episcopal, Presbyterian, or Congregational. Given the racial and religious complexities of *fin de siècle* America, it is not surprising that some settlements found it difficult to accept residents or visitors of different backgrounds. Catholic and Jewish groups established settlements, either because they hoped to further their religious aims or because they felt unwelcome at settlement houses with a Protestant orientation. There were 22 Catholic settlements (and many more urban missions) and a handful of Jewish ones in the larger cities.

Few early settlements welcomed African Americans who established their own institutions. The Urban League, founded in 1911 by the National League for the Protection of Colored Women, the Committee on Urban Conditions, and the New York Committee for Improving the Industrial Conditions of Negroes, actively promoted settlement houses in black neighborhoods. The Atlanta Neighborhood Union, founded in 1908 by Lugenia Burns Hope, epitomized the broad approach taken by southern black reformers when it opened a medical clinic alongside its recreational and vocational programs. African-American women pioneered the rural settlement, bringing education, childcare training, and improved hygiene standards to members of their race in isolated country districts.

While many urban settlement houses eschewed controversy in deference to wealthy donors, Hull House and New York's Henry Street Settlement played a leading role in the child labor reform movements, provided meeting rooms for trade union organizers, and challenged urban political machines. In addition to clubs and classes, day nurseries and sports facilities, settlement house workers lobbied for improved municipal sanitation, tenement house legislation, factory inspection, and better working conditions. They demonstrated modern methods of housekeeping to immigrant women, agitated for better municipal housekeeping for government, and projected women's domestic concerns into the political arena. The women of the Neighborhood Union tackled the racial biases in Atlanta's municipal services with some success despite being doubly disfranchised by race and gender.

Florence Kelley, whose undergraduate thesis at Cornell University examined children's changing legal status, observed the abuse of child laborers during her period of residence at Hull House from 1892–9. An active campaigner for working women's rights in Philadelphia in the 1880s, she established the New Century Working Women's Guild and joined with the Century Club and Philadelphia Working Women's Society to fight for shorter working hours for women and children. She supported women's right to work while arguing that poor working conditions harmed men, women, and children alike. Kelley served as a factory inspector for the state of Illinois and urged the state legislature to abolish child labor.

Along with settlement house residents Julia Lathrop and Lillian D. Wald, Kelley was instrumental in the establishment and operation of the Children's Bureau in 1912. Working with a small group of dedicated women, the Bureau under Lathrop's leadership investigated infant mortality, child labor, widows' pensions, and maternal and infant health. It was a strong voice for women's concerns within the federal government, although its influence waned in the 1920s. The Children's Bureau became the center of female activism in Washington, achieving an improvement in child heath standards but having less success in its effort to obtain a Constitutional amendment prohibiting children's employment. Regulation of child labor remained a state affair through the 1920s, only succumbing to federal intervention during the Great Depression. Even then, there was little effort to regulate the work children did on farms so that young rural workers, especially from racial minority groups, continued to toil in the fields once their urban counterparts had left the factories.

Mary White Ovington, head resident at New York's Greenpoint Settlement between 1895 and 1903, W. E. B. DuBois, Mary Church Terrell, and Ida B. Wells-Barnett were among the founders of the National Association for the Advancement of Colored People in 1908. Initially organized to protest a race riot in Springfield, Illinois, the NAACP drew heavily upon the talents of African-American women such as Kathryn Johnson, its first field secretary, and club women and educators Mary Talbert, Mary McLeod Bethune and Nannie Helen Burroughs. Men held most of the leadership positions, but women constituted a significant portion of the grass-roots membership, using their experiences in church and benevolent groups to raise funds and provide services.

What all these groups had in common was their effort to enlist public support on behalf of women's politicized domestic agenda.

Female guardianship of the family and public and private morality gave women reformers a platform on which to lobby for social betterment. By the early twentieth century they had established kindergartens, improved municipal health through the installation of sewers and clean water supplies, and regulated railroads, monopolies, and labor conditions. Increasingly, these activists sought the vote as a means to accomplish their aims, believing that they needed direct political input as well as influence.

CIVIC RIGHTS

The fight for women's legal rights continued after the Civil War, when differences on how to integrate emancipated slaves into civic life divided the old abolitionist–women's rights coalition. In 1866, abolitionists of both sexes founded the American Equal Rights Association (AERA) in order to remove racial and gender restrictions from state constitutions. The organization floundered as tactical debates turned into policy disputes between female suffrage advocates and those favoring enfranchisement of African-American men. Male leaders of the AERA, including Wendell Phillips and Horace Greeley, jettisoned what they perceived as the heavy baggage of women's suffrage in order to ensure the adoption of the Fourteenth Amendment which guaranteed equal protection before the law for all persons and penalized states which denied the vote to "any of the male inhabitants of such State." Together with the Fifteenth Amendment, which declared that the right of citizens to vote shall not be "denied or abridged by the United States or by any State on account of race, color, or previous condition of servitude," these two amendments introduced sex into the Constitution for the first time and were interpreted as precluding female suffrage.

Many abolitionists preferred to work with the Republican Party in order to obtain votes for freedmen, believing they would be a pro-Republican force in the South. Adding women to the ballot would (given the preponderance of white women in southern states) dilute prospects for Republican control. They felt it was "the Negro's hour" and that women's rights could wait. Sojourner Truth pointed out the fallacy of this logic in 1867. She wanted women "to have their rights," lamenting "in courts women have no right, no voice; nobody speaks for them." Civil rights for African-American men would not protect the interests of all freed people. "There is a great stir about colored men getting their rights, but not a word about the colored women; and if colored men get their rights, and not colored women theirs . . . it will be just as bad as it was before." African-American women caught "the vision of freedom" by participating in Republican party politics in the South, but suffered abuse at the hands of whites when they attempted to exercise political rights.

Women's suffrage advocates made few gains in the 1860s and 1870s despite vigorous campaigning. In 1867, Kansas put two suffrage referenda on the ballot; one proposing suffrage for African-American men and the other enfranchising all women. Once the state's Republican Party began to campaign against votes for women, suffragists in the state, and those from the Equal Rights Association crusading on their behalf, turned to the Democratic Party for assistance. This drove a wedge between proponents of African-American rights and those who gave primacy to female equality since many Democrats opposed votes for black people.

Women engaged in the post-bellum suffrage struggle emphasized natural rights as the basis for equality and participation in the public sector. Susan B. Anthony and Elizabeth Cady Stanton regarded the vote as crucial to women's advance in the world. Their preoccupation with suffrage led them to search for allies who agreed with them on this issue and to abandon those who did not. According to historian Ellen C. DuBois, Anthony's willingness to abandon the abolitionist–women's rights coalition approach of the previous two decades demonstrated her political desperation over the future of the woman suffrage movement (the term used by Anthony and her associates), not just in Kansas, but nationally.

The Republicans believed an anti-woman suffrage stance would improve the chances for universal manhood suffrage in Kansas. Newspaperman Horace Greeley spoke out against female voting, declaring that public sentiment neither demanded nor supported this "revolutionary and sweeping" innovation which involved such a radical transformation in social and domestic life. The voters concurred, but also rejected suffrage for African-American men, defeating both referenda.

The Kansas debacle severed the women's rights–abolitionist alliance. Anthony stated flatly that she would "cut off this right arm of mine before I will ever work for or demand the ballot for the Negro and not the woman." Frederick Douglass argued that voting rights for African-American men must come first in order to ensure the physical safety of his race. He drew a chilling portrait of southern freed people's lives in 1869.

When women, because they are women, are dragged from their homes and hung upon lamp-posts; when their children are torn from their arms and their brains dashed to the pavement; when they are objects of insult and outrage at every turn; when they are in danger of having their homes burnt down over their heads; when their children are not allowed to enter schools; then they will have an urgency to obtain the ballot.

A voice from the back of the audience asked if all that was not true of black women? To which Douglass replied, "Yes, yes, yes; it is true of the black woman, but not because she is a woman, but because she is black." The divisions of race, rather than the similarities of gender, held sway in Kansas.

Two separate women's rights organizations emerged from the Kansas defeat. In May 1869, Susan B. Anthony and Elizabeth Cady Stanton established the National Woman Suffrage Association (NWSA). They restricted membership to women, believing that men would dominate a mixed organization. The American Woman Suffrage Association (AWSA), launched by Lucy Stone, Henry Blackwell, and Julia Ward Howe in November 1869, thought it politically expedient to lobby first for voting rights for African-American men and to tackle women's suffrage afterwards. The American campaigned on a state by state basis, while the National favored a Constitutional amendment to overcome state voting restrictions. The two organizations remained separate and mutually antagonistic until 1890 when they merged to form the National American Woman Suffrage Association (NAWSA).

Other tensions divided the suffrage organizations; the American was more conservative, concentrating narrowly on suffrage. The National opposed the "aristocracy of sex," Stanton's description of the prevailing gender hierarchy, favored family limitation and female sexual autonomy. This stance attracted the flamboyant reformer Victoria Claflin Woodhull, whose sexual radicalism and scandalmongering found little favor with the general public. The hostility generated by Woodhull's antics, her advocacy of legalized prostitution, free love, and dress reform restricted the platform on which female activists were willing to speak or mobilize. Sexual ridicule easily tainted women challenging male authority. Woodhull's declaration, "We mean treason; we mean secession . . . We are plotting revolution; we will [overthrow] this bogus Republic, and plant a government of righteousness in its stead" unless women receive the vote, alienated the intensely patriotic members of the NWSA, leading them to stick closely to voting rights and abandon other issues, at least publicly.

The Kansas debacle notwithstanding, most initial suffrage victories came in the West. While northeastern women's rights advocates quarreled over tactics, sparsely populated Wyoming Territory in 1869 became the first state or territory to grant voting rights to women. Historians differ in their analysis of the suffrage victory in Wyoming. Some attribute it to a desire to attract women into the territory, noting that Wyoming lacked a formally organized women's movement at this time. Others put it down to the influence of a few exceptional women. Esther McQuigg Morris, Julia Bright, and other women's rights advocates lobbied their husbands and neighbors in the nascent Wyoming legislature to include suffrage in the territorial constitution. Morris subsequently became the first female justice of the peace.

Wyoming law also included women on juries from 1870 onwards and treated them as civil equals in matters of property rights and pay for teachers. Twenty years after women received the right to vote in Wyoming Territory it applied for statehood. The territorial legislature wired a Congress sceptical about its female voters (and whose Democratic members wanted to block the admission of another Republican state) "We will remain out of the Union a hundred years, but we will not come in without woman suffrage." Congress narrowly ratified its statehood.

Utah enfranchised women in 1870. This followed the precedent set by the Mormon church giving women an important public role in welfare matters. Two other factors help explain the early incorporation of female suffrage into Utah legislation. The church wished to demonstrate that polygamy did not oppress women and it wanted to bolster its position within the Utah territory as more (mostly male) gentiles settled there. Enfranchising women accomplished both objectives. Mormon women, including influential newspaper editor Emmeline Blanche Woodward Wells of the *Woman's Exponent,* were active suffrage proponents. Wells journeyed to Washington to argue

against the 1887 Edmunds–Tucker Act which banned plural marriages and withdrew suffrage from women in Utah. Women regained
the vote following Utah's admission to statehood in 1896.

While women in the west achieved suffrage victories, eastern and
midwestern women suffered several important defeats. In 1871 and
1872, Susan B. Anthony and some 150 other women tried to vote,
using an argument put forward by Victoria Woodhull that the
Fourteenth and Fifteenth Amendments granted the vote to all citizens, including women. In most cases, polling officials refused
women access to the ballot box, but Anthony and her comrades in
Rochester registered and voted. The judge denied Anthony permission to speak at her trial for "wrongful and unlawful" voting in a federal election and ordered the jury to find her guilty. Anthony never
paid the fine, but was not permitted to appeal because the state feared
the Supreme Court would overturn the verdict, given the judge's
gross violations of due process.

In 1875 Virginia Minor sued Missouri for the right to vote. The
Supreme Court ruled that women citizens did not have voting rights
unless a state specifically chose to grant them, and states could con-
stitutionally ban women from the polls. After the failure of this
approach, NWSA lobbied Congress for a suffrage amendment.
Sympathetic representatives, usually from western states, presented
the so-called Anthony amendment annually from 1878 onwards.
AWSA persevered with its state by state campaign with little success.
Between 1870 and 1890, eight states held women's suffrage referenda, and all were defeated.

Legislation removed many of women's specific legal disabilities in
the late nineteenth century, yet women made little progress on voting
rights. Married women gained ownership of their property in 33
states by 1890. They obtained legal guardianship of their children
and the right to make contracts in about half the states and sat on
juries in a few. They were entitled to keep their earnings in two-
thirds of the states, although most southern states retained restrictive
legal codes. Between 1870 and 1910, there were nearly 500 campaigns in 33 states to place women's suffrage before the voters, but
despite staggering efforts by dedicated workers, a mere 17 referenda
actually made it onto the ballot papers, and women obtained the franchise only in Colorado and Idaho.

Limited suffrage, usually on school, tax, or bond issues, achieved
a wider distribution. Twenty states permitted widows with school age

children to vote by 1890, while another three gave women the right to vote on bond issues. Partial suffrage could be a poisoned chalice because it made women subject to party discipline on all matters, including expanding the franchise, which neither national party favored. Even when women obtained partial suffrage, hostile voting officials, crowds, and unsuitable polling stations (notably saloons) deterred women from using their ballot.

The basis on which women fought for the vote changed at the turn of the century. In keeping with the growth of politicized motherhood, many suffragists emphasized women's special roles as mothers and the application of their housekeeping skills for the public good rather than women's equal rights as citizens. They shifted from arguments based upon inherent equality or equity to those based upon women's special role as mothers and their civic virtue. While proponents of women's suffrage had utilized both arguments from mid-century, by 1900 the balance had tilted towards the "difference" rather than the "sameness" side of the equation. Mass membership altered the crusade from a general campaign for women's rights to a more specific advocacy of suffrage. Moreover, suffrage was now tied to obtaining other goals. Temperance advocates, for example, supported women's suffrage so that they might vote for prohibition. It was thus seen as a means to an end, rather than a manifestation of women's equality.

Working women and reformers, high school and college-educated women had less patience with the narrow view of women as men's dependents. As Dr. Mary Putnam-Jacobi wrote in her 1894 pamphlet *"Common Sense" Applied to Woman Suffrage,* published in support of adding female suffrage to the New York State constitution, employed women needed legal protection to safeguard their working conditions. Rather than indirect representation by husbands, fathers, or brothers, they should vote directly for the officials who made and enforced such laws.

Progressive women regarded the franchise as a method of achieving reform and implementing woman-centered social policies. Jane Addams deployed maternal rhetoric even though she never married or had children. She explained her interest in politics and social reform by stating "housewifely duties logically extended to the adjacent alleys and streets." Some suffragists used the language of separate spheres to justify their participation in politics and social reform. Nebraska Populist Luna Kellie believed that "a decent mother might wish very much to vote on local affairs" such as school board elections, although she had been brought up to believe that it was "unwomanly to concern oneself with politics."

Radical critics of society, including Emma Goldman and Elizabeth Gurley Flynn, eschewed the organized women's movement and rejected the franchise as relevant only to the middle class. Viewing capitalism as the root of working-class problems, "Mother" Mary Harris Jones, who campaigned for miners' and textile workers' rights, regarded suffrage as a diversion from her primary objectives and a tool in class warfare. "The plutocrats have organized their women. They keep them busy with suffrage and prohibition and charity." Workers needed to strike directly at the bosses, not tinker around the edges of social justice.

Mother Jones notwithstanding, the plutocrat class contributed some virulent opponents of female suffrage. The early twentieth-century anti-suffrage movement consisted of many local organizations, with 25 state associations combined to form the National Association Opposed to Woman Suffrage. The Massachusetts Association Opposed to the Further Extension of Suffrage to Women (MAOFESW), the New England Anti-Suffrage League and the Illinois Association Opposed to Woman Suffrage drew their members from wives of the business elite. MAOFESW broadcast its anti-suffrage message through its journal *The Remonstrance* between 1890 and 1920, and issued numerous anti-suffrage pamphlets during and after the 1895 referendum on municipal suffrage for women in Massachusetts. Other anti-suffrage periodicals included the *Anti-Suffragist* (1908) and *Woman's Protest* (1912).

Female suffrage opponents feared that party politics would undermine women's special role as keepers of the domestic hearth. They dreaded the potential merging of male and female characteristics and the destruction of the existing social order. Roman Catholic bishops, antagonized by the nativist tone of many suffrage proponents, worried that woman suffrage would harm the family. Immigrants had ambivalent responses to suffrage. Russian Jewish immigrants overwhelmingly approved of votes for women, according to a 1915 survey conducted on New York's Lower East Side. New York State referenda on suffrage both in 1915 and 1917 attracted the support of most Jewish immigrants and some Italians, but the Irish were strongly opposed.

While newer Americans divided on suffrage, native-born white southern Democrats resolutely opposed it. Having succeeded in disfranchising African-American men through legislation and racial terrorism, white male southerners rejected any dilution of their political and economic control. They linked suffragists with the regulation of child labor, antipathy to big business, and protective labor legislation, all of which seemed antithetical to the economy and politics of the New South. They also feared that women's suffrage would alter the balance of power within the home.

Anti-suffragists pointed to the supposedly harmful legislative consequences wrought by women voting or, conversely, women voters' lack of legislative impact. Many big businesses worried that female voters would overset their accustomed way of doing things by legislating against child labor, inequality in the workplace, or alcohol. Northern and southern politicians alike feared suffrage as another weapon in the arsenal of politicized motherhood, taking seriously the suffrage movement's claims that full citizenship would enable women to defend their interests at the polls. Florence Kelley drew a close connection between suffrage and the battle to end child labor by noting that "until the mothers in the great industrial States are enfranchised" the nation would not be free of the sweating system that had children "carrying bundles of garments from the factories to the tenements, little beasts of burden, robbed of school life that they might work."

Jane Addams advanced a similar line of reasoning by noting that a woman's simplest duty was "to keep her house clean and wholesome and to feed her children properly" which she could not do if local politicians did not regulate housing and sanitary conditions. Suffrage would enable women to implement their maternal goals but anti-suffragists rejected politicized motherhood. As former President Grover Cleveland described it, "the refining, elevating influence of woman, especially in her allotted sphere of home and in her character of wife and mother, supplements man's strenuous struggles in social and political warfare." To give women the vote would embroil women in public battles (in which many women already involved themselves) and it would also "give to the wives and daughters of the poor a new opportunity to gratify their envy and mistrust of the rich."

Grover Cleveland notwithstanding, not all poorer women favored suffrage; some female trade unionists believed enfranchisement might curtail protective legislation. Nevertheless many working women supported suffrage because as wage earners they believed they had a legitimate place in the public sphere. During the

California suffrage campaign of 1896, working women raised funds and stuffed envelopes to help the cause. Commissioner of Labor Carroll D. Wright made explicit the connection between women's poor economic circumstances and their exclusion from the political process. "The lack of direct political influence constitutes a powerful reason why women's wages have been kept at a minimum." Mary Duffy of the Overall Makers' Union told New York legislators "we need every help to fight the battle of life, and to be left out by the State just sets up a prejudice against us." Voting would help achieve industrial democracy.

The women's suffrage campaign accelerated after the turn of the century. The unification of the two suffrage associations into the National American Woman Suffrage Association in 1890, the passing of the old guard, and the election of a new president of the National American Woman Suffrage Association shifted attention from the state by state approach back to a federal woman suffrage amendment. Women built coalitions between organizations so that each group could support suffrage for its own reasons. This helped to overcome the nativism and racism epitomized by Laura Clay in Kentucky and Carrie Chapman Catt of NAWSA. Catt had argued that giving immigrant and African-American men the vote but denying it to genteel white women made them into "subjects." NAWSA never supported whites' only suffrage, but feared losing white southern women's support more than alienating African Americans. As a result, according to historian Mary Martha Thomas, white women tended to support limited educated suffrage while African Americans supported universal suffrage.

The South lagged behind on voting rights for women. The connection with abolitionism and the threat to the prevailing race–gender hierarchy tainted suffrage to southern whites. As the white South reconstructed itself after the Civil War, white men defined masculinity as male authority over women, not only supporting separate spheres, but arranging them hierarchically so that the world of male politics dominated the female world of the home. Neither the planter elite nor the manufacturing interests of the New South favored women's suffrage, fearing regulation of wages, child labor, and working conditions.

Women's suffrage campaigns made a bit of headway in the South after 1900, although the "southern strategy" overtly pandered to racism. Some suffrage advocates believed that enfranchising women would consolidate white supremacy by restricting the extended franchise to educated, white women. Laura Clay argued that woman suffrage could "neutralize all the alarming elements of the race question" by enfranchising all literate women. This would bring a preponderance of white women to the polls, while African-American women, with their lower literacy levels, would benefit in small numbers. The southern strategy drew strength from a growing national acceptance of racial difference. Henry Blackwell, a former abolitionist, authored a pamphlet in 1895 entitled "A Solution of the Southern Problem" which endorsed educational qualifications for voting. This tactic played upon the widespread fear of ignorant and presumably easily manipulated voters, whether female, working class, immigrant, or African American.

At Clay's behest, NAWSA established a Southern Committee in 1892, a move which attracted support from elite white community activists who also worked for prohibition, the WCTU, the Confederate Memorial Association, and various charities. Most had been active in reform and charity organizations as well as their churches and the WCTU. They distanced themselves from African-American women both in organizational terms and in their disdain for African-American legal rights.

African-American women criticized the hostility of white suffrage advocates, North and South, to extending voting rights to them as well as their willingness to countenance racial discrimination in all its manifold forms. While the National Association of Colored Women and other African-American women's organizations endorsed women's suffrage, they encountered indifference or opposition from many white suffrage advocates. Mary Church Terrell, head of the NACW, and Walter White of the NAACP agreed that if white women "could get the Suffrage Amendment through without enfranchising colored women, they would do it in a moment."

A NAWSA executive confirmed this view in 1919, declaring that if NAWSA accepted the membership of the African-American Northeastern Federation of Women's Clubs "the enemies can cease from further effort – the defeat of the amendment will be assured." White suffragists showed their racism by trying to segregate black suffragists at the back of the 1913 suffrage parade in Washington, DC Ida Wells-Barnett refused to be segregated and joined the Illinois delegation as it strode down Pennsylvania Avenue.

There were some notable exceptions to the exclusion of black women from the suffrage crusade. The New York Woman's Suffrage Party elected African-American suffragist Annie K. Lewis as its vice-chairman in 1917. Other northeastern and midwestern states, including Massachusetts and Illinois, also had vigorous black women's suffrage clubs and some integrated organizations. Wells-Barnett herself fought for both racial justice and women's suffrage, founding the Alpha Suffrage Club in 1913.

While suffrage activists succeeded in five states between 1900 and 1913, the new generation of leaders deplored the rut in which the movement seemed stuck. Inspired by the militancy of British suffrage advocates, Elizabeth Cady Stanton's daughter Harriot Stanton Blatch emulated their publicity-garnering tactics. No longer content to speak only to friends in their drawing rooms, and rejecting the slow drip, drip of education efforts, Blatch organized parades, secured the cooperation of labor unions, and recruited well-known progressive and union reformers.

The Congressional Union, founded in 1913 by Alice Paul and Lucy Burns (renamed the National Woman's Party in 1916), adopted British suffragists' single-minded devotion to the cause. Its younger, militant cross-class membership courted controversy. The first NWP parade turned into a shoving match as hostile crowds blocked the suffragists' path. Despite a parade permit they received little police protection, which outraged public opinion and secured publicity for the cause. Paul and her followers held the party in power responsible for suffrage and worked to defeat Democratic candidates in states where women had the vote, tactics that alienated the more conservative NAWSA but made suffrage front page news.

NAWSA welcomed the decision of the General Federation of Women's Clubs to support women's suffrage in 1914. In 1915, Carrie Chapman Catt declared her "winning plan," to work wholeheartedly to amend the Constitution and waste no more time on statewide campaigns. Following America's entry into World War I, Catt presented woman suffrage as a war measure that would ensure women's cooperation. President Wilson, a late convert to the cause, agreed, declaring that it was "vital to the winning of the war." Certainly women's expanded range of economic activity during the war made such cooperation seem essential.

Despite Catt's use of the war as a means of justifying female suffrage, American women reformers were not united in its support. When war broke out in Europe, Charlotte Perkins Gilman and some

1500 other women marched down New York's Fifth Avenue urging peace. One year later, Jane Addams, Carrie Chapman Catt, and other women peace advocates formed the Women's Peace Party, which had about 3000 members. The International Congress of Women met at the Hague, with Addams proclaiming that it was "fitting that women should meet and take counsel" to bring about peace. Catt downplayed her own pacifist sentiments in order not to alienate public opinion and key political officials. Radicals Elizabeth Gurley Flynn and Emma Goldman sought to keep America outside the war, while Alice Paul and her supporters picketed the White House with signs asking President Wilson what he would do for women's suffrage and questioning how long women would have to wait for liberty. Goldman received five years in prison for her opposition to the draft while Paul and other members of the NWP were given short sentences for obstructing the sidewalk. Their arrest and subsequent forced feeding prompted a surge of sympathy for suffragism.

Catt and other moderate female political activists presented themselves to wartime government as ready, willing, and able to participate in the fight on all fronts. At the same time, NAWSA continued to pressure the President and Congress to pass a woman suffrage amendment. New York and Illinois enacted suffrage laws in 1917 as did South Dakota, Michigan, and Oklahoma in 1918. Women worked actively for the defeat of anti-suffrage senators, ensuring a more receptive climate at the federal level. The growing number of states where women could already vote helped persuade Congress to amend the Constitution in 1919.

The subsequent battle for ratification by state legislatures was hard fought, but NAWSA had its battle plan ready. They sent telegrams to state governors to convene special sessions of those legislatures which were not sitting or to submit the amendment urgently to those which were about to go into recess. By getting the more sympathetic western states to vote quickly, NAWSA activists generated a bandwagon effect which encouraged other states to take favorable action. Opponents of women's suffrage tried to force statewide referenda on the issue, but the Supreme Court rejected this challenge.

When women finally got the vote in 1920, they did so more as a measure of gratitude for their participation in the war effort than as a matter of social justice. Nevertheless, the incremental changes over the previous 50 years finally made it possible to accept women's place in the polity, as citizens with voting rights. Female suffrage thus recognized women's special contributions as well as their equality before the law. African-American social welfare reformer Fannie Barrier Williams favored women's suffrage as a test of "our womanly worth," believing that women had a special responsibility to create a better world. Many women of all races and ethnic groups worked toward this goal through a variety of organizations. They believed the vote was an important tool for creating a better world, but so were the voluntary organizations in which many of them had worked for the public good.

Whether suffrage enabled women to achieve their social and political agenda in the decades between World War I and World War II is open to question. Incorporation into the major political parties co-opted women and subjected them to party discipline over a wide range of issues. In the decades between the Civil War and the suffrage amendment, women had been outside the mainstream of American party politics but had nevertheless managed to imbue politics with their concerns for the less fortunate, for their families, and for social welfare. The maternalist political agenda bore fruit in the form of numerous charities, the Children's Bureau, and myriad city, state, and federal laws designed to protect women and children. Yet suffrage was not a panacea; many women, especially African Americans, remained effectively disfranchised for decades to come and only with the resurgence of feminism in the mid-twentieth century did women once more become a political force.

PART III
From the Vote to World War II

9 Economic Activity during Boom, Bust, and War

Between 1920 and 1945, the economy of the United States endured major upheavals in adjusting to peacetime prosperity, cataclysmic depression, and war mobilization. Social acceptance of female economic activity fluctuated with the business cycle, yet a growing number of women worked regardless of hostile public opinion because they or their families needed the money. Wartime labor demands ended the Great Depression, opened new types of employment to women, and encouraged more married and older women to enter the labor market. Female labor force participation levels declined after World War II, but they were still higher than before the war, social pressure to stay at home notwithstanding. As the productive value of women's labor within the home declined, family sizes shrank, and Americans placed a higher value on education and consumption, more women went out to work. Race, ethnicity, age, and marital status continued to have an impact on the proportion of each group holding jobs outside the home and the type of work they did. There was some convergence in employment levels between groups of women and many fewer women undertook remunerated work within the home (taking in boarders or doing industrial homework), so that the household became a more purely domestic place for women, a point which will be explored further in the next chapter.

THE DIFFERENTIAL LABOR MARKET

The female labor force remained complex and fragmented, with more white women working at the same time that African-American women's levels of economic activity declined. Twice as many married white women worked in 1940 as in 1920, while married black women's employment levels declined by 16 percent. This decline probably stemmed from the movement of African-American families to cities where men had an opportunity to earn a regular cash income, something few sharecroppers had been able to do. In contrast, sociologists Robert and Helen Merrell Lynd reported in 1925 that the habit of (white) married women's working spread; they exhibited growing economic independence by staying in the labor force after marriage. Despite public hostility to married women's employment which surfaced during the Depression, the uncertain economic climate prompted women to hold onto jobs "just in case" or seek paid work when other family members became unemployed.

Women's role within the family economy altered in this era: more took jobs outside the home and replaced children under the age of eighteen as ancillary breadwinners in white families. Their expanded presence in the labor market resulted from several long-term trends including higher educational levels, smaller families, and altered expectations. Mothers worked to pay for their children's education and help buy the consumer items inter-war families demanded. They

Table 9.1   Gainfully employed women by race, nativity, and marital status for women aged 15 and over

	1920 (%)	1930 (%)	1940 (%)
All Women	23.7	24.8	25.8
Single	46.4*	50.5	45.5
Married	9.0	11.7	13.8
White Women	21.6	23.7	24.5
Single	45.0*	48.7	45.9
Married	6.5	9.8	12.5
Non-white Women	43.1	43.3	37.6
Single	58.8*	52.1	41.9
Married	32.5	33.2	27.3

* Includes widowed and divorced women, and thus understates the proportion of never-married women in the labor force.

Sources: US Department of Commerce, Bureau of the Census, Fourteenth Census of the US: 1920, Vol. IV, *Occupations* (Washington DC, Government Printing Office, 1923).

US Department of Commerce, Bureau of the Census, Fifteenth Census of the US: 1930, *Occupational Statistics* (Washington DC, Government Printing Office, 1932).

US Department of Commerce, Bureau of the Census, Sixteenth Census of the US: 1940, Population Vol. III *The Labor Force*, Part I (Washington DC, Government Printing Office, 1943).

US Department of Commerce, Bureau of the Census, US Census of Population, 1950, Vol. IV, *Special Reports,* Part I (Washington DC, Government Printing Office, 1953).

also stayed at work in order to use their education and because there was less house- and childcare once their (fewer) children started school. The proportion of young workers decreased as 15 and 16 year olds stayed in school, especially during the Great Depression when there were few jobs for teenagers, and education through high school became a necessary credential for employment.

Increasingly, married women, especially immigrants, substituted wage labor for taking in boarders. Greater affluence resulted in fewer people willing or needing to share a room in someone else's home. As Dorta explained to a young Slovak widow in *Out of this Furnace*, Thomas Bell's realistic 1941 novel about immigrant steel workers in Western Pennsylvania, "keeping boarders isn't what it was when you came to America. Then they were coming by the boatload, you could put six in a room, feed them pork chops and *halushki*, and make a little money." World War I and immigration restrictions dried up the supply of potential lodgers and the remaining few wanted "carpets and lace curtains in their rooms, a different dish at every meal, and God knows what else." The shift to employment outside the home attests to the changes in women's economic activity and the near demise of earning through household endeavors.

Additionally, the proportion of employed women reflected their higher level of economic activity before marriage. Claudia Goldin's cohort analysis of women workers shows that the inter-war generation of women had higher levels of employment when single and continued to be well represented among the ranks of the employed, especially as young married women. Better educated women wanted to stay in the labor market to utilize their hard-won credentials, which also contributed to higher levels of married and older women working.

FEMALE OCCUPATIONS IN THE 1920s AND 1930s

Women's employment expanded most strongly in the clerical and professional sectors of the economy with the proportion of female workers in industry fluctuating as other jobs opened and industrial production waned and waxed. White women consolidated their hold on white-collar occupations but had a sizeable presence in textiles, clothing manufacture, and food processing, with small inroads on the fringes of heavy industry including sewing seat covers and other "nimble-fingered" tasks in car and truck factories. Women's wages improved but nevertheless lagged behind men's; for example, female auto workers earned much less than their male counterparts despite the unskilled nature of some men's work and the more intricate tasks performed by women. Women who worked at home or in small tenement factories still labored long hours for low pay notwithstanding protective legislation designed to curtail such practices because many employers ignored the law. States required employers to keep registers of homeworkers, but few did. Factory owners evaded labor laws in large ways and small: one Greensboro, North Carolina, rayon worker wrote to Secretary of Labor Frances Perkins protesting that "women on standing jobs have no rest stools," even though North Carolina law mandated them.

The exclusion of some key industries, domestic service, and agriculture also reduced the effectiveness of protective legislation. Maryland laws limited female operatives to a ten hour day and six day week, but exempted the economically powerful canning industry which employed thousands of women in the processing and packing sheds. In practice, the hours worked by the sexes differed little because employers cut men's hours when legislation controlled women's. Protective legislation kept women out of certain industrial occupations and higher paying jobs, while gendering rights of contract and remedies for poor employment practices.

In 1920, 39 percent of all employed women held professional, managerial, clerical, and sales positions, rising to 45 percent in 1940. Women college graduates expanded their range of occupations to include personnel management and business careers. Women also made some progress in gaining significant government posts during Franklin D. Roosevelt's presidency, including Frances Perkins, the first woman to attain Cabinet rank, as Secretary of Labor.

Yet women and men still occupied distinct niches in the white-collar world. Women taught in elementary schools while men dominated high school and college teaching; women were nurses and men were doctors. The proportion of clerical workers rose for both sexes, doubling for men (from 3 to 6 percent between 1900 and 1940), but quintupling for women (from 4 to 21.5 percent). By the end of the Great Depression women vastly outnumbered men in this sector, comprising 54 percent of all clerical and kindred workers. White-collar work itself altered as the proliferation of business correspondence resulted in new ways of handling paperwork and certain functions

Table 9.2   Occupational distribution of women workers, 1920–40

	1920 (%)	(%)	1930 (%)	(%)	1940 (%)	(%)
White Collar	38.8		44.2		44.9	
Prof.Man.		13.8		16.5		16.1
Clerical		18.7		20.9		21.5
Sales		6.3		6.8		7.3
Manual and Serv.	47.7		47.3		51.1	
Operatives		23.9		19.8		21.5
Domestic Serv		15.8		17.8		18.1
Other Service		8.1		9.7		11.3
Agricultural		13.5		8.4		4.0

Source: US Department of Commerce, Bureau of the Census, *Historical Statistics of the United States from Colonial Times to 1957* (Washington, DC, Government Printing Office, 1960), 74.

became mechanized. By 1920, clerical work had been transformed from a stepping stone to management to dead-end female employment in stenography, typing, and filing. Men dominated senior office positions or those requiring physical labor, while women increasingly filled repetitious, routine, or junior slots in the office hierarchy.

Even the position of secretary, previously a way to learn the business and advance through it, evolved into the position of "office wife," emulating the service and caring functions of the "home wife." Contemporary movies, *His Secretary* (1925) and *The Office Wife* (1930), emphasized the decorative and romantic side of women's office work once private secretary had become the top female business position rather than a springboard to management. For the declining number of men who undertook clerical work, the office hierarchy remained open at the top with a number climbing from clerical to managerial positions.

Large companies recruited both sexes into entry level positions but routed them quite differently in their induction procedures, training women destined for clerical positions in how to dress, good manners, and personal hygiene. Men, intended for promotion through the ranks, were taught the nature of the business, the firm's ethos and corporate strategy. Thus new employees might start in similar positions, but firms promoted men and held women back, and even where the sexes performed the same or similar jobs women received lower wages.

The gentility of department store work and the possibility of some upward mobility within the store hierarchy made this work especially desirable. Popular fiction depicted sales work as glamorous and appropriate for married women. Women clerks in department stores enjoyed prestige, but not necessarily large salaries. The sexes rarely sold the same goods in large stores, with men being more likely to sell "big ticket" items on a salary plus commission basis. Some department stores provided opportunities for advancement for their female workers within the segregated departments, and a small number moved up the store hierarchy from the sales floor into managerial and executive positions including those of buyer, floorwalker, personal shopper, and stock controller. A few even made it to the top ranks of the department store hierarchy; when Dorothy Shaver was appointed president of Lord & Taylor's in 1945 she became one of the highest paid women of her day and a notable exception to female exclusion from executive positions.

RACIAL AND ETHNIC EMPLOYMENT

Access to white-collar jobs was restricted on a racial, and to a lesser extent, ethnic basis. While ethnic bias lessened as newer immigrant groups assimilated into the fabric of American life, racial discrimination persisted throughout the inter-war years and beyond. A snapshot of employment by racial group for 1930 indicates the extreme variation in occupations, with women of color having higher levels of agricultural and service employment and European-American women dominating clerical and professional jobs. Over one-half of all gainfully employed white women in 1930 wore white blouses to work, compared with about 6 percent of nonwhites.

African-American women had the most skewed employment profile of all women of color. Urbanization led to more domestic and fewer farm jobs, but these two occupations still accounted for 85 percent of their employment in 1930. Some gains had been made during World War I in manufacturing employment, but "strong prejudice" subsequently prevented African-American women from gaining "more skilled and better paid kinds of work, which was reserved for white women," according to the Department of Labor. Many women of color employed in manufacturing either had janitorial positions or did the hardest, heaviest work and received the lowest wages. Black

Table 9.3   Women's employment by race and occupation, 1930

Occupational Group	White (%)	African American (%)	Native American (%)	Mexican (%)	Chinese (%)	Japanese (%)
White Collar	52.4	5.9	10.8	17.3	55.7	24.9
Prof.Man.	19.2	4.6	5.8	6.8	32.0	13.6
Clerical	25.1	0.6	3.3	2.8	11.7	3.7
Sales	8.1	0.6	1.7	7.7	12.0	7.6
Manual & Serv	43.0	69.4	63.0	61.6	41.7	52.2
Operatives	22.7	8.4	37.6	24.7	20.8	12.2
Domestic & personal serv	12.2	61.0	25.4	36.9	20.9	40.0
Agricultural	4.6	24.7	26.1	21.2	2.5	22.9

Totals do not always add to 100 due to rounding.

Source: as for Table 9.1.

stemmers in the North Carolina cigarette factories, for example, earned about half the wages paid to white women. Few African-American women obtained white-collar jobs, either in the rural South or the urban North. About 5 percent were teachers or nurses, and some truly exceptional women ran stores, as did Maya Angelou's grandmother in Stamps, Arkansas, or had office jobs.

Asian women had low overall levels of labor force participation, but were distributed more evenly across the occupational spectrum than blacks in 1930. They advanced in professional and managerial employment, yet the Japanese still had a significant presence in the fields and kitchens. The Census counted relatively few Native American women as gainfully employed since so many lived on reservations or subsistence holdings. Those in the labor market clustered in handicrafts, agriculture, and domestic service. Many Mexican women had factory jobs or were domestic servants, although a sizeable number worked in the increasingly commercialized agriculture of the Southwest.

The labor force participation of non-white women (98 percent of whom were African American in 1920) decreased in the inter-war years with the drop being particularly acute among single women. In 1920 about three-fifths of all single non-white women had jobs; by 1940 this declined to about two-fifths. The shift from rural South to urban North had a profound impact on African-American women's employment patterns. Urbanization enabled them to substitute school for field work in the 1920s, accounting for some of the decline in economic activity, especially for 10–15 year olds who were no longer "working out" by the age of 10, as southern black girls had done routinely at the turn of the century. Married women also withdrew from the labor force, the proportion falling from 33 percent in 1920 and 1930 to 27 percent by 1940. Cash incomes in the North permitted some African-American women to stay out of the labor force, although the difficulty they had in finding work during the Depression could also explain some of this decline.

Racial discrimination remained rife in all sectors of the economy. Working conditions for agricultural workers deteriorated, even before the Depression, especially for women of color, as the boll weevil and rising international competition undermined domestic cotton production. Discriminatory employers paid lower wages per hour to Mexican- and African-American women, both in domestic service and in agriculture. Hispanic women workers in California's walnut groves in the 1920s earned less per hour than white workers, as did black women in the pecan industry. Although women of color routinely received lower pay, employers nevertheless fired them during the Depression when white women felt compelled to work for any wages they could get and took service jobs which they previously avoided.

LABOR UNIONS AND WOMEN

The attitudes of union leaders in the 1920s scarcely reflected the changed nature of the female labor force. Despite the rising proportion of married women in the labor force union bosses still regarded women as a temporary labor force that took jobs away from "real" workers, that is, men. Women's increased commitment to employment throughout their lives should have made them more valuable union members, yet union organizers were slow to recognize their expanded constituency, partly because their main strength still came from skilled workers who regarded women as competitors for their jobs.

The American Federation of Labor (AFL) did little to encourage female participation in this era. Its executive council had no female delegates, even though women comprised a significant proportion of the membership in a few large unions, including the International

Ladies' Garment Workers' Union. Some AFL branches, such as the International Molders' Union, overtly excluded women and expelled members who taught women their trade. The Women's Trade Union League (WTUL) continued to lobby on behalf of women workers. It had close links with the Women's Bureau whose first head, Mary Anderson, had been a WTUL organizer and vigorously defended women's right to work at the jobs of their choice.

There were a number of gendered barriers to effective organizing in the increasingly industrialized South. Efforts to unionize garment and textile workers there depended upon women's cooperation, but the social structure of southern textile mill communities strongly resisted female labor organization. Indeed some southern mill village churches actually banned female union members in the 1920s. The complete dependence of mill families upon the local textile factory also impeded unionization. Unlike northern cities where family members might work in different industries or establishments, mill families tended to have jobs in the same factory, thus a strike deprived the family of its entire income.

Women in southern mills contributed about 30–40 percent of the household income. As working conditions deteriorated in the 1920s with the introduction of new machinery and higher production quotas, workers became more militant. A wave of strikes began in 1929 when the women at a rayon spinning plant in East Tennessee walked off the job. The largely male leadership of the United Textile Workers framed their strike demands in the 1920s and 1930s in terms of the family wage, wanting men to be paid wages sufficient to support a family, although they also favored equal pay for women and children. Union organizer Ella May Wiggins wrote "Mill Mother's Lament" before she was murdered by armed thugs in Bessemer City, North Carolina in 1929.

> How it grieves the heart of a mother,
> You every one must know,
> But we can't buy for our children,
> Our wages are too low.
> . . .
> But understand, all workers,
> Our union they do fear,
> Let's stand together, workers,
> And have a union here.

Mothers worked for the same reason as fathers: to earn sufficient wages to support their families. They wanted a union for the same reasons, too: to raise wages and improve working conditions. Employer resistance and terrorism brought the strike wave to an end, but racial and gender divisions within the labor force also undermined the effectiveness of the southern labor movement.

While male union officials paid little attention to the plight of women workers, many white workers also ignored the plight of African-American and Mexican women who worked long hours for low wages. Employer manipulation of racial and gender divisions discouraged interracial cooperation. A Durham, North Carolina, tobacco worker recalled the invidious nature of racial prejudice: "You're over here doing all the nasty dirty work . . . The white women over there wear white uniforms . . . And you're over here handling all that old sweaty tobacco." Under such circumstances it was difficult for workers to join together in common cause.

Organized labor had little interest in the predicament of workers outside conventional union settings. Few black women who sewed for a living worked in factories, and most of the washerwomen worked for private customers rather than commercial laundries. African-American activist Mary Church Terrell tried to convince the Women's Bureau to set up a Colored Women's Division in the early 1920s, only to be told by the director Mary Anderson that "colored women" were not a large factor in industry. Given such neglect, it is not surprising that when women of color tried to establish domestic workers' unions to fight for higher wages and better working conditions their unions were short lived, even though they achieved some successful strikes.

Belatedly in the late 1920s the International Ladies' Garment Workers' Union made some efforts to recruit African-American sewing machine operators. Other women of color, including the cannery workers of California and the cigar workers of Texas, organized in the 1920s and early 1930s. The United Cannery, Agricultural, Packing, and Allied Workers of America had strong female leaders in the late 1930s, including Luisa Moreno, who fought hard to get equal pay for equal work clauses inserted in their contracts. Other interracial union organizing took place in the pecan factories of St. Louis where black and white women struck successfully against low wages and racially based wage differentials. The company had high profits even during the Depression and could well afford to raise the rates paid. The strike resulted in the tripling of take-home pay to some middle-aged black women and inspired labor activism among other multiracial labor forces. Interracial cooperation also resulted in the unionization of commercial laundries as the Congress of Industrial Organizations enrolled thousands of women into the United Laundry Workers during the 1930s. Unions were slow to link the personal with the political and few transcended the racial and gendered prejudices which gave primacy to men in the work place. Yet women such as Ella May Wiggins and those who walked the picket lines were keenly aware that until those connections were made, the union movement would not serve women's interests.

THE GREAT DEPRESSION

The Great Depression dented employment prospects for women of all classes and races at the same time that popular culture inveighed against female employment outside the home and women sought work to keep themselves and their families in basic necessities. Unemployment levels for men were, by and large, higher than women's since the Depression initially hit hardest at heavy industry (a male preserve). The 1930 Census showed that 4.7 percent of female and 7.1 percent of male wage earners had been unemployed in the preceding year. Joblessness rose among women in the early thirties, reaching 20 percent in 1931, but still tended to be lower than men's. By 1937, about two-thirds of the women out of work came from the ranks of clerical workers, factory operatives, and domestic servants, but teachers and businesswomen also faced uncertain prospects.

Widespread unemployment had relatively little impact on racial and gender stratification in the labor market. The sexes existed in largely separate labor markets which the Depression did little to undermine. Moreover, the actual number of women in the labor market continued to rise despite magazine articles declaring "You Can Have My Job: A Feminist Discovers Her Home" and similar suggestions from some educators, politicians, and cultural commentators that women should not be economically active. Most employers did not substitute cheaper female employees for more expensive male ones, rather they laid off male workers until demand picked up. Nor did they necessarily substitute lower waged non-white employees for higher paid white women. In racially complex cities, employers laid off white women but rarely replaced them with African or Mexican Americans whom they deemed inappropriate for office and factory jobs. Some white women "traded down," taking jobs as domestics when they could not get manufacturing jobs, temporarily reversing the white exodus from the nation's kitchens, and making it more difficult for women of color to get work.

The proportion of unemployed women varied between racial groups and sections of the country. A 1931 study of urban areas indicated that African-American women had unemployment levels two to four times greater than white women, with much greater variations between women of different racial groups than for men. Women in service occupations particularly suffered as affluent women stretched their household budgets by either reducing servants' wages or firing them. The Kentucky Department of Labor discovered in 1933 that over half of all domestic workers in Louisville lost their jobs as a result of the Depression and the rest suffered wage cuts.

The abundance of labor drove wages down for women in other occupations as well. Mexican pecan shellers in Texas who made $6 or $7 a week in the 1920s, earned only $2 or $3 during the 1930s. This work had previously supplemented agricultural jobs, but as these disappeared, it provided women and families with their only income. Rural women pickled and preserved, stripped tobacco, and picked cotton for pay or for their own families. Many urban women spent their days waiting for jobs, according to Meridel LeSueur's account of female unemployment, "Women on the Breadlines," in 1932. They sat for hours in the employment bureau "waiting for a job. There are no jobs."

Female factory operatives suffered displacement and short-time working as industrial production declined. Women at the bottom of the occupational hierarchy might find themselves displaced by those only one or two rungs above them. Employers speeded up machinery and forced workers to work faster for the same or less money. Many textile factories let their workers go or employed them for only part of the week, a pattern replicated in the canning, meatpacking, and candy industries throughout the nation. Mills in Fall River and Amoskeag produced only a fraction of the cloth they had made earlier. They cut women's wages by one-quarter in 1931, and the great Amoskeag mills closed entirely in 1936, leaving a generation of mill workers stranded.

There was fierce competition for the few jobs that did exist. The female textile workers of Amoskeag took jobs in shoe factories or as domestic servants. Maids in New York City waited on street corners hoping that a potential employer would come by to give them a day's work, while others traveled great distances in search of a job. In this economic climate, resentments against women's employment grew. More specifically, the myth that married or even single women worked for "pin money" delegitimized women's quest for employment. Cartoons in labor newspapers depicted strong men in overalls sheltering their wives who wore aprons and frequently had one child in their arms and several more hanging on their skirts. The inference was clear: the good union man provided for the family while his wife looked after it.

At the same time that more married women desperately searched for jobs they encountered widespread disapproval. Less than one-fifth of respondents to a 1936 Gallup poll approved of married women working full time. Popular commentator Norman Cousins articulated the attack on female employment, making little distinction between married or single women workers. He thundered that there were "10 000 000 out of work in the United States . . . and there are also 10 000 000 or more women, married and single, who are job-holders. Simply fire the women, who shouldn't be working anyway, and hire the men." Then "Presto! No unemployment. No relief rolls. No depression." Such solutions ignored the different types of work done by the sexes and the jobs available, but also stirred resentment against women as workers.

Local, state, and national governments all legislated against married women's employment. A number of cities and states attempted to dismiss either all married women or those with employed husbands. The 1932 National Economy Act restricted federal jobs to one per family. Passed over the opposition of the National Woman's Party and business and professional women's clubs, this act established a precedent for depriving married women of government employment. Given women's lower wages, families sought to maximize their income while complying with the act by withdrawing women from federal jobs. Families sometimes had no choice about who worked; managers simply fired their married female staff. Married women in local government also fared badly. Over three-quarters of the nation's schools would not hire married women as teachers and half fired women when they married.

The widespread segregation of the labor market and the very small overlap between male and female occupations meant that dismissing married women would not provide jobs for men. It might, however, provide employment for single women, and in the cutthroat economic climate of the Great Depression single women severely criticized their married sisters' presence in the labor force, even picketing with signs demanding "Fire Married Women: Hire Needy Single Women." Single women in the automobile industry resented married sisters with seniority who kept their jobs while unattached women lost theirs. United Auto Workers' officials supported seniority rights, but colluded with laying off married women by subscribing to the principle of local autonomy. Adherence to the family wage ideology subverted their commitment to job protection based on length of service. Rather than defend married women's right to work, unions such as the Brotherhood of Railway and Steamship Clerks (whose jobs could easily be done by either sex) proclaimed that married women with able-bodied husbands should not work outside the home.

WOMEN AND NEW DEAL WORK PROGRAMS

Women benefited from federal employment, relief programs, and welfare programs, both as their subjects and their administrators, but New Deal programs concentrated primarily upon men rather than women. Most programs were designed with men in mind; women received secondary consideration and less imaginative treatment. As a resolution sent to Frances Perkins commented, women were "thrown out of jobs as married women, refused relief as single women, discriminated against by the N.R.A. [National Recovery Administration] and ignored by the C.W.A. [Civil Works Administration]." New Deal program administrators assumed that the family wage was the natural state of family finances, that men should support their families, and that women and children should be economically dependent upon them. While many if not most Americans believed that men should be the main breadwinners, the rise in married women's labor force participation during the 1920s indicated that a growing number valued women's employment outside the home. The New Deal, by harking back to an earlier era, negated that choice and privileged men in the work place.

Early job creation schemes overlooked women's economic activity. The Public Works Administration (PWA) spent $3.3 billion in 1933 building schools, roads, hospitals, dams, bridges, courthouses, and other public buildings, employing thousands of carpenters, plumbers, construction workers, and architects, but few stenographers, typists, or domestic servants. Similarly the Federal Emergency Relief Administration (FERA), which dispensed money from Washington for projects run by state and local governments at the start of the New Deal, gave reasonably paid employment to men on construction projects but made small relief payments to women.

Many New Deal programs overlooked the discrepancy between female need and available assistance. Women accounted for only 7 percent of CWA workers nationwide and in some cities virtually no CWA jobs went to women. A network of female reformers, including Eleanor Roosevelt, the President's wife, had some small success in obtaining public work relief for women in the CWA in 1933–4, but the most popular employment program ignored women altogether. The Civilian Conservation Corps (CCC) provided rural jobs for young men from 1933 onwards, feeding, housing, and paying them while they worked upon rural conservation and restoration projects. Unemployment camp administrator Hilda W. Smith argued for the "she–she–she" to match the CCC and eventually about 8000 women attended CCC-style camps, but they received little education and lower wages than men, and the program was abandoned in 1937 when Congress cut its appropriation.

New Deal employment and relief programs maintained the gendered wage differentials common in private industry before the Depression. The 12 percent of FERA workers who were women received lower wages than men. Most women worked on educational programs and those designed for people receiving relief, remunerated at the lowest level of all FERA jobs, 30 cents an hour, compared with 40 cents an hour for unskilled construction workers and $1.00 an hour for skilled workmen. Women disproportionately found themselves getting FERA relief handouts rather than jobs.

The wage differentials regularized by the FERA for work relief had their counterpart in the National Industrial Recovery Act codes which were supposed to ensure a fair deal for workers by regulating wages and hours. Codes covering industrial establishments set minimum wages and maximum hours for thousands of job categories. Although historian Susan Ware concludes that women "stood to gain more from minimum wage standards" since they had lower wages, many employers institutionalized wage differentials by allocating women and men to distinct job classifications. The NRA accepted that workers paid less than the NRA minimum in July 1929 (predominantly women) could still receive wages below the supposed minimum. NRA wage codes omitted domestic servants, farm laborers and "employees engaged in light and repetitive work," a euphemism for female workers, mostly in the textile industry. Underpaid workers continued to earn a pittance and women doing work similar to men received lower wages. "Jacket, Coat, Reefer and Dress Operators, Male" had an agreed wage of $1.00 an hour while "Jacket, Coat, Reefer and Dress Operators, Female" earned 90 cents. While this conformed to "long-established customs," it placed the federal stamp of approval in the form of the NRA Blue Eagle on wage discrimination.

In keeping with progressive reform opposition to the combination of domestic and industrial work, many NRA codes curtailed or banned industrial homework in the belief that it undermined sound labor standards. Female reformers from the National Consumers' League, the Women's Trade Union League, and the Democratic Party joined social workers and government officials in an effort to regulate out of existence practices they viewed as detrimental to family life and industrial recovery. In doing so, they further gendered the recovery by eliminating one way women combined employment with looking after their homes and families. Poorly paid piece workers, many of them mothers with family care responsibilities, undercut factory workers and drove down wages. The outcry from women who worked at home making "a few dollars a week to keep a home together" for their children who would otherwise be placed in an orphanage, according to one outraged homeworker, led President Roosevelt to issue an executive order permitting the elderly, ill, and disabled and those who cared for them to continue doing hand work at home.

American women did not passively accept their relegation to the economic sidelines by either the Great Depression or the New Deal. The National Woman's Party, National Federation of Business and Professional Women's Clubs and League of Women Voters remonstrated over the wage differentials with NRA administrator Hugh Johnson and the Labor Advisory Board, but to little avail. In late 1933 and 1934, women's groups pressured the administration to improve female employment prospects in New Deal programs.

Eleanor Roosevelt's White House Conference on the Emergency Needs of Women focused attention on the unfair nature of CCC and NRA programs. Top women in the Roosevelt administration, including Secretary of Labor Frances Perkins and Ellen Woodward, who directed many of the female employment projects, sought to assure women that they were not intentionally discriminated against, but even Harry Hopkins (head of relief) admitted in 1934 that the CWA hadn't "been particularly successful in work for women."

The Works Progress Administration (WPA) which replaced earlier relief and work programs in 1935 stereotyped gender roles and wages. State administrators employed married women reluctantly because they believed that "the husband is the logical head of the family," so only if the husband were disabled could a wife be certified as the "economic head" of the household and thus eligible for work relief. Female WPA workers earned $3 per day compared with $5 for men, assuming they could even get a place on a project, since many administrators limited the proportion of women on job creation programs to less than one-fifth of the total. In 1936, Harry Hopkins ordered the Colorado WPA to eliminate half its female employees because they constituted 27 percent of the rolls instead of the 16 percent national average.

The WPA restricted the jobs open to each sex. Most female WPA projects reinforced traditional female occupations with more than half the female WPA workers stitching in its sewing rooms. There was a serious mismatch between the types of jobs available and the employment background of women workers. In 1930, over two-fifths of all working women had white-collar jobs, but only one-sixth of WPA jobs fell into this category. Professional women competed for positions in WPA art and educational programs, in libraries, adult education, the Federal Theatre Program, the Federal Writers' Project, and the Federal Arts' Project.

With these notable exceptions, the WPA was essentially a national construction project in which men built roads, bridges, municipal facilities, public buildings, and sewage systems. An exhaustive inventory of public work relief available in Muncie, Indiana, demonstrated the construction orientation of New Deal programs: 13 of its 16 projects were construction based and employed men only. A small number of jobs permitted women to take an inventory of local housing, supervise recreational facilities, make mattresses and bedding for the needy, and supplement the staffs of health and welfare agencies and the public library.

Women of color had particular difficulty getting public relief since WPA officials invariably viewed them as fit only for domestic service and relegated them to domestic training programs which were short and inexpensive to run. After a brief course, the trainees were placed as maids at half the usual wages paid to unskilled workers. In five years this program trained 18 000 women as domestics, sending nearly three-quarters to work in private households. Administrators removed African-American women who refused a domestic placement from the welfare rolls but not whites. Such race and gender discrimination meant that white men constituted 74 percent of WPA workers; black men were 14 percent; white women, 11 percent; and black women only 2 percent. Virtually no women from other races obtained WPA jobs.

Labor legislation during the Great Depression advanced the role of organized labor and helped unionize the female labor force. NRA codes encouraged shorter working hours for both sexes and instituted minimum wages which increased women's wages especially in the southern cigarette and textile industries. Employers responded by cutting the wages they paid to skilled workers to compensate for raises to the unskilled. They also speeded up production lines in order to augment output, thus offsetting wages against productivity, according to the industrial workers who attended Bryn Mawr College's summer school for working women.

Employers in a number of industries used the instability of the Great Depression as an excuse to substitute capital for labor, upgrade equipment, and lessen the skill required to accomplish some processes. Cigar manufacturers turned to machinery as a way of displacing troublesome skilled (male) workers and enhancing productivity; in the process the industry shifted from a largely male one to a more even gender balance. A similar process occurred in the automobile plants where manufacturers replaced men with lower paid women in certain parts of their plants, raising the proportion of female auto workers from 7 to 11 percent during the 1930s. Such increases, while small, exacerbated fears that women would displace men and led male auto workers to demand separate seniority lists for each sex. In contrast, the International Ladies' Garment Workers' Union responded to rising women's employment in its sector by actively encouraging women to join the union as a means of resisting employer intimidation and exploitation. It employed effective organizers such as Rose Pesotta to appeal to women workers, with the result that membership quintupled in the early years of the Depression.

The NRA encouraged union organization as did the National Labor Relations Act of 1935 which established the National Labor Relations Board to certify unions as bargaining agents. It required employers to bargain in good faith and permitted closed (union only) shops. These acts stimulated union growth, fostered the expansion of industrywide unions, and encouraged union bosses to take female membership more seriously. The Congress of Industrial Organizations, formed by workers in the mass production industries in 1935, became a bastion of female labor organization. Its president John L. Lewis supported equal pay for equal work, although not all labor union organizations were so enlightened. A United Auto Workers' local official spoke for many when he said that "the working wife whose husband is employed should be barred from industry." Such local officials provided tepid support for female members regardless of national policy.

Female militancy burgeoned as department store clerks and cannery workers joined textile, garment, and tobacco industry workers in organizing. Some CIO member unions, such as the United Cannery, Agricultural, Packing, and Allied Workers of America, sought to make union membership representative of the labor force by recruiting people of color and women of all races into the membership and leadership. Domestic workers in New York and Washington, DC, succeeded in forming unions which raised wages significantly, while the Southern Tenant Farmers' Union in Arkansas and Mississippi had both black and white women members. The net result of these organizing drives was to increase female union membership from about 250 000 in 1929 to approximately 800 000 in 1939.

Despite these very real gains, not all women workers benefited from a New Deal climate favorable to employees. Both NRA codes and the Social Security Act of 1935 ignored the plight of agricultural and domestic workers who, unlike the elderly and organized (mostly male) factory workers, lacked a politically significant constituency and were disproportionately African American and female. The sister of a Quincy, Illinois, maid expressed outrage in her letter to Secretary of Labor Frances Perkins in 1937 over their exclusion from old age annuities, minimum wages, and maximum working hours. She asked "What about the poor domestics, both in private homes and private institutions? What have you done for them? NOTHING . . . Why should the government disregard this element when they are already the under-dogs, and at the same time represent such a large element of our population, especially the female population?"

An aide to Miss Perkins replied that their exclusion resulted not from those who wrote the initial legislation but stemmed from "compromises which are forced when the legislation is being passed." This response captured the difficulties encountered by the White House in trying to get controversial legislation through a sceptical Congress. Southern Democrats controlled key committees and adamantly opposed the incorporation of African-American occupations into national employment legislation, fearing this would raise wages and encourage federal intervention into regional labor practices. The Social Security Act had an explicitly gendered construction, assumed that men would support their wives, and excluded many occupations dominated by women or people of color. Thus while many women in the manufacturing sector benefited from New Deal legislation, those in agriculture, domestic service, and many white-collar jobs received little or no assistance.

THE ARMED FORCES

The New Deal ameliorated the effects of the Depression, but World War II ended it, causing a sharp spike in women's employment levels and encouraging even more older and married women into the labor market. It also opened military service to women on a mass basis for the first time. As the conflict loomed, Congresswoman Edith N. Rogers introduced a bill which sought to establish a noncombatant Women's Auxiliary Army Corps. Although the bill failed for lack of support from either the military or Congress, serious personnel shortages after the bombing of Pearl Harbor led the Army Chief of Staff to thunder "I want a women's corps right away and I don't want any excuses." Congress authorized female units for each service: the Women's Auxiliary Army Corps (WAAC), Naval WAVES (Women Accepted for Volunteer Emergency Service), Coast Guard SPARS (the name derived from the Coast Guard motto *Semper Paratus*), and (nicknameless) Women's Marine Corps attested to the top brass's realization that female soldiers could release men for military combat since between one-fifth and one-third of all service personnel engaged in paperwork rather than warfare.

Over 350 000 women served in the US military during World War II. They tended to be better educated than male service personnel, largely because they could not enlist until they were 20 (men were drafted at 18) and because the services were highly selective in the women they accepted. Two-fifths of Army women were high school graduates while another fifth had been to college. Servicewomen came disproportionately from the North, since southern women deemed military service "more at variance with their customs and traditions," according to the director of the Women's Marine Corps. Regardless of region, women in the military experienced one very real benefit from serving their country: higher wages than in civilian life. Almost all female service personnel worked before entering the military, but many had been underpaid and undervalued.

Women officers had the difficult job of learning to be officers with no senior female personnel as role models. The services limited their authority by not permitting them to be in charge of men. This created operational difficulties, so the military decreed that female officers issued orders on behalf of a higher ranking male officer. Military women also encountered continued indignation from male officers and enlisted men who felt that women's presence demeaned the services. As a result women were barred from combat zones, weapons training, and many aspects of warfare. They could go no higher than Lieutenant Colonel or Commander, even in the nurses' corps. While they served valiantly, they also served in a sex-segregated military which transposed highly gendered notions of appropriate work to women in uniform.

In addition, the conservative, southern-dominated officer corps brought racial quotas to military life, demonstrating a marked reluctance to enlist African-American women. The Women's Army Corps remained segregated during the war and only 6 percent were black. The Navy, which restricted African-American men to a few occupations, refused to accept black women until forced to do so by President Roosevelt in 1944. The Marine Corps kept its door firmly shut to black women, while the Coast Guards accepted only a handful.

Women in uniform challenged the traditional macho image of the armed services and adjustment to their presence, even as nurses, was not easy. Widespread resentment of women in the forces made recruiting sufficient numbers difficult. There were innumerable rumors about the promiscuity of servicewomen and their sexual orientation. Women suspected of lesbian "tendencies" or relationships were court-martialled and given bad conduct discharges. The extreme suspicion of same-sex relationships meant that one could be discharged upon a psychiatrist's statement or for displaying physical affection by hugging or kissing. Women could also be dismissed from the services for becoming pregnant. While few did so early in the war, by the time the war was drawing to a close, the number of women "devolunteering" through pregnancy started to rise as women wished to return to civilian life.

Women in uniform performed similar jobs to the civilian labor force as clerks, typists, telephone operators, dieticians, nurses, and laundresses. A small number flew planes as Women's Airforce Service Pilots, but had civilian rather than military status and received decidedly inferior treatment. Congress accepted the high command's wishes to retain female service personnel after the war, but limited them to 2 percent and refused to countenance their promotion to the higher ranks. Servicewomen did receive veterans' benefits and, like their male counterparts, went to college on the GI bill. Overall, the experience of women in the services showed both how much they could accomplish and the extent to which gendered assumptions constrained their performance.

WOMEN IN THE WARTIME LABOR FORCE

The war increased the number and variety of jobs open to women in the civilian labor force, raised the proportion of women who worked, encouraged the employment of older women and those with family responsibilities, and greatly expanded the number in heavy industry. Encouraged by government propaganda campaigns featuring Rosie the Riveter and movies such as *Swing Shift Maisie* (1943), which depicted patriotic women working on the assembly line, the number of women workers rose by 50 percent between 1940 and 1944. Both younger and older women responded to the call for war workers. Twice as many 14–19 year olds held jobs in 1944 as in 1940 and the increase for women over 45 was only slightly smaller. Evidence from

1950 suggests that older women maintained their elevated employment levels although young women's returned to their pre-war levels. In 1940, 17 percent of women ages 55–64 had jobs outside the home, but by 1960, the proportion had doubled, suggesting that wartime accelerated an ongoing trend.

During World War II employment became much more typical for women. Nearly half (48 percent) held a job at some time during 1944, rising to 53 percent among urban women. Many older women workers had previously been employed but left the labor force after marriage or children or had been discouraged by the previously unfavorable economic climate. Married women now constituted a growing proportion of gainfully employed women. In 1940 one-third of all female workers were married; by 1950 more than half were. Although women left the labor force in large numbers at the end of the war, the proportion of wives who worked edged up from 15 percent in 1940, to 19 percent in 1944, and 22 percent in the post-war period.

The war accelerated women's penetration of the clerical labor market, while it also increased their presence in manufacturing, especially heavy industry. The federal government alone absorbed 800 000 female workers, while city and state governments relaxed their ban on married female employees. The service and retail sectors of the economy grew quickly, but private household service declined, as former domestics seized the opportunity to work in better paying industrial settings. Black women's employment prospects improved markedly in government service and industry, but once hired, black women endured abuse from white colleagues who resented their presence. Mazetta Clanagan, one of the first African-American women hired at the Westinghouse Airbrake Company in Pittsburgh, described how white workers jeered at her as she walked across the catwalk over their heads. Tina Hill, who worked at North American Aircraft in Los Angeles, recalled "all the Negroes went to Department 17 because there was nothing but shooting and bucking rivets." The wages they earned in industrial establishments, while frequently lower than whites', were nevertheless far higher than their earnings as domestic servants.

Few women had access to industrial training programs designed to suit peacetime workers for the war industries as the nation geared up for battle. The Vocational Training for War Production Workers program enrolled no women despite the protests of the War Manpower

Commission's Women's Advisory Committee. Initially few industrial work places welcomed women. Shipyards, aircraft factories, foundries, and armament manufacturers only accepted women once the supply of surplus men dried up, and then only in a small number of job classifications.

Employers ran training programs for their female recruits, taught them how to shoot and buck rivets, drill, and hammer, and modified complex tasks and processes to accommodate inexperienced workers. Skilled male workers resented this de-skilling process and pressed unions to negotiate separate seniority lists for the sexes, so that when peace came, men would retain or get their old jobs back while women were let go. Women joined unions in large numbers during the war, especially in the wartime industries such as armaments, aircraft and shipbuilding, but some unions (construction, railroading, and mining) refused to accept female members. Even those unions, such as the United Auto Workers whose national leadership strongly favored equality between the sexes at work, had an uneven record at the local level regarding women's employment issues.

Female union membership climbed from 9 percent of women workers in 1940 to 22 percent in 1944, with some unions working strongly to incorporate women's interests into their programs. Nancy Gabin's study of the auto workers found that the female share of membership jumped from 15 to 40 percent in the United Electrical Workers and comprised one-third of their organizers. The National War Labor Board endorsed equal pay for equal work in a suit brought against General Motors by the United Electrical Workers and the United Auto Workers. This suit indicated both a commitment to equality and a fear that employers would replace men with cheaper female labor unless wage parity existed within occupational classifications. Women's wages in the automotive industry rose during the war, even in all-female job titles, from 67 percent of men's in 1940 to 79 percent in 1943. Nevertheless, even enlightened unions continued their masculine orientation over wage and bargaining matters, believing that women would leave the labor force (or at least jobs in heavy industry) after the war.

Virtually all the workers fired at the end of the hostilities were women. This took place despite female seniority in many plants and occupations because unions did not consider women to be "bona fide members of the Union" and frequently did not support their job claims. Federal law gave preference in employment to returning male, but not female, veterans. The Women's Advisory Committee to the War Manpower Commission was disbanded and with it, a measure of federal protection for women in the work place. Women in certain industries, especially those covered by the United Auto Workers' union, resisted sex-based layoffs with some assistance from their union, but most received less support and found themselves out of work.

Other factors impelled women to leave the labor force, at least temporarily. It was hard enough to sustain family and employment commitments during the war when some special services for female defense workers existed, but the abolition of those services made women's juggling act even more difficult. Women who did war work to protect their loved ones overseas had less incentive to work once the war ended. As the troops returned home and the birth rate skyrocketed, women signaled their desire for domestic normality by leaving the defense plants to care for their young families. A Roper Poll conducted in 1943 found that a majority of young single women wished to continue working in the same occupation after the war, but married women had a more ambivalent attitude.

The war had accelerated many long-term trends in women's employment, including the growing presence of older and married women in the labor force. In a process which had taken a century to complete, "work" now took place outside the home and almost no women combined income production with housekeeping through industrial homework or taking in boarders. Those who wanted or needed to augment family incomes did so by taking jobs, leading to a rise in married women's employment. Strong racial variations in female employment patterns remained, although some convergence occurred as more married white women entered the labor market and the number of employed married non-white women declined. In 1920, five times more married women of color had jobs than their white counterparts; by 1940, about twice as many did so.

The number of women workers rose throughout the twentieth century, apart from a brief dip after World War II, but the gendered basis of women's employment remained its most important characteristic. Women and their families rationalized female employment in terms of family need, throughout prosperity, depression and war. The basis of the family economy changed, as mothers replaced children as ancillary breadwinners, allowing them to continue their education. A desire to purchase the consumer goods which proliferated in the twentieth century also impelled women to work. Pundits advised women to leave the labor force during the Great Depression, but they stayed put because their families needed the money. During World War II, patriotism and good wages justified female employment in a wide range of occupations, but employers, unions, government, movies, and women's magazines envisaged jobs only for the duration. The sharp drop in the number of women in the peacetime labor market proved temporary as many returned to work once their children went to school. Women's employment levels returned to their wartime peak by 1960, but in a narrower range of occupations. Although the war opened jobs in heavy industry to black and white women, this proved to be an exceptional circumstance. After the war these jobs closed to women and occupational segregation accelerated with women workers relegated to the white- and pink-collar ghettos. Women who had once welded airplane wings could not get jobs welding car panels; instead they set hair or filed papers.

Although more married women had jobs, women's social roles still inflected their economic ones. Domesticity had a strong hold over women, for even if women had jobs outside the home they remained responsible for running the home itself. Women's role in the American economy thus had a complexity which men's did not, with two shifts being the norm: one in the factory, office, shop, hospital, or school, and the other as housewife and mother at home. This dual burden characterized women's work as much as did occupational segregation or movement in and out of the labor market depending on marital status or children's ages. Depression, war, and prosperity reinforced the duality of female economic roles but also confirmed women as wage workers in a sex-stratified economy.

10 Family and Migration, 1920–1945

The 1920s to the 1940s witnessed the most dramatic political and social events of the twentieth century. Prohibition, the Great Depression, consumerism, advertising, radio, movies, Freudian psychology, World War II, contraception, and adolescent culture produced a torrent of contradictory messages about women's social and economic roles, pulling them between paid employment and the demands of home and family, showing them glamorous life styles and how to use new domestic appliances, but insisting that they should put family first. These forces interacted not to liberate women from the home but to entrench them within it. They became "crypto-servants" (in economist John Kenneth Galbraith's analysis) with ever-greater responsibility for the emotional and physical well-being of their families and longer hours of domestic labor regardless of supposedly labor-saving devices. The interplay between women's responsibilities in the family and the economic and cultural forces during the inter-war years illustrates the tensions inherent in their dual roles.

Despite, or rather because of, women's increased labor force participation, social pundits, manufacturers, government officials, and magazine editors continually told women their place was in the home, fearing "the home will suffer a kind of domestic suicide," if married women took jobs. These women entered the labor market because the new consumer society required sufficient income to buy the items promoted by national advertising. This resulted in a dual role in which they retained responsibility for household well-being although their extra-household interests expanded. Each woman tried to blend love, marriage, and self-expression in order to satisfy "her personal ambitions, but she wants a husband, home and children, too," observed lawyer and reformer Crystal Eastman, who wondered "how to reconcile these two desires in real life?" A plethora of experts advised women to opt for domesticity over economic activity, but women's own behavior suggested a complex balancing act rather than a simple preference for family or employment. Indeed falling birth rates indicate that women and their partners at the very least wished to shape fertility to suit their needs, rather than passively accepting large families and unalloyed domesticity to please social or political pundits.

THE FAMILY IN THE INTER-WAR YEARS

This era contained many paradoxes for women, as William Chafe noted in his history of American women in the twentieth century. The shrill public emphasis on the importance of the home and women's place within it accompanied steadily falling fertility and rising employment levels. Even elite women's colleges such as Vassar declared that women's "chief interests and responsibilities, motherhood and the home" should be their primary focus rather than employment. While 90 percent of Vassar students in 1923 believed that marriage was "the biggest of all careers" they undertook it on their own terms. The birth rate, which declined steadily from the end of the Civil War until World War I, tumbled at an unprecedented rate through the 1920s and 1930s. Childlessness became more prevalent as women disregarded popular opinion such as that expressed by a 1925 Indiana newspaper which condemned the voluntarily childless as "reasonable targets for popular opprobrium." In 1900 about one couple in ten had no children; by 1940 this proportion had risen to one in five as more women preferred employment, leisure, and higher standards of living to the demands of childcare.

Contraceptive usage increased among all groups, despite the opposition of the Catholic Church and the obstacles some states placed in their way. Connecticut banned birth control even for married couples until the Supreme Court ruled in *Griswold vs. Connecticut* (1965) that the right of privacy precluded state interference in couples' bedrooms and extended this right to single people in 1972. Family sizes fell most sharply among the urban business and professional classes as couples used diaphragms, condoms, or *coitus interruptus* to have fewer children and to increase the spacing between them. By 1940, urban white women gave birth to an average of two children, compared with three for urban black women and five or slightly more for rural women of both races.

Having fewer children, women wished to maximize what they

believed to be the chances of each birth being successful. They accepted the medical profession's propaganda and articles appearing in women's magazines which depicted home births as barbaric and dangerous. Instead they joined the trend in which childbirth was "lifted out of the realm of darkness into the spotlight of new science," as *Good Housekeeping* magazine asserted, by having their children in the maternity ward of their local hospital, delivered under anesthesia by doctors, rather than at home with a midwife or "granny" in attendance.

By 1940, 55 percent of all births took place in hospitals where childbirth became a complex disease supervised by specialists who induced labor to suit doctors' and patients' schedules and drugged mothers with Nembutal and scopolamine. Such hospital births could be dangerous. The death rates from puerperal fever rose in supposedly antiseptic wards, only declining in the 1940s when hospitals improved their practices through the use of safer spinal anesthetics, and antibiotics became available to curb infections. Rural women continued to have their babies at home with a female relative or neighbor to look after the home and children.

Maternal and infant health had been the subject of much concern during the Progressive Era. The United States ranked seventeenth in maternal mortality and eleventh in infant deaths among 20 leading industrial nations in 1918. These statistics prompted Children's Bureau Chief Julia Lathrop to propose a federal maternal and infant health bill during World War I, modelled in part on the Little Mothers' Leagues of large cities which aimed to teach immigrant girls to be scientific mothers and transmit their knowledge to their own mothers. Women of all social backgrounds supported this legislation, alarmed by high maternal and infant death rates, and believing that the state should promulgate high standards of health for mothers and babies. The Women's Joint Congressional Committee, led by Florence Kelley, lobbied actively for the legislation as did women's magazines and women doctors, the Daughters of the American Revolution, and the YWCA. These groups favored state support for mothers and infants and insisted that the program be run by women.

Passed as the Sheppard–Towner Maternity and Infancy Protection Act in 1921, this innovative legislation provided matching grants to states with maternity and infancy protection plans. As Molly Ladd-Taylor observes, Sheppard–Towner "exemplified the political philosophy and program of maternalism," extending it to urban and rural communities and all racial and ethnic groups, protecting women and children within the family, but "it did not challenge married women's economic dependence on men or try to empower mothers in other social roles." Despite a commitment to improved women's and children's health, southern states segregated their maternity and infant care programs or restricted them to whites. Nevertheless the clinics instructed mothers on infant care and provided health demonstration centers, although not regular sustained health care. Designed and implemented by women, the Maternity and Infancy Protection Act exemplified politicized motherhood, had widespread support from women across the nation, and contributed to the decline in infant deaths from 75 per 1000 live births to 64 per 1000 in the 1920s. It funded nearly 3000 prenatal care centers and over 3 million home visits, with 162 000 women participating in mothers' classes in 43 states.

New child-rearing practices spread by baby clinics, doctors, and women's magazines included feeding babies on rigid schedules which were supposedly better for the baby but could be excruciatingly painful for both mother and infant. Such fashions did not reach the tenant farm women of the rural South who, according to Margaret Hagood's sociological study during the Depression, found this notion "incomprehensible." Other trends supported dedicated motherhood even after the funding for Sheppard–Towner terminated in 1929. Freudian theories of subconscious bonds between parents and children and a more scientific approach to childcare made motherhood a full-time occupation despite smaller families. Expert advisers stressed the quality of child-rearing and the importance of the mother–child bond, making women feel guilty if they did not devote themselves totally to their children. Women substituted intensive maternity for the physically demanding household production their mothers and grandmothers had undertaken.

New theories of childcare required constant attention to nutrition, health, and social development which only mothers could provide. The emphasis, as the Lynds noted in their study of Muncie, Indiana, shifted from childbearing to child-rearing since fewer mothers had domestic assistance and repeatedly read in the popular press not to trust "uneducated" help. Middle-class mothers spent significantly more time with their children than their own mothers did. They played ball with them, helped with homework, and took them to music and dance classes. Female attendance at parenting classes,

Parent–Teachers' Association and National Congress of Mothers meetings attested to motherhood's central place in their lives. Even women who belonged to other organizations such as the Women's Christian Temperance Union focused on motherhood in the talks they listened to and committees they joined.

HOUSEWIFERY, DOMESTIC TECHNOLOGY, AND DOMESTIC ADVICE

By the 1920s, housewifery had become divorced from the manufacture of goods and services. Highly skilled and specialized production in the home had been replaced by a combination of domestic technology, mass consumption, and cheap products readily available in the market place. New appliances made housework less arduous and more acceptable as a daily occupation for a broad range of women, but housewifery remained, in Dorothy Dix's words, "a life sentence of hard labor in her home. [The housewife's] work is the most monotonous in the world and she has no escape from it." Machines eliminated some physical drudgery but made little difference to the amount of time spent on housework because affluent housewives substituted electricity for the help they previously received from servants or children.

Fewer homemakers had live-in maids at their beck and call in the inter-war years as young white women used their education to obtain other types of work and African-American women, especially in northern cities, resisted residential service jobs. They preferred living with their own families and communities to being stranded in a white neighborhood with a tiny bedroom off the kitchen or in the attic. Day work also enabled them to go to church and maintain community ties which live-in service rarely permitted. This suited employers and efficiency experts who increasingly valued privacy and believed that a daily cleaning woman provided the "greatest advantage" in terms of getting the job done effectively. Household adviser Christine Frederick regarded being without resident help as an "opportunity to manage the home according to one's own highest standards of thrift, efficiency, sanitation, and family happiness." By inference, the presence of live-in servants detracted from these high standards, but their absence also meant more work for mother.

Labor-saving devices, domestic science instruction in schools, and women's magazines disrupted "the sequence of mother–daughter inheritance" and devalued women's old-fashioned practices. Even during the depths of the Great Depression women turned to cookery and household manuals such as Fannie Farmer's *New England Cookery Book* and Irma Rombauer's *Joy of Cooking* to acquire new techniques to exploit modern appliances and cook inviting meals. Home economists and domestic efficiency experts taught scientific housekeeping, nutrition, childcare, and household management in schools, colleges, and the mass media, emphasizing that the "successful mother . . . delegates to electricity all that electricity can do," in the words of one midwestern electric company. Mother "cannot delegate the one task most important. Human lives are in her keeping, their future is molded by her hands and heart," but she could buy a vacuum cleaner and spend more time with her children.

As with other female-based professions such as teaching, nursing, and social work, the professional practitioners of home economics felt it necessary to denigrate amateurs by emphasizing the scientific side of consuming, cooking, and childcare. The Smith–Lever Act of 1914 gave federal sanction to home economics as a science by establishing cooperative extension courses at land grant universities. In 1923, the Department of Agriculture incorporated a Bureau of Home Economics "to study practical home problems" as a means of "improving and bettering" living conditions. The Smith–Hughes Vocational Education Act of 1917 defined "homemaking as a basic vocation for women," channeling women into the domestic sphere rather than other careers.

Ruth Schwartz Cowan's history of housework describes post-World War I home care as an emotional "trip" in which washing clothes indicated love, cooking encouraged familial loyalty and affection, and cleaning the bathroom kept the family safe from germs. Meals took on an added significance because automobiles, the development of a teen culture, and a plethora of after school activities diverted attention from the family home. Families used the dinner table as their main focus, their "General Headquarters," because they were all so busy with separate activities that it was the only place they gathered during the day. Cooking took on emotional importance since a bad meal threatened the sanctity of the family unit as well as its vitamin levels. With other family members so heavily involved in activities outside the home, women bore the brunt of maintaining family life, protecting and defending their children through a germ-free environment and nutritionally balanced meals.

Rural women found domestic advice more difficult to follow in the inter-war years because electrification and sanitary plumbing reached the countryside slowly. In 1920, less than 10 percent of rural homes had central heating, electricity, hot and cold running water, and indoor toilets. Three-quarters of urban households had complete bathrooms at the start of the Depression compared with one-third of rural homes. Lacking electricity, rural women also lacked the supposedly labor-saving devices that actually resulted in more time devoted to housework. In 1923, 10 percent of farm homes had vacuum cleaners, 2 percent had electric sewing machines, and less than 1 percent had refrigerators although electric irons were near-universal in towns and over one-third of urban dwellers had electric washing machines. Rural women worked hard but not as long as city dwellers, stopping their chores once night fell rather than working by artificial light later into the evening. New Deal agencies such as the Rural Electrification Administration and the Tennessee Valley Authority brought power to rural Americans, so that by 1944 two-fifths had electricity, climbing to three-quarters by 1949, with a consequent increase in time devoted to housework.

There were also racial differences in household expenditures with African Americans spending much less than whites on domestic goods. Throughout the inter-war years African Americans endured very low standards of living and poor household conditions, both in urban and rural areas. Black farm families lived in unplastered houses, sometimes without windows and almost always without screens to keep out flies. Most of their furniture was homemade; they relied upon open hand-dug wells, and few had privies, let alone flush toilets. Through World War II urban African-American dwellings frequently lacked sanitary conveniences. African-American teacher training colleges and extension agents recognized the racially inflected differences in living standards by using coal in their cooking demonstrations, rather than gas or electricity as used by similar institutions for white women.

Women who lived in modern dwellings escaped some of the physical labor performed by their mothers (or their mothers' servants). It took over two hours a day to maintain a wood or coal stove, carrying fuel, lighting and cleaning the stove, and taking out the ashes. Gas and electric stoves merely required a wipe down with a damp rag and occasional oven cleaning. Washing clothes on a scrub board meant bringing water inside, heating it, pouring it into the tub, and then scrubbing each garment separately. Early washing machines had an automatic agitator and used commercially available washing powder which eliminated the laborious process of making soap, although they still required attention (adding soap powder, attaching the drain pipe, and feeding the clothes through the wringer). The electric iron also eased washday blues since one no longer had to stand next to a hot stove heating irons. Indoor plumbing, of course, also decreased household labor – no more hauling water, heating it, or emptying slops.

Why, then, did the hours worked by women in modern homes not decrease? The answer lies in rising standards and the increased responsibility women bore for housework, as they had sole charge of the home, with little help from employees or other family members. Advertisers and magazine editors stressed the emotional importance of housewifery. Christine Frederick declared that husbands should not be asked to help at home, believing it unfair to ask a man who worked "hard and faithfully at his task of earning money during his working day" to turn "choreman" as soon as he came home. Mothers might ask their children to help out, but after school activities and independent socializing made them unreliable assistants.

Sociologist Talcott Parsons observed in the 1940s that industrialization enlarged the world outside the home, but for women it meant "an involution of the world into the space of the home . . . with the modern role of housewife" emerging as the "dominant mature feminine role" in the twentieth century. This statement encapsulated the widespread belief that women retained responsibility for the smooth running of the household and performance of domestic tasks. Technology did not liberate, rather it concentrated housework on the housewife as she justified the investment in machines by doing work that previously had been delegated. At the turn of the century nearly nine-tenths of affluent women either sent their clothes to a commercial laundry or employed a laundress. By the 1920s, six out of ten used an electric washing machine and in the 1930s almost all (85 percent) did, with the net result that these women did more work rather than less. Expanded wardrobes, washable fabrics, and more frequent clothing changes meant that women washed clothes more often than earlier in the century. Where spring cleaning had once sufficed, daily dusting and vacuuming became the norm. Children used to be bathed weekly, but with hot running water they were scrubbed every day. Housework proliferated to fill the time available and justify the purchase price of domestic technology.

Shopping also took up more time as domestic advisers urged women to throw out "much that is still useful, even half-new, in order to make room for the newest 'best'" and to buy items that their mothers would have made. Few women baked their own bread in the 1920s, preferring to shop for it and other convenience foods at the new self-service supermarkets such as Piggly Wiggly and the A & P. Women's magazines colluded with the manufacturers' and advertisers' manipulation of women's emotions, using guilt to sell products. Profiting from the amount of advertising copy they sold, magazines emphasized the precarious emotional nature of family life, telling women that the wrong laundry powder or mouthwash would cost them their children's love. Conversely, careful shopping enabled mothers to fulfill their role as the emotional linchpin of the family by buying products which would help their children grow strong and healthy.

Women retained responsibility for housework even when they worked outside the home. A 1934 study of gainfully employed married women homemakers discovered that women workers still performed most, if not all household duties. They tended to do tasks weekly rather than daily, devoting their weekends to housework instead of leisure. They received little support from their families in meal preparation, shopping, or taking out the trash, but had some assistance with doing the dishes, sweeping, and dusting. Surveys of American buying habits concluded that the working wife's income narrowed class differentials in consumption patterns as these women bought vacuum cleaners, toasters, and irons, with the result that patterns of housewifery converged across social classes.

Housewifery underwent de-skilling in the inter-war years as women lost their special expertise and became the handmaidens of technology, processed food, and consumption. Instead of being the source of domestic feminism, the home became a boring place where repetitive chores smothered independence. In Sinclair Lewis's *Main Street* (1920) the very chairs squealed "Choke her–choke her–smother her" at Carol Kennicott, the eponymous housewife-heroine who gave up her career as a librarian to marry a doctor in Gopher Prairie. In a foretaste of Betty Friedan's post-war suburban "problem that had no name," Lewis depicted housework as unsatisfying repetitive toil performed with "puerile methods" by an unequal partner. Caring for her home did not satisfy career-oriented Carol; it bored her to distraction.

Many women found technologized housewifery less fulfilling than their mother's production of preserves, bread, hams, cheeses, clothes, and bedding, and yet, because homemaking had an emotional, almost sacred, function, few women felt they could relinquish their domestic tasks at this time. Moreover, their experiences in the 1930s and 1940s underscored the importance of domesticity, as families turned back the clock, using female labor to make what they could no longer afford to buy or could not find in the shops. With the return of affluence in the late 1940s and 1950s women again perceived their household labors as somehow trivial and repetitive and began to question the housewifely role as the essence of their being.

CHANGING GENDER ROLES IN THE 1920S AND 1930S

The end of World War I saw the emergence of the "New Woman" of the 1920s. Stereotyped as flappers, young women rid themselves of the corsets and elaborate hairstyles of their mothers' generation, as they drank, smoked, wore cosmetics, and bobbed their hair. *Life* magazine illustrator John Held portrayed flappers in rolled-down nylon stockings, shiny shift dresses, long necklaces, and high-heeled shoes going to speakeasies, drinking illicit cocktails, and riding in fast cars. Worried that their popularity would be affected by old-fashioned or out-of-date garments, female high school and college students throughout the country emulated big city flappers and bought mass produced stylish clothes. Social commentators deplored falling moral standards and what the Pittsburgh *Observer* described as "the serious ethical consequences of immodesty in girls' dress." These women left the narrow confines of the home behind in search of the same pleasures men enjoyed, trying to bring the glamour of movie heroines into their lives.

Movies, popular magazines, and prolonged adolescence for high school and college students promoted an independent youth culture and helped to establish romantic love as the most satisfactory basis for marriage. Bombarded with highly sexual cinematic images, young women had unparalleled social freedom, going on unchaperoned dates and engaging in "petting parties" just like the boys.

Young people met at youth clubs, church socials, and public dances, with automobiles greatly enhancing their mobility. Although women still had less social and sexual latitude than their male peers and went out less frequently, sexual morality shifted in this era from the rigid emphasis on purity before marriage which characterized women born before the turn of the century to a more liberal attitude. Levels of pre-marital virginity declined from about three-quarters of the women born between 1890 and 1900 to less than one-third for those born after 1910.

Social commentators used the phrase "companionate marriage" to describe marriage in the 1920s. It implied a union of equals that met both partners' sexual, emotional, and personal needs based upon mutual affection and sexual attraction, rather than economic need or religious dogma. Along with the psychiatrists and psychologists of the 1910s and 1920s, advocates of such relationships asserted women's sexuality as natural and to be encouraged. Popular novels showed companionate marriage to be the ideal throughout the social spectrum. Zora Neale Hurston's powerful novel about rural African Americans in the Great Depression, *Their Eyes Were Watching God*, has Janie picking beans with Tea Cake (her third husband and a younger man) not because he forced her to, but because she enjoyed his companionship throughout the day. When they finished in the fields "Tea Cake would help get supper afterwards."

The logical consequence of companionate marriages was that they should end when they no longer met the partners' need. Women of all groups demonstrated a heightened willingness to leave unsatisfactory relationships, and levels of divorce continued their upward trajectory throughout the 1920s. The Great Depression brought a temporary decline as fewer couples could afford to institute divorce proceedings, but as soon as the economy picked up so did marital separations. States responded by tightening the grounds upon which they granted divorces, but more marriages dissolved in the late 1940s and 1950s as hasty wartime unions came unstuck.

Rising divorce levels indicated higher expectations of marriage and a reaction to greater levels of family violence. Historian Peterson Del Mar concludes that modern wives became more vulnerable to violence in the inter-war years as society seemed more accepting of it. Kevin White describes youth culture of the early twentieth century as encouraging displays of excessive masculinity which easily slipped over into abuse. In the early part of the century social service

agencies tried to keep families together by reforming husbands' sexual, drinking, and spending habits, but by the 1930s, social workers
had less sympathy for abused women and more frequently blamed
them for marital discord by adopting modern psychiatric theories in
an effort to put case work on a supposedly scientific basis.

Freudians looked upon sexual violence as indicative of women's
desire to be dominated which justified abuse, while gangster and
cowboy movies frequently portrayed violence against women as part
of relationships. Movie critic Molly Haskell describes 1930s films
Little Caesar, Public Enemy, and *Scarface* as "the most violently
machismo, woman-bruising films in history," representing force as a
means of controlling women. Money problems during the Depression
also exacerbated male abuse and resentment against female independence. As the social climate changed, police and protection agencies
seemed less sympathetic to women's problems so women walled off
their souls from the pain. Hurston wrote that after Janie's second
husband slapped her "until she had a ringing sound in her ears" she
"packed up and put away [her thoughts and feelings] in parts of her
heart where he could never find them." Many women endured the
violence because they believed it to be women's lot, saw no way to
get out of the abusive relationship, or believed it better for their children to be raised by both parents, despite the marital problems.
Smaller family sizes, a culture which accepted violence, and
increased privacy and separation from neighbors and relations all
exacerbated female vulnerability.

MIGRATION IN BOOM, BUST, AND WARTIME

Population mobility also increased women's isolation. The boom
time of the 1920s accelerated urbanization, while the Great
Depression and World War II contributed to population turmoil.
Educational opportunities, bright lights, and employment drew young
people to the cities. In particular, the weakening rural economy
forced out African Americans, who left the South in large numbers,
heading for New York, Pittsburgh, Chicago, and other northern cities.
Encountering resistance to their presence, they moved into racially
homogeneous districts. Harlem, newly served by a subway line and
undergoing rapid housing construction, became the "race capital" of
America, offering employment for African-American women within

it and serving as a base for those who found jobs in white homes downtown.

During the Great Depression housing conditions deteriorated, with eviction rates running as high as one family in four being thrown out of their homes for non-payment of rent or mortgage arrears. Foreclosures rose ten-fold in some cities in the first few years of the Depression, forcing families to move. Homeowners or renters might let or sublet a portion of their dwelling to avoid foreclosure, eviction, or the sale of their home for tax arrears. A number of families took to what was euphemistically termed light housekeeping, where they rented part of a home in order to cut their housing costs. This all contributed to overcrowding and to dwellings in a poor state of repair.

Those who could not pay, moved in with relatives or, if their family were unwilling to take them in, took to the road or built a shack in one of the many "Hoovervilles" that sprang up on waste ground in the early 1930s. A Kentucky-born woman living in Oklahoma after the 1929 oil boom dried up, recalled families living "in everything from pup tents, houses built out of cardboard boxes and old pieces of metal that they'd pick up – anything that they could find to put somethin' together to put a wall around 'em to protect 'em from the public." They lived in rusted-out car bodies, packing crates, whatever they could construct to keep the rain off. Even under such circumstances many women tried to keep their homes in order and establish their domestic environment.

Women, men, and families all took to the highways and railroads, searching for better prospects. Some, like Box-Car Bertha Thompson, made famous by her autobiography published in 1937, rode the rails seeking work, companionship, or just a change from grim circumstances, and sometimes sold their bodies for money or food. Others traveled in family groups like the fictional Joad family in John Steinbeck's *Grapes of Wrath*, packing their meager belongings into a decrepit pickup with "horsehair curling out of seat cushions, fenders battered and hammered back," heading for California or wherever there might be work picking crops. The lucky ones stopped in government camps with solid wooden dwellings and washing facilities while they harvested produce. These camps provided services for the migrants, and, as one woman reminisced to oral historian Studs Turkel, advisers showed the women how to stuff mattresses and make clothing. The unlucky ones camped along the side of the road, got run out of towns and counties for vagrancy, and could not find work.

MARRIED WOMEN'S ROLES DURING THE DEPRESSION

The Great Depression simultaneously heightened gender roles and undercut them as women's housekeeping skills made a crucial difference in family survival, but married women also sought jobs outside the home to sustain families in the face of widespread unemployment. Married women believed their family's economic needs justified their continued presence in the labor force. Many were sole, main, or significant contributors to their family's income. They sought work because, as one carpenter's wife wrote to Eleanor Roosevelt, they really needed the work; their husbands "did not draw much salary and don't get much work at that."

The household economics of most families were stark as income levels fell by half between 1929 and 1933. Mary Anderson, head of the Women's Bureau, believed that families needed an income of $1500 to exist in reasonable dignity; any less than that justified women's presence in the labor force. Just before the Depression, two-fifths of American families subsisted on less than $1500 per year; by 1935–6 nearly two-thirds did. Women had two responses to this decline in living standards: they could either go to work or redouble their economizing efforts in the home. Estimates vary, but approximately one-third of all married women workers were the sole support of their families while over half augmented the income earned by other family members.

The Great Depression reinforced female domesticity, even as it weakened women's ability to conform to the domestic ideal. Gwendolyn Hughes' 1925 study of *Mothers in Industry* stated the perceived ideal, namely that "women's place is in the home" and that men would provide for their families. The Depression, and the rising level of married women's employment outside the home during the 1920s, contradicted that ideal. Despite individual and family variations, social commentators such as Dorothy Dix continued to advise women that men were the family decision makers, reinforcing what they believed to be traditional roles and values. Married women who worked were labeled "thieving parasites" and blamed for all manner of social ills including juvenile delinquency and battered male egos.

While these complaints were not new, they acquired an added edge during the Depression as society cast around for scapegoats and easy solutions.

The Depression constrained family economic strategies by curtailing the previously common practice of using children as full-time wage earners. New Deal efforts to eliminate child labor, especially in manufacturing, succeeded despite objections from textile corporations, newspaper publishers, a strict constructionist Supreme Court, and families that relied upon young workers. Between 1930 and 1940 the proportion of 14- and 15-year-old workers fell by 41 percent, with a smaller decline among older teenagers. Those children who worked were more likely to have part-time jobs and provided basic necessities only in "severely deprived families," according to sociologist Glen Elder's study of Oakland, California. This made families more dependent upon adult breadwinners and reinforced the family wage ideology where a single wage earner (the husband/father) had responsibility for supporting dependent kin.

Historian Susan Ware believes that the Depression had less of an impact on women than men; it accentuated women's domestic and home economic skills while undermining men's ability to meet their family support obligations. Women returned to producing goods and services in the home; home canning enjoyed a boom; and female labor once more substituted for electrical appliances, whose sales declined. Radio cooking programs featuring Betty Crocker and Aunt Sammy taught women to prepare healthy food inexpensively. Strong social pressure reinforced this domesticity and devalued women's rising employment levels and willingness to work in low-waged jobs to support their families. According to Eleanor Roosevelt, "wives and mothers are the inspiration of the homes, the persons for whom men really work," but not the wage earners.

When the Lynds returned to Muncie to assess the impact of the Depression on midwestern families in 1935, they found families turned against themselves, with "men defending a battered personal status against the sharp words of reproachful wives and children." Certainly, families turned inwards, spending more time together as the unemployed father helped Johnny "with his homework in the long evenings" and mother devoted "more of her time to cookbooks" and less to writing the papers with which she "formerly bored her fellow club women," according to a 1933 Indiana newspaper. A New York City father put a less sanguine face on events when he asked

"What's wrong with me, that I can't protect my own children?" Although more women sought employment, public responses to the economic crisis reinforced traditional gender roles as New Deal work relief, social assistance, and retirement legislation all assumed a wage-earning father, domestic mother, and dependent children. Thus although more married women had jobs, they had to justify their working according to family need rather than their own desires or right to work.

GENDER AND ASSISTANCE

Government divided the poor who needed assistance along gender lines into those eligible for employment and those for whom relief seemed the appropriate response. The solutions to poverty adopted under the New Deal followed the paths pioneered by mothers' pensions during the 1910s and 1920s, incorporating their basic philosophy and establishing a federal–state partnership in which the federal government provided the money but the states controlled the administrative mechanisms and distribution. New Deal social welfare legislation incorporated the family wage ideology and made support for women contingent upon their maternal and marital status. The Social Security Act of 1935 codified and expanded extant state welfare legislation providing assistance to dependent children and their mothers and incorporated the assumptions and values of existing widows' pension programs with very little debate. Anxiety about men's status as economic household heads led to the refraction of women's economic activities and needs through the prism of the family, regardless of individual circumstances. Once the Social Security Act came into force, welfare authorities removed single mothers from work relief and put them on Aid to Dependent Children (ADC) whether they wanted to work or not.

Most jurisdictions granting aid to widows and the elderly in the early years of the Depression preferenced the elderly in number and amount of pensions given. In 1931, when state funding for widows' pensions and old age pensions peaked, widows and dependent children in 85 urban areas received nearly $46 per month for an average family of four people (about $11.50 per person). Old age pensioners received $30 per person. By 1935 payments to both groups had declined: the average monthly allowance for widows' families had dropped to $40 ($10 per person) while that of the elderly was $21 per person.

Racial discrimination also harmed the female poor since southern states granted few pensions to African-American mothers and had fewer places for African-American children in public institutions, while southwestern states routinely discriminated against Mexican Americans. In 1932, the city of New Orleans simply stopped accepting applications for care from African Americans. The New Orleans Family Service Society informed the Family Welfare Association of America that it was powerless to help poor African Americans because of its own financial situation, so "Negro families are said to be suffering greatly." Southern welfare workers concluded that "the Negro is bearing the brunt of the depression in the South" because many public authorities overtly ignored African-American women's applications for relief. An African-American woman from Georgia complained to the federal government in 1935 that when she tried to obtain help the welfare authorities "talk to me like a dog." Assistance was routinely refused throughout the South, according to sociologist John Dollard, for fear that it would "take the pressure off Negro families to seek employment on the farms or in the white households."

In the absence of work or relief, these poor women survived by taking in a little washing, begging, and picking over trash cans and dumps for discarded vegetables and fruit. Neighbors and church organizations sustained those in particularly straitened circumstances. Black women who worked in white people's kitchens "bring them white folks' pots home" to feed their own families and their neighbors, reported one domestic servant who had to threaten to quit in order to get her employer to let her take home the kitchen scraps. Extended and augmented families helped out by pooling their resources and child-minding for those in work. The informal exchange of goods and services sustained rural and urban African-American families who suffered high rates of unemployment and low rates of assistance throughout the Depression.

Social Security legislation reflected prevailing sentiments about the family wage and the need for mothers to remain at home with their children. It provided an insurance-based unemployment and retirement system, primarily for the industrial working class, and a welfare-based support system for mothers with young children. The levels of support for retired men were higher ($30 per person) than the welfare provision for mothers and their young children ($18 for the first child and $12 for subsequent children). Women who worked outside the home received no separate benefits if they were married to men who qualified for Social Security retirement pensions. Linda Gordon posits that the low levels of support for women and children came not from some "transhistorical patriarchy," but from the assumption that supporting men and the family wage would translate into higher standards of living for women and children. The poverty of ADC came from providing funds only for children while making no demands on behalf of their maternal caretakers and from idealizing full-time domesticity as the only appropriate role for mothers. Because ADC was a child welfare measure, a high degree of state supervision over maternal behavior was justified, even though Old Age Assistance entailed no welfare investigations, checks upon spending patterns, or regulation of personal relationships.

The provisions of the Social Security Act limited it largely to white people by omitting agricultural laborers and domestic servants. It benefited more male than female wage earners by excluding female-dominated occupations such as teaching and philanthropy. There was another glaring omission from the coverage of the welfare legislation. Despite calling the subsection giving assistance to families "Aid to Dependent Children" and later, "Aid to Families with Dependent Children," it covered only mothers and children. The authors of the legislation and subsequent interpretations (until *Weinberger vs. Wiesenfeld* in 1975) refused to extend provisions of the act to include fathers bringing up children on their own. As had been the case with widows' pensions, the family model upon which this law was based assumed that mothers brought up children and provided no social support for different family forms, such as widowed fathers with young children. Their own families might help them, but charities frequently pressured widowers and other single fathers to place their children in orphanages or give them up for adoption. Social Security legislation reinforced conventional social roles and penalized family units which did not conform to the norm.

FAMILIES DURING WORLD WAR II

World War II simultaneously accentuated and undermined domesticity; employment of mothers became an economic and patriotic necessity, so more women faced the difficult act of balancing paid work, household management, and childcare with little support from husbands away at war or set in their ways. Shortly after the United States entered the war, the government propaganda machine targeted older women and those with children for employment in defense plants, emphasizing their patriotic duty and need to support the men on the battlefield. Childcare posed real problems for those Rosie the Riveters with young children since government nursery programs neither provided sufficient places nor suited shift workers. Other women took jobs which fitted around children's timetables such as waitressing and teaching, especially after labor shortages forced school systems to accept married women as teachers.

However, Rosie the Riveter was a temporary employee, riveting aircraft wings or welding boilerplate until the war ended. Planning for peace stressed the need to reintegrate men back into their old jobs, for as President Franklin D. Roosevelt said in one of his fireside chats, "they must not be demobilized into an environment of inflation and unemployment, to a place on the breadline or on a corner selling apples." Women were invited to help the war effort for the sake of their men, their families, and the nation, but only "for the duration," thus preventing any significant restructuring of gender roles.

In any case, older women found their transition from housewife or part-time worker to war worker fraught with obstacles. Many husbands did not want them to work, but they persisted because they had sons at the front, needed the money to pay off debts accumulated during the Depression, or felt a patriotic duty to assist the war effort. Employers initially resisted older women's presence in the labor force, preferring to hire men or younger women, but a shortage of workers helped break down the barriers. Being younger than the female population as a whole, servicemen's wives were well represented among the ranks of employed women, with over half this group working in 1944. A combination of patriotism and financial considerations encouraged them to work in defense plants, since few women married to enlisted men could support their families or themselves on the $50 per month they received from the government. Officers' wives fared better because their husbands had higher wages and could send more home.

The proportion of employed service wives might have been higher still but for two factors. Women who followed their husbands from army camp to army camp could find themselves in remote districts or small towns with few sources of work. Frequent moves made it difficult to hold on to jobs for very long. Employers complained that they left "at the drop of a hat" if family matters needed their attention, their husbands returned home from the front, or if they were posted to another location. Over 7 million women moved during wartime, either to take defense industry jobs or to follow their men as they moved between army camps. The war thus severed family ties and created social instability. Nurse Frances Krantz married a doctor just before the war began. She continued to work as an operating room nurse in Manhattan until the Army posted her husband to South Carolina and subsequently to Indiana. When he shipped out to the Far East, she returned with their infant daughter to Connecticut to live with her widowed mother and grandmother. Other women whose families could not or would not take them in fended for themselves in distant communities.

Like many mothers of young children, this highly trained nurse chose not to enter the labor market even though she had vitally needed skills. The Army would not consider placing her in uniform since she was married to an officer and had a baby. Civilian employment would have been a possibility except that she, like millions of other mothers, considered her primary responsibility was to her daughter and husband. In 1940, less than 8 percent of married women with children under the age of 10 had jobs, rising to 12 percent by 1944.

Childcare difficulties explain why women with older children and single women formed the bulk of new female workers. Working mothers typically used members of their extended family, neighbors, husbands, or friends to look after their children, but wartime mobility severed many of these ties. Some employed paid babysitters, but relatively few used day care centers. The pervasive belief that mothers should look after young children at home when coupled with Congressional inaction impeded the systematic provision of childcare. Until it was disbanded in 1943 the WPA ran a children's nursery program which gave jobs to unemployed women at the same time that it cared for poor women's children.

The wartime labor emergency prompted the Federal government to expand these facilities under the terms of the Lanham Act in 1942. The Federal Works Administration organized childcare facilities for women working in defense plants, operating 3000 nurseries with 130 000 children. These centers had limitations since they did not accommodate shift work, and bureaucratic infighting and complicated procedures made it difficult for local communities to qualify for funds. Women workers in the defense industry pressed hard for nursery facilities tailored to the needs of production workers. The United Auto Workers, with many assertive female employees who were also committed union members, held a conference in 1943 urging the extension of federally funded day nurseries. A sweeping childcare bill sponsored by Oklahoma Senator Elbert D. Thomas in 1943 fell foul of interagency bickering and disagreements over whether to place the children of working mothers in institutions or care for them at home.

Communities such as Seattle and Detroit, which tried to introduce group after school facilities for children, found that parents were unwilling to use them. Karen Anderson's study of these programs discovered that relatively high fees, intrusive questionnaires, and children's resentment at being in school after the school day ended undermined these efforts. Seattle after school programs enrolled 1200 children in 30 centers, but few other cities matched these numbers. Indeed some cities found it almost impossible to keep their educational systems intact, resorting to half-day sessions as student numbers outpaced buildings and staff. This, of course, placed additional pressure on those with childcare responsibilities since their children had fewer hours in school and more free time in which to get up to mischief.

Women served the nation in many capacities during World War II, not just in the defense plants or theaters of war. Most wives and mothers contributed to the war effort through enhanced domesticity and voluntary activities. Arguably, women's greatest service was that they gave up their sons or husbands to the war effort. With over 400 000 men killed in action and another 671 000 wounded, Gold Star mothers and wives paid a high price for peace. Millions of women planted Victory Gardens to grow what they could no longer buy. Government efforts to curtail inflation resulted in strict rationing of commodities deemed to be essential, including gasoline, clothing, meat, butter, nylons, soap, and shoes. Ration coupons did not guarantee the availability of scarce items. Half of all housewives reported they could not buy sufficient food and shortages of key commodities such as sugar and meat made it difficult to feed their families and preserve garden produce.

Women canned vegetables, patched old clothes, made their own soap, and wore socks or painted black lines up the back of their legs to simulate seams. Poor people with no reserves of clothing suffered especial hardships, although the affluent had enough clothes to see them through the war. All women found themselves doing more sewing and mending, making over what they might once have discarded. Shopping took up more of their time as they searched for scarce commodities. Women in small towns and rural areas had fewer shops in which to look for essential items but they had land upon which they could grow vegetables and, perhaps, keep a few chickens, unlike women in large cities who depended upon what they could purchase.

Wartime housing proved a particular nightmare for women upon whom the burden of finding and maintaining a home fell. There were few dwellings built during the war, so many war workers' families lived in inadequate and unsanitary temporary accommodation. Willow Run, Michigan, housed thousands of workers at the Ford bomber plant in tents, trailers, shanties, basements, and subdivided homes and apartments. African Americans moving north to take defense jobs encountered extreme difficulty in finding housing; attempts to place them in a previously white neighborhood resulted in riots in Detroit in 1942. Few cities tried to integrate public housing, even when there were units to let, so that black neighborhoods suffered overcrowding as recent migrants had nowhere else to go. Families with children, regardless of race, suffered especially restricted housing choice as many landlords refused to rent to them.

Newly built wartime housing fell far short of minimum standards, while the trailer parks which sprang up near defense plants frequently lacked playgrounds, laundry, and sanitary facilities. With memories of the Depression still fresh in their minds, older residents resented and feared the newcomers who paid no property taxes on their mobile residences and crowded into local schools. Conditions in the trailer parks were particularly hard for women who had to keep their children quiet while shift workers slept, who were far from shops, and who kept house under cramped and unsanitary conditions.

The war narrowed class differentials in standards of living, opened factory jobs to African and Mexican Americans of both sexes, and provided the children of immigrants with stable incomes. Unemployment virtually ended, so that the previously un- and under-employed found jobs at reasonable wages. Between 1935 and 1944 the incomes of the poorest third of the American population rose by nearly 50 percent while those of the wealthiest third rose by about 30 percent, narrowing the gap between the poor and the privileged. The fortification of basic foodstuffs, including flour, bread, and milk, with vitamins, improved nutrition levels and health. In 1936, the poorest third of the population had a caloric intake that was 82 percent of that of the richest third, while that of the middle third was 89 percent as high. By 1948, there was no difference between the middle and most affluent population groups, while the poorest urban dwellers now took in nearly the same number of calories (96 percent) and greatly increased their meat consumption.

Women participated in formal and informal support activities for the war effort, joining the Red Cross to roll bandages and assist servicemen's families. They participated in the activities of the United Service Organization (USO) which sponsored social activities for the military. Both these organizations largely depended upon white middle-class volunteers and reflected their unfortunate prejudices. The Red Cross had racially segregated blood banks; despite pressure from the White House, especially from Mrs. Roosevelt, it only hired African Americans in a menial capacity or to assist black soldiers overseas. The USO, formed by major religious organizations to boost service people's morale, provided socially approved escorts to dance with soldiers and pour tea. It excluded blacks from its premises, leading African-American women to form a parallel organization and to campaign for the "Double V," victory against fascism abroad and racism at home. According to D'Ann Campbell only the American Women's Voluntary Services, founded in New York in 1940, was racially integrated. Campbell concludes that voluntary activities may have made a negative net contribution to the war effort. Bandage rolling provided women with something to do, but could have been done more effectively by machines, while the voluntary welfare activities reinforced social divisions.

By the end of the war, women had demonstrated tremendous resilience and adaptability. Many combined employment and motherhood and used their domestic skills to cope with wartime shortages. Yet some pundits blamed them for a perceived rise in juvenile delinquency and others attacked them for being overprotective mothers. In 1942, Phillip Wylie launched a broadside against women, coining the derogatory term "momism" to describe smothering love which prevented children from growing up. *Generation of Vipers* launched a series of anti-woman diatribes lambasting mothers for the emotional disorders of their sons whom they tried to keep tied to their apron strings. Ferdinand Lundberg and Marynia Farnham's *Modern Woman: The Lost Sex* (1947) took this critique one stage further, asserting that "rejecting, over-solicitous, or dominating" mothers produced "the delinquents, the behavior problem children, and some substantial portion of criminals." Motherhood, at least in the eyes of these commentators, became a social problem rather than a solution.

Domesticity and motherhood remained central to women's lives throughout this era although women sought to shape both to suit their economic and social circumstances. The age of marriage fell and birth rates soared at the end of the war, indicating that women were opting for motherhood over continued employment or even higher education. Following a catastrophic depression, the war had placed great strain on American families, with about one in six enduring long separations. Rosie the Riveter returned home urged by women's magazines, government, and manufacturers to provide a ready market for peacetime consumer goods in her new house in the suburbs. This unalloyed domesticity lasted only for a decade and was undercut by consistently rising employment levels, especially among the mothers of young children.

The dual nature of women's lives and the tensions between home and family grew stronger throughout these years, with the strongest social approval going to full-time mothers. After a short sharp drop in employment levels more women entered the labor market, rationalizing their employment in terms of their families' needs and (by the 1960s and 1970s) as a means of using their education. The war underscored the twin foci of women's lives, but accelerating long-term trends in married women's labor force participation spread employment more broadly across the classes and races. The balance between home and work shifted after the war, yet a growing number of women perceived a fluidity between home and work and imbued their daughters with a belief that they could combine both aspects in a liberated, less gender-bound synthesis of roles.

11   Education and Culture, 1920–1945

The seesaw of gendered participation in education and cultural activities tipped up and down in the inter- and post-war years as prosperity, poverty, war, peace, and lingering prejudice expanded, constricted, and shaped expectations and opportunities. Women obtained greater access to secondary schooling, but higher and professional education varied with the economic and social climate, as an increasingly conservative social mood impeded female aspirations. In the early 1920s many women believed they had been fully accepted as scientists, yet as historian of science Margaret Rossiter observes, they made little progress in the next two decades because social and economic patterns "systematically channeled women into secondary roles." The same strictures applied to most educational, scientific, professional, literary, sporting, and artistic endeavors, although some exceptional women flourished, especially in gender-specific occupations such as acting or singing in which being female was a requirement for certain parts. Generally, women did not succeed in moving up professional hierarchies into positions of authority over others, whether as doctors or directors, and at times they actually lost ground.

EDUCATION

Education promised a route out of poverty to the children of immigrants and the rural poor, with high school graduation becoming the norm for both sexes after 1920. For young women in cities and remote areas of the country, high school, business college, or university represented the route to a white-collar job. The desire for better education prompted rural families to move to the cities and provided some of the impetus for the Great Migration of African Americans out of the South.

Many girls took vocational and commercial rather than academic courses so that although they comprised just over half the students in high school, they lagged behind men in post-secondary education, with the gap worsening during the Depression and post-war years. In 1920, about 8 percent of all 18–21-year-old women enrolled in colleges and universities, and comprised 47 percent of all undergraduates. In the 1930s and 1940s, the number of men in college increased rapidly; two-fifths of undergraduates in 1940 were women but only three-tenths were in 1950, a ratio on a par with that of 1880. Not until the late 1970s did the proportion of female undergraduates approximate that of the 1920s. Nevertheless, by 1940, there were over 600 000 women college students.

Women's colleges provided role models for their students; women comprised 72 percent of the academic staff at the largest women's colleges in 1940 compared with only 3 percent at men's colleges. Female faculty presence in all academic institutions peaked in 1940 at 28 percent and fell sharply in the post-war era, even in women's colleges. As more women students attended coeducational institutions they had less chance to see women in positions of authority or fusing political with academic education as Vassar economist Mabel Newcomer did when she chaperoned students to a suffrage rally. The head of her hall, a former classmate of suffragist Harriot Stanton Blatch, took her to task for this because "women's education was still on trial and must not be confused with other doubtful causes." Such activities spurred then Vice President Calvin Coolidge to attack women's colleges as "hotbeds of radicalism," making their staffs cautious about their political connections. Female academics also received significantly lower pay than their male counterparts, even at women's colleges, and were confined to lower grades which deterred women from academic careers.

Inexpensive or free higher education during the Depression encouraged the children of immigrants despite restrictive admissions policies in many colleges and nurses' training courses. Catholic and Jewish immigrants' children enrolled in state universities in the inter-war years although Ivy League college administrators regarded the large number of talented applicants as a problem and discriminated against them. Sectarian institutions also accommodated aspiring students from diverse backgrounds. The number of Catholic women's colleges increased from 14 to 37 between 1915 and 1925 and reached 116 by 1955, enabling Catholic women to advance their education in a setting acceptable to themselves, their parents, and their church.

More African-American women also attended college in the interwar years, mostly in segregated institutions. The attitude of northern colleges varied from tolerance to active hostility, while southern ones kept the races apart. A six-fold expansion in African-American college graduates occurred between 1917 and 1927, with female attendance levels rising faster than male since women could obtain jobs teaching in segregated schools but prejudice against African-American men undermined the utility of higher education. Families made great sacrifices to educate their daughters; nearly half of all African-American college students in the 1930s came from the families of unskilled workers, compared with less than one in twenty white college students.

As the economy deteriorated, many students took part-time jobs or turned to federal programs for support. The National Youth Administration (NYA) underwrote the tuition and living expenses for approximately one in eight college students during the Great Depression and was one of the few New Deal agencies to assist women and African Americans on the same basis as white men. Female students comprised 45 percent of those aided by the NYA, slightly more than their actual percentage in the undergraduate population. Mary McLeod Bethune, director of the Negro division of the NYA, ensured that African-American students benefited from educational grants, traveling extensively to encourage local NYA directors to include students of all racial groups. At her urging, the NYA established a special Negro Higher Education Fund to facilitate college attendance.

The actions of the NYA indicate the high level of acceptance of education for both sexes, especially at the high school level, although the tone of women's higher education altered. As in high schools, college women demanded a less restrictive environment and more active social lives by seeking an end to curfews, mandatory church services, and bans on smoking and drinking. Women joined sororities to enhance friendships and obtain housing, but their exclusivity reinforced religious, ethnic, and class divisions. Many campuses, especially Catholic and African-American ones, maintained dress codes in order to emphasize student respectability, although in the mid-1920s women students at Fisk finally managed to persuade the administration that cotton stockings and gingham aprons were outmoded. Colleges also permitted greater contact between the sexes in the 1920s and 1930s, holding dances and dropping strict chaperonage requirements.

Women's colleges shifted away from a purely academic education by putting home economics and nursing on the curriculum, and many female students expressed their wish to combine education and careers with marriage. A 1936 *Fortune* poll discovered that three-fifths wanted to marry shortly after graduation and two-fifths wanted to work after marriage. Some post-war educators abandoned the career orientation altogether. Lynn White, Jr., president of the all-female Mills College, called for a curriculum which permitted a woman to "foster the intellectual and emotional life of her family and community," to furnish her home with taste and beauty, and cook gourmet meals for her family. His speech to the American Association of University Women in 1947 received a hostile reception from members who believed that women should be educated for their own purposes rather than as ornaments or housekeepers.

White's comments underscore the backlash against women's education and employment as higher education became heavily male-dominated in the late 1940s. The number of women doing science and medicine surged during the war, but declined sharply in the post-war years, as did the proportion obtaining advanced degrees. Veterans enrolled in large numbers on post-war campuses, frequently supported by wives who worked to augment veterans' benefits. GI educational provision distorted higher education by paying for many white and some black men to attend university, but women comprised less than 3 percent of veteran-students. Since there were few African-American women in the military, they did not receive any federal assistance towards their education after the war, and their numbers decreased.

Some women succeeded in carving out academic careers, although prejudice certainly limited their progress. Mary Ritter Beard pioneered women's history in the 1930s and attempted to establish a World Center for Women's Archives. Critics derided her scholarship and subsumed her authorship under that of her husband Charles (with whom she published some joint works), yet Mary Beard was, as she titled one of her books, a "force in history" through her scholarship on women. Other notable female scholars of the inter-war years included anthropologists Ruth Benedict and Margaret Mead, and sociologist Helen Merrell Lynd, co-author of the studies on Muncie, Indiana, and a noted teacher at Sarah Lawrence. Mead's field work in New Guinea discovered a great range of behavior accepted as "natural" for each sex, leading her to conclude that "passivity, responsiveness, and willingness to cherish children" were not sex-linked aspects of behavior.

Despite these women's efforts, occupational segregation in the professions increased in the 1930s and 1940s. Rosalind Rosenberg notes, "Margaret Mead kept the light of feminist scholarship burning," yet the light flickered in subsequent decades. The proportion of female doctors, professors, and dentists declined while that of librarians, nurses, and social workers rose as educational institutions retained or raised their discriminatory policies. Most notoriously, medical schools limited women to around 5 percent of their intake, if they accepted them at all. In 1910, 6 percent of all doctors were women; by 1930 this had fallen to 4 percent. When the military accepted female doctors during World War II, medical schools reluctantly opened their doors a crack. By 1950, women again comprised 6 percent of all physicians, but medical schools reinstated discriminatory admissions policies in the 1950s and the proportion of female physicians fell.

Hospitals made it difficult for women to practice medicine effectively by refusing to hire them or accommodate their patients. In 1914, the American College of Surgeons admitted 1065 members, with only two women among them, prompting obstetrician and surgeon Bertha Van Joosen to establish the American Women's Medical Association in 1915. This society helped female doctors retain a sense of solidarity but had little success in prizing open the doors to equality in the medical profession. A 1929 American Medical Association survey discovered that nine-tenths of hospitals still barred women physicians, although World War II forced their temporary acceptance.

Families and educational establishments urged women with a vocation for healing to become nurses rather than doctors. Particularly during the hard times of the Great Depression, nurses' training had the added advantage of offering a modest wage, room, and board. The daughter of Russian Jewish immigrants, Frances Krantz entered Hartford Hospital Training School in 1934 and received $7 per month for the duration of her training. As the Depression deepened, hospitals withdrew student nurses' stipends but still furnished free accommodation. Graduate nurses also had the opportunity for further study and specialization, which was especially attractive as competition sharpened for private duty and head nurse positions during the Depression. Frances Krantz, RN (registered nurse) moved to New York City in 1938 to take up advanced training as an operating room nurse, ensuring steady employment and higher wages.

While the armed forces reluctantly accepted female physicians in 1943, they welcomed women in white. Nearly one-third of all professional nurses joined the Army or Navy Nurse Corps during World War II, eventually enjoying full military rank and better pay than civilian nurses. Recruited through the Red Cross, rather than directly through the armed forces, they generally served behind the front lines. Medical corpsmen and male doctors dealt with the wounded on the battlefield and sent them to hospitals away from the fighting. Racial segregation persisted in the uniformed medical services. African-American nurses served in segregated units only looking after men of their race.

Nursing courses expanded rapidly once Congress established the Cadet Nurse Corps in 1943. The Bolton Act paid for student nurses' training in return for military service and nursing for the duration of the war and greatly expanded the number of non-white nurses. Prewar training programs tended to be racially segregated, but the number of African-American nurses doubled in the 1940s and by 1950, the number of nursing schools accepting black students had risen from 42 to 330. Prompted by staff shortages, many hospitals hired non-white nurses for the first time during the war, expanding employment opportunities and encouraging more women of color to undertake post-secondary education.

The greatest expansion of women's education and training in this era occurred in a limited number of fields and undermined the optimism of educated women in the 1920s that they were on the way to equality. Women experienced great difficulties in obtaining advanced education, medical, legal, or scientific credentials, and academic positions in the 1930s and 1940s. Girls comprised a majority of high school graduates, yet there were nearly two men in college for every woman in the mid-1950s and a smaller proportion of doctorates went to women in the 1940s than in the 1920s. This educational segregation and marginalization contributed to the determination of the next generation of women to obtain better credentials in a wider range of fields, sustained by their own mothers' commitment to their daughters' education and their willingness to go out to work to pay for it.

WOMEN'S WRITING

Women's place in American cultural life was a mixture of individual triumphs and gendered setbacks in high culture, accompanied by a wide audience for their popular writing, especially in children's and adolescent fiction. Laura Ingalls Wilder's *Little House on the Prairie* series and the popular mystery stories about "girl detective" Nancy Drew, first authored by Carolyn Keene (Edward Stratemeyer) and later by his daughter Harriet Stratemeyer Adams, attracted a mass market by depicting female independence and integrity. Nancy Drew, an affluent motherless student, regularly got herself in and out of scrapes as she solved mysteries. While she had a boyfriend and several good female friends, she provided both the brains and motivation to resolve the crimes and misdemeanors. Such plucky heroines had a long lineage in American fiction with Louisa May Alcott's Jo as their progenitor.

Nursing also became the subject of popular fiction in the 1930s and 1940s. Helen Dore Boylston's *Sue Barton* and Helen Wells' *Cherry Ames* highlighted women's abilities and professional commitment, although they also contained an element of romance. In *Sue Barton: Senior Nurse* (1937), the heroine declares herself to be "terribly fond" of her boyfriend, whom she expected to marry someday, but "Please not now. I'm busy!" As literary critic Deborah Philips notes, Barton's training carefully followed that proposed by nurse educator and social welfare activist Lavinia Lloyd Dock, who worked at the Henry Street Settlement where the fictional Sue studied community health nursing. These stories grew out of inter-war attitudes which accepted female vocations, if not occupations, and inspired girls and young women to take their own interests seriously.

Young women read these series voraciously, yet woman writers aiming at the adult market experienced difficulties. The number of women writing remained buoyant, but they lost critical acclaim as new male-dominated literary movements made their work seem old-fashioned, sentimental, and backward looking. Willa Cather still explored themes of female independence at a time when male writers ignored women or depicted them as one-dimensional. F. Scott Fitzgerald's classic novel of the Roaring '20s, *The Great Gatsby* (1925), portrays female characters as shallow money seekers and archetypal flappers looking for good times and a meal ticket. In Dorothy M. Brown's analysis such female characters had no moral integrity, unlike Edith Wharton's Kate Clephane who, in *The Mother's Recompense,* forgoes her own happiness in order to make up for past mistakes and ensure her daughter's well-being. Wharton won a Pulitzer Prize in 1921, but resided abroad for the rest of her life. Willa Cather felt estranged from the literary generation which succeeded her, telling them in *Not Under Forty* (1936) that they would not understand her values. Ellen Glasgow's reputation surpassed that of Wharton and Cather by the mid-1930s. She was elected to the American Academy of Arts and Letters in 1940 and received the Pulitzer Prize for fiction in 1942.

Women participated to varying degrees in the cultural life of the 1920s and 1930s. Part of the Algonquin Round Table – a group of writers who exchanged *bon mots* – Dorothy Parker wrote short stories like "Big Blonde" and was drama critic for *Vanity Fair.* Lila Acheson Wallace co-founded *Reader's Digest,* bringing fiction, shortened books, and lighthearted commentaries to homes and dentists' waiting rooms across the nation. Pearl Buck's novel *The Good Earth* was a best seller in the bleak days of 1931 and 1932. She was the first American woman to win the Nobel Prize for Literature (1938), achieving greater recognition than the arguably more enduring fiction of Cather or Wharton.

Female poets fell out of fashion, criticized for writing poetry rooted in personal experience and emotion. Edna St. Vincent Millay had enjoyed great popularity in the 1920s, winning the Pulitzer Prize for poetry in 1923 for verse that expressed the freedom and gaiety of the flapper era, claiming that her "candle burns at both ends" and would not last the night. She also campaigned vigorously to overturn the unjust convictions of Sacco and Vanzetti for supposed involvement in the murder of a paymaster in Massachusetts. As her poetry increasingly pondered social issues in the 1930s, critics dismissed it along with Sara Teasdale's and Louise Bogan's work, comparing them unfavorably with male British and American poets W. H. Auden, T. S. Eliot, and Wallace Stevens.

Millay, like a number of female authors, turned to journalism, working as *Vanity Fair's* foreign correspondent during the 1920s while Dorothy Thompson became head of the New York *Evening Post's* Berlin office in 1924. Martha Gellhorn, a Bryn Mawr graduate and daughter of a suffrage campaigner, wrote extensively for American magazines during the Spanish Civil War and World War II, reporting from as close as she could get to the front line. Despite her years of war reporting, when *Collier's* magazine found it could only accredit one correspondent for the D-Day landings, it chose her then-husband Ernest Hemingway, leaving her to find her own passage, and to send back incisive reports.

The Harlem Renaissance and the rise of ethnic writers such as Phillip Roth questioned the predominance of the WASP aesthetic in American literature between the wars, as the women of these communities struggled to place their concerns on the literary agenda. The Harlem Renaissance, largely dominated by men, was an urban movement of educated African Americans celebrating "The New Negro's" freedom from the racist constraints of southern life. Unlike their male counterparts, many African-American women authors explored issues of gender as well as race. Jessie Redmond Fauset, literary editor of the NAACP's *Crisis*, delineated a hierarchical world in which "men had a better time of it than women, colored men than colored women, white men than white women" in her novel *Plum Bun* (1929). Perhaps such truth-telling made uncomfortable reading since neither Fauset nor Zora Neale Hurston received the same acceptance as Langston Hughes or James Weldon Johnson. The rural orientation of *Their Eyes Were Watching God* (1937), its frank exploration of wife abuse, and its facility with southern dialect, placed it outside the mainstream of the urban androcentricity of her contemporaries.

Hurston modeled the African-American community in *Their Eyes* after Eatonville, the all-black town in which she grew up, taking gender relations and the achievement of a good marriage through equality and sharing as her themes. Her characterization of rural life in the Great Depression differed sharply from that of John Steinbeck's *Grapes of Wrath* (1939) which showed Ma Joad as a nurturing, domesticated earth mother who deserved "a whipping" for undermining her husband's authority. Steinbeck's novel ends with Ma telling her daughter, Rose of Sharon, to suckle a dying man, to submerge her grief at her baby's death in an effort to sustain the living. This depiction of the family which endures through women's sacrifices contrasts with Hurston's recognition of the limitations of traditional family structures. Hurston neither romanticizes the family nor suggests that women should unilaterally relinquish their interests in order to sustain failed marriages or other people's dreams.

Born in Plinsk near Warsaw, Anzia Yezierska immigrated with her family to New York in the early 1890s. Her writing reflects upon her ethnic heritage in trenchant studies of class, gender, and assimilation in New York City. Yezierska's heroines explored their new country and the immigrants' difficult and painful route to success in stories which encapsulate the conflict between generations and cultures. Her characters trade the communal spirit of the old world for the individualism of the new, rejecting the limitations of their upbringing to find "the soul – the spirit – of America!" Yet American culture posed dangers for the unwary; its officials lacked understanding and sympathy for the newcomers. The Russian immigrant woman aspiring to be a teacher in "Soap and Water" is refused her diploma because she is ill-kempt from working eight hours a day in a laundry to support herself.

Yezierska repudiates the Jewish community's ordained fate for women, marriage and working for the family, preferring independence and individual identity. Family ties and marriage did not necessarily bring happiness in Yezierska's world. As Shenah Pessah tells Sam Arkins when she rejects his love, "You can't make me for a person. It's not only that I got to go up higher, but I got to push myself up by my own strength." The dual nature of the female immigrant's experience, longing to be a part of American culture, yet never capable of complete assimilation, imposes a tension and sadness on her stories. Sara Smolinsky's pious father denounces her career aspirations and independence: "She's only good to the world, not to her father. Will she hand me her wages from school as a dutiful daughter should?" Strength and independence were the best foundations for relationships with individual self-worth valued over self-sacrifice.

Impoverished during the Depression, Yezierska obtained work with the Federal Writers' Project of the WPA, churning out her quota of 2000 words a day. The proletarian fiction of other women writers in the 1930s explored poverty from a female perspective through independent female characters who supported their families. Meridel LeSueur, Tillie Olsen, and Agnes Smedley challenged conventional male proletarian fiction in which women served the working-class struggle through homemaking and looking after the domestic side of the revolution. These social protest writers explored family relationships and emotions along with job prospects and labor disputes. LeSueur wrote of "Women on the Breadlines" for the *New Masses* in 1932, showing them to be betrayed both by men and capitalism. Smedley traveled to Europe and China, wrote sympathetic accounts of the communist attempts to overthrow Chiang Kai-shek, marched with the Red Army in the 1930s, and published numerous books and newspaper articles on China. Smedley, especially in her thinly veiled autobiography, *Daughter of Earth,* depicted traditional motherhood as limiting female autonomy, preferring the mothers of the Red Army who fought alongside their children to the destructive relationship she had with her own mother.

Strikes and labor activism inspired female authors. In 1929, textile workers at Loray Mill in Gastonia, North Carolina, walked off the job when union activists of both sexes were fired for trying to organize the mill. *Strike* by Mary Heaton Vorse (1930), *To Make My Bread* (Grace Lumpkin, 1932) and *The Gathering Storm* by Dorothy Myra Page (1932) combined female militancy with everyday existence in mill villages. Myra Page also wrote *Daughter of the Hills,* an account of women's struggle in the coal fields of Appalachia which blended the romance and family life of its protagonists, Dolly Hawkins and John Cooper, with the fight to bring pure water, medical attention, and unions to the Cumberland Mountains between the wars. These works share a willingness to confront issues of gender, class, and sometimes race from the vantage point of women who fused their roles in the family with earning a living under hostile economic circumstances.

In the 1930s and 1940s new female authors came to prominence as Katherine Anne Porter, Carson McCullers, and Mary McCarthy began publishing. The most celebrated author, though not necessarily the one who received the most critical acclaim, was Margaret Mitchell whose *Gone with the Wind* (1937) sold over a million copies in its first six months and won the Pulitzer Prize for literature. Quickly made into a movie, starring Vivien Leigh and Clark Gable, it enthralled millions of readers and movie fans with its romanticized version of the Old South and its strong female characters. Yet, as Laura Hapke observes, *GWTW* and similar novels of the 1930s "create a dialectic between erasure and celebration" of women's careers, simultaneously lauding and condemning Scarlett's strength and determination.

Events surrounding the cinematic production of *GWTW* also erased and celebrated women's work. Hattie McDaniel became the first African-American woman to win an Oscar for her portrayal of Mammy, but the director worried that white southerners would be offended by the presence of African-American actors and refused to let her or other black cast members attend the premier in Atlanta. *GWTW's* ambivalence toward female ambition reinforced the widespread concern about women's place in the home and the world of work which recurred during the Great Depression. Despite the popularity of the book and the movie, and women's centrality to the story, women were nevertheless ambiguous characters, hedged by gendered and racial restrictions on their behavior and ambitions. Female authors of diverse ethnicities, races, and classes included the female perspective in their writings, achieving great popularity between the wars, if not always critical acclaim. They occupied a central place in popular literature but an uncertain status in *belles lettres*.

FINE ARTS

Women participated in music and the arts primarily as performers or artists, helped establish museums and were patrons of artistic endeavors but had difficulty in getting their pictures hung or their symphonies performed. Abby Aldrich Rockefeller founded the Museum of Modern Art in 1929 at a luncheon with other socially prominent women, contributing several thousand paintings to its collections. Gertrude Vanderbilt Whitney encouraged young artists by giving them studio space, exhibitions, and financial support. A sculptor who worked both in the United States and Europe, she opened the Whitney Museum of American Art in 1931. Some female artists incorporated feminist themes into their work, notably sculptor Adelaide Johnson whose marble statue, "The Woman Movement," was dedicated in 1921 at a reception held in the US Capitol. In 1936, her sculpture of Susan B. Anthony served as the basis of a 3 cent postage stamp.

Georgia O'Keeffe was one of the leading artists of the inter-war years. Her painting included several important trends of the early twentieth century, notably the precisionist emphasis on geometric form and line which characterized the work of other noted artists of the period such as Charles Sheeler and Edward Hopper. Born in Sun Prairie, Wisconsin, in 1887, O'Keeffe studied at the Art Institute of Chicago and at the Art Student's League of New York City. During the 1920s she painted a series of gigantic flowers in which the enlargement transformed the flowers into abstract compositions. Works such as *Black Iris* (1926) captured the vastness of the American landscape through coloration and bold pattern. Moving to the Southwest in the 1930s, O'Keeffe incorporated the local landscape into her work.

Women also achieved fame as photographers in the 1930s. Margaret Bourke-White (associate editor of *Fortune* magazine, 1929–33), Berenice Abbott, and Dorothea Lange specialized in documentary photography and photo-journalism, contributing lasting images of depression and war. Bourke-White documented the droughts in the Midwest, writing that the plight of the farmers, "jolted me into the realization that a man is more than a figure to put into the background of a photograph for scale." Subsequently she teamed up with Erskine Caldwell to produce *You Have Seen Their Faces* (1937), an indictment of the sharecropping system in text and photographs. Another of her powerful pictures silhouetted a line of African Americans waiting for food handouts after the 1937 Louisville flood against a billboard proclaiming "World's Highest Standard of Living: There's no way like the American Way" with a smiling, prosperous white family in their shiny car. She defended the right of women to work as men's equals, stating that it was "the excellence of the results which counts."

After 12 years as a studio photographer Dorothea Lange took her camera to the streets, farms, and migrant labor camps. Hired by the Director of the California State Emergency Relief Administration to chronicle the experiences of migrant laborers, Lange talked to her subjects, found common ground with them, and recorded their comments on their situation. She later toured the United States for the Farm Security Administration to bring the plight of the poor to the eyes of the nation. Lange's stark images isolated subjects against fields and sky, drawing the eye into the frame. During World War II, she worked for the War Relocation Authority documenting the Japanese internment as the government, encouraged by hostile mobs, forced them out of their homes in California and into camps in the interior.

Female artists joined together in the National Association of Women Painters and Sculptors, which in 1934 admitted Augusta Savage as its first African-American member. Savage later received a commission from the New York World's Fair Corporation for which she created "The Harp," widely known as "Lift Every Voice and Sing," after the text of James Weldon Johnson's poem which it featured. Savage opened an art school in Harlem and also served as an assistant supervisor in the Federal Art Project (FAP) sponsored by the Works Progress Administration. The FAP offered work to unemployed artists and, like a number of other New Deal cultural programs, was particularly sensitive to female practitioners, who constituted 40 percent of all professional artists in the United States during the 1930s and a similar proportion of FAP artists. The range of public art during the Depression included murals, Native American crafts, sculpture, and paintings.

However, the public art of the New Deal displayed in public buildings mostly portrayed men at work and rarely included women in its portraits of workers and work sites. This erasure of the female dovetailed with the New Deal legislative emphasis on male as producer and female as dependent. The construction projects built under the Public Buildings Administration devoted 1 percent of their budgets to "embellishments." Almost without exception these depicted well-muscled male laborers, with women in family groups, protected by heroic men, or nurturing children. During World War II, Rosie the Riveter joined the assembly line, as a thirtyish, white woman, with useful muscles and a desire to defeat Hitler. When the country needed woman power, art was pressed into service to expand the range of acceptable gender roles, while in peace or depression it showed women with families and ignored their economic contributions.

DRAMA, MUSIC, AND SPORTS

Women took part in drama, music, and sports as players and, less frequently, as writers, composers, bandleaders, or managers. Many leading stage performers in this period were household names, including Ethel Barrymore, Fanny Brice, and Helen Hayes. Women's talents as playwrights also received recognition: *Abby's Irish Rose* by Anne Nichols ran for 2327 performances on Broadway in the 1920s. Examining a pupil's accusations of lesbianism against two teachers, Lillian Hellman's *The Children's Hour* was a controversial Broadway hit in 1934, as was *The Little Foxes* (1939). Hellman served as the urbane model for detective Nora Charles in Dashiel Hammett's *Thin Man* detective stories featuring a witty upper-class couple who, with their dog Asta, solved crimes. The movie versions appeared in the 1930s and 1940s, starring Myrna Loy and William Powell as the sophisticated, egalitarian partners.

Hallie Flanagan produced plays while in college in the early 1920s and won a Guggenheim fellowship to compare production methods internationally. In 1935, the Roosevelt administration asked her to direct the Federal Theater Project (1935–39) designed to alleviate the impact of the Depression on the legitimate theater, actors, and backstage staff. Radio and the movies had also damaged theater attendance so that by 1933, half of New York City's theaters had closed and many actors were unemployed, a situation duplicated across the nation. The Federal Theater had five subsections and played to over 25 million people. The living newspaper dramatized current events, while the new plays' division gave unknown playwrights an opportunity to mount theatrical works. There was an experimental theater, a tryout theater, and a Negro Theater which produced plays across the United States, including a production of *Macbeth* with an entirely African-American cast. Plays were also produced in Yiddish for the benefit of the immigrant Jewish audience which spoke little English. Congress terminated the program in 1939 amid allegations of communist infiltration including an accusation that Marlowe, the greatest dramatist before Shakespeare, was a communist.

Female musicians succeeded as jazz, popular, and opera singers but rarely as instrumentalists, symphony players, composers or conductors in the inter-war years. Few orchestras hired female instrumentalists; barely 100 women held professional positions with New York City's symphonies and orchestras compared with 17 000 men. A few women transcended taboos limiting them to decorative or genteel roles. Concert pianist Ethel Leginska established and conducted the Boston Philharmonic Orchestra in the 1920s and headed the Boston Women's Symphony Orchestra. Amy Marcy Beach broke new ground for women when she founded and became first president of the Association of American Women Composers in 1926, while opera singer Mary Garden was appointed as head of the Chicago Opera Company in 1921. In 1930, Ruth Crawford Seeger won a Guggenheim fellowship in composition. Although Crawford stopped composing after her marriage, she and her husband jointly collected over 1000 folk songs, preserving an important part of America's musical heritage.

African-American women attempting classical careers encountered the twin barriers of race and gender. Hazel Harrison toured Europe, played with the Berlin Philharmonic as a concert pianist in the 1920s, and taught music in Chicago, before joining the staffs of Tuskegee Institute and Howard University. Marian Anderson began her singing career in her church Sunday School. Her family could not afford singing lessons, but supported by family friends and her church, Anderson obtained classical tuition at home and in Europe. In 1939, the Daughters of the American Revolution barred her from performing at Constitution Hall. Anderson professed herself "shocked beyond words to be barred from the capital" of her country after performing in "almost every other capital in the world." After a groundswell of public protest and the intervention of Eleanor Roosevelt, she sang to 75 000 people at the Lincoln Memorial on Easter Sunday.

Female blues and jazz singers performed alongside the big bands and small ensembles of the inter-war years. Ma Rainey, Bessie Smith, and Billie Holiday carved out a niche for themselves as vocalists, despite the problems of race and gender which abounded in the world of popular music. Ma Rainey, the first woman to rise to fame as a Blues singer, started in touring minstrel shows, gaining the sobriquet, "Mother of the Blues." She recorded for Paramount records in the 1920s, selling by mail order in the South and in shops in the North. Many of the songs she recorded were her own compositions, distinguishing her from vocalists who merely sang others' words. Rainey's career ended in the 1930s when her record company went bankrupt, and the segregated vaudeville and minstrel circuit collapsed.

The appeal of Bessie Smith, the "Empress of the Blues," transcended racial barriers, giving her a following on radio, records, and stage. Many of Smith's compositions had a topical theme, including "Rent House Blues," "Nobody Knows You When you're Down and Out," and a number of songs about prison life. As with Ma Rainey, the Depression seriously harmed her career. Smith continued to perform in small venues, but died as the result of injuries sustained in a car crash in Mississippi in 1937.

Torch singer Billie Holiday sang about love lost, rarely mentioning racial problems, which white audiences would have found unacceptable. She toured with Artie Shaw's band, but there was a white back-up singer available should venues not permit integrated performances. Holiday memorialized the haunting song "Strange Fruit" which tells of the lynchings in the South, as well as singing her own compositions, including "God Bless the Child," and popular love songs and ballads. She recorded for the race record label, Brunswick, and also appeared in several movies where her maid's character sang.

Female singers and actresses had an obvious niche in the performing arts, although endemic racial discrimination in the United States led Josephine Baker, among others, to develop careers abroad. In contrast, female athletes and explorers had to carve a new way for themselves. Women expanded their sporting activities during the inter-war years, with some becoming national heroines for their prowess and daring. In 1927, Ruth Nicols was one of the first women to win certification from the Department of Commerce as a pilot. Amelia Earhart flew over the Atlantic in 1928 as a crew member and was the first woman to pilot a plane across the ocean (in 1932). Like many other women attracted to flying, Earhart barnstormed the United States and participated in cross-country races. She disappeared near Howland Island in the Pacific with her crew on a flight around the world in 1937. Hostile reaction from male pilots stifled women's attempts to make the transition to commercial flying as the all-male pilot's union refused them admission. By the early 1930s, airlines limited women who wanted to fly solely to caring for passengers, hiring trained nurses to reassure travelers, and creating the role of stewardess. Women continued to obtain pilot's licenses but, denied access to military and commercial aviation, flying could only be an expensive hobby for women, not a career.

The replacement of earlier generations' informal spontaneous pastimes with formal sports and recreation discouraged active participation and marginalized women, according to the Lynds' study of leisure time pursuits in Muncie. There were many highly structured activities for males, but relatively few for females apart from the YWCA and intramural sports. Even though more women played sports in the 1920s than in the 1890s, schools and communities focused primarily upon male athletic contests and devoted most of their resources to them. Women's participation in sports grew along different lines with social advisers in the popular press adjuring young sportswomen to "lose gracefully" so as not to intimidate sensitive male egos. They played more individual and fewer team sports and had less opportunity for inter-school competition. The growing importance of male high school and college sports starved women's athletic programs.

In the early 1920s "graceful" sports such as tennis, golf, and swimming grew in popularity. Ice skating garnered publicity and participants when Olympic medallist Sonja Henie appeared in magazines and newsreels, and had her own ice skating show in the 1930s. The best-known female athlete of the era was Babe Didrickson who played basketball, a wide range of athletic events, and, most famously, golf. Co-founder of the post-war Ladies' Professional Golf Association, Didrickson helped popularize the game for women and regularized the situation of those who wanted to play for a living.

Women also played baseball, basketball, and softball on an amateur, club, and (occasionally) professional level. Softball was particularly popular among women; there were thousands of leagues across the United States in the 1930s. An all-woman basketball club known as the Red Heads (after the wigs they wore) played exhibition games in the late 1930s. Philip K. Wrigley established the All-American Girls' Baseball League when the military drafted all the male players during World War II. With attendance reaching the one million mark in the late 1940s, this midwestern league paid salaries considerably in excess of those usually earned by women, although much lower than those paid to male baseball stars. In order to ensure that baseball did not impair their femininity, the owners insisted the players attend charm courses, wear skirts, and behave in a "ladylike" manner off the diamond. By 1954, competition from television and men's sports had killed off women's professional baseball.

RADIO

Female vocalists had widespread popular followings, especially after the new medium of radio brought inexpensive entertainment to millions. Newspaper circulation declined during the 1920s as people turned to the radio for news, entertainment, and music. The first commercial radio station was founded in Pittsburgh in 1920; by 1922 there were over 500 stations across the country. At the start of the Great Depression about 13 million American households had radios and by World War II, there were over 50 million radio sets and 900 stations. The growth of radio networks boosted the market share of large manufacturers who advertised nationally. Almost all programs had commercial sponsors so the new medium brought consumer products into millions of homes. Advertisers told children to ask their mothers to buy their products, boosting sales of household items and secret decoder rings alike.

Radio stations and the new network of stations sought to fill the airwaves with programs with mass appeal in order to attract an audience for the commercial advertisers. Cooking programs helped housewives provide inexpensive nourishing meals during the

Depression. The "Betty Crocker Hour" told women how to econo-mize, promoting General Mills' products while broadcasting cost-saving ideas and recipes. Radio also adapted vaudeville acts such as George Burns and Gracie Allen, entertaining millions who could not afford to see live stage shows. During World War II, the federal gov-ernment used radio to get its patriotic and nutritional messages across to women, sponsoring radio programs to improve the nation's health through the use of vitamin-rich foods and a balanced diet. Soap operas, programs backed by Procter & Gamble and other mak-ers of household products, were especially popular with the female audience. They provided serialized dramas of domestic life which women listened to avidly while they cooked, ironed, washed and mended.

The first of these serials was *The Rise of the Goldbergs* which fea-tured the everyday trials and tribulations of a Jewish family. Characteristically, soap operas featured a strong female lead, usually a mother, who tried to solve her family's and community's problems. One of the most popular of these domestic dramas was *Ma Perkins* which ran from 1933 until 1960. Ma was a spirited widow who reopened her late husband's lumber yard, provided employment for the men who had worked there, and sustained her family with its profits. *Ma Perkins* appealed to a wide audience in Depression (and post-Depression) America, according to Virginia Payne, the actress who played Ma. Listeners identified closely with the serial; "the con-tinuity of the program helped people during the Depression. We were their link and we were something to cling to." *Ma Perkins* and other radio serials provided a comforting world in which problems got sorted out and endings were happy.

Dependence upon commercial sponsorship and the growing national scope of radio networks fostered timidity in programming. Program makers worried about not offending what they perceived to be key constituencies such as white southerners. They frequently pre-sented stereotyped views of African Americans, and confined African-American women to the part of domestic servant or nagging shrew. Hattie McDaniel played Beulah on the show of the same name, while Ernestine Wade depicted Sapphire in the *Amos 'n Andy Show* in the broken English forced upon her by the popular serial's white producers.

Although there were notable exceptions, such as *Ma Perkins,* many of the female characters on radio had little scope to demonstrate the diversity of female experience and abilities. Radio shows such as the Jack Benny program projected a fantasy world with clear hierarchies of race, class, and gender. In other productions, especially those featuring vocalists, women might have central roles. Kate Smith, for example, had her own radio show in which she was the featured singer. She brought the song *God Bless America!* by Irving Berlin to public attention, and it became closely associated with her. Yet radio constructed a limited set of roles for women, an example which television later followed.

CINEMA

To an even greater extent than radio, movies dominated American popular culture from the 1920s through to the 1940s. During the Depression, 60–90 million people went to the movies at least once a week with urban school children even spending their lunch money in order to escape for a few hours before the silver screen. Magazines such as *Movie Screen* and *True Confessions* provided information about the stars on and off the screen, to glamour-hungry fans. Particularly during the Depression, movies brought excitement into otherwise drab lives. Their popularity raised concern over the images they disseminated as the Legion of Decency and Hollywood Production Code attempted to regulate morality and sexuality on the big screen. The images of women they disseminated contained overt and covert messages about gender.

Women acted in, directed, and occasionally produced movies in the inter-war years, but as the big studios came to dominate Hollywood, women were increasingly limited to acting in front of the cameras. There were of course exceptions to this. Mary Pickford, co-founder of United Artists, managed her own career and picked her movie roles and directors with care before she became a producer. Her on-screen persona was that of an innocent young woman with spirit, an image which resonated well with her fans. In her own words: "I am a woman's woman. My success has been due to the fact that women like the pictures in which I appear." America's Sweetheart, as she was known, had an astute business brain and made the transition from star to producer successfully.

Dorothy Arzner was one of the few women to work as a director for a major studio, directing 17 pictures between 1927 and 1943, including Paramount's first talkie, *The Wild Party*, with Clara Bow in 1929. Female screenwriters were more numerous than directors, including Anita Loos and Frances Marion, yet film critic Molly Haskell concludes that their vision was neither particularly feminist, nor a slavish submission to a male ethos. Instead, it reflected and possibly improved upon what women wanted to see, namely a confirmation of the choices they had made. Loos produced lighthearted comedies from 1912 (*The New York Hat*) until 1953 (*Gentlemen Prefer Blondes*), with many of her female characters having a sharp tongue and a shrewd sense of how to get on in the world. Marion, who started as a stunt double, numbered *Rebecca of Sunnybrook Farm* (1917), *Pollyanna* (1920), *Anna Christie* (1930; Greta Garbo's first talkie), and *Stella Dallas* (1937) among her 136 screen plays.

Female roles in the 1920s tended to be either vamps or virgins. The innocent parts played by Mary Pickford and Lillian Gish contrasted with the sexually aware and sensuous Theda Bara and Clara Bow, "the 'It' girl." Clara Bow's flapper roles appealed to Jazz Age urban dwellers as distinct from the rural sweethearts portrayed to such effect by Pickford and Gish. Haskell describes the dialectic of 1920s silent movies as between "new" and "old fashioned" women, but new and old fashioned simply referred to the techniques used for attracting men. The flappers created by Anita Loos and other screenwriters had no interest in politics or women's rights, the burning issues of their era; instead they kept their brains hidden under their cloche hats. This stemmed, in part, from the limitations of silent movies, where visual imagery conveyed movie messages, but it also reflected the narrow range of roles and ideas Hollywood permitted female characters. Women rarely participated in the slapstick comedy pioneered by Charlie Chaplin, Buster Keaton, and Laurel and Hardy. They might be the butt of the gags, but did not perpetrate them. In this, as in so much else, women existed as components in a world of relationships and emotional entanglements, rather than as individuals.

Talkies gave women more scope for expression and widened the range of parts they played, but still featured them mostly as girlfriends, wives, and mothers. In the early thirties, female emancipation seemed confined to sexuality. Marlene Dietrich in *Blue Angel* (1930) and Mae West in *She Done Him Wrong* (1933) deployed sensuality to entice men, sometimes to their destruction. West's screen persona combined allure with wisecracking in a series of independent characters who selected their partners and prospered through their own pluck and gumption. She enjoyed particular popularity during the Great Depression when Americans desperately wanted to believe that determination would bring success. Her suggestive one-liners, as much as her physical presence, made female sexuality assertive and independent of marital relationships. When Cary Grant asks in *She Done Him Wrong,* if she ever met a man who could make her happy, she responds, "Sure. Lots of times." West pointed to a core truth about intimate relationships, "When a girl goes wrong, men go right after her," showing that both sexes engaged in erotic activities, despite social conventions which reacted strongly against female sexual transgressions.

Other movies from the early 1930s also depicted overt female sexuality as normal rather than aberrant, mirroring the rise in pre-marital intercourse occurring in American society. In *Design for Living* (1933) the heroine, Miriam Hopkins, falls in love with two men while living in Paris. She marries one, but sleeps with the other, and subsequently lives with both. By 1934, such behavior had been restricted by the Production Code, which established moral standards for the cinema in a backlash against the overt eroticism of Dietrich, West, Jean Harlow, and other *femmes fatales.*

The Motion Picture Producers and Distributors Association responded to pressure from the Legion of Decency and the threat of government censorship in the early 1930s with rules stating that movies should not lower moral standards; "correct standards" should be presented; and that law "divine, natural or human" should not be ridiculed. Married couples slept in twin beds; crime did not pay; and villains either repented of their misdeeds or suffered the consequences. Sexuality became limited to kisses and chaste embraces; revealing clothing was banned. Even animals' genital organs had to be hidden, so the chimps in the Tarzan movies wore body stockings. Hollywood's censors curbed female sexual expression, which perhaps ironically, opened up more varied parts for women during the 1930s and early 1940s. Women's careers took on greater significance in movies once the Production Code repressed sexual flamboyance and bawdy behavior.

Romance continued to dominate the cinema, but women worked for a living in the movies as they did in the real world. Rosalind Russell played a journalist in *His Girl Friday* (1940) and an advertising executive in *Take A Letter, Darling.* The actresses and dancers of

Golddiggers of 1933 supported each other in the economically precarious world of the theater, successfully combining job- and husband-hunting. Busby Berkeley's lavish choreography reduced women into cogs in elaborate song and dance sequences. In a message calculated to appeal to Depression-era audiences Ginger Rogers sings "We're in the Money", while chorus girls appear as oversized dancing coins. Even though the heroines find husbands and jobs, *Golddiggers* shows the Depression turning former soldiers into forgotten men and women into streetwalkers and impoverished tenement dwellers. In an emotionally charged finale, "Remember My Forgotten Man," powerful marching music accompanies men, but not women, on the breadline, savagely undercutting the lighthearted approach to unemployment in the rest of the movie.

The genre of screwball comedies which emerged in this era featured women and men competing as equals in the battle of the sexes. With their fast-paced dialogue, movies such as *It Happened One Night,* starring Claudette Colbert, and *Bringing Up Baby* with Katherine Hepburn, helped Americans laugh their way out of the Depression. Among the most glamorous of all were romantic comedies featuring Ginger Rogers and Fred Astaire, dancing debonairly through a series of misunderstandings and mishaps.

Movies of the early 1940s portrayed women taking part in the war effort. *Swing Shift Maisie* (1943) depicts Ann Sothern doing her part in making bombers. *Since You Went Away* demonstrated how hard war was on those left behind, while *Keep Your Powder Dry* with Lana Turner and *So Proudly We Hail* captured the valiant efforts of women who enlisted. As the war ended, a backlash against female independence occurred in the cinema as well as in society generally. During the forties, *film noir* displayed women paying for their independence by sacrificing either their families or their happiness. *Mildred Pierce* (1945) condemned businesswoman Joan Crawford for attempting to combine motherhood with a career. In other *film noir* women are either treacherous (*Maltese Falcon)* or victims (Barbara Stanwyck in *Sorry, Wrong Number*). 1950s comedies such as *It's a Woman's World* firmly placed women in the domestic realm, as did the popular television series *I Love Lucy* which ridiculed Lucille Ball's efforts to work outside the home.

Animated cartoons presented visions of womanhood which paralleled those of live actresses and increasingly marginalized female characters or omitted them. Two distinct versions of animated womanhood took root: the vampish Betty Boop and the passive, minor character who was peripheral to the main story. Minnie Mouse set the standard for cartoon girlfriends, occasionally putting Mickey in his place. In *Plane Crazy* (1928) she bails out using her panties as a parachute rather than suffer his advances, but more often he rescues her from unpleasant situations. In her high heels, ruffled panties, and sexless body, Minnie rarely had an active role in the cartoon proceedings; she was the sidekick not the focal point of the action.

Betty Boop, created in 1930 by Max and David Fleischer to be Bimbo the Dog's companion, soon had a feature role. Unlike Minnie, Betty took center stage as an overtly sexual flapper with a short skirt, garters, and a costume that revealed distinctly female anatomy. The Betty Boop cartoons contained sexual innuendo and urban sophistication, signaled by using Cab Calloway and Louis Armstrong on the soundtracks and in the animations. Fearless Fred sometimes rescues Betty from the hands of lecherous men, but she also escapes on her own. Several of the cartoons acknowledge the Depression, notably *Any Rags* in which the rag and bone man collects household scraps and *Betty Boop's Big Boss*, in which Betty and hundreds of other women apply for a secretarial job. Betty's provocative costume and independent sexuality fell foul of the Production Code, forcing the Fleischers to put her in a long skirt, apron, and modest blouse. By 1937, after depicting her as a babysitter, school teacher, secretary, and nurse, the Fleischers lost interest in the now tame spinster character and dropped her.

Feature length cartoons occupied an important place in the Hollywood of the 1930s and 1940s. *Snow White and the Seven Dwarfs*, *Dumbo*, and *Bambi* (Walt Disney, 1937, 1941, 1942) expanded the range of animated females, while etching the archetypes deeply. *Snow White* pits a young innocent female against a malevolently beautiful middle-aged woman. Snow White wins a place in the dwarfs' cottage through her housekeeping skills and waits for her prince, singing "I'm Wishing for the One I Love to Find Me Today," a paradigm of female passivity. Mrs. Jumbo, in *Dumbo*, waits forlornly for the stork to bring her little bundle of joy. Maternal overprotectiveness results in madness as Mrs. Jumbo turns on her son's tormentors. She is chained up and it is left to a male mouse to rescue the little elephant with the big ears. Bambi's mother is shot, leaving Bambi to discover the perils and delights of the forest on his own. Mothers are missing or inadequate in all these cartoons; true femininity is passive, while active women (such as the Wicked Queen in Snow White) are associated with evil.

The situation of women in the Disney empire in the inter-war years illustrated the problems they faced in the movie industry. In a highly gendered division of labor, Disney only hired women to voice the characters and paint the cels, the most tedious and repetitive part of the animation process. Women had made real strides in educational and cultural activities, but their presence in Hollywood betokened the problems they encountered in expanding the range of their activities. Women sought new outlets for their talents, their educational levels rose, but gendered constraints continued to shape their careers and cultural representations.

From the optimism of the 1920s, through the Depression of the 1930s, and the wartime exigencies of the 1940s, women's educational and cultural activities expanded and contracted in a complex swirl of patterns which partially recognized female ambition, but primarily channeled it into a limited number of roles. Women went to high school to prepare themselves for jobs, but hard times and post-war backlash limited their participation in higher education and traditionally male-dominated professions. Popular magazines captured many of the contradictions of women's lives during wartime, praising them for working on airplanes, but adjuring them not to lose their femininity. This tension permeated American culture, with the seesaw sometimes tipped more toward individual aspirations and at other times emphasizing women's place in the family and restricting their ambitions. Education, high and popular culture encapsulated these tensions, but firmly rejected Margaret Mead's notion that behavior in these areas was anything but sex linked.

12   Reform and Politics, 1920–1945

After ratification of the Nineteenth Amendment in 1920 granting women the vote, Carrie Chapman Catt declared, "We are no longer petitioners, we are not wards of the nation, but free and equal citizens." Women won the vote, but the battle for political integration and full citizenship still had to be fought since obtaining the franchise did not resolve issues of women's economic and financial status or their role in public life. Anti-suffragists transformed opposition to suffrage into a prolonged campaign to restrict women's citizenship rights throughout the inter-war years. They contested women's claims to full economic protection by the state, equal property and nationality rights, trial by their peers through inclusion on juries, and custody over their children. Laws which accepted wage differentials, racial bias, and unequal citizenship also perpetuated discrimination against women. While the primary focus in this chapter is on women's political status, the use of federal and state legislation to enhance or diminish women's place in the economy is also examined because increasingly government rather than contracts between worker and employer controlled the economic treatment of women.

The former suffrage coalition split over basic tensions between operating within the existing political framework and parties or forming a separate party which would place women's interests first. Seeing suffrage won, many women spread their reforming efforts into diverse causes, further diffusing female public activities. These varied strategies complicated the quest for a solution to women's place in the polity and have led to an undervaluing of female political endeavors after the Nineteenth Amendment. Although some historians have viewed the era between the wars as a quiet, if not quiescent, period for female activism in which the search for personal sexual freedom and consumerism replaced crusading, in fact women struggled to consolidate their political position on myriad fronts. The continued resistance to women's claims to full citizenship meant that the inter-war years were marked by vigorous efforts to obtain equal access to the mechanisms of the state by pressing for non-discriminatory legislation and inclusion in party politics.

This period contained a number of large-scale political, social, and economic controversies which pro- and anti-feminists disputed in legislation and lobbying, conducted against a background of state by state and issue by issue conflicts and resolutions. The genuine and intense disagreement between those who thought that only further constitutional change would achieve real equality for women and those who wanted to function within the existing legislative framework considerably complicated the feminist crusade. Two major events disrupted the debate, creating outcomes by *force majeur*. The Great Depression resulted in a stream of social legislation which conformed to the male-worker, women-caretaker stereotypes, but also enhanced employment rights. Subsequently, in World War II, intensive propaganda efforts encouraged millions of women to work in defense plants with little enabling legislation or public outcry. When the war ended, government and industry expected women to return home, but they took with them aspirations and attitudes which sowed the seeds for the second wave of feminism.

THE NATURE OF WOMEN'S POLITICAL PARTICIPATION

Ironically getting the vote threatened the coherent basis upon which women participated in the affairs of state. Women had "domesticated" politics in the nineteenth and early twentieth centuries, in Paula Baker's analysis, by urging government to incorporate their reform agenda. By 1900, their activism centered on social welfare and the quest for suffrage. Women fought for the vote on contradictory grounds: to be treated the same as men, or alternatively be able to implement female values distinguishing them from men. This discrepancy pulled the women's movement in different directions over the best way to obtain a fair deal for women after they won the vote. Once they were incorporated into the electorate, it became harder to argue that female difference justified a special place in civic matters.

NAWSA's successor, the League of Women Voters (LWV), reflected the dilemmas facing women voters, especially over integration into the political parties. Jane Addams favored women acting as a separate group in order to retain a female perspective on civic matters. Carrie Chapman Catt, former NAWSA president, preferred women to join organizations as "free and equal" citizens. The League attracted hostility from those opposed to women's political participation in the first place. The governor of New York state declared that "there is no proper place for a *league of women voters*" since there was no league of men voters. Moreover, any group other than a political party which attempted to exert political influence was "a menace to our free institutions and to representative government." This attack staggered members of the New York LWV, including Eleanor Roosevelt and Carrie Chapman Catt, who observed that some male politicians were bitter towards the former suffragists "because we are women" presaging the obstacles they faced in gaining political acceptance.

Female voters, as represented by the League, initially favored a gender-based plan of action, which distinguished it from the National Woman's Party which wished to abolish all sex-based legislation whether it "protected" women or not. The NWP favored "conscious sex loyalty" which restricted its membership to a few thousand, white, middle-class women focused on obtaining an Equal Rights Amendment to the Constitution. The League's first agenda contained dozens of proposals to improve women's and children's legal status and welfare, citizenship education, and election law reform. Shocked by women's low turnout in 1920, LWV leaders concluded voter education should take priority and that women needed time and encouragement to acquire the voting habit. It urged women in 1924 to "Vote as you please, but vote!"

The League turned into a better government organization, concentrating on voter registration, efficient government, women's legal status, and international cooperation to prevent war. Although it made little reference to its origins in the suffrage crusade, it sought to further women's interests and integrate women into politics. Its nonpartisan stance offended some male party activists and organizations, including the National Civic Federation which felt that independent voting weakened the party system. A confidential memorandum from this business-led group warned that the League had "a more or less radical, sentimental program for the so-called betterment of women in industry" which threatened its members' interests. Female independence was, in this view, more threatening than partisanship, which could be controlled by the existing parties.

The League attracted a small proportion (5–10 percent) of former suffragists, yet women retained their activist stance through membership in other organizations. As Nancy Cott observes in *The Grounding of Modern Feminism*, women's domestic political culture continued from the nineteenth century into the 1920s and 1930s. Voluntary and reform groups continued to expand post-suffrage, working towards incremental reform in the tradition of earlier movements. Women's organizations proliferated in the late 1910s and 1920s, with new ones emerging as older ones lost their purpose or went out of fashion. J. Stanley Lemons concludes that business and professional women's organizations partially displaced social concerns among women, but female service societies such as the Altrusa, Quota, Zonta, and Soroptimists Clubs also fought for civic issues.

Female voter registration remained lower than men's in the 1920s, possibly because rampant political corruption left many women "thoroughly disgusted" with electoral politics, according to one midwestern businesswoman in 1924. Yet this feeling was not limited to women, as the Teapot Dome oil scandal (over leasing naval oil reserves to Republican Party contributors) and other corruption scandals evoked cynicism about politicians' probity from both sexes. Female political activity, measured by membership in interest groups, grew. The PTA alone expanded to over 1.5 million members in the 1920s and had over 22 000 branches by 1931. Concern over education was an accepted part of the fabric of American life, but women also spoke out on controversial issues which addressed national and international problems. The Association of Southern Women for the Prevention of Lynching challenged racial/gender hegemonies while the Women's International League for Peace and Freedom asserted a gendered dimension to international relations.

The anti-lynching crusade, which originated in Ida B. Wells-Barnett's courageous stand in the 1890s, surged in the 1920s as black and white women mobilized for a federal law to stop the bloodshed. Mary B. Talbert, a former teacher and president of Buffalo's Phyllis Wheatley Club, chaired the NAACP anti-lynching campaign and, when Congress failed to pass an anti-lynching bill in 1921, encouraged women to vote against Congressmen who opposed it. The president of the Palmer Memorial Institute in North Carolina, Charlotte Hawkins Brown, sought inter-racial cooperation in the crusade, and urged the white North Carolina Federation of Women's Clubs to pass an anti-lynching resolution. The National Council of Women also took a stand against lynching in the 1920s. In 1930, Jessie Daniel

Ames brought many white southern women into the fight against injustice through the Association of Southern Women for the Prevention of Lynching. By the early 1940s the vast majority of Americans, regardless of race, favored making lynching a federal crime, although the government never legislated against it.

Women's International League for Peace and Freedom (WILPF) and Women's Committee for World Disarmament campaigns kept the cause of world peace on the domestic and international agendas in the 1920s, led to a reduction in defense spending, and provoked conservative opposition to women's influence in affairs of state. Senior army officers and the Secretary of War (an opponent of women's suffrage whose senatorial campaign had been defeated by the Massachusetts Woman Suffrage Association) attacked female peace campaigners as disloyal. The infamous 1924 Spider Web Chart of subversive organizations on which women's groups figured prominently emanated from Brigadier General Amos A. Fries' Chemical Warfare Service. It attacked the patriotism of the WILPF, Women's Joint Congressional Committee, American Association of University Women, National Council of Jewish Women, YWCA, National Consumers' League, American Home Economics Association, and Women's Christian Temperance Union (among others) as part of the "socialist-pacifist movement" and "international socialism."

These charges galvanized a serious backlash. A growing number of women joined conservative patriotic groups, including the Daughters of the American Revolution (DAR), the American Legion's women's auxiliary, and American War Mothers, which demanded that the WILPF be barred from the National Council of Women. As red-baiting tactics turned against the women's movement, organizations grew cautious about linking peace and gender issues, and the General Federation of Women's Clubs and the PTA disaffiliated from the WILPF in 1922.

By no means all women succumbed to right-wing pressure. Jane Addams gave the money from her 1931 Nobel Peace Prize to the Women's International League for Peace and Freedom. Attacks on women's groups continued in the 1930s when Elizabeth Dilling published *The Red Network: A "Who's Who" of Radicalism for Patriots* (1934) which targeted the WILPF, YWCA, League of Women Voters, and Women's Trade Union League, and many female reformers. Such diatribes diverted women's attention from the fight for equality and, as with the furore over Victoria Claflin Woodhull's flamboyant sexuality in the nineteenth century, narrowed the issues over which feminists felt they could fight.

GENDERED CITIZENSHIP

As separate political entities, feminists argued they should no longer be subsumed under their husband's nationality or financial status. A series of legal challenges in the 1920s and 1930s sought full citizenship and political rights, including the right to choose where to live, to control wages and property, and serve in public office and on juries. The campaign to establish individual rights for women continued for decades and underscores the crucial role of government in establishing (or preventing) equality between the sexes as well as the resistance to that equality.

The right to individual nationality status was one of several campaigns waged to establish women as full and distinct legal entities. In 1907, at the height of immigration from southern and eastern Europe, the federal government decided that any woman who married a foreigner took his citizenship, even if she were native born. Women not only lost their citizenship, but suffered the civic penalties that restricted foreigners' rights. In some states these included an inability to own land, practice certain professions, run for public office, take civil service exams, or, of course, vote.

The Women's Joint Congressional Committee, comprised of the League of Women Voters, General Federation of Women's Clubs, Women's Christian Temperance Union, National Consumers' League, and Women's Trade Union League, joined with the Association of Women Lawyers to pressure Congress for separate and independent citizenship. Under the Cable Act (1922), US women who married foreigners became naturalized Americans who could lose their citizenship if they resided abroad. In 1930, Congress revoked this prohibition. Native-born women married to aliens ineligible for naturalization finally got the right to retain their pre-marital nationality status in 1931.

Certain aspects of women's campaign for equal citizenship encountered great opposition and engaged female activists' attention throughout the 1920s. Only 5 of the 16 states where women voted before 1920 allowed them to serve on juries. After enfranchisement, another 15 states permitted women to undertake jury duty, while the rest assumed the Nineteenth Amendment applied solely to voting. The Massachusetts Supreme Court kept women off juries until 1931, despite legislation stating that being qualified to vote meant one was "liable to serve as a juror." The Court held that since women did not vote when the law was enacted they could not be jurors without specific enabling legislation. Denying women the right to sit on juries meant women were not tried by their peers and limited judgment over criminal and civil crimes to men.

Women were divided over whether they should sit in judgment. Republican women in Connecticut opposed female jury service, claiming that "women should be more concerned over the breaking down of homes than over the breaking down of the jury system," that they were less suited to jury service than men, and did not want to sit on juries, in any case. Connecticut blocked female jury service until the late 1930s. The last state prohibition on female jurors succumbed to judicial challenge in 1966. Even then, less than half required jury service on an equal basis, attesting to the continued tendency to gender citizenship.

Childcare problems, the nature of the crime, and inadequate courthouse facilities constituted grounds for female demurral from jury service. In some states, women (but not men) had to register with the clerk of court to be placed on the jury list. The Supreme Court accepted this practice through 1961 because "woman is still regarded as the center of home and family life" so a state could act "in pursuit of the general welfare, to conclude that a woman should be relieved from the civic duty of jury service unless she herself determines that such service is consistent with her own special responsibilities." Presumptions about female weakness and family status implied jury service would harm women, and that looking after children or a home precluded full citizenship.

Discrimination against married women remained commonplace in matters of domicile (legal place of residence), upon which participation in civic life depended. A married woman's domicile was legally subsumed in the husband's; he determined where all family members resided, voted, ran for political office, paid taxes, or served on juries. Married women also had less control over property than their husbands or single people. Community property states routinely gave men the right to manage joint property. Until the mid-1960s, 11 states restricted the capacity of married women to make contracts or dispose of property and 5 required court approval before they could run a business. States also gave husbands superior rights in divorce; a man could sue for divorce on the grounds of improper sexual behavior before marriage, but a wife could not. Many legal inequalities remained in place throughout the inter-war years and succumbed only to the changed legal climate wrought by the women's liberation movement.

NATIONAL WOMAN'S PARTY AND THE EQUAL RIGHTS AMENDMENT

The National Woman's Party introduced the Equal Rights Amendment (ERA) in 1923 to overcome laws hampering full participation in economic and political life. Women's continued legal disadvantages and the slow pace of selection and election for public office persuaded the NWP that only a constitutional amendment would end discrimination. Controversy raged within feminist circles as social feminists committed to gradualism and protective legislation fought with militant feminists favoring equal individual rights. Led by the National Woman's Party, militant feminists asserted women's and men's complete social and economic equality. The NWP persuaded Congressman Daniel Anthony, nephew of Susan B. Anthony, to introduce the Equal Rights Amendment in 1923. The deceptively simple wording – "Men and women shall have equal rights throughout the United States and every place subject to its jurisdiction" – belied the controversy it stirred up. Social feminists from the National Consumers' League, Women's Trade Union League, League of Women Voters, Women's Joint Congressional Committee, and female industrial workers worried that the ERA would negate protective legislation and favored collaborating within existing political organizations to improve women's situation.

Social feminist Dr. Alice Hamilton, the pioneer of industrial medicine, believed that working women had special needs which they could not attain unaided. In a letter to *Equal Rights*, Hamilton warned the NWP that if they "succeeded in rescinding all the laws in the country and future protective laws, you will have harmed a far larger number of women than you will have benefited and the harm done to them will be more disastrous." Social feminists with a progressive social welfare agenda wished to extend the restraints on hours and working conditions to all workers, while the business and professional women who dominated the NWP believed that only complete legal equality would enable women to advance.

By 1925 almost all states restricted women's working hours; one-third defined minimum wages or working conditions. Social feminists considered that physical differences and the difficulties of combining wage earning and family life warranted special treatment by the state. Militant feminists countered that protective legislation denied women jobs and ignored agricultural and domestic laborers who toiled longer hours than industrial workers. It excluded women from particular (frequently better paying) jobs but ignored abuses elsewhere. A Connecticut statute forbade women from working as waitresses after 10 p.m. when wages and tips were highest but did not prevent women from scrubbing office floors or nursing late at night.

Militant feminists vigorously opposed efforts to include business and professional women in protective laws. Alice Paul regarded gender-based labor laws as "another handicap for women in the economic struggle" since not all women are mothers and even mothers did not need constant "maternity protection." Nevertheless working-class mothers benefited from labor legislation which recognized their social dilemmas and shielded them from abuses they had been unable to fight any other way. The state intervened at the urging of social reformers because male systems of labor protection such as unions and individual contracts rarely safeguarded women. According to reformer Florence Kelley there were inherent and permanent differences between the sexes. "Women will always need many laws different from those needed by men."

The only state to enact equal rights legislation (Wisconsin, 1921), tried to reconcile protection and equality through a clause guaranteeing equal rights except where this would "deny to females the special protection and privileges they now enjoy for the general welfare." No state emulated this compromise and few passed broad equality legislation.

Political acceptance for the ERA grew during the Depression and World War II. Many branches of the Business and Professional Women's Club supported it in the late 1920s and 1930s, joined by associations of women lawyers, doctors, dentists, pilots, civil servants, and certified public accountants. The Republican Party endorsed it in 1940, followed by the General Federation of Women's Clubs and the Democratic Party in 1944. Once the Supreme Court accepted the principle of protecting wages and hours for industrial workers of both sexes, the argument that the ERA would expose women workers to harsh and harmful conditions lost its force. By the mid-1940s social feminists who struggled hard to improve working women's lot in small ways when larger avenues seemed blocked began to view the ERA more favorably; most notably, Eleanor Roosevelt withdrew her opposition to it in 1946.

GOVERNMENT REFORMS AND THE STATUS OF WOMEN

Social feminists succeeded in "institutionalizing the protective impulse," in Theda Skocpol's phrase, first in the Children's Bureau and then in the Women's Bureau, the successor to the Women in Industry Service established in 1918. The Children's Bureau, the main bastion of social-feminist sentiment in the federal government in the 1910s and 1920s, had children's health and welfare as its primary interest and perceived women mainly as mothers rather than as individuals with separate needs. That said, Children's Bureau staffers genuinely cared about the mothers with whom they corresponded and for whom they wrote advisory pamphlets. Julia Lathrop and Grace Abbot led Children's Bureau campaigns against child labor and for better health care for children and pregnant women. These stances provoked controversy as conservative religious leaders and industrialists opposed child labor laws because, they said, such intervention would destroy the sanctity of the home.

Under Mary Anderson's leadership the Women's Bureau investigated the conditions of women in the labor force, primarily in industrial occupations. It lobbied continuously throughout the 1920s and 1930s for protective labor legislation and against the ERA. The compartmentalization of women's interests into separate bureaus institutionalized a fragmented view of women as either workers or mothers, but did not recognize the legitimacy or desirability of combining employment with motherhood, which women increasingly did.

Maternal and infant health legislation demonstrated the early successes achieved by women after suffrage and the pitfalls awaiting social feminist reformers in the 1920s. Congress passed the Sheppard–Towner Act by a large majority in 1921, but compromises meant its appropriations only lasted for five years, then had to be renewed. In the seven years in which it operated maternal and infant death rates decreased, but Congress terminated the program nevertheless.

A number of interrelated factors accounted for the demise of Sheppard–Towner. Politicians in 1921 believed women would vote as a group, but overestimated their unity and voting strength. The almost entirely white, male medical establishment vehemently opposed the use of lay women, social workers, and public health nurses as child and maternal health educators and practitioners. The American Medical Association stigmatized Sheppard–Towner as state interference in medicine, attacked it as "an imported socialistic scheme," and lobbied for its demise. They followed a medicalized model of health that denied that poverty or lack of education contributed to high infant and maternal death rates and believed health care should be solely their province.

Another factor preventing Sheppard–Towner's renewal, according to Molly Ladd-Taylor, was the hostility of former anti-suffragists and opponents of "politicized motherhood," who believed it was husbands' duty to ensure women received proper medical care. Conservatives felt federal programs undermined the family and made "mothers believe that Uncle Sam instead of their own husbands, ought to take care of them." Its opponents also attacked the Children's Bureau for not conforming to appropriate gender roles. They were "a few single ladies holding Government jobs." Mothers should teach such old maid reformers how to catch husbands and have babies of their own, critics ridiculed.

The 1924 Congressional elections propelled less progressive Representatives and Senators into office, while former supporters of Sheppard–Towner such as the Daughters of the American Revolution adopted a more right-wing stance. Physicians denounced federal maternal and infant health care programs as "the beginning of Communism in medicine" while the Woman Patriots claimed it embodied "nationalized, standardized care of children." State interference in the family seemed suspect to this coalition of conservative lawmakers, doctors, and patriotic organizations.

The medicalization and masculinization of welfare programs was complete by the end of the Great Depression. Under the Children's Bureau social worker-maternalist ethos, women had headed almost all the early state child welfare programs and had worked as volunteers in mother and baby health clinics. While female social welfare activism did not disappear altogether, the Great Depression made social work more attractive to men, and government funding turned formerly voluntary positions into paid jobs. Social welfare programs originated by women became part of state and federal bureaucracies largely run by men. In the late 1930s, three-quarters of state child welfare programs had male doctors and public health officials at their helm, further undermining women's place in public life as advocates of social welfare. Indeed, the New Deal inadvertently damaged voluntarist-reformist groups such as the Women's Trade Union League and the National Consumers' League which had campaigned for social justice. New Deal labor legislation seemed to obviate their crusading functions, while financial stringencies made it more difficult to raise funds. World War II subsequently diverted attention from these issues and after the war women were much less likely to join women-only organizations. The WTUL disbanded in 1950 as the older generation of social feminists died out, and no younger women replaced them.

The shift to male-centered public programs and women's seeming lack of success at the polls led the editors of *Ladies' Home Journal* to conclude in 1928 that women's suffrage had made little difference in the political parties or the quality of office holders. Female voters tended to have the same allegiances as the men in their families, fragmenting along fault lines of race, class, religion, and region. As one midwestern woman declared in the late 1920s, "It seems perfectly natural for me to be a Democrat. My family were always Democrats, and so it doesn't seem strange to me."

The pessimistic picture of women's civic involvement depicted by 1920s magazines in articles entitled "Is Woman's Suffrage a Failure?" or "Are Women a Failure in Politics?" needs to be examined against the resistance women met when they attempted to join existing political structures. States had to rewrite laws and reinterpret voters' registration statutes in 1920. Some jurisdictions denied women the ballot because they could not meet residency requirements between the passage of the Nineteenth Amendment and polling day. Women who married had to re-register in their married names, while in rural districts getting to the polls conflicted with domestic responsibilities; husbands went into town for the day, but wives could not leave their children or chores that long and stayed home.

Women's participation depended upon "local conditions rather than general causes" according to Kristi Andersen's research on women voters which discovered a high correlation between the length of time women had the vote and their willingness to use it. Poorer women, recent immigrants, and those in rural areas tended to have lower voting levels in some but not all states. Female voter turnout was higher where women had engaged in voluntary organizations, even if they previously opposed women's suffrage. As the Southern Women's League for the Rejection of the Anthony Amendment declared in 1920, "the time for debating the rights and wrongs of the amendment has passed and now it is time for the women to qualify as voters."

National political parties encouraged female membership but presence on the women's committee rarely translated into female candidates or influence over policy. The Republican Party created a National Women's Executive Committee and a Women's Division in 1918. Women asked for equal representation on the National Committee but settled for "adequate" numbers, getting about 8 percent of delegates. Democratic women fared marginally better with around 12 percent of the delegates. Women fought hard for representation at the executive committee level, with Democratic women achieving this in 1920 and Republican women in 1924.

The Republicans made a conscious effort to mobilize African-American women, enlisting the aid of the National Association of Colored Women, who favored Republicans as the party of Lincoln. Black women joined together in the National League of Republican Colored Women in 1924, and in 1927 Nannie Burroughs, the head of the NLRCW, attended the party's first meeting of women leaders. She also campaigned actively for Herbert Hoover's election in 1928, although racial prejudice kept African Americans out of the Inaugural Ball.

Some state political machines found it to their advantage to mobilize female voters. Joan Jensen's research on New Mexico found that the Mexican-American sector of the Republican Party moved swiftly to register women and incorporate them into the party machinery. By the mid-1940s, the sexes had achieved parity on political committees in 11 states. In some states, legislation required equal numbers of both sexes on party committees, but where parties could organize their own affairs, women had better representation on Democratic committees than on Republican ones.

Eleanor Roosevelt (ER) exemplified women's place in politics in this era, as she achieved influence and a power base in the Democratic Party but not elected office. ER, finance chair of the Women's Division of the Democratic Party, fought hard to get the party to agree that women, rather than male party leaders, should name their own delegates to the 1924 presidential nominating convention. As chair of the women's platform committee she coordinated a progressive social welfare program which the all-male Resolutions Committee rebuffed. Despite this setback, ER worked on Al Smith's gubernatorial campaign in her native New York State because he was committed to social reform and to demonstrate women's commitment to working within the party political process. Although Smith was a Tammany Hall politician he also had a sincere respect for women reformers, having relied upon reformer Belle Moskowitz to marshal the women's vote for his 1918 campaign and to be his closest adviser.

Women's electoral role expanded further in the 1928 presidential campaign with ethnicity and temperance figuring largely in the contest. The battle between Al Smith, a Roman Catholic "Wet", and Herbert Hoover, a rural white "Dry" Protestant, drew women from immigrant stock, rural districts, and the middle class to the polls to support their respective candidates. Eleanor Roosevelt and Wyoming Governor Nellie Tayloe Ross co-directed the Democratic National Women's Committee, canvassing vigorously for Smith. ER appointed Molly Dewson, a former social worker, Consumers' League member, and probation officer to manage Smith's midwestern campaign, thrusting her onto the national stage and establishing her position within the Democratic Party.

Some attorney generals and governors refused to permit female candidates, insisting on specific enabling legislation. A suit brought in Michigan claimed that a married female justice of the peace had no right to her office, being "sexually unable to do so as a matter of nature and as a matter of law." The judge who heard the case dismissed it, stating that the Nineteenth Amendment settled that issue. Recalcitrant states took years to agree; Oklahoma only amended its constitution in 1942 to permit elected female officials.

Generally, women achieved greater electoral success at the local and state level. The closer to home, literally and metaphorically, the more likely a woman would be elected or appointed to public office, succeeding in local government because it seemed an extension of the municipal housekeeping efforts in which women had engaged for years. In the 1920s thousands were elected to city and county offices, compared with a few hundred elected to state legislatures and a handful to Congress. In 1921, there were 37 female legislators in 26 states; by the early 1930s there were 146 from 39 states, and in the mid-1940s, 234 women held office. The only female governors were stand-ins for their husbands, "Ma" Ferguson in Texas and Nellie Tayloe Ross in Wyoming, although Jeanette Rankin from Montana was elected to Congress in her own right in 1916, and Ross became a Democratic Party activist.

Women tended to serve in education, finance, and welfare, but rarely as attorney general or in the judiciary. By the 1940s, women had finally been elected to the Senate as well as the House of Representatives, although it took decades for there to be more than a handful of Congresswomen or one or two female Senators. The integration of women into politics, then, took decades to accomplish. A significant change occurred when the Roosevelt administration, rooted both in conventional party politics and social welfare reform, expanded the power of the federal government and incorporated women and racial minorities to a greater extent than previously.

WOMEN, POLITICS, AND REFORM DURING THE NEW DEAL

The New Deal included groups previously excluded from the political mainstream and incorporated progressive social welfare assumptions about gender roles into legislation. Many female appointees had a background in social work, social reform movements, and voluntary activities and were, for the most part, members of an extended women's network of reformers. Frequently college educated, they brought a common set of experiences and expertise to federal government programs plus a shared perspective honed in the settlement houses and early forays into party politics. The network centered on Eleanor Roosevelt, a politician and Democratic Party activist in her own right. While ER never held elected office, she was crucial to getting women appointed to public positions and to ensuring that elected and appointed officials heard their ideas.

Described as "the most influential woman of our times," ER lobbied vigorously for the poor and dispossessed throughout FDR's administration. Coming from a wealthy if unhappy family, ER did not attend college, but undertook voluntary work in a New York settlement house before marriage to her distant cousin Franklin. While raising her family, she coordinated the League of Women Voters' legislative program, belonged to the National Consumers' League and Women's Trade Union League, and organized women within the Democratic Party. ER kept the interests of women, minorities, and the poor on the federal agenda throughout the New Deal, pressing her husband to incorporate them into his legislative programs and to find jobs for them.

Molly Dewson occupied a central place in the women's network and within the circle of advisers upon whom the Roosevelts relied. Like a number of the women's network, she had a long-standing and happy relationship with another woman, living in what was sometimes termed a Boston Marriage, a union between two women. Dewson was Director of the Women's Division of the Democratic National Committee (1932–4), Chairman of the Women's Division Advisory Committee (1934–7), and sat on the Social Security Board from 1937 to 1938. She expanded patronage politics and helped place women in important government positions.

Rooted in the social welfare reformist tradition, Dewson believed that women and men had different political concerns, a view shared by ER. Both presumed that women concentrated on social welfare while men focused more on power and their careers. This view of women as disinterested activists reflected their class background (mostly affluent) and continued exclusion from elected positions as much as the politics of difference which shaped their reform careers. Dewson declared she was "not a feminist. I am a practical politician out to build up the Democratic Party where it sorely needs it." For her this entailed getting as many women as possible into federal office, but she had to fight hard for each one.

Dewson suggested Frances Perkins for Secretary of Labor, organizing a letter writing campaign to garner support for her appointment. Educated at Mount Holyoke, and the first woman to hold Cabinet rank, Perkins came from a social reform background. She worked as the Consumers' League's lobbyist to the New York State legislature in the 1910s and principal investigator on the New York State Factory Commission set up in the aftermath of the Triangle Shirtwaist Company fire in 1911. Perkins served as Industrial Commissioner in New York, making a favorable impression on Franklin Roosevelt, then a state senator and later governor of New

York. She accepted the appointment in the belief that she had a "duty to other women to walk in and sit down on the chair that was offered."

Women gained most places in new agencies where they encountered less prejudice and could "forge ahead more rapidly" to higher administrative posts, Frances Perkins claimed. Women comprised about half of all employees in the Civil Service Commission, Works Progress Administration, and Social Security Board, but a much smaller proportion of the "construction" agencies such as the Public Works Administration and Tennessee Valley Authority. Ellen Woodward, Hilda Worthington Smith, Florence Kerr, and Lorena Hickok held key positions at the Works Progress Administration, as did Mary McLeod Bethune at the National Youth Administration.

Despite some political advances, few women of color had access to electoral politics throughout this era. Chinese and Japanese immigrants were ineligible for citizenship. Racial bias in the South, manifested through violence, intimidation, whites-only primaries, grandfather clauses and literacy tests, limited African-American voting. As late as 1952, 87 percent of southern black women could not vote. Both New Mexico and Arizona barred Native Americans from voting through the 1940s although the Indian New Deal, Indian Reorganization Act of 1934, and the Indian programs of the Civilian Conservation Corps encouraged Native American women's political activity within their own communities. Seminole women voted for tribal cattle trustees during the 1930s; the Colorado River Tribes, among others, elected women to the tribal councils; and women took part in the National Congress of American Indians for the first time in 1944. Native American women held supervisory and administrative positions in the Indian Work Camps of the CCC, the Civil Works Administration and the Works Progress Administration. The Commissioner of Indian Affairs also accepted the quite distinct gender base of Native American customs by incorporating gardening and farming as part of the educational programs for women.

Mary McLeod Bethune was the highest ranking African-American woman serving in government but was never considered a part of the women's network. She organized the Federal Council on Negro Affairs, also known as the Black Cabinet, which provided a collective voice for African Americans in government. Bethune, who was President of Bethune–Cookman College in Daytona, Florida, led registration drives to enroll African-American women to vote despite Ku

Klux Klan opposition, and headed the National Council of Negro Women, which campaigned for integration and a federal anti-lynching statute. Although successful at the NYA, she and other campaigners for civil rights made little impact on New Deal labor and welfare programs because southern Democrats blocked efforts to include farm and domestic workers in such legislation.

Bethune "visualized dozens of Negro women coming after me, filling positions of high trust and strategic importance" just like white women. Yet women of all races comprised a small portion of public office holders as the politics of difference still held sway. Mrs. Roosevelt stated "women *are* different from men. They are equals in many ways, but they cannot refuse to acknowledge the differences." Female New Dealers believed the sexes had diverse political and social perspectives, distinct economic roles, and needed special forms of public assistance. New Deal programs incorporated the belief that women were, as Ellen Woodward put it, "family conscious" and built upon the politics of difference, incorporating progressive beliefs in the need for state intervention in labor legislation and social welfare and traditional notions of the family, with male breadwinners and female dependents.

Female New Dealers labored under serious constraints. Grace Abbott, former head of the Children's Bureau, believed that the men who ran New Deal agencies took their advice lightly and assumed that an individual woman's inadequacy meant all women were incompetent. Ellen Woodward struggled against male intransigence in the Federal Emergency Relief Administration and the Works Progress Administration where she headed the Women's and Professional Projects division and tried to create meaningful work programs for women of all races. Despite her efforts, women received relatively little work relief and tended to be shunted into means-tested benefits.

The Social Security Act (SSA) of 1935 and its revisions in 1939 epitomized the incorporation of gender-based attitudes into American law. As the competition for jobs sharpened during the Great Depression, resentment against female employment increased. While principally directed against married women, these sentiments questioned the legitimacy of all women in the work place. "Debate over the 'new woman' of the previous decade, who combined work and family, was completely subsumed," according to Lois Scharf, by the national concern "over the 'forgotten man' who combined no work with a possibly demoralized and disintegrating family." New Dealers building upon the politics of difference and concerned for the stability of the nation, developed programs which served male breadwinners, assuming this would provide for women as part of families.

The Social Security Act granted old age pensions, unemployment insurance, and aid to families with dependent children. Based on a traditional family wage model, it used women's Social Security contributions to keep the system solvent. Rather than balancing the needs or rights of different family members, the Social Security Act viewed wage earning as an unusual and possibly undesirable activity for mothers and discounted women's waged contributions to their families. The Act incorporated separate spheres into federal law. President Roosevelt believed that it was a measure for children, "designed to release from the wage-earning role the person whose natural function is to give her children the physical and affectionate guardianship necessary . . . to rear them into citizens capable of contributing to society."

The Committee on Economic Security (CES) which drew up the Social Security Act wished to keep costs down. The act provided relatively well for certain individuals whom it defined as workers, while relegating others, mostly women, to poorly funded, locally controlled programs. Frances Perkins acknowledged that the Social Security Act excluded too many workers, but its passage was politically fraught and realpolitik prevailed. Southern congressmen spoke against the Social Security bill because it threatened to upset the existing racial balance. They did not want federal funds going directly to African Americans, impinging upon white control over agricultural and domestic workers. Their fears reflected concern over the transfer of power from the states to the central government and the potential costs of these measures. In practice, the SSA excluded over three out of every five employed African Americans. Women comprised 60 percent of workers not covered at a time when they were less than 30 percent of the labor force, with African-American women faring very badly: only 20 percent had jobs which entitled them to Social Security benefits.

The amendments to the Social Security Act in 1939 did little to alter the racial configuration of old age pensions, but did extend benefits to the surviving widows of pensioned men and to the children of men in pensionable occupations. The chairman of the Social Security Board described the new benefits as "a family concept. You just cannot think of these people as individuals. You have to think of them in their family relationships." Coverage expanded, but regarded women as men's dependents, not as individual economic persons. In fact, married women could not receive a pension based upon their own earnings if their husbands drew retirement benefits. Their contributions subsidized the pensions which went to non-employed wives. Moreover, unless a husband depended completely on his wife for support, neither he nor their children could obtain a pension based on her earning record. Women in receipt of survivors' benefits who remarried lost the pension based upon their late husband's entitlement.

The calculation of how much a widow received was gender-biased. A male retiree received 100 percent of the pension to which he was entitled. He was credited with 50 percent more for his wife when she reached retirement age. When he died, she received a widow's pension of half the combined amount, that is, 75 percent of a man's. The American Social Security system differed from other systems in this regard. The British old age pension system, for example, granted the same pension to both sexes, but the American system reduced the widow's standard of living following the death of her husband. The Federal Advisory Council which reviewed the Social Security Act queried why a widow should receive less than a single man and was told by the Social Security actuary "she can look after herself better than he can." Such assumptions meant that for all the good old age and widows' pensions accomplished, gendered perceptions disadvantaged women.

Social Security legislation assumed that women married men for economically venial reasons. Congress and the Social Security Board worried that women would entrap men into wedlock to get their Social Security benefits. The amended act stipulated that the supplementary wife's pension would be paid only if the marriage had occurred before the husband reached the age of 60 and excluded divorced and separated women from retirement benefits based upon their ex-husband's earnings. Rising divorce levels in the mid- and late twentieth century disadvantaged women whose marriages broke down, displacing homemakers who had no career other than their family and no entitlement to retirement pensions if they divorced.

The SSA differentiated between two groups of mothers and children with drastic consequences. The first group consisted of impoverished lone mothers and dependent children, who received small

ADC (Aid to Dependent Children) payments. The second group contained the widows of men covered under the provisions of Social Security retirement clauses; they received higher survivors' benefits. The removal of widows from the ADC roster under the 1939 amendments stigmatized the program by deleting those traditionally regarded as the morally acceptable worthy poor. The amended act disadvantaged non-white women, whose late husbands were largely outside the covered occupations, as well as women whose children were born out of wedlock.

Despite the number of women who came to Washington during the Depression, or perhaps because their social reformer perspective enshrined gender difference as the basis of legislation, New Deal measures incorporated a family-centered outlook while expanding public provision. In this social and economic emergency, men got work, women got dole. Men were workers; women were mothers. The amended Social Security Act provided assistance for widows only while they had young children or if they and their husbands had reached retirement age. It stranded women between motherhood and old age as displaced homemakers, with no pension, no job, and nowhere to turn. The Social Security system demanded the same payments from women and men, but provided lower returns to working women on their retirement contributions. The lack of coverage for African-American dominated occupations left this group particularly vulnerable. Even with these limitations, the Social Security Act did transfer some resources to older widows through survivors' benefits. One can note the Social Security Act's inadequacies and racial and gender biases while still recognizing that it gave widows (at least those whose husbands had been in covered occupations) a guaranteed subsistence in old age.

The history of labor legislation during the New Deal attests to the importance of the federal government in regulating women's employment. Prior to the New Deal, virtually all labor legislation was enacted locally, so there were great variations between cities, states, and regions. The first major New Deal labor legislation, the National Industrial Recovery Act passed in 1933, accepted "long established customs," permitted wage codes which discriminated against women, and divided women and men into different job categories. Such provisions were accepted despite the presence of women's network member and union activist Rose Schneiderman on the NRA's Labor Advisory Board, the statistical evidence presented by the

Women's and Children's Bureaus, and the testimony of Women's Trade Union League witnesses.

After the Supreme Court ruled the NRA unconstitutional, two subsequent pieces of labor legislation had long-term significance for women. The National Labor Relations or Wagner Act (1935) legitimized collective bargaining and gave federal sanction to labor unions. It boosted the union movement by forcing employers to recognize and bargain in good faith with their employees. It was particularly important for un- and semi-skilled workers, especially women. The largely female membership of the International Ladies' Garment Workers' Union increased five-fold after its passage.

The Fair Labor Standards Act of 1938 further consolidated the role of the federal government in labor relations, establishing minimum wages and maximum working hours throughout industry, without regard to workers' sex. Largely drafted by Frances Perkins with contributions from Katherine Lenroot of the Children's Bureau, the act prohibited child labor, although it still did not cover farm laborers or domestic servants as a result of conservative southern Democrats' amendments. By regulating the labor of women and men on the same basis, the act began to reverse the gender-differentiated approach to protecting workers.

Women achieved a greater presence in the federal government and had more input during the Roosevelt presidency than ever before. Why, then, did some pieces of legislation serve women so poorly? Three women sat on the Social Security Advisory Council and Molly Dewson was a member of the Social Security Board, but none of them queried the inequality built into the SSA and its revisions. Instead, as Alice Kessler-Harris posits, "influential women social reformers had long since accepted that providing security of the family was the most likely way to safeguard women." The SSA benefited single women (insofar as it included the occupations in which they worked and if they never married) but subsumed married women under the domestic umbrella. This was the logical outcome of the social reformist strategy which envisaged women's security as deriving from the family. Dewson believed that Social Security's principal objective was to "establish a greater measure of security in the life of the family" and thus to create "the well-being of the Nation." Despite the advances in office holding and the acceptance of labor legislation which applied equally to women and men, the New Deal rejected the radical feminism of the National Woman's Party and persisted in viewing women as part of a family, not as individuals.

WOMEN'S WAR AND ITS AFTERMATH

The issue of World War II as a turning point for American women has vexed historians. Susan Hartman describes the 1940s as bringing "the most serious attention to women's status under the law since the days of the women's suffrage campaign." William Chafe characterizes the war as "a strange paradox" with minimal legal changes despite a massive influx of women into the labor market. Women might have been "heroines of the homefront," to use D'Ann Campbell's phrase, but they also remained at war with America, subject to unequal treatment and, as the post-war era indicated, dissatisfied with gendered hindrances to their participation in public life.

The war opened opportunities for women even as it sidelined the reform concerns of the women's network and demonstrated that men had no intention of allowing women to influence industrial or military policy. The United States relied upon women's labor at home, in the workplace, and, to a lesser extent, in theaters of war to defeat the Axis powers, but it allowed women little say in the conduct of the war at home or abroad. Government agencies largely ignored female expertise; few women served on the production, labor force, or food agencies. The labor mobilization programs drawn up by the men who ran the war ignored the Women's Bureau's detailed knowledge of women workers and the challenges confronting women who combined work and family life. When international rather than domestic issues confronted the nation, women's expertise was deemed irrelevant and discounted.

The President appointed a Women's Advisory Committee (WAC) to the War Manpower Commission (WMC) which, according to Mary Anderson, was simply a device to put women "off in a corner" and gave them little input or decision making power. Chaired by Margaret Hickey, the WAC had been appointed over the protests of the head of the WMC who "didn't want them . . . but there had been so much pressure . . . he finally had to yield." The Manpower Commission showed its disdain for its female advisers by ignoring them or informing them of decisions already taken. Despite assuring Mary Anderson that Hickey would be a full member of the Labor

Management Committee whose task was to coordinate factory labor, it barred her from some meetings because it did not wish to give any "minority" special privileges. Hickey concluded that there might be nothing discriminatory in government policy, but "in the practice – that is where we have difficulty." The WMC accepted wage differentials between the sexes and was ambivalent about mothers working.

Discriminatory assumptions also excluded women of color from high ranking government positions and crucial committees. The Women's Interest Section, a female public relations unit in the War Department, omitted African-American women entirely. Mary McLeod Bethune protested this exclusion to the Women's Advisory Committee, forcing the War Department to reverse itself. The National Council of Negro Women served as a major conduit between the government and African-American women, but white women's organizations tended to shut women of color out of their coalitions and were insensitive to their needs and sometimes to issues of class as well.

Class–race tensions came to a head over childcare and military service. Elite women's organizations such as the National Association of Business and Professional Women and the American Association of University Women (AAUW) led the campaign for women to enter the military but showed little concern over the discrimination encountered by women of color in the services. The AAUW lobbied for the transfer of day care centers from the Federal Works Administration to the Children's Bureau and state education agencies, believing they would provide a higher standard of early childhood education. African-American women opposed this reorganization because these agencies had a history of racial neglect and discrimination. In 1945, the AAUW platform favored the establishment of a permanent Fair Employment Practices Commission, but many of its local branches refused to admit women of color. After the war, African-American women continued to fight for equal rights through the NCNW and the NAACP, among other organizations, and played an important role in the civil rights movement.

Japanese women living on the West Coast lost their rights during the war. The combination of racial prejudice and fear of invasion resulted in the Army removing all persons of Japanese ancestry to inland centers. Even in this emergency, gender influenced events, with men regarded as the determiners of nationality. The families of white men married to Japanese women were permitted to retain their residence, even though Caucasian women with Japanese husbands were evacuated. The evacuees were held under barbaric conditions, crammed into horses' stalls at racetracks commandeered for the purpose. Mine Okubo, a *Nisei* (second-generation) artist, described the conditions in her illustrated book *Citizen 13660*. Families were crammed into hastily whitewashed stables where "huge spikes and nails stuck out all over the walls." Conditions were little better in the desert camps. The Army admitted the housing facilities were unsuitable for families and planned no schools for the children or activities for the adults. Instead, barbed wire and armed guards surrounded the internees. *Nisei* women married to servicemen were permitted to leave the camps before the general population, but most evacuees only left at the beginning of 1945 when the Supreme Court decided that detainment violated their constitutional rights.

The war devastated the Japanese community, but its impact on other women was less clear cut. The concept of equal pay for equal work became more widespread, but not all employers adhered to it. The war certainly encouraged more women into the labor force, but there was no compulsion for women to take jobs, especially if they had young children. Instead, as Leila Rupp's study of wartime propaganda has shown, the public was encouraged to "accept the participation of women in unusual jobs without challenging basic beliefs about women's roles" because the propagandists emphasized the transitory, emergency nature of their work.

The number of women in elected office did increase during the war; there were 144 women in state legislatures in 1941 and 228 in 1945, and 249 in 1950, although some states persistently elected only men. The number of women serving in Congress increased slightly, with more women elected in their own right, rather than as substitutes for their late husbands. There was also some increase in the number of women appointed to public office, although Harry S. Truman, who succeeded to the presidency following Franklin D. Roosevelt's death, refused to have a woman in the cabinet. Post-war Presidents Truman and Eisenhower each appointed more women than their predecessors, yet their appointees lacked the supportive women's network which existed under the Roosevelt administration and did not act directly on women's behalf. Presidents acceded to requests from the women's committees of their respective parties to appoint more women, but these were token appointments which recognized women without giving them power.

Between 1920 and 1945 women's political participation underwent significant changes. The vote had been won, but the war over integration raged on. It took four decades before legal impediments to full citizenship had been removed in all parts of the nation, before women could serve on juries, be elected to office, have equal property rights, and vote regardless of skin color. The organized women's movement splintered into social and militant feminists, with the much larger social feminist group opting for integration into the existing party political system, and the smaller National Woman's Party adopting a separatist strategy to obtain an equal rights amendment. A third group, labeled the Women's Bureau coalition by Cynthia Harrison, sought to improve the situation of working women while believing that men should support their wives. A fourth group of organized women (Daughters of the American Revolution and similar patriotic societies) took a conservative stance, largely opposing government assistance to women or children. Women working for racial equality comprised a fifth group, never fully integrated into the feminist movement and ambivalent about the ERA's effectiveness.

Disagreements persisted between these groups over the extent to which women should work through separatist or integrationist strategies, or whether they should identify as women's groups at all. In 1945, Margaret Hickey, president of the National Business and Professional Women's Club, had declared that the "old strident, selfish feminism" was dead. In the anti-communist ferment of the late 1940s and early 1950s, fewer women identified themselves as feminists, although women serving as elected representatives did introduce legislation to remove specific legal disabilities. Integration into the party system left women at the bottom of political party hierarchies, receiving a small number of appointments to public office and perceived as tokens rather than as full and equal members with an important constituency.

The politics of difference had served women's interests in the early part of the century. Progressive legislatures and officials had recognized women's expertise, but a more conservative climate, the incorporation of welfare programs into government (increasingly run by men), and a post-war emphasis on families all diminished this as a route to power for women. The post-war era subsumed women's interests into those of the family in an attempt to create normalcy after the horrors of depression and war. A reinvigorated feminist movement in the 1960s, based upon the politics of equality, strove to accomplish what the first feminist movement had not: the complete integration of women into American economic, social, and political life based upon the equality of the sexes rather than their presumed differences.

Epilogue – The Feminine Mystique

In 1946, the anthropologist Margaret Mead wrote that: "women – and men – are confused, uncertain and discontented with the present definition of women's place in America." The aftermath of World War II left both sexes yearning for a normal world, frequently defined through a nostalgic haze as one in which men supported their families and women cared for them. After 16 years of depression and war, people sought a less troubled home and family life. Husbands who had tolerated wives' employment during the war pressured them to return to the home and full-time housewifery once the emergency ended. As one former California defense worker explained, "my husband didn't want me to work when he was able to keep me at home. Of course, during the war, there wasn't any question about it because everybody was needed."

Whatever individual husbands or wives felt about women's employment outside the home, powerful economic, social, and political forces converged to shape a society in which women's primary focus was within the household, at least for much of the next generation. Women's economic and social choices were not inevitable outcomes of the war, but were created by manufacturers seeking lasting markets for consumer goods, by a government which feared unemployment among veterans, and by millions of individuals who wanted to build a good life for themselves and their families as quickly as possible.

Public sentiment swung against (married) women's work outside the home in the post-war era as movies attacked female employment and Freudian psychoanalysts condemned working women as unnatural, reinforcing whatever doubts women themselves had about trying to balance family and career commitments. The chilling anti-communist political climate of the late 1940s and early 1950s also impeded women's civic activism, as did the massive immersion in domesticity and the baby boom, yet by the late 1950s and early 1960s a significant female presence in the civil rights, student, and anti-war movements presaged the women's liberation movement which significantly altered women's place in American life.

Whether World War II represented a turning point in American women's history, as William Chafe has argued, is still debated by historians. Like the Civil War, it greatly expanded women's range of experience, especially in the sorts of jobs held by women, but in other areas, such as education and politics, if anything it deflected or diminished women's involvement. The demographic response to long years of depression and war was two-fold: an unprecedented surge in fertility and a move to the suburbs which reshaped the contours of American life and defused movements which had their origins in the cities. There was great pressure on women to conform to the supposedly traditional status of homemaker and mother in post-war America, although as this study of women's economic and social situation has made clear, such roles were highly fluid and somewhat mythical. Both the Great Depression and World War II indicated to women, if not to society as a whole, that they could undertake a wide variety of occupations and successfully balance home and work. The clash of gendered ideology and economic forces during the 1920s, 30s, and 40s demonstrated both the continuity of old social values and their systematic undermining by individual and national need.

The duality of World War II propaganda encouraged women's labor force participation while upholding traditional family values. The country needed women's muscle in the workplace, but it provided meager social backup so that childcare and household chores remained stumbling blocks for working women. By late 1944, as the war wound down, images appeared encouraging female domesticity. Advertising by appliance makers stressed women at home, standing by the sink, stove, and refrigerator rather than in the factory, tightening bolts or making guns. Women's magazines stressed the virtues of home life, lauding early marriage and large families. While many women left their wartime jobs voluntarily, others were pushed out by the Selective Service Act which guaranteed old jobs back to veterans, by propaganda which emphasized that a woman's place was in the home, and by the difficulties of caring for young children and maintaining a job. Paradoxically, women wanted to hold jobs but could only justify this by necessity rather than choice.

In the absence of equal opportunities legislation, post-war employers could hire whom they wished at whatever salary would be accepted, and they demonstrated a strong preference for male workers.

Between three- and four-fifths of all vacancies listed with employment services in the late 1940s were designated "men only," with women limited to domestic service and clerical work. Women's pay declined as employers refused to hire them on an equal basis with men. Seven-tenths of female job vacancies attracted the minimum wage, while only one in four male jobs paid that poorly. These factors combined to cut women's share of the labor market from its wartime high of 36 percent to 28 percent in 1950. Yet this was a temporary interruption to the long-term trend toward rising employment levels as women sought to use their education and improve their families' standard of living. By 1960, women's employment had recovered its wartime peak and has grown steadily ever since. Although evicted from their relatively high-paying jobs in heavy industry, women's wartime experience contributed to the subsequent militancy in the union, civil rights, and women's liberation movements in the post-war period.

Having come of age during the end of the Depression and war years, newlyweds idealized the larger families of their grandparents' generation, helped by pervasive images in magazines, television, movies, and newspapers of happy families with working fathers and contented mothers caring for home and children. Reversing earlier trends, birth rates among the affluent exceeded those of the less well-off. Big families confirmed female domesticity and heightened gender distinctions with the all-American mom replacing the spunky career woman as the leading female role in the movies and on television.

Few women remained single; instead they achieved "deepest satisfaction" according to *McCall's* magazine, by marrying young, having a large family and a house in the suburbs. They did all this by forgoing advanced education, quitting part-way through college, or doing all they could to ensure they had a diamond on their ring finger when they graduated. Early marriages, large families (four children under the age of 5 or 6 was not uncommon), and geographical mobility (moving away from one's own family during the war or to the suburbs afterwards) fostered a reliance upon parenting authorities such as Dr. Spock, who told women to be completely devoted to their children and held them entirely responsible for their upbringing.

Domesticity occupied women's time as they tried to create ideal homes in the new suburbs. Decentralized residential patterns made children dependent upon their mothers for transport to their activities while a lack of childcare facilities (other than the family home) meant mothers had little alternative to complete immersion in the household. Togetherness became the watchword of the 1950s, with family happiness (according to *McCall's*) accomplished by sharing "a common experience." Even though women may have preferred employment to what some saw as stultifying domesticity (described in 1963 by Betty Friedan as "the problem that had no name"), popular commentators and academic authorities firmly pushed them into the home.

Ferdinand Lundberg and Marynia Farnham's *Modern Woman* declared in 1947 that it was women's nature to be passive and dependent. Female happiness, in their view, came from motherhood; their employment outside the home would destabilize society. They preached biological predestination in which only acceptance of pregnancy and dependence upon men promised happiness and put a Freudian spin on the family wage ideology by equating feminism with a neurotic rebellion against female destiny. Psychiatrist Helene Deutsch urged women to accept their true feminine nature by rejecting masculinity, staying at home, and accepting the world as brought to them by their husbands and children. These commentators deplored women who questioned this psychobiological construction of femininity as neurotic and castrating.

Post-war fears of changing gender roles led to public affirmation of motherhood as the central female role or, as Ashley Montagu wrote in the *Saturday Review* in 1958, "no woman with a husband and small children can hold a full-time job and be a good homemaker" at the same time. Fearing social disintegration, women's magazines and popular culture created an idealized family type, the family of nostalgia, in which men supported their families in single family dwellings in the suburbs, while women provided the domestic services for their families.

Television programs including *Father Knows Best* told women and children that the husband ruled the roost and brought wisdom home from the office each day in his briefcase. Women who attempted to trespass into the male world of work became the butt of sitcom jokes. Lucille Ball in *I Love Lucy* (1953–5) repeatedly used her superb comic timing to get a job on stage and screen only to be rebuffed by her husband. It is possible to read *Lucy* against the grain, emphasizing the woman who tries to find work rather than the woman viewers laugh at because she fails, but whichever interpretation one chooses, clearly a woman's place in the early post-war labor force was equivocal at best.

So was women's place in education. In a world where schooling and credentials grew steadily more important, women had been marginalized. Institutions of higher learning expanded, but served many more men than women. The federal government poured money into the sciences (dominated by men), but neglected the arts and humanities, which had more female students. In the aftermath of World War II the proportion of women in higher education had dropped as the government supported veterans' higher education. Since the level of subsidy was insufficient to support a family, the wives of many former service personnel worked so that their husbands could study. This deflected their own career aspirations, but also encouraged married women to take jobs. The net result was to make college campuses a more male-dominated environment, at least until the baby boomers started in tertiary education.

In 1950, the share of female undergraduates was lower than it had been at any point since 1870. A smaller proportion of women studied for advanced degrees in post-war America than at the turn of the century. The proportion of female faculty, especially in senior positions, receded steadily after World War II, reaching its nadir in the early 1970s, when a new generation of educated women began knocking at the gates of academe. The women who managed to get into university found themselves channeled into a few stereotyped courses: three-fifths took secretarial, nursing, home economics, or education degrees.

Women's access to higher education expanded in the 1960s and 1970s, first at the undergraduate and then at the post-graduate and professional level as they began using legal remedies and sustained political pressure to force open campus facilities and programs. The Civil Rights Act of 1964 (Title VII) mandated that all women and people of color had to receive equal consideration in educational institutions (and in employment) to white men. No longer could colleges refuse to accept women because they had filled their quota of female slots for certain programs; nor could colleges legally require women to obtain higher grades or test scores than men in order to be admitted. As a result, the number of women enrolled in American colleges and universities increased by 45 percent between 1970 and 1975.

Changes in federal law were crucial to women's quest for advancement in the post-war era, yet women's political activity did not return readily to its pre-war levels. Women lost their separate political base when the New Dealers aged and were replaced or evicted from public office. The social feminist generation had no obvious successors. They had, as Susan Ware observes in *Beyond Suffrage*, trained no successors because they thought of themselves as setting an example for others to follow. Yet the lack of female political organizations and the integration (or submergence) of the women's divisions of both the Republican and Democratic parties left women battling against indifferent or hostile party hierarchies. Women were still less likely to vote than men in the 1950s and constituted a tiny fraction of elected officials. They received little encouragement from public officials in their political activities. In 1948, President Harry S. Truman addressed a centennial celebration of the Seneca Falls Women's Rights Declaration, entitled "The American Woman: Her Changing Role: Worker, Homemaker, Citizen," tellingly inverting the title so that Homemaker came first.

Female politicians battled to retain their place in public life in the face of such attitudes. Lacking an organized support network, they were rarely nominated or, as India Edwards, director of the Women's Division of the Democratic Party put it, were put forward because the party "thinks it's a lost cause." Female candidates also suffered red-baiting in the 1940s and 1950s. Richard Nixon defeated Helen Gahagan Douglas for a California Senatorial seat in 1950 by smearing her as the "Pink Lady." Senator Joseph McCarthy attacked the lawyer and American representative to the United Nations Commission on the Status of Women, Dorothy Kenyon, as a fellow traveler in 1950, ending her public career. Senator Margaret Chase Smith (Republican, Maine) bravely stood up to McCarthy's tactics, by calling upon legislators to reject "fear, ignorance, bigotry and smear."

In the chilly atmosphere of post-war politics few people were as brave as Smith. Women's voluntary organizations, those representing racial minorities, or with overseas affiliations, were especially suspect. The Zionist Pioneer Women came under suspicion, as did the National Council of Negro Women. Suburban housewives withdrew from ethnic societies, fearing they might be tainted with the subversive label. These organizations attempted to prove their patriotism, partly by shunning feminist demands. Cold warriors emphasized the importance of the domestic hearth in achieving victory over communism, a process Elaine Tyler May refers to as "domestic containment." Membership in the League of Women Voters and the Consumers' League plummeted after the war, although the League still served as an important training ground for women interested in civic affairs and public office.

Even though support for the Equal Rights Amendment had grown during World War II and the number of women elected to public office increased in the early 1940s, there was a tapering off of female elected office holders through the 1960s. Less than a dozen women served in Congress, but they were more likely to be elected in their own right rather than filling out their late husband's term of office. Once women began serving on important Congressional committees, they introduced legislation to benefit women and expand their opportunities. Yet support for the Equal Rights Amendment remained equivocal. While Republican Representatives tended to favor the ERA, Democratic women still advocated protective legislation. The Senate passed the ERA in 1950 and 1953, but not with a large enough majority to send it to the states for ratification despite the continued support from the Business and Professional Women's Clubs, the General Federation of Women's Clubs, and the National Woman's Party.

Even though the women's movement barely "survived in the doldrums" according to Leila J. Rupp and Verta Taylor, African-American women were engaged in the struggle for racial equality and played crucial roles in the civil rights movement. They ran NAACP offices, brought suit to obtain admission to segregated schools and universities, and put themselves in physical danger for their beliefs. Rosa L. Parks, secretary of the NAACP chapter in Montgomery, Alabama, sparked the bus boycott by refusing to give up her seat to a white man in 1955, thus violating the city's bus segregation ordinance. The boycott, which lasted for over a year, focused attention on the daily indignities faced by southern blacks. Young African-American women who had little or no access to state-supported secondary or higher learning in the South, fought for admission to high schools and colleges, enduring jeering mobs in Little Rock, Arkansas, and elsewhere in their determination to obtain an education.

The women's movement which had faltered during the 1940s and 1950s awakened in the 1960s as a new generation of college-educated civil rights and anti-war protesters asserted women's rights to equality. Throughout the inter-war years, the politics of difference had been the dominant paradigm. Yet the 1950s showed the limits of even affluent domesticity without feminism, as women reacted against the problem that had no name, against social injustice, and against social, political, and economic systems which treated them unfairly. Women emerged from the war seeking individual rather than political solutions to the challenges of mid-twentieth-century life, but within a generation they (and their daughters) had fused the personal with the political in the civil rights and women's liberation movements. Once women realized that the ideal home in the suburbs was not a solution to the nameless dissatisfaction many felt with their lives, they sought collective, political solutions to the problems they encountered. This paved the way for the women's liberation movement, which with all its successes and failures, forced Americans to confront the enduring importance of gender in all aspects of life in the United States.

Bibliography

The proliferation of scholarship on women since the 1970s means that only a portion of the relevant works can be included in this bibliography. The current interest in women's experiences reflects a concern for the diversity of experiences, the typical and ordinary, and the impact of grand events upon everyday folk as well as elites. The books and articles described here capture the richness and diversity of women's experiences, emphasizing how those experiences varied by race, region, and ethnicity, while still exploring the common threads of education, employment, and political participation. Many of the works cited overlap chronologically and topically. To avoid repeating material, readers are urged to consult topics across the chronological divides and to examine them for relevant information between topics. The beginning of this bibliography provides an overview and general sources.

One of the first works to explore the historiography of women is Gerda Lerner's "Placing Women in History: Definitions and Challenges," which appeared in *Feminist Studies*, III (Fall, 1975), 5–14; reprinted in Mary Beth Norton (ed.), *Major Problems in American Women's History* (Lexington, Mass., D.C. Heath, 1989). Joan Kelly's important question, "but was it a Renaissance for women?" can be found in her collected essays, *Women, History, and Theory: The Essays of Joan B. Kelly* (Chicago, University of Chicago Press, 1988). Other examinations of the practice of studying women in the past can be found in Ellen DuBois, Mari Jo Buhle, Temma Kaplan, Gerda Lerner, and Carroll Smith-Rosenberg, "Politics and Culture in Women's History: A Symposium," *Feminist Studies*, 6 (Spring 1980), 26–84; Gerda Lerner, *The Majority Finds Its Past: Placing Women in History* (Oxford, Oxford University Press, 1979); Nancy Hewitt, "Beyond the Search for Sisterhood: American Women's History in the 1980s," *Social History* 10 (October 1985); Joan W. Scott, "Gender, a Useful Category of Historical Analysis," *American Historical Review*, 91 (1986), 1053–75; Linda K. Kerber, "Separate Spheres, Female Worlds, Women's Place: The Rhetoric of Women's History," *Journal of American History*, 75 (1988), 9–39; Elsa Brown Barkley, "'What Has Happened Here': The Politics of Difference in Women's History and Feminist Politics," *Feminist Studies*, 18 (1992), 295–312; and Bonnie G. Smith, "Gender and the Practices of Scientific History: The Seminar and Archival Research in the Nineteenth Century," *American Historical Review*, 100 (1995), 1150–76.

Useful essay collections include Ellen Carol DuBois and Vicki L. Ruiz (eds), *Unequal Sisters: A Multi-cultural Reader in U.S. Women's History* (New York, Routledge, 1990) and Linda K. Kerber, Alice Kessler-Harris, and

317

Kathryn Kish Sklar (eds), *U.S. History as Women's History: New Feminist Essays* (Chapel Hill, University of North Carolina Press, 1995). Susan Armitage and Elizabeth Jameson (eds), *The Women's West* (Norman, University of Oklahoma Press, 1987) concentrates on the western female experience as does Lillian Schlissel, Vicki L. Ruiz and Janice Monk (eds), *Western Women: Their Land, Their Lives* (Albuquerque, University of New Mexico Press, 1987). Patricia Albers and Beatrice Medicine (eds), *The Hidden Half: Studies of Plains Indian Women* (Lanham, MD, University Press of America, 1983) is an excellent anthology of writings about one group of Native American women. Catherine Clinton (ed.), *Half Sisters of History: Southern Women and the American Past* (Durham, NC, Duke University Press, 1994); Virginia Bernhard, Betty Brandon, Elizabeth Fox-Genovese, and Theda Perdue (eds), *Southern Women: Histories and Identities* (Columbia, University of Missouri Press, 1992); and Anne Firor Scott, *Unheard Voices: The First Historians of Southern Women* (Charlottesville, University of Virginia Press, 1993) explore the gendered dynamics of life in the South and southern history. Darlene Clark Hine (ed.), *Black Women in American History* (New York, Carlton, 1990) presents an important resource on African-American women. Paula E. Hyman and Deborah Dash Moore (eds), *Jewish Women in America: An Historical Encyclopedia* (London, Routledge, 1997) is a counterpart on Jewish women in the United States.

Women's voices can be heard most loudly when they speak in their own words. Gerda Lerner (ed.), *Black Women in White America: A Documentary History* (New York, Pantheon, 1972) includes letters to newspapers, articles, organizations' papers, correspondence, and speeches. W. Elliot Brownlee and Mary M. Brownlee (eds), *Women in the American Economy: A Documentary History* (New Haven, Conn., Yale University Press, 1971) deploy documents and letters to explore women's economic lives. Gretchen M. Bataille and Kathleen M. Sands (eds), *American Indian Women: Telling Their Lives* (Lincoln, University of Nebraska Press, 1984) contains Native American women's autobiographies. Paula Gunn Allen, *The Sacred Hoop: Recovering the Feminine in American Indian Traditions* (Boston, Beacon Press, 1986) examines legends and accounts of Indian women's lives, as does Carolyn Niethammer, *Daughters of the Earth: The Lives and Legends of American Indian Women* (London, Collier-Macmillan Books, 1977).

Kirstin Olsen, *Chronology of Women's History* (Westport, Conn., Greenwood Press, 1994) supplies a year by year account of major events in women's history. Major biographical dictionaries include *Notable American Women, 1607–1950*, ed. Edward T. James, Janet Wilson James, and Paul S. Boyer (Cambridge, Mass., Belknap Press, 1971) and its sequel *Notable American Women: The Modern Period: A Biographical Dictionary* (Cambridge, Mass., Belknap Press, 1980), ed. Barbara Sicherman and Carol Hurd Green with Ilene Kantrov and Harriette Walker; and Darlene Clark Hine, Elsa Barkley Brown, and Rosalyn Terborg-Penn (eds), *Black Women in America: An Historical Encyclopedia* (Brooklyn, NY, Carlson, 1993). Rayna Green, *Native American Women: A Contextual Bibliography* (Bloomington, University of Indiana Press, 1984) and Gretchen M. Bataille and Kathleen

M. Sands, *American Indian Women: A Guide to Research* (Brooklyn, NY, Carlson, 1991) supply detailed bibliographies on Native American women.

Almost all the tabular material in this book comes from the United States Census. Collected every ten years since 1790, the Census contains a wealth of information about women's work, mobility, family relations, race, ethnicity, naturalization status, mortality, and household patterns. *Historical Statistics of the United States: Colonial Times to 1970* issued by the Bureau of the Census (Washington, DC, Government Printing Office, 1975) presents historical data over time, with especially detailed information on population, vital statistics, education, consumer expenditure, and social statistics. Other government agencies, such as the Women's Bureau and the Children's Bureau, are fruitful sources for the twentieth century.

There are a number of overviews of women in the economy. Edith Abbott wrote one of the first economic histories of women, *Women in Industry* (New York, D. Appleton, 1910) examining the relationship between economic changes and gender roles. Reprinted by Arno Press in 1969, it remains a useful resource. Alice Kessler-Harris, *Out to Work: A History of Wage-Earning Women in the United States* (Oxford, Oxford University Press, 1982) integrates the study of laboring women with major economic, social, political, and cultural events in a comprehensive analysis of women's economic activity. Claudia Goldin, *Understanding the Gender Gap: An Economic History of American Women* (Oxford, Oxford University Press, 1990) correlates employment with specific stages of women's life cycles, the changing economic role of married women, and the political economy of gender. Elizabeth Faulkner Baker, *Technology and Women's Work* (New York, Columbia University Press, 1974) surveys the impact of technology on women's work in the nineteenth and twentieth centuries. Valerie Kincade Oppenheimer, *The Female Labor Force in the United States: Demographic and Economic Factors Governing its Growth and Changing Composition* (Berkeley, University of California Press, 1969) analyzes supply and demand factors, the discrete nature of the male and female labor markets, and the demographic factors which led to the expansion of employment for older and married women.

Chapter 1

Several essay collections cover the range of women's work in the United States. Carol Groneman and Mary Beth Norton (eds), *"To Toil the Livelong Day:" America's Women at Work, 1780–1980* (Ithaca, NY, Cornell University Press, 1987) and Milton Cantor and Bruce Laurie (eds), *Class, Sex, and the Woman Worker* (Westport, Conn., Greenwood Press, 1977) contain useful essays. Native American women's economic roles are explored in Nancy Shoemaker (ed.), *Negotiators of Change: Historical Perspectives on Native American Women* (London, Routledge, 1995); Kathryn E. Holland Braun, "Guardians of Tradition and Handmaidens to Change: Women's Roles in Creek Economic and Social Life During the Eighteenth Century," *American Indian Quarterly,* 14 (1990), 239–58. Louise Lamphere, "Historical and Regional Variability in Navajo Women's Roles," *Journal of*

Anthropological Research 45 (1989), 117–29 probes differences in women's roles between different groups. Ramon A. Gutiérrez, *When Jesus Came the Corn Mothers Went Away: Marriage, Sexuality, and Power in New Mexico, 1500–1846* (Stanford, Calif., Stanford University Press, 1991.) investigates the impact of European colonization on sex roles as does Theda Perdue, *Cherokee Women: Gender and Culture Change, 1700–1835* (Lincoln, University of Nebraska Press, 1998).

Women's role in agriculture receives careful consideration from Joan M. Jensen, *Loosening the Bonds: Mid-Atlantic Farm Women, 1750–1850* (New Haven, Conn., Yale University Press, 1986). In *With These Hands: Women Working on the Land* (New York, Feminist Press and McGraw-Hill, 1981), Jensen presents accounts of women's agricultural experiences, including Native American women, African Americans (both slave and free), Hispanic women, and native- and foreign-born white women. Nancy Grey Osterud, *Bonds of Community: The Lives of Farm Women in Nineteenth Century New York* (Ithaca, NY, Cornell University Press, 1991) investigates gender relations and work on family farms in upstate New York. Jeanne Boydston, *Home and Work: Housework, Wages, and the Ideology of Labor in the Early Republic* (Oxford, Oxford University Press, 1990), discusses changing definitions of work in the nineteenth century.

The literature on African-American women and slave agriculture has grown in the last two decades. Claire Robertson, "Africa into the Americas? Slavery and Women, the Family, and the Gender Division of Labor," in David Barry Gaspar and Darlene Clark Hine (eds), *More Than Chattel: Black Women and Slavery in the Americas* (Bloomington, Indiana University Press, 1996), pp. 3–43 examines the carryovers from Africa into slavery in the Americas. Betty Wood, *Women's Work, Men's Work: The Informal Slave Economies of Low Country Georgia* (Athens, University of Georgia, 1995) also probes African carryovers and how enslaved women managed to produce economic goods for their families' benefit. Jacqueline Jones, *Labor of Love, Labor of Sorrow: Black Women, Work, and the Family from Slavery to the Present* (New York, Basic Books, 1985) delves into the working of the slave economy as experienced by black women. Dorothy Sterling, *We Are Your Sisters: Black Women in the Nineteenth Century* (New York, Norton, 1984) and Deborah Gray White, *Arn't I a Woman? Female Slaves in the Plantation South* (New York, Norton, 1985) cover some of the same ground. Charles L. Perdue, Jr., Thomas E. Arden, and Robert K Phillips present former slaves' testimony on their experiences in *Weevils in the Wheat: Interviews with Virginia Ex-Slaves* (Charlottesville, University of Virginia Press, 1976). This volume and other Works Progress Administration interviews with former slaves in the 1930s furnish the slaves' side of the story, but are filtered through the racial politics of the time and the long lens of distant memory.

Early accounts of women's experiences in the factories include Lucy Larcom, *A New England Girlhood* (New York, Corinth Books, 1961 [orig. 1889]); Harriet H. Robinson, *Early Factory Labor in New England* (1889) and her autobiography, *Loom and Spindle* (1898). Robinson is also the subject of a historical biography, *"A Good Poor Man's Wife" Being a Chronicle of Harriet Hanson Robinson and Her Family in Nineteenth Century New England* (Hanover, NH, University Press of New England, 1981) by Claudia L. Bushman. Edith Abbott's *Women in Industry* contains a wealth of quantitative and qualitative data by one of the pioneering investigators into women's employment outside the home. More recent examinations include Thomas Dublin, *Women at Work: The Transformation of Work and Community in Lowell, Massachusetts, 1820–1860* (New York, Columbia University Press, 1979); Daniel Walkowitz, *Worker City, Company Town: Iron and Cotton Worker Protest in Troy and Cohoes, New York, 1855–1884* (Urbana, University of Illinois Press, 1978); Susan Estabrook Kennedy, *If All We Did Was to Weep at Home: A History of White Working-Class Women in America* (Bloomington, Indiana University Press, 1979). Mary H. Blewett, *Men, Women, and Work: Class, Gender, and Protest in the New England Shoe Industry, 1780–1910* (Urbana, University of Illinois Press, 1988) investigates employment inside and outside the home and the way that marriage changed women's relation to the labor force. Philip S. Foner (ed.), *The Factory Girls* (Urbana, University of Illinois Press, 1977) is particularly useful since it contains many of the original writings of New England textile workers. Mary H. Blewett, *We Will Rise in Our Might: Workingwomen's Voices from Nineteenth-Century New England* (Ithaca, NY, Cornell University Press, 1991) also includes women's speeches and letters.

Chapter 2

Carl Degler, *At Odds: Women and the Family in America from the Revolution to the Present* (Oxford, Oxford University Press, 1980) provides a comprehensive demographic history of women's lives. Combining an analysis of fertility, family structure, employment, and political and social activism, this volume helps integrate women's experience with changes in the economic, social, and demographic structures of American life. Other general histories of the family include Steven Mintz and Susan Kellogg, *Domestic Revolutions: A Social History of American Family Life* (New York, Free Press, 1989); Joseph R. Peden and Fred R. Glahe, *The American Family and the State* (San Francisco, Pacific Research Institute for Public Policy, 1986); Barrie Thorne (ed.), *Rethinking the Family: Some Feminist Questions* (New York, Longman, 1982); Michael Gordon (ed.), *The American Family in Social-Historical Perspective* (New York, St. Martin's Press, 1978).

Robert V. Wells, *Revolutions in Americans' Lives: A Demographic Perspective on the History of Americans, Their Families, and Their Society* (Westport, Conn., Greenwood Press, 1982) furnishes an overview of the demographic changes which powerfully shaped women's lives in the early nineteenth century. Lisa Wilson, *Life After Death: Widows in Pennsylvania, 1750–1850* (Philadelphia, Temple University Press, 1992) investigates widowhood. James Trussell and Richard Steckel, "The Age of Slaves at Menarche and Their First Birth," *Journal of Interdisciplinary History,* 8 (1978), 477–505; Richard H. Steckel, "Antebellum Southern White Fertility: A Demographic and Economic Analysis," *Journal of Economic History,* 40 (1980), 331–50; Maris A. Vinovskis, "Socioeconomic Determinants of

Interstate Fertility Differentials in the United States," *Journal of Interdisciplinary History*, 6 (1976), 375–96; Richard A. Easterlin, "Population Change and Farm Settlement in the Northern United States," *Journal of Economic History*, 36 (1976), 45–75 all investigate birth rates.

Herbert Gutman, *The Black Family in Slavery and Freedom* (New York, Pantheon, 1976); Robert Fogel and Stanley Engerman, "Recent Findings in the Study of Slave Demography and Family Structure," *Social Science Research*, 63 (1979), 570–7; Eugene D. Genovese, *Roll, Jordan, Roll: The World the Slaves Made* (New York, Pantheon, 1976); Todd L. Savitt, *Medicine and Slavery: The Diseases and Health Care of Blacks in Antebellum Virginia* (Urbana, University of Illinois Press, 1978 all examine the racial patterns of ante-bellum population trends.

Nancy F. Cott, in *The Bonds of Womanhood: Woman's Sphere in New England, 1790–1835* (New Haven, Conn., Yale University Press 1977), establishes the background for this period. There are many studies of women's changing roles within the family from the Age of Jackson until the Civil War. Barbara Welter's pioneering article, "The Cult of True Womanhood," *American Quarterly*, 18 (1966), 151–74, details the basic concepts which underpinned middle-class women's lives in this era. Kathryn Kish Sklar, *Catharine Beecher: A Study in American Domesticity* (New York, Norton, 1973); Jeanne Boydston, Mary Kelley, and Ann Margolis (eds), *The Limits of Sisterhood: The Beecher Sisters on Women's Rights and Woman's Sphere* (Chapel Hill, University of North Carolina Press, 1988); and Barbara Epstein, *The Politics of Domesticity* (Middletown, Conn., Wesleyan University Press, 1981) all explore domesticity and the propounders of this ideology. Harriet Beecher Stowe's essay, "The Lady Who Does Her Own Work" is reprinted in Gail Parker, *The Oven Birds: American Women on Womanhood, 1820–1920* (New York, Anchor Doubleday, 1975).

Mary Ryan, *The Cradle of the Middle Class: The Family in Oneida County, New York, 1780–1865* (Cambridge, Cambridge University Press, 1981); Richard Meckel, "Educating a Ministry of Mothers: Evangelical Maternal Associations, 1815–1860," *Journal of the Early Republic, 2* (1982), 403–23; and Bernard Wishy, *The Child and the Republic: The Dawn of Modern American Child Nurture* (Philadelphia, University of Pennsylvania Press, 1968) all examine family life in the early nineteenth century. John Mack Faragher, *Men and Women on the Overland Trail* (New Haven, Conn., Yale University Press, 1979), and *Sugar Creek: Life on the Illinois Prairie* (New Haven, Conn., Yale University Press, 1986); Julie Roy Jeffrey, *Frontier Women: The Trans-Mississippi West, 1840–1880* (New York, Hill and Wang, 1979) investigate the migration process. Christine Stansell, *City of Women: Sex and Class in New York, 1789–1869* (New York, Alfred A. Knopf, 1986) concentrates on working-class women and their family relations.

The first half of John D'Emilio and Estelle B. Freedman's *Intimate Matters: A History of Sexuality in America* (New York, Harper & Row, 1988) scrutinizes pre-industrial family systems, the private world of families in the early industrial era, and the developing socio-sexual world of utopian communities. Its examination of sexual politics encompasses same-sex intimacy, pointing out, as does Carroll Smith-Rosenberg, "The Female World of Love and Ritual: Relations between Women in Nineteenth-Century America," in Nancy F. Cott and Elizabeth H. Pleck (eds), *A Heritage of Her Own* (New York, Simon and Schuster, 1979), pp. 322–42, that homosocial friendships may or may not include sexual relations. See Marilyn Wood Hill, *Their Sisters' Keepers: Prostitution in New York City, 1830–1870* (Berkeley, University of California Press, 1993) for an economic and social analysis of prostitution.

Birth control and abortion are the subjects of Linda Gordon, *Woman's Body, Woman's Right: A Social History of Birth Control in America* (New York, Grossman, 1976); James C. Mohr, *Abortion in America: The Origins and Evolution of National Policy, 1800–1900* (New York, Oxford University Press, 1978); James Reed, *From Private Vice to Public Virtue: The Birth Control Movement in American Society Since 1830* (New York, Basic Books, 1978). On childbearing see Judith Walzer Leavitt, *Brought to Bed: Childbearing in America, 1750–1950* (New York, Oxford University Press, 1986); Richard W. Wertz and Dorothy C. Wertz, *Lying-In: A History of Childbirth in America* (New York, Free Press, 1977); Jane B. Donegan, *Women and Men Midwives: Medicine, Morality, and Misogyny in Early America* (Westport, Conn., Greenwood Press, 1978).

The changing practices of housewifery are explored by Glenna Matthews, *Just a Housewife: The Rise and Fall of Domesticity in America* (New York, Oxford University Press, 1987); Ruth Schwartz Cowan, *More Work for Mother: The Ironies of Household Technology from the Open Hearth to the Microwave* (New York, Basic Books, 1983); Nancy Folbre, "Unproductive Housewife: Her Evolution in 19th Century Economic Thought," *Signs*, 16, (1991), 463–84. The interaction between middle-class women and their domestic help in the early nineteenth century is the focus of Daniel Sutherland, *Americans and Their Servants: Domestic Service in the United States from 1800 to 1920* (Baton Rouge, Louisiana State University Press, 1981) and Faye Dudden, *Serving Women: Household Service in the Nineteenth Century* (Middletown, Conn., Wesleyan University Press, 1983). Gillian Brown, *Domestic Individualism: Imagining Self in Nineteenth-Century America* (Berkeley, University of California Press, 1990) and Clifford E. Clark, Jr., *The American Family Home, 1800–1960* (Chapel Hill, University of North Carolina Press, 1989) investigate the domestic environment.

Racial variations in family experience are the focus of many historical works, including many already cited. Readers are referred to Robert Fogel, *Without Consent or Contract: The Rise and Fall of American Slavery* (New York, W. W. Norton, 1989); Elizabeth Fox Genovese, *Within the Plantation Household: Black and White Women of the Old South* (Chapel Hill, University of North Carolina Press, 1988); Charles Joyner, *Down by the Riverside: A South Carolina Slave Community* (Urbana, University of Illinois Press, 1984); Suzanne Lebsock, *The Free Women of Petersburg: Status and Culture in a Southern Town, 1784–1860* (New York, W. W. Norton, 1984); James Oliver Horton, "Freedom's Yoke: Gender Conventions among Antebellum Free Blacks," *Feminist Studies*, 12 (1986), 51–76. The white plantation mistress's perspective is expressed by Mary Boykin Chesnut, *A Diary from Dixie*, ed. Ben Ames Williams (Boston, Houghton Mifflin, 1949).

Native American culture and the place of women within it varied from region to region and according to its economic and geographical foundations. James T. Axtell, *The Indian Peoples of Eastern America: A Documentary History of the Sexes* (New York, Oxford University Press, 1981); Patricia Albers and Bea Medicine, *The Hidden Half: Studies of Plains Indian Women* (Washington, DC, University Press of America, 1983); Gretchen M. Bataille and Kathleen M. Sands, *American Indian Women: Telling Their Lives* (Lincoln, University of Nebraska Press, 1984); Beverly Hungry Wolf, *The Ways of My Grandmothers* (New York, Morrow, 1980); Joan Jensen and Darlis A. Miller, *New Mexico Women: Intercultural Perspectives* (Albuquerque, University of New Mexico Press, 1986); Claudia Lewis, *Indian Families of the Northwest Coast: The Impact of Change* (Chicago, University of Chicago Press, 1970); Frank B. Linderman, *Pretty Shield: Medicine Woman of the Crows* (New York, John Day, 1972 [orig., 1932]) examine diverse family patterns among Native Americans.

Joan Hoff, *Law, Gender, and Injustice: A Legal History of U.S. Women* (New York, New York University Press, 1991); Leo Kanowitz, *Women and the Law: An Unfinished Revolution* (Albuquerque, University of New Mexico Press, 1969); Carole Shammas, Marylynn Salmon, and Michel Dahlin, *Inheritance in America: From Colonial Times to the Present* (New Brunswick, NJ, Rutgers University Press, 1987); Marylynn Salmon, *Women and the Law of Property in Early America* (Chapel Hill, University of North Carolina Press, 1987); Michael Grossberg, *Governing the Hearth: Law and the Family in Nineteenth-Century America* (Chapel Hill, University of North Carolina Press, 1985) all cover legal issues.

Chapter 3

Linda Kerber's discussion of *The Women of the Republic: Intellect and Ideology in Revolutionary America* (Chapel Hill, University of North Carolina Press, 1980) explores the impact of the American Revolution on education in the post-Revolutionary era. Barbara Miller Solomon, *In the Company of Educated Women: A History of Women and Higher Education in America* (New Haven, Conn., Yale University Press, 1985) looks at the development of college education for women, beginning with the private academies of the early nineteenth century. Andrea Wyman, *Rural Women Teachers in the United States: A Sourcebook* (Lanham, MD and London, Scarecrow Press, 1997) contains a bibliography on women in education and in rural areas with a state by state bibliography of diaries and collections of letters.

Specific analyses of women's education include Maris A. Vinovskis and Richard M. Bernard, "Beyond Catharine Beecher: Female Education in the Antebellum Period," *Signs,* 3 (1978), 856–69; Anne Firor Scott, "What, Then, Is the American: This New Woman?" *Journal of American History,* 65 (1978), 679–703; and "That Ever Widening Circle: The Diffusion of

Feminist Values from the Troy Female Seminary, 1822–1872," *History of Education Quarterly,* 19 (1979), 3–27.

Education figures prominently in the discussions of female activists in Eleanor Flexner, *Century of Struggle: The Woman's Rights Movement in the United States* (New York, Atheneum, 1974 [orig., 1959]); Janet Zollinger Giele, *Two Paths to Women's Equality: Temperance, Suffrage, and the Origins of Modern Feminism* (New York, Twayne Publishers, 1995); Barbara Welter, *Dimity Convictions: The American Woman in the Nineteenth Century* (Athens, Ohio University Press, 1976); Keith Melder, *Beginnings of Sisterhood: The American Woman's Rights Movement, 1800–1850* (New York, Schocken Books, 1977); and Anne Firor Scott, *The Southern Lady: From Pedestal to Politics, 1830–1930* (Chicago, University of Chicago Press, 1970).

Ann Douglas, *The Feminization of American Culture* (New York, Knopf, 1977) offers a wide-ranging overview of women's role in the development of American culture in the century. Elaine Showalter, *Sister's Choice: Tradition and Change in American Women's Writing* (Oxford, Clarendon Press, 1991) goes beyond the title to include a study of quiltmaking as well as analyzing women's writing, while Elsa Barkley Brown also considers quilting in "African-American Quilting: A Framework for Conceptualizing and Teaching African-American Women's History," *Signs,* 14 (1989), 921–38. Faye E. Dudden, *Women in the American Theatre: Actresses & Audiences, 1790–1870* (New Haven, Conn., Yale University Press, 1994) examines the constriction of opportunity for actresses by the middle of the nineteenth century.

Mary Kelley, in *Private Woman, Public Stage: Literary Domesticity in Nineteenth Century America* (Oxford, Oxford University Press, 1984) explores the development of women as authors in the nineteenth century. Also see Nina Baym, *Women's Fiction: A Guide to Novels by and about Women in America, 1820–1870* (Ithaca, NY, Cornell University Press, 1978); Sally Allen McNall, *Who Is In the House: A Psychological Study of Two Centuries of Women's Fiction in America, 1795 to the Present* (New York, Elsevier, 1981); Kristin Herzog, *Women, Ethnics, and Exotics: Images of Power in Mid-Nineteenth Century Fiction* (Knoxville, University of Tennessee Press, 1983); Nina Baym, *Feminism and American Literary History: Essays* (New Brunswick, NJ, Rutgers University Press, 1992).

There are numerous studies of specific women authors, including Carolyn L. Karcher, *The First Woman in the Republic: A Cultural Biography of Lydia Maria Child* (Durham, NC, Duke University Press, 1994) which concentrates on Child's literary output while her activism takes precedence in Deborah Pickman, C*rusader for Freedom: A Life of Lydia Maria Child* (Boston, Beacon Press, 1992). Other studies include Jean Pfaelzer, *Parlor Radical: Rebecca Harding Davis and the Origins of American Social Realism* (Pittsburgh, University of Pittsburgh Press, 1996); Frances Smith Foster, *Written by Herself: Literary Production by African American Women, 1746–1892* (Bloomington, Indiana University Press, 1993); Shirley Samuels, *The Culture of Sentiment: Race, Gender, and Sentimentality in 19th Century America* (Oxford, Oxford University Press, 1992). Paula Blanchard,

Margaret Fuller: From Transcendentalism to Revolution (Reading, Mass., Addison-Wesley, 1988) explores the background to Margaret Fuller's *Woman in the Nineteenth Century.*
There is an entire industry devoted to Harriet Beecher Stowe and analyses of her most noted book, *Uncle Tom's Cabin.* See Joan D. Hedrick, *Harriet Beecher Stowe: A Life* (Oxford, Oxford University Press, 1994); Mason I. Lowance, Jr., Ellen E. Westbrook, and R.C. De Prospo (eds), *The Stowe Debate: Rhetorical Strategies in Uncle Tom's Cabin* (Amherst, University of Massachusetts Press, 1994); Eric J. Sundquist (ed.), *New Essays on Uncle Tom's Cabin* (Cambridge, Cambridge University Press, 1986).

Chapter 4

The literature on female reformers, political activity, and religious movements in the early nineteenth century is voluminous. There are a number of overviews of women's political participation in its broadest sense. Paula Baker, "The Domestication of Politics: Women and American Political Society, 1780–1920," *American Historical Review,* 89 (June 1984), 620–47, shows how women's interest in public affairs simultaneously altered their own status and politics. Other surveys of women in politics include Mary P. Ryan, *Women in Public: Between Banners and Ballots, 1825–1880* (Baltimore, Johns Hopkins University Press, 1990) who concentrates on the era covered in this chapter; Glenna Matthews, *The Rise of Public Woman: Woman's Power and Woman's Place in the United States, 1630–1970* (New York, Oxford University Press, 1992) covers a much broader chronological period.
The essays in Jean Fagan Yellin and John C. Van Horne (eds), *An Untrodden Path: Women's Political Culture in Antebellum America* (Ithaca, NY, Cornell University Press, 1994) and in Louise A. Tilly and Patricia Gurin (eds), *Women, Politics, and Change* (New York, Russell Sage, 1992) illuminate the dimensions of female political participation. Elizabeth R. Varon, "Tippecanoe and the Ladies, Too: White Women and Party Politics in Antebellum Virginia," *Journal of American History,* 82 (September 1995), 494–521 demonstrates the nature of female involvement in organized politics in the years before the Civil War. Victoria E. Bynum, *Unruly Women: The Politics of Social and Sexual Control in the Old South* (Chapel Hill, University of North Carolina Press, 1992) explores gender and gendered politics in the South, while Elizabeth Ann Bartlett, *Liberty, Equality, Sorority: The Origins and Interpretation of American Feminist Thought: Frances Wright, Sarah Grimké, and Margaret Fuller* (New York, Carlson, 1994) explores the southern and northern origins of feminist thinking.
Eleanor Flexner's *Century of Struggle: The Woman's Rights Movement in the United States* (Belknap Press of Harvard University, 1975 [orig. 1959]) remains as illuminating on feminism as when first published. Christine Bolt, *The Women's Movements in the United States and Britain from the 1790s to the 1920s* (New York, Harvester Wheatsheaf, 1993) covers the sweep of the women's movement. Ellen Carol DuBois, *Feminism and Suffrage: The Emergence of an Independent Women's Movement in America, 1848–1869*

(Ithaca, New York, Cornell University Press, 1978) is an outstanding account of the origins of the women's movement in the United States. Also see Barbara J. Berg, *The Remembered Gate: Origins of American Feminism: The Woman and the City, 1800–1860* (Oxford, Oxford University Press, 1978); Keith Melder, *The Beginnings of Sisterhood: The American Woman's Rights Movement, 1800–1850* (New York, Schocken, 1977); Jane Rendall, *The Origins of Modern Feminism: Women in Britain, France, and the United States, 1780–1860* (Basingstoke, Macmillan, 1985).

Lori D. Ginzberg, *Women and the Work of Benevolence: Morality, Politics and Class in the Nineteenth Century United States* (New Haven, Conn., Yale University Press, 1990); Nancy Hewitt, *Women's Activism and Social Change: Rochester, New York, 1822–1872* (Ithaca, New York, Cornell University Press, 1984) examine aspects of female reform in the early nineteenth century. Jean E. Friedman, *The Enclosed Garden: Women and Community in the Evangelical South, 1830–1900* (Chapel Hill, University of North Carolina Press, 1985) and Scott, *The Southern Lady*, both examine women's participation in reform and benevolence in the South.

Utopian and religious reformers are the subject of Celia Morris, *Fanny Wright: Rebel in America* (Urbana, University of Illinois Press, 1992); Caroll Smith Rosenberg, *Religion and the Rise of the American City: The New York City Mission Movement, 1812–1870* (Ithaca, Cornell University Press, 1971); Nancy Hewitt, "Feminist Friends: Agrarian Quakers and the Emergence of Woman's Rights in America," *Feminist Studies*, 12 (1986), 27–49; Jean M. Humez, *Mother's First-Born Daughters: Early Shaker Writings on Women and Religion* (Bloomington, Indiana University Press, 1993). Thomas J. Brown, *Dorothea Dix: New England Reformer* (Cambridge, Mass., Harvard University Press, 1998) contains a portrait of a female activist who kept her distance from both the abolitionist and women's rights movements.

Gerda Lerner, *The Grimké Sisters from South Carolina: Rebels Against Slavery* (Boston, Houghton Mifflin Company, 1967) and Larry Ceplair (ed.), *The Public Years of Sarah and Angelina Grimké: Selected Writings, 1835–1839* (New York, Columbia University Press, 1989) examine these pioneers of women's speaking in public. Other accounts of specific reformers include D. C. Bloomer, *Life and Writings of Amelia Bloomer*, with a new introduction by S. J. Kleinberg (New York, Schocken Books, 1975) which details the life and writings of the temperance reformer whose name became synonymous with dress reform in the mid-nineteenth century. Ruth Bordin, *Woman and Temperance* (Philadelphia, Temple University Press, 1981) explores the connections between feminism and temperance.

The linkages between anti-slavery and women's political participation are the subject of Angela Davis, *Women, Race, and Class* (New York, 1983); Blanche Hersh, *The Slavery of Sex: Feminist-Abolitionists in America* (Urbana, University of Illinois Press, 1978); Jean Fagan Yellin, *Women and Sisters: The Anti-slavery Feminists in American Culture* (New Haven, Conn., Yale University Press, 1989); Shirley Yee: *Black Women Abolitionists: A Study in Activism, 1820–1860* (Knoxville, University of Tennessee Press, 1992); Debra Gold Hansen, *Strained Sisterhood: Gender and Class in the*

Boston Female Anti-Slavery Society (Amherst, University of Massachusetts Press, 1993). Julie Roy Jeffrey, *The Great Silent Army of Abolitionism: Ordinary Women in the Antislavery Movement* (Chapel Hill, University of North Carolina Press, 1998) explores the role of ordinary women in the abolitionist movement and how their activism changed over time.

The role of women in the Civil War has received growing recognition from historians. Early studies include Mary Elizabeth Massey, *Bonnet Brigades: American Women and the Civil War* (New York, Alfred A. Knopf, 1966) and Bell Irvin Wiley, *Confederate Women* (Westport, Conn., Greenwood Press, 1975). Also see Catherine Clinton and Nina Silber, *Divided Houses: Gender and the Civil War* (New York, 1992); Drew Faust, "Altars of Sacrifice: Confederate Women and the Narratives of War," *Journal of American History,* 76 (1990), 1200–28; and Elizabeth D. Leonard, *Yankee Women: Gender Battles in the Civil War* (New York, Norton, 1994). Lee Ann Whites, *The Civil War as a Crisis in Gender: Augusta, Georgia, 1860–1890* (Athens, University of Georgia Press, 1995) examines race and gender in the reconstruction of the South.

The Journal of Charlotte L. Forten, ed., with introduction and notes, Ray Allen Billington (London, Collier-Macmillan, 1969) gives a fascinating account of growing up in Salem and Philadelphia as part of a leading African-American abolitionist family, then travelling to the South Sea Islands to work with the freedwomen and men. Biographical accounts of nineteenth-century feminists include Kathleen Barry, *Susan B. Anthony: A Biography of a Singular Feminist* (New York, Ballantine Books, 1988); Elisabeth Griffith, *In Her Own Right: The Life of Elizabeth Cady Stanton* (Oxford, Oxford University Press, 1984); Nell Painter, *Sojourner Truth: A Life, A Symbol* (New York, Norton, 1996).

Chapter 5

The primary sources on women's work in the late nineteenth and early twentieth centuries are especially rich. Special Census monographs such as *Statistics of Women at Work Based on Unpublished Information Derived from the Schedules of the Twelfth Census, 1900* (Washington, DC, Government Printing Office, 1907) and *Women in Gainful Occupations, 1870 to 1920* by Joseph A. Hill (Census Monographs, No. 9. Washington, DC, Government Printing Office, 1929) and various state bureaus of labor (especially the larger states such as Illinois, New York, and Massachusetts) contain detailed analyses of women's employment.

US Congress, Senate, *Report on Condition of Woman and Child Wage-earners in the United States*, 19 Volumes (Washington, DC, Government Printing Office, 1910–13) contains a wealth of information. Vol. 1: *Cotton Textile Industry*; Vol. 2: *Men's Ready-Made Clothing*; Vol. 5: *Wage-Earning Women in Stores and Factories*; Vol. 10: *History of Women in Trade Unions* are especially useful for those wishing to counter the somewhat dated argument that women did not participate actively in union organizing. Vol. 9 of this series by Helen L. Sumner, *History of Women in Industry in the United States* (1910) contains an illuminating overview of women industrial workers, as does Edith Abbott, *Women in Industry*. These volumes were reprinted as part of an Arno Press series, *Women in America: From Colonial Times to the Twentieth Century*, issued in 1974.

Other contemporary accounts of women workers include Annie Marion MacLean, *Wage-Earning Women* (New York, Macmillan, 1910); Elizabeth Beardsley Butler, *Women and the Trades: Pittsburgh, 1907–1908*, With a New Introduction by Maureen Weiner Greenwald (Pittsburgh, University of Pittsburgh Press, 1984); Katherine Anthony, *Mothers Who Must Earn* (New York, Russell Sage Foundation, 1914); Elizabeth Beardsley Butler, *Saleswomen in Mercantile Stores: Baltimore, 1909* (New York, Charities Publication Committee, 1912); and Louise Odencrantz, *Italian Women in Industry: A Study of Conditions in New York City* (New York, Russell Sage Foundation, 1919).

Many secondary analyses of female employment in the late nineteenth and early twentieth centuries encompass this period. Elyse Rotella, *From Home to Office. U.S. Women at Work, 1870–1930* (Ann Arbor, University of Michigan Press, 1981); Robert Smuts, *Women and Work in America* (New York, Columbia University Press, 1959); and Kessler-Harris provide overviews. Martha May, "Bread Before Roses: American Workingmen, Labor Unions and the Family Wage," in Ruth Milkman (ed.), *Women, Work, and Protest: A Century of US Women's Labor History* (London, Routledge & Kegan Paul, 1985) details the ideological climate which surrounded women's work at the turn of the century, while S.J. Kleinberg, *The Shadow of the Mills: Working Class Families in Pittsburgh, 1870–1907* (Pittsburgh, University of Pittsburgh Press, 1989) examines women's work in a male-dominated employment environment.

Examinations of women in specific industries include Mary H. Blewett, *Men, Women, and Work: Class, Gender, and Protest in the New England Shoe Industry, 1780–1910* (Urbana, University of Illinois Press, 1988); Tamara Hareven and Randolph Langenbach, *Amoskeag: Life and Work in an American Factory-City* (New York, Pantheon Books, 1978); Ruth Rosen, *The Lost Sisterhood: Prostitution in America, 1900–1918* (Baltimore, Johns Hopkins University Press, 1982). Margery W. Davies, *Woman's Place is at the Typewriter: Office Work and Office Workers, 1870–1930* (Philadelphia: Temple University Press, 1982) examines the growing importance of office work for female employees. Eileen Boris, *Home to Work: Motherhood and the Politics of Industrial Homework in the United States* (Cambridge, Cambridge University Press, 1994) explores the interstices of motherhood and work for pay within the home. Joanne J. Meyerowitz, *Women Adrift: Independent Wage Earners in Chicago, 1880–1930* (Chicago, University of Chicago Press, 1988) examines self-supporting women living apart from their families.

Studies of African-American women in the labor force include Jacqueline Jones, *Labor of Love, Labor of Sorrow: Black Women, Work and the Family from Slavery to the Present* (New York, Basic Books 1985); Roger Ransom and Richard Sutch, *One Kind of Freedom: The Economic Consequences of Emancipation* (Cambridge, Cambridge University Press, 1978), Victoria Byerly, *Hard Times Cotton Mill Girls* (Ithaca, NY, ILR Press, 1986); Paula

Giddings, *When and Where I Enter: The Impact of Black Women on Race and Sex in America* (New York, William Morrow and Company, 1988); David Katzman, *Seven Days a Week: Domestic Service in Industrializing America* (New York, Oxford University Press, 1978); Tera W. Hunter, *To 'Joy My Freedom: Southern Black Women's Lives and Labors after the Civil War* (Cambridge, Mass., Harvard University Press, 1997).

The literature on women's work in other ethnic/racial groups includes: Evelyn Nakano Glenn, *Issei, Nisei, War Bride: Three Generations of Japanese American Women in Domestic Service* (Philadelphia, Temple University Press, 1986); Lucie Cheng Hirata, "Chinese Immigrant Women in Nineteenth Century America," in Carol Berkin and Mary Beth Norton (eds), *Women of America: A History* (Boston, Houghton Mifflin, 1979) and Hirata, "Free, Identured, Enslaved: Chinese Prostitutes in Nineteenth Century America," *Signs*, 5 (1979), 339–57. Sarah Deutsch, *No Separate Refuge: Culture, Class, and Gender on an Anglo-Hispanic Frontier in the American Southwest, 1880–1940* (New York, Oxford University Press, 1987) compares women's work experiences by ethnic group. Mario T. Garcia, "The Chicana in American History: The Mexican Women of El Paso, 1890–1920," *Pacific Historical Review*, 49:2 (1980), 315–37, examines the experiences of Mexican women in an urban setting, while Glenda Riley, *Women and Indians on the Frontier, 1825–1915* (Albuquerque, University of New Mexico Press, 1984) concentrates on cultural interaction.

Accounts of white ethnic women include Susan Estabrook Kennedy, *If All We Did Was to Weep at Home: A History of White Working Class Women in America* (Bloomington, Indiana University Press, 1979); Hasia R. Diner: *Erin's Daughters in America* (Baltimore, Johns Hopkins University Press, 1983); Virginia Yans McLaughlin, *Family and Community: Italian Immigrants in Buffalo, 1880–1930* (Ithaca, NY, Cornell University Press, 1977); Eva Morawska, *For Bread with Butter: Life Worlds of East Central Europeans in Johnstown, Pennsylvania, 1890–1940* (Cambridge, Cambridge University Press, 1985); Tamara Hareven, *Family Time and Industrial Time: The Relationship between the Family and Work in A New England Industrial Community* (Cambridge, Cambridge University Press, 1982); Susan A. Glenn, *Daughters of the Shtetl: Life and Labor in the Immigrant Generation* (Ithaca, NY, Cornell University Press, 1990); Elizabeth Ewen, *Immigrant Women in the Land of Dollars: Life and Culture on the Lower East Side, 1890–1925* (New York, Monthly Review Press, 1985).

Women's labor protest figures in many of these volumes but readers should also see Vivien Hart, *Bound by Our Constitution: Women, Workers, and the Minimum Wage* (Princeton, NJ, Princeton University Press, 1994) for an examination of the legal aspects of women's work. Diane Kirkby, *Alice Henry: The Power of Pen and Voice: The Life of an Australian-American Labor Reformer* (Cambridge, Cambridge University Press, 1991) and Nancy Schrom Dye, *As Equals and As Sisters: Feminism, the Labor Movement and the Women's Trade Union League of New York* (Columbia, University of Missouri Press, 1980) investigate cross-class organizing. Theresa S. Malkiel, *The Diary of a Shirtwaist Striker*, With an Introductory Essay by Francoise Basch (Ithaca, NY, ILR Press, 1990 [orig. 1910]) gives a lightly fictionalized account of labor struggles in the New York garment industry, while Ardis Cameron, *Radicals of the Worst Sort: Laboring Women in Lawrence, Massachusetts, 1860–1912* (Urbana, University of Illinois Press, 1993) explores working women's culture in the textile mills.

Chapter 6

The US Census is also an excellent source of information about family structure in this period. As with women's work, it facilitates comparisons of family structure across ethnic and racial groups and over time. There were numerous sociological investigations of family life at the turn of the century, including Margaret Byington, *Homestead: The Households of a Milltown* (Pittsburgh, University of Pittsburgh Press, 1974 [orig. 1910]); Emily Balch, *Our Slavic Fellow Citizens* (New York, Charities Publications Committee, 1910); Robert Coit Chapin, *The Standard of Living among Workingmen's Families in New York City* (New York, Russell Sage, 1909).

Carroll D. Wright, *A Report on Marriage and Divorce in the United States, 1867 to 1886* (Washington, DC, Government Printing Office, 1889) is the first systematic study of marriage and divorce, while William O'Neill, *Divorce in the Progressive Era* (New York, Franklin Watts, 1973) contributes a historical perspective. Secondary analyses of family relations include Mark J. Stern, *Society and Family Strategy, Erie County, New York, 1850–1920* (Albany, State University of New York Press, 1987); Kleinberg, *The Shadow of the Mills*; Kenneth W. Godfrey, Audrey M. Godfrey, and Jill Mulvay Derr, *Women's Voices: An Untold History of the Latter-Day Saints, 1830–1900* (Salt Lake City, Utah, Deseret Book Company, 1982). Also see Maureen Ursenbach Beecher and Lavina Fielding Anderson (eds), *Sisters in Spirit: Mormon Women in Historical and Cultural Perspective* (Urbana, University of Illinois Press, 1987).

Herbert Gutman, *The Black Family in Slavery and Freedom* and Jacqueline Jones, *Labor of Love, Labor of Sorrow: Black Women, Work, and the Family from Slavery to the Present* (New York, Basic Books, 1985) focus on the African-American family. Peter W. Bardaglio, *Reconstructing the Household: Families, Sex, and the Law in the Nineteenth Century South* (Chapel Hill, University of North Carolina Press, 1995) presents a regional review of family ideals and legal matters. Steven Ruggles, *Prolonged Connections: The Rise of the Extended Family in Nineteenth Century England and America* (Madison, University of Wisconsin Press, 1987) contrasts family structure in the two countries. Amy E. Holmes, "'Such is the Price We Pay': American Widows and the Civil War Pension System," in Maris A. Vinovskis, *Toward a Social History of the American Civil War: Exploratory Essays* (Cambridge, Cambridge University Press, 1990), pp. 171–95, examines the development of the Civil War pension system.

Elizabeth H. Pleck, *Domestic Tyranny: The Making of Social Policy Against Family Violence from Colonial Times to the Present* (New York, Oxford University Press, 1987); Linda Gordon, *Heroes of Their Own Lives: The Politics and History of Family Violence, 1880–1960* (New York, Viking, 1988); David Peterson del Mar, *What Trouble I have Seen: A History of*

Violence against Wives (Cambridge, Mass., Harvard University Press, 1996) furnish an overview of violence. Kleinberg, *Shadow of the Mills*, chapter 7; Pamela Haag, "The 'Ill-Use of a Wife': Patterns of Working Class Violence in Domestic and Public New York City 1860–1880," *Journal of Social History*, 25 1992), 447–77; and Betsey Downer, "Battered Pioneers: Jules Sandoz and the Physical Abuse of Wives on the American Frontier," *Great Plains Quarterly*, 12 (1992), 31–49, examine violence in particular locations. C. Kirk Hudson, "'Whackety Whack, Don't Talk Back': The Glorification of Violence Against Females and the Subjugation of Women in Nineteenth Century Southern Folk Music," *Journal of Women's History*, 8 (1996), 114–42, examines femicide in the ballads of the South.

Histories of housework in this era explore changing technology. See Susan Strasser, *Never Done: A History of American Housework* (New York, Pantheon, 1982); Matthews, *Just a Housewife;* Cowan, *More Work for Mother;* S. J. Kleinberg, "Technology and Women's Work: The Lives of Working Class Women, Pittsburgh, 1870–1900," *Labor History*, 17 (1976), 58–72. On family strategies see Claudia Goldin, "Family Strategies and the Family Economy in the late Nineteenth Century," in Theodore Hershberg, *Philadelphia: Work, Space, Family and Group Experience in the Nineteenth Century* (New York, 1981) and Sharon Harley, "For the Good of Family and Race: Gender, Work and Domestic Roles in the Black Community, 1880–1930," *Signs*, 15 (1990), 254–65.

Joan Morrison and Charlotte Fox Zabusky, *American Mosaic: 140 First Generation Americans Talk about Why they Came to This Country, What They Endured, the Dreams They Cherished and the Realities They Found* (New York, New American Library, 1980) contains first-hand accounts of immigrant experiences. Isaac Metzker (ed.), *A Bintel Brief: "A Bundle of Letters"* to the Jewish Daily Forward (New York, Ballantine Books, 1971) is a selection of the letters to the advice column of New York's leading Yiddish-language newspaper, featuring the problems of the immigrant generation.

Sucheng Chan, Douglas Henry Daniels, Mario T. Garcia, Terry P. Wilson (eds), *Peoples of Color in the American West* (Lexington, Kentucky, D. C. Heath, 1994) contains many relevant articles. Janice L. Reiff, Michel R. Dahlin, and Daniel Scott Smith, "Rural Push and Urban Pull: Work and Family Experiences of Older Black Women in Southern Cities, 1880–1900," *Journal of Social History,* 16 (1983), 39–48, examines African-American women's residential mobility.

Vincent N. Parillo, "The Immigrant Family Securing the American Dream," *Journal of Comparative Family Studies,* 22 (1991), 131–45 investigates the role of the family in employment and assimilation. Yans McLoughlin, *Family and Community;* Hareven, *Family Time;* Morawska, *Bread with Butter;* and John Bodnar, Roger Simon, and Michael P. Weber, *Lives of Their Own: Blacks, Italians, and Poles in Pittsburgh, 1900–1960* (Urbana, University of Illinois Press, 1982) investigate the relation between the family, immigration, and women's roles. Yuji Ichioka, *The Issei: The World of the First Generation Japanese Immigrants, 1885–1924* (New York, Free Press, 1988) also concentrates on family migration processes and assimilation for the Japanese. Florette Henri, *Black Migration: Movement North, 1900–1920* (New York, Doubleday, 1976); Elizabeth H. Pleck, *Black Migration and Poverty, Boston, 1865–1900* (New York, Academic Press, 1979); Joe William Trotter, Jr. (ed.), *The Great Migration in Historical Perspective: New Dimensions of Race, Class, and Gender* (Bloomington, Indiana University Press, 1991); Carole Marks, *Farewell, We're Good and Gone: The Great Black Migration* (Bloomington, Indiana University Press, 1993); and Peter Gottlieb, *Making Their Own Way: Southern Blacks' Migration to Pittsburgh, 1916–1930* (Urbana, University of Illinois Press, 1987) all examine the complex process of African-American migration with varying emphasis on women's experiences and the interaction between family relationships and the migration process. Vicki L. Ruiz, *From Out of of the Shadows: Mexican Women in Twentieth-Century America* (New York, Oxford University Press, 1998) undertakes a similar task for Mexican women.

The westward migration has been the subject of many studies, most of them written from the viewpoint of European Americans. Exceptions to this are Janet A. McDonnell, *The Dispossession of the American Indian, 1887–1934* (Bloomington, Indiana University Press, 1991) and Nell Irvin Painter, *The Exodusters: Black Migration to Kansas after Reconstruction* (New York, Alfred A. Knopf, 1977). Reminiscences of western life include Hilda Faunce, *Desert Wife* (Providence, Little Brown, 1928) about a white woman's life on a trading post. Elinore Pruitt Steward, *Letters of a Woman Homesteader* (Lincoln, University of Nebraska Press, 1961) recalls the struggle of a widowed woman with a small child to earn a living in Colorado and Wyoming. Nannie T. Alderson and Helena Huntington Smith, *A Bride Goes West* (Lincoln, University of Nebraska Press, 1969) follows the adventures of a southern newlywed who accompanied her husband to an abandoned miner's cabin in Montana

A delightful volume by Marjorie Kreidberg, *Food on the Frontier: Minnesota Cooking from 1850 to 1900 with Selected Recipes* (St. Paul, Minnesota Historical Society, 1975) is an illustrated goldmine of recipes, rural practices, and mechanical contrivances. Lillian Schlissel (ed.), *Women's Diaries of the Westward Journey* (New York, Schocken, Books, 1982) offers an overview of these diaries and their significance, as do Elizabeth Hampsten, *Read This Only to Yourself: The Private Writings of Midwestern Women* (Bloomington, University of Indiana Press, 1982); Sharon Niederman (ed.), *A Quilt of Words: Women's Diaries, Letters, and Original Accounts of Life in the Southwest, 1860–1960* (Boulder, Col., Johnson Books, 1988); Dean L. May, *Three Frontiers: Family, Land, and Society in the American West, 1850–1900* (Cambridge, Cambridge University Press, 1994) provides a demographic account of the lives of those who settled in the West in the late nineteenth century.

Chapter 7

Contemporary accounts of American education can be found in US Department of the Interior, Bureau of Education, *Negro Education: A Study of the Private and Higher Schools for Colored People in the United States*

(Washington, DC, Government Printing Office, 1917); Sara A. Burstall, *Impressions of American Education in 1908* (London, Longmans, Green, 1908); Vera verPlank North, "Pittsburgh Schools," in Paul U. Kellogg, *The Pittsburgh District: The Civic Frontage* (New York, Survey Associates, 1914), pp. 217–305; and US Congress, *Reports of the Immigration Commission*, Vols 14 and 16: *Children of Immigrants in Schools*, Vols 2 and 4. S. Doc. 749, 61st Cong. 3rd sess. (Washington, DC, Government Printing Office, 1911). State and local boards of education in this era published reports on schooling, with some information categorized by sex.

Paula S. Fass, *Outside In: Minorities and the Transformation of American Education* (New York, Oxford University Press, 1989); James D. Anderson, *The Education of Blacks in the South, 1860–1935* (Chapel Hill, University of North Carolina Press, 1988); Ileen A. DeVault, *Sons and Daughters of Labor: Class and Clerical Work in Turn-of-the-Century Pittsburgh* (Ithaca, NY, Cornell University Press, 1990) examine education from race, gender and class perspectives.

Educational histories focusing on women include Mabel Newcomber, *A Century of Higher Education for Women* (Washington, DC, Zenger, 1959); Thomas Woody, *A History of Women's Education in the United States* (New York, Science Press, 1929); Jane Roland Martin, *Reclaiming the Conversation: The Ideal of the Educated Woman* (New Haven, Conn., Yale University Press, 1985); Lynn D. Gordon, *Gender and Higher Education in the Progressive Era* (New Haven, Conn., Yale University Press, 1990). Joyce Antler, *Lucy Sprague Mitchell: The Making of a Modern Woman* (New Haven, Conn., Yale University Press, 1986) and Rosalind Rosenberg, *Beyond Separate Spheres* (New Haven, Yale University Press, 1982) look at women in the academy.

Robert A. Trennert, "Educating Indian Girls at Nonreservation Boarding Schools, 1878–1920," in DuBois and Ruiz, *Unequal Sisters*, pp. 224–37, addresses the issue of cultural assimilation in his analysis of the Bureau of Indian Affairs' efforts to remove Native Americans from their families for education in Euro-American ways. Ann Metcalf, "From Schoolgirl to Mother: The Effects of Education on Navajo Women," *Social Problems, 23* (1976), 535–44, addresses the same issues, as does George J. Sanchez, "'Go After the Women': Americanization and the Mexican Immigrant Woman, 1915–1929'"; see also in DuBois and Ruiz, *Unequal Sisters*, pp. 250–63, for Hispanic women. Devon A. Miheusuah, *Cultivating the Rosebuds: The Education of Women at the Cherokee Female Seminary, 1851–1909* (Urbana, University of Illinois Press, 1993) documents the tensions manifest in schools run by Native Americans for their own purposes, but as K. Tsianina Lomawaima shows in *They Called It Prairie Light: The Story of Chilocco Indian School* (Lincoln, University of Nebraska Press, 1994) such tensions ran even higher in schools run by outsiders.

Bert Lowenberg and Ruth Bogin (eds), *Black Women in Nineteenth Century Life: Their Thoughts, Their Words, Their Feelings* (University Park, Pennsylvania State University Press, 1976); Jeanne L. Noble, *Beautiful Also Are the Souls of My Sisters: A History of the Black Woman in America* (Englewood Cliffs, NJ, Prentice-Hall, 1978); R. E. Butchart, *Northern*

Schools, Southern Blacks, and Reconstruction: Freedmen's Education, 1862–1875 (Westport, Conn., Greenwood Press, 1980) reflect on African-American women's education. On European immigrant children's education see Maxine Seller, "The Education of the Immigrant Woman, 1900–1935," in Linda Kerber and Jane Mathews (eds), *Women's America: Refocusing the Past* (New York, Oxford University Press, 1982).

The collection of essays in Judith Walzer Leavitt, *Women and Health in America* (Madison, University of Wisconsin Press, 1984) provides an overview of women's role in health, as healers and as patients. Mary Roth Walsh, *Doctors Wanted: No Women Need Apply: Sexual Barriers in the Medical Profession, 1835–1975* (New Haven, Conn., Yale University Press, 1977) and Regina Markell Morantz-Sanchez, *Sympathy and Science: Women Physicians in American Medicine* (New York, Oxford University Press, 1985) investigate doctoring. Studies of nursing include Richard Harrison Shryock, "Nursing Emerges as a Profession," *Clio Medica*, 3 (1968), 131–47; Susan Reverby, *Ordered to Care: The Dilemma of American Nursing, 1850–1945* (Cambridge, Cambridge University Press, 1987); Barbara Melosh, *"The Physician's Hand": Work Culture and Conflict in American Nursing* (Philadelphia, Temple University Press, 1982); Darlene Clark Hine, *Black Women in White: Racial Conflict and Cooperation in the Nursing Profession, 1890–1950* (Bloomington, Indiana University Press, 1989). I am grateful to Frances Krantz, RN, for her willingness to be interviewed over the years about her experiences as a nurse. On midwives see: Judy Barrett Litoff, *American Midwives, 1860–the Present* (Westport, Conn., Greenwood Press, 1978); Barbara Ehrenreich and Deidre English, *Witches, Midwives, and Nurses: A History of Women Healers* (Old Westbury, NY, Feminist Press, 1973). Richard W. Wertz and Dorothy C. Wertz: *Lying-In, A History of Childbirth in America* (New York, Free Press, 1977) and Frances E. Kobrin, "The American Midwife Controversy: A Crisis of Professionalization," *Bulletin of the History of Medicine*, 40 (1966), 350–63, also examine childbirth and midwifery.

Other studies of female attempts to infiltrate the professions include Barbara Harris, *Beyond her Sphere: Women and the Professions in American History* (Westport, Conn., Greenwood Press, 1978); Dee Garrison, *Apostles of Culture: The Public Libraries and American Society* (New York, Macmillan, 1979); Roy Lubove, *The Professional Altruist: The Emergence of Social Work as a Career* (Cambridge, Mass., Harvard University Press, 1965). B. Collier-Thomas, "The Impact of Black Women in Education: An Historical Overview," *Journal of Negro History,* 51 (1982), 173–80, and Jacqueline Jones, *Soldiers of Light and Love: Northern Teachers and Georgia Blacks, 1865–1873* (Chapel Hill, University of North Carolina Press, 1980) explore teaching. Sheila M. Rothman, *Woman's Proper Place: A History of Changing Ideals and Practices, 1870 to the Present* (New York, Basic Books, 1978) discusses the home economics movement as do Barbara Ehrenreich and Deirdre English, *For Her Own Good: 150 Years of Experts' Advice to Women* (New York, Doubleday, 1989), while D. Kelley Weisberg, "Barred from the Bar: Women and Legal Education in the United States," *Journal of Legal Education,* 38 (1977), 485–507, discusses the profession in which women made little headway until late in the twentieth century.

Women's contributions to culture took many forms. Karen J. Blair, *The Clubwoman as Feminist: True Womanhood Redefined, 1868–1914* (New York, Holmes and Meier, 1980) and Cynthia Neverdon Morton, *Afro-American Women of the South and the Advancement of the Race, 1895–1925* (Knoxville, University of Tennessee Press, 1989) both discuss how educated women put their knowledge to work in the service of their communities. Literary overviews of women as authors in this period include: Nina Baym, *Women's Fiction: A Guide to Novels by and about Women in America, 1820–1870* (Ithaca, NY, Cornell University Press, 1978); Carole McAlpine Watson, *Prologue: The Novels of Black American Women, 1891–1965* (Westport, Conn., Greenwood Press, 1985); Kristin Herzog, *Women, Ethnics, and Exotics: Images of Power in Mid-Nineteenth Century Fiction* (Knoxville, University of Tennessee Press, 1983).

Louisa May Alcott has been the subject of numerous studies. Madeleine B. Stern, *Louisa May Alcott* (Boston, Northeastern University Press, 1998) contains evidence of Alcott's feminism. Also see: Sarah Elbert, *A Hunger for Home: Louisa May Alcott and "Little Women"* ((Philadelphia: Temple University Press, 1984); Martha Saxton, *Louisa May: A Modern Biography of Louisa May Alcott* ((New York, Avon Books, 1978); Madeleine B. Stern (ed.), *Critical Essays on Louisa May Alcott* (Boston, G. K. Hall, 1984); Gloria T. Delamar, *Louisa May Alcott and "Little Women": Biography, Critique, Publications, Poems, Songs, and Contemporary Relevance* (Jefferson, NC: McFarland, 1990); Barbara Sicherman, "Reading *Little Women*: The Many Lives of a Text," in Kerber et al., *US History as Women's History*, pp. 245–66 examines the ways in which Alcott resonated with mid-twentieth century audiences. Nina Auerbach, "Austen and Alcott on Matriarchy: New Women or New Wives?" in Mark Spilka (ed.), *Towards a Poetics of Fiction* (Bloomington, Indiana University Press, 1977), pp. 266–85, explores concepts of family in *Little Women*. On Emily Dickinson see Vivian R. Pollak, *Dickinson: The Anxiety of Gender* (Ithaca, NY, Cornell University Press, 1984), and Michael Allen, *Emily Dickinson as an American Provincial Poet* (Brighton, British Association for American Studies, 1985).

Willa Cather's depictions of women in the West have been the subject of many literary histories. In addition to reading *O, Pioneers!* (1913), *Song of the Lark* (1915), and *My Antonia* (1918), all of which were written during the period under discussion here, readers may wish to consult "Willa Cather" by Herbie Butterfield, in Richard Gray (ed.), *American Fiction: New Readings* (London, Vision Press, 1983); Dorothy Van Ghent, *Willa Cather* (Minneapolis, University of Minnesota Pamphlets on American Writers, No. 36); Harold Bloom (ed.), *Willa Cather* (New York, Chelsea House Publishers, 1985); Sally P. Harvey, *Redefining the American Dream: Novels of Willa Cather* (Rutherford, NJ, Fairleigh Dickinson University Press, 1995); Frances W. Kays, *Isolation and Masquerade: Willa Cather's Women* (New York, Peter Lang, 1992); Marilyn Arnold, *Willa Cather: A Reference Guide* (Boston, G.K. Hall, 1986).

Judith Fryer, *Felicitous Space: The Imaginative Space of Edith Wharton and Willa Cather* (Chapel Hill, University of North Carolina Press, 1986) compares the two authors and their construction of space. Readers should consult Wharton's own autobiography, *A Backward Glance* (New York, Charles Scribner's Sons, 1934); also Shari Benstock, *No Gifts from Chance: A Biography of Edith Wharton* (London, Penguin, 1995); R.W. B. Lewis's authorized biography, *Edith Wharton: A Biography* (New York, Harper and Row, 1975); Harold Bloom (ed.), *Edith Wharton* (New York, Chelsea House, 1986); Penelope Vita-Finzi, *Edith Wharton and the Art of Fiction* (London, Pinter, 1990); Carol Wershovan, *The Female Intruder in the Novels of Edith Wharton* (Rutherford, NJ, Fairleigh Dickinson Press, 1982).

Laura Ingalls Wilder's children's novels of life in the West were written in the 1930s and 1940s about her own childhood and her parents' marriage in the second half of the nineteenth century. There are numerous analyses of Wilder's world and intentions. See, for example, Laura Ingalls Wilder and Rose Wilder Lane, *A Little House Sampler,* ed. William T. Anderson (Lincoln, University of Nebraska Press, 1988). Anderson is the author of many works about the Little House books, their author, and her family. Also see Ann Romines, "*The Long Winter*: An Introduction to Western Womanhood," *Great Plains Quarterly,* 10 (1990), 36–47; William Holtz, "Closing the Circle: The American Optimism of Laura Ingalls Wilder," *Great Plains Quarterly,* 4 (1984); John E. Miller, *Laura Ingalls Wilder's Little Town: Where History and Literature Meet* (University Press of Kansas, 1994); Kathryn Adams, "Laura, Ma, Mary, Carrie and Grace: Western Women as Portrayed by Laura Ingalls Wilder," in Susan Armitage and Elizabeth Jameson, *The Women's West* (Norman, University of Oklahoma Press, 1987), pp. 95–110.

Studies of African-American women writers in the late nineteenth and early twentieth centuries refute the notion that literary production was exclusively white or male. Hazel Carby, *Reconstructing Womanhood: The Emergence of the Afro-American Woman Novelist* (New York, Oxford University Press, 1987) indicates that these authors subverted the paradigms of (white) womanhood as a means of reflecting upon (black) women's experiences. Claudia Tate, *Domestic Allegories of Political Desire: The Black Heroine's Text at the Turn of the Century* (Oxford, Oxford University Press, 1992) explores the themes upon which Frances Ellen Watkins Harper, Pauline E. Hopkins, and other African-American women authors reflected.

Other female contributions to American cultural life are discussed in Kathy Preiss, *Cheap Amusements: Working Women and Leisure in Turn-of-the-Century New York* (Philadelphia, Temple University Press, 1986); Elaine Hedges, "The Nineteenth Century Diarist and Her Quilts," *Feminist Studies,* 8 (1982), 293–308; Jean Gordon, "Early American Women Artists and the Social Context in Which They Worked," *American Quarterly,* 30 (1978), 54–69; Kathleen D. McCarthy, *Women's Culture: American Philanthropy and Art, 1830–1930* (Chicago, University of Chicago Press, 1991); Karen Blair, *The Torchbearers: Women and Their Amateur Arts Associations in America, 1890–1930* (1994).

Chapter 8

Among the many excellent collections of articles on women reformers in this era, readers are referred to Nancy Hewitt and Suzanne Lebsock, *Visible Women: New Essays in American Activism* (Urbana, University of Illinois Press, 1994); Kerber, Kessler-Harris, and Sklar, *U.S. History as Women's History*; Seth Koven and Sonya Michel, *Mothers of a New World: Maternalist Politics and the Origins of Welfare States* (London, Routledge, 1993); Kathleen D. McCarthy, *Lady Bountiful Revisited: Women, Philanthropy, and Power* (New Brunswick, NJ, Rutgers University Press, 1990); and Linda Gordon (ed.), *Women, the State, and Welfare* (Madison, University of Wisconsin Press, 1990). Laura E. Edwards, *Gendered Strife and Confusion: The Political Culture of Reconstruction* (Urbana, University of Illinois Press, 1997) focuses on the period immediately after the Civil War. Rebecca Edwards, *Angels in the Machinery: Gender in American Party Politics from the Civil War to the Progressive Era* (New York, Oxford University Press, 1997) considers the extent of women's political participation.

Accounts of the struggle for the vote not already cited include Anne Firor Scott and Andrew M. Scott, *One Half the People: The Fight for Woman Suffrage* (Philadelphia, Lippincott, 1975); William O'Neill, *Everyone Was Brave: A History of American Feminism* (Chicago, Quadrangle, 1969); Sara Hunter Graham, *Woman Suffrage and the New Democracy* (New Haven, Yale University Press, 1996); and Rita J. Simon and Gloria Danziger, *Women's Movements in America: Their Successes, Disappointments, and Aspirations* (New York, Praeger, 1991). Jane Jerome Camhi, *Women Against Women: American Anti-Suffragism, 1880–1920* (New York, Carlson, 1992) and Michael Levin, "Exalted by Their Inferiority: Arguments Against the Female Franchise," *Research in Social Movements, Conflict and Change*, 13 (1991), 199–220, examine the opposition to suffrage.

The writings of suffragists and their opponents can be found in Aileen S. Kraditor, *The Ideas of the Woman Suffrage Movement, 1890–1920* (New York, Columbia University Press, 1965); Carrie Chapman Catt and Nettie Rogers Shuler, *Woman Suffrage and Politics: The Inner Story of the Suffrage Movement* (Seattle, University of Washington, 1970); Aileen Kraditor (ed.), *Up From the Pedestal: Selected Writings in the History of American Feminism* (Chicago, Quadrangle, 1968); Ellen Carol DuBois (ed.), *Elizabeth Cady Stanton/Susan B. Anthony Correspondence, Writings, Speeches* (New York, Schocken Books, 1981); and Mari Jo Buhle and Paul Buhle (eds), *The Concise History of Woman Suffrage: Selections from the Classic Work of Stanton, Anthony, Gage, and Harper* (Urbana, University of Illinois Press, 1981).

Regional and (auto)biographical accounts of suffrage include Alan P. Grimes, *The Puritan Ethic and Woman Suffrage* (Westport, Conn., Greenwood Press, 1980) and Abigail Scott Duniway, *Pathbreaking: An Autobiographical History of the Equal Suffrage Movement in the Pacific Coast States* (New York, Source Book Press, 1970) on the relative ease with which western states accepted woman suffrage. Paul E. Fuller, *Laura Clay and the Woman's Rights Movement* (Lexington, University of Kentucky Press, 1975) and Majorie Spruill Wheeler, *New Women of the New South: The Leaders of the Woman Suffrage Movement in the Southern States* (New York, Oxford University Press, 1993) analyse the southern ambivalence to suffrage. On African-American women and suffrage see in particular Rosalyn Terborg-Penn, "Discontented Black Feminists; Prelude and Postscript to the Passage of the Nineteenth Amendment," in Lois Scharf and Joan Jensen (eds), *Decades of Discontent* (Westport, Conn., Greenwood Press, 1983) and Paula Giddings, *When and Where I Enter: The Impact of Black Women on Race and Sex in America* (New York, Morrow, 1984).

On temperance see Ross Evans Paulson, *Women's Suffrage and Prohibition: A Comparative Study of Equality and Social Control* (Chicago, Scott, Foresman, 1973); Jack S. Blacker, *"Give to the Winds Thy Fears": The Women's Temperance Crusade* (Westport, Conn., Greenwood Press, 1985); Ruth Brigitte Anderson, *Women and Temperance: The Quest for Power and Liberty, 1873–1900* (Philadelphia, Temple University Press, 1981). Also see: Naomi Black, *Social Feminism* (Ithaca, NY, Cornell University Press, 1989); Steven Buechler, *The Transformation of the Woman Suffrage Movement* (New Brunswick, NJ, Rutgers University Press, 1986); Wil A. Linkugel and Martha Solomon, *Anna Howard Shaw: Suffrage Orator and Social Reformer* (Westport, Conn., Greenwood Press, 1991); Andrea Moore Kerr, *Lucy Stone: Speaking Out for Equality* (New Brunswick, NJ, Rutgers University Press, 1992); Mary Martha Thomas, *The New Woman in Alabama: Social Reforms and Suffrage, 1890–1920* (Tuscaloosa, University of Alabama Press, 1992); Alice Sheppard, *Cartooning for Suffrage* (Albuquerque, University of New Mexico Press, 1994); Suzanne M. Marilley, *Woman Suffrage and the Origins of Liberal Feminism in the United States* (Cambridge, Mass., Harvard University Press, 1996).

Accounts of women in the settlement houses include Allen F. Davis, *Spearheads for Reform: the Social Settlements and the Progressive Movement, 1890–1914* (New York, Oxford University Press, 1967); Mina Carson, *Settlement Folk: Social Thought and the American Settlement Movement, 1885–1930* (Chicago, University of Chicago Press, 1990); Elizabeth Lasch Quinn, *Black Neighbors: Race and the Limits of Reform in the American Settlement House Movement, 1890–1945* (Chapel Hill, University of North Carolina Press, 1993); Ruth Hutchinson Crocker, *Social Work and Social Order; The Settlement Movement in Two Industrial Cities, 1889–1930* (Urbana, University of Illinois Press, 1992); Rivka Shpak Lissak, *Pluralism and Progressives: Hull House and the New Immigrants 1890–1919* (Chicago, University of Chicago Press, 1989).

For biographies of the generation of reformers emerging from the settlement house and progressive movements see: Allen Davis, *The American Heroine: The Life and Legend of Jane Addams* (New York, Oxford University Press, 1973); Mary Jo Deegan, *Jane Addams and the Men of the Chicago School, 1892–1918* (New Brunswick, NJ, Transaction Books, 1988); Jane Addams, *My Friend Julia Lathrop* (New York, Macmillan, 1935); Kathryn Kish Sklar, *Florence Kelley and the Nation's Work: The Rise of Women's Political Culture, 1830–1900* (New Haven, Conn., Yale

University Press, 1995); Jacqueline Anne Rouse, *Lugenia Burns Hope: Black Southern Reformer* (Athens, University of Georgia Press, 1989); Lillian D. Wald, *The House on Henry Street* (New York, Henry Holt, 1938 [orig. 1915]).

Glenda Elizabeth Gilmore, *Gender and Jim Crow: Black Women and the Politics of White Supremacy in North Carolina, 1896–1992* (Chapel Hill, University of North Carolina Press, 1996); Alfreda M. Duster (ed.), *Crusade for Justice: The Autobiography of Ida B. Wells* (Chicago, University of Chicago Press, 1980); Ida B. Wells-Barnett, *Southern Horrors: Lynch Law in All Its Phases* (New York, New York Age Print, 1892); Jacquelyn Dowd Hall, *Revolt against Chivalry: Jesse Daniel Ames Daniel and the Women's Campaign against Lynching* (New York, Columbia University Press, 1979) investigate the politics of race–gender relations.

The literature on women as pioneers of systematic welfare provision for other women has many facets. Theda Skocpol, *Protecting Soldiers and Mothers: The Political Origins of Social Policy in the United States* (Cambridge, Mass., Belknap Press of Harvard University Press, 1993) examines voluntary organizations and state formation. Robyn Muncy, *Creating a Female Dominion in American Reform, 1890–1935* (New York, Oxford University Press, 1991) and Regina G. Kunzel, *Fallen Women, Problem Girls: Unmarried Mothers and the Professionalization of Social Work, 1890–1945* (New Haven, Conn., Yale University Press, 1993) probe the niches women carved out for themselves. Linda Gordon, "Black and White Visions of Welfare: Women's Welfare Activism, 1890–1945," *Journal of American History,* 78 (1991), 559–90; Stephen Diner, "Chicago Social Workers and Blacks in the Progressive Era," *Social Service Review,* 44 (1970), 393–410; John H. Ehrenreich, *The Altruistic Imagination: A History of Social Work and Social Policy in the United States* (Ithaca, NY, Cornell University Press, 1985); Mimi Abramovitz, *Regulating the Lives of Women: Social Welfare Policy from Colonial Times to the Present* (Boston, South End Press, 1988) provide overviews of welfare.

Alisa Klaus, *Every Child a Lion: The Origins of Maternal and Infant Health Policy in the United States and France, 1890–1920* (Ithaca, NY, Cornell University Press, 1993) analyzes the development of child welfare programs in health terms. Kathryn Kish Sklar, "The Historical Foundations of Women's Power in the Creation of the American Welfare State, 1830–1930," in Koven and Michel, pp. 43–93 explores the significance of maternalist sentiment in the development of American welfare. Linda Gordon, *Pitied But Not Entitled: Single Mothers and the History of Welfare* (New York, Free Press, 1994) details the gendered construction of welfare. Also see Ann Shola Orloff, *The Politics of Pensions: A Comparative Analysis of Britain, Canada, and the United States, 1880–1940* (Madison, University of Wisconsin Press, 1993). On poor women themselves see Beverly Stadum, *Poor Women and Their Families: Hard Working Charity Cases, 1900–1930* (Albany, NY, State University of New York Press, 1992).

On rural reformers see Jane Taylor Nelsen (ed.), *A Prairie Populist: The Memoirs of Luna Kellie* (Iowa City: Iowa University Press, 1992). Peggy Pascoe, *Relations of Rescue, The Search for Female Moral Authority in the*

American West, 1874–1939 (New York, Oxford University Press, 1990) examines a different facet of western women's reform activity. Estelle Freedman, *Their Sisters' Keepers: Women's Prison Reform in America, 1830–1930* (Ann Arbor, University of Michigan Press, 1981); Patricia Hill, *The World Their Household: The American Woman's Foreign Mission Movement and Cultural Transformation, 1870–1920* (Ann Arbor, University of Michigan Press, 1985); Kathleen McCarthy, *Noblesse Oblige: Charity and Cultural Philanthropy in Chicago, 1849–1929* (Chicago, University of Chicago Press, 1982); Katherine M. B. Osburn, *Southern Ute Women: Autonomy and Assimilation on the Reservation, 1887–1934* (Albuquerque, University of New Mexico Press, 1998); Anne Firor Scott, *Natural Allies: Women's Associations in American History* (Urbana, University of Illinois Press, 1991); Darlene Clark Hine, *Black Women in the Middle West: The Michigan Experience* (Ann Arbor: Historical Society of Michigan, 1990); Dorothy Salem, *To Better our World: Black Women in Organized Reform 1890–1920* (New York, Carlson, 1990); Karen J. Blair, *The Clubwoman as Feminist: True Womanhood Redefined, 1868–1914* (New York, Holmes and Meier, 1980); Sheila Rothman, *Woman's Proper Place: A History of Changing Ideals and Practices, 1870 to the Present* (New York, Basic Books, 1978); Evelyn Brooks Higginbotham, *Righteous Discontent: The Women's Movement in the Black Baptist Church, 1880–1920* (Cambridge, Mass., Harvard University Press, 1993) all examine women's voluntary associations.

On war and peace activities see Maurine Weiner Greenwald, *Women, War, and Work: The Impact of World War I on Women Workers in the United States* (Westport, Conn., Greenwood Press, 1980) and Barbara Moench Florence (ed.), *Lella Secor: A Diary in Letters, 1915–1922* (New York, Burt Franklin, 1978) details the experiences of one of the organizers of the American Neutral Conference Committee and the Emergency Peace Foundation, which tried to keep the United States out of World War I.

Chapter 9

Race, Gender, and Work: A Multicultural Economic History of Women in the United States (Boston, Mass., South End Press, 1991) by Teresa L. Amott and Julie A. Matthaei contains an ethnically and racially sensitive overview of the twentieth-century economy. Also see Lois Scharf, *To Work and To Wed: Female Employment, Feminism, and the Great Depression* (Westport, Conn., Greenwood Press, 1980). Caroline Manning, *The Immigrant Woman and Her Job,* US Department of Labor, Women's Bureau, Bulletin of the Women's Bureau No. 74 (Washington, DC, Government Printing Office, 1930) and Cecyle S. Neidle, *American's Immigrant Women* (Boston, Twayne Publishers, 1975) examine women immigrants in the labor force.

Jessie Clark and Gertrude E. McDougaild, *A New Day for the Colored Woman Worker: A Study of Colored Women in Industry in New York City* (New York, np, 1919) looks forward to a time when African-American women would find industrial jobs easier to obtain. The reality for the overwhelming majority was continued relegation to the ranks of domestic service until World War II. See Elizabeth Clark-Lewis, "'This Work Had a End':

African-American Domestic Workers in Washington, DC, 1910–1940," in *"To Toil the Livelong Day": America's Women at Work, 1780–1980*, ed. Mary Beth Norton and Carol Groneman (Ithaca, NY, Cornell University Press, 1987). Phyllis Palmer, *Domesticity and Dirt: Housewives and Domestic Servants in the United States, 1920–1945* (Philadelphia, Temple University Press, 1989) examines how domestic work changed between the wars. Brenda Clegg Gray, *Black Female Domestics During the Depression in New York City, 1930–1940* (New York, Garland, 1993) and Evelyn Nakano Glenn, "The Dialectics of Wage Work: Japanese American Women and Domestic Service, 1904–1940," in Dubois and Ruiz, pp. 345–72, investigate housework from the servants' perspective.

Judith A. Baer, *The Chains of Protection: The Judicial Response to Women's Labor Legislation* (Westport, Conn., Greenwood Press, 1978); Philip S. Foner, *Women and the American Labor Movement: From World War I to the Present* (New York, Free Press, 1980); Elizabeth Faue, *Community of Suffering and Struggle: Women, Men, and the Labor Movement in Minneapolis, 1915–1945* (Chapel Hill, University of North Carolina Press, 1991); Nancy Gabin, *Feminism in the Labor Movement: Women and the United Auto Workers, 1935–1975* (Ithaca, NY, Cornell University Press, 1990); Vicki L. Ruiz, *Cannery Women, Cannery Lives: Mexican Women, Unionization, and the California Food Processing Industry, 1930–1950* (Albuquerque: University of New Mexico Press, 1987) investigate protective legislation and union women.

Liston Pope, *Millhands and Preachers: A Study of Gastonia* (New Haven, Conn., Yale University Press, 1942) traces the dynamics and aftermath of the strike in which so many women participated. Jacquelyn Dowd Hall, James Leloudis, Robert Korstad, Mary Murphy, LuAnn Jones, and Christopher B. Daly, *Like a Family: The Making of a Southern Cotton Mill World* (New York, Norton, 1987) delineates the textile industry in the South. Dolores E. Janiewski, *Sisterhood Denied: Race, Gender, and Class in a New South Community* (Philadelphia, Temple University Press, 1985) probes the intersection of these three critical variables in structuring women's employment while Tamara Hareven, *Family Time, Industrial Time,* explores ethnicity and gender among the work rhythms of Manchester, New Hampshire.

The transition to white-collar employment is documented in Lisa M. Fine, *The Souls of the Skyscraper: Female Clerical Workers in Chicago, 1870–1930* (Philadelphia, Temple University Press, 1990); Susan Porter Benson, *Counter Cultures: Saleswomen, Managers, and Customers in American Department Stores, 1890–1940* (Urbana, University of Illinois Press, 1986); Margery Davies, *Woman's Place Is at the Typewriter: Office Work and Office Workers, 1870–1930* (Philadelphia, Temple University Press, 1982); Cindy Sondik Aron, *Ladies and Gentlemen of the Civil Service: Middle Class Workers in Victorian America* (New York, Oxford University Press, 1987); Sharon Hartman Strom, *Beyond the Typewriter: Gender, Class, and the Origins of Modern American Office Work, 1900–1930* (Urbana, University of Illinois Press, 1992).

Brian Gratton, *Urban Elders: Family, Work, and Welfare among Boston's Aged, 1890–1950* (Philadelphia, Temple University Press, 1986) investigates employment among that city's elderly. On the other end of the age spectrum, see the Arno Press reprints of *The Working Girls of Cincinnati* (1974); Anne Mann, *Women Workers in Factories* [orig. 1918]; Frances Ivins Rich, *Wage Earning Girls in Cincinnati* [orig. 1927]; Frances R. Whitney, *What Girls Live on – And How* [orig. 1930].

The working lives of rural women are covered by Deborah Fink, *Agrarian Women: Wives and Mothers in Rural Nebraska, 1880–1940* (Chapel Hill, University of North Carolina Press, 1992); Wava G. Haney and Jane B. Knowles, *Women and Farming: Changing Roles, Changing Structure* (Boulder, Col., Westview Press, 1988); Dee Garceau, *The Important Things of Life: Women, Work, and Family in Sweetwater County, Wyoming, 1880–1929* (Lincoln, University of Nebraska Press, 1997); Carolyn E. Sachs, *The Invisible Farmers: Women in Agricultural Production* (Totowa, NY, Rowman and Allanheld, 1983).

Margaret Hagood, *Mothers of the South: Portraiture of the White Tenant Farm Woman* (New York, W. W. Norton, 1977 [orig. 1939]) tells rural poor white women's side of the Great Depression. Maya Angelou's account of her childhood in Stamps, Arkansas, during the Great Depression, *I Know Why the Caged Bird Sings* (New York, Random House, 1970), indicates how a few exceptional African-American women managed to transcend the limitations imposed by a racist society to own their own businesses. Studs Terkel, *Hard Times: An Oral History of the Great Depression* (New York, Pantheon Books, 1986) and Gerald Markowitz and David Rosner (eds), *"Slaves of the Depression": Workers' Lettters about Life on the Job* (Ithaca, NY, Cornell University Press, 1987) supply oral and written testimony by women and men on how the Depression affected them.

Susan Ware, *Holding Their Own: American Women in the 1930s* (Boston, Twayne Publishers, 1982) focuses on the particular impact of the Depression on women. Ruth Milkman, "Women's Work and Economic Crisis: Some Lessons of the Great Depression," *Review of Radical Economics,* 8 (Spring, 1976), reprinted in Cott and Pleck, *A Heritage of Her Own,* pp. 507–42, believes that official statistics understated female unemployment. I would argue that official statistics missed the unknown but clearly large number of women who shifted from their normal employment into lesser jobs such as domestic work. See Julia Kirk Blackwelder, *Women of the Depression: Caste and Culture in San Antonio, 1929–1939* (College Station, TX, Texas A & M Press, 1984) and Jo Ann E. Argersinger, *Toward a New Deal in Baltimore. People and Government in the Great Depression* (Chapel Hill, University of North Carolina Press, 1988).

Federal government documents contain many sociological analyses conducted during the Depression. See for example, US Department of Labor, Women's Bureau, *Wage-Earning Women and the Industrial Conditions of 1930: A Survey of South Bend,* Bulletin No. 92 (Washington, DC, 1932); *Women Unemployed Seeking Relief in 1933,* Bulletin No. 139 (Washington, DC, Government Printing Office, 1936), *Unattached Women on Relief in Chicago, 1937* (Washington, DC, Government Printing Office, 1936), and Jean Collier Brown, *The Negro Woman Worker,* Bulletin No. 165 (Washington, DC, Government Printing Office, 1939).

William Chafe, *The American Woman: Her Changing Social, Economic, and Political Roles, 1920–1970* (New York, Oxford University Press, 1972) views the war as a turning point for American women. Ruth Milkman, *Gender at Work: The Dynamics of Job Segregation by Sex during World War II* (Urbana, University of Illinois Press, 1987), the oral histories in Sherna Berger Gluck, *Rosie the Riveter Revisited: Women, The War, and Social Change* (Long Beach, California State University Long Beach Foundation, 1983), and Karen Anderson, "Last Hired, First Fired: Black Women Workers During World War II," *Journal of American History*, 69 (1982) 82–97, document female employment experiences during the war.

Chapter 10

Many of the works already cited also include information about women's role in the family from World War I until World War II. Other studies include Day Monroe, *Chicago Families: A Study of Unpublished Census Data* (Chicago, University of Chicago Press, 1932); Winifred D. Wandersee, *Women's Work and Family Values, 1920–1940* (Cambridge, University of Cambridge Press, 1981); Elaine Tyler May, *Great Expectations: Marriage and Divorce in Post-Victorian America* (Chicago, University of Chicago Press, 1980); Judith E. Smith, *Family Connections: A History of Italian and Jewish Immigrant Lives in Providence, Rhode Island, 1900–1940* (Albany, State University of New York Press, 1985); Kimberly L. Phillips, "'But it is a Fine Place to Make Money': Migration and African-American Families in Cleveland, 1915–1929," *Journal of Social History*, 30 (1996), 393–414.

The ideology of modernity and the new woman are the subjects of Roland Marchand, *Advertising the American Dream: Making Way for Modernity, 1920–1940* (Berkeley, University of California Press, 1985) and Richard Wightman Fox and T. Jackson Lears, *The Culture of Consumption: Critical Essays in American History, 1880–1980* (New York, Pantheon, 1983). June Sochen, *The New Woman in Greenwich Village, 1910–1920* (New York, Quadrangle Books, 1972); Dolores Hayden, *The Grand Domestic Revolution: A History of Feminist Designs for American Homes, Neighborhoods, and Cities* (Cambridge, Mass., MIT Press, 1981); Estelle Freedman, "The New Woman: Changing Views of Women in the 1920s," *Journal of American History*, 61 (1974), 372–93; and Sean Dennis Cashman, *America in the Twenties and Thirties: The Olympian Age of Franklin Delano Roosevelt* (New York, New York University Press, 1989) scrutinize gender roles and social change. On cookbooks see Frank Stricker, "Cookbooks and Lawbooks: The Hidden History of Career Women in Twentieth Century America," *Journal of Social History*, 10 (1976), 1–19.

Changing attitudes of and towards children are documented by Paula Fass, *The Damned and the Beautiful: American Youth in the 1920s* (New York, Oxford University Press, 1977); Glen Elder, Jr., *Children of the Great Depression: Social Change in Life Experience* (Chicago, University of Chicago Press, 1974); Beth Bailey, *From Front Porch to Back Seat: Courtship in Twentieth-Century America* (Baltimore, Johns Hopkins University Press, 1988); John Modell, "Dating Becomes the Way of

American Youth," in Leslie Page Moch and Gary D. Stark (eds), *Essays on the Family and Historical Changes* (College Station, Texas A & M Press, 1983). On the difficulties of dating the sexual revolution see Daniel Scott Smith, "The Dating of the American Sexual Revolution: Evidence and Interpretation," in Gordon, *American Family*, 2nd edn, pp. 426–38. The most important sociological documentation of these changes can be found in Robert and Helen Merrell Lynd, *Middletown: A Study of Contemporary American Culture* (New York, Harcourt, Brace, & World, 1956 [orig. 1929]). See Dorothy Parker, *The Collected Dorothy Parker* (New York, 1973) for trenchant views of changing mores.

Susan Ware, *Holding Their Own: American Women in the 1930s* (Boston, Twayne Publishers, 1982) supplies a synthesis of women's lives during this era, written from the point of view that women did sustain the gains of earlier decades. Cheryl Lynn Greenberg, *Or Does It Explode? Black Harlem in the Great Depression* (New York, Oxford University Press, 1991) investigates one urban black community's responses to the Great Depression. Contemporary sociological studies of Depression-era life enable readers to test Ware's assumptions for themselves. See, Charles S. Johnson, *Shadow of the Plantation* (Chicago, University of Chicago Press, 1934) on rural African-Americans and Robert and Helen Merrell Lynd on midwestern whites in *Middletown in Transition: A Study in Cultural Conflict* (New York, Harcourt, Brace, and World, 1937).

Other contemporary documents on families during the Depression include James Agee and Walker Evans, *Let Us Now Praise Famous Men: Three Tenant Farm Families* (Boston, Houghton Mifflin, 1989 [orig. 1939]) which depicts Depression life for both sexes and includes Farm Security Administration photographs. Ruth S. Cavan and Katherine H. Ranck, *The Family and The Depression: A Study of One Hundred Chicago Families* (Chicago, University of Chicago Press, 1938) and Mirra Komarovsky, *The Unemployed Man and His Family: The Effects of Underemployment upon the Status of Men in Fifty-Nine Families* (New York, Institute of Social Research, 1940) both examine impoverished families in large cities. Komarovsky's work is indicative of the popular and academic mindset which viewed unemployment as primarily a male problem.

On the politics of sexuality and marriage see: Kristin Luker, *Abortion and the Politics of Motherhood* (Berkeley, University of California Press, 1984); David M. Kennedy, *Birth Control in America: The Career of Margaret Sanger* (New Haven, Conn., Yale University Press, 1970); Carole R. McCann, *Birth Control Politics in the United States, 1916–1945* (Ithaca, NY, Cornell University Press, 1994) and Kevin White, *The First Sexual Revolution* (New York, New York University Press, 1993).

Discussions of changing attitudes toward motherhood can be found in Gwendolyn Mink, *The Wages of Motherhood: Inequality in the Welfare State, 1917–1942* (Ithaca, NY, Cornell University Press, 1995); Ann Dally, *Inventing Motherhood: The Consequences of an Ideal* (London, Burnett Books, 1982); Maxine L. Margolis, *Mothers and Such: Views of American Women and Why They Changed* (Berkeley, University of California Press, 1984); Molly Ladd-Taylor and Lauri Umansky, *"Bad" Mothers: The Politics of Blame in Twentieth-Century America* (New York, New York University Press, 1998).

Christine Frederick, *Household Engineering: Scientific Management in the Home* (Chicago, American School of Home Economics, 1920) told women how to manage their homes. On the growth of home economics see Marjorie East, *Home Economics: Past, Present, and Future* (Boston, Allyn and Bacon, 1980). Various authors discuss housewifery in this period. Katherine Jellison, *Entitled to Power: Farm Women and Technology, 1913–1963* (Chapel Hill, University of North Carolina Press, 1993) emphasizes government agencies' pressure on farm women to emulate urban housewives while ignoring their productive work on the farm. Jeanne Westin, *Making Do. How Women Survived the '30s* (Chicago, Follett Publishing, 1976) researches women's strategies for coping with the economic cataclysm in a series of interviews with survivors. Lois Rita Helmbold, "Beyond the Family Economy: Black and White Working-Class Women during the Great Depression," *Feminist Studies*, 13 (1987), 629–55, compares the experiences of poor women, while US Department of Labor, Women's Bureau, *The Effects of the Depression on Wage Earners' Families. A Second Survey of South Bend* by Harriet A. Byrne, Bulletin No. 108 (Washington, DC, Government Printing Office, 1936), supplies a statistical overview of one typical midwestern city.

Susan M. Hartmann, *The Home Front and Beyond: American Women in the 1940s* (Boston, Twayne Publishers, 1982) is a history of women's participation in the events of this momentous decade. Karen Anderson, *Wartime Women: Sex Roles, Family Relations, and the Status of Women during World War II* (Westport, Conn., Greenwood Press, 1981) explores how women managed to combine work inside and outside the home as do D'Ann Campbell, *Women at War with America: Private Lives in a Patriotic Era* (Cambridge, Mass., Harvard University Press, 1984) and Michael E. Stevens (ed.), Ellen D. Goldlus, asst. ed., *Women Remember the War 1941–1945* (Madison, State Historical Society of Wisconsin, 1993). Leila J. Rupp, *Mobilizing Women for War: German and American Propaganda, 1939–1945* (Princeton, NJ, Princeton University Press, 1978) examines propaganda and the images used to encourage women to accomplish their country's wartime aims.

Chapter 11

The somewhat depressing picture of stagnation or reversal in women's education derives from Mabel Newcomer's *A Century of Higher Education for American Women* (New York, Harper, 1959) written at the trough of female participation in higher education. Newcomer's view is reinforced by Margaret W. Rossiter, *Women Scientists in America: Struggles and Strategies to 1940* (Baltimore, Johns Hopkins University Press, 1982) who documents the battles fought by women to obtain access to higher education and recognition as scientists. Distinguished sociologist Jessie Bernard writes on *Academic Women* (Cleveland, Meridian Books, 1966). Barbara Miller Solomon, *In the Company of Educated Women*, remains the best overview of the subject. Some of my remarks about unequal admissions policies come from the experience of my own high school class of 1965 which discovered that institutions such as Cornell University required higher grades from women than men. Charlotte William Conable, *Women at Cornell: The Myth of Equal Education* (Ithaca, Cornell University Press, 1977) takes up that story once women arrived on the campus.

On women historians see Nancy F. Cott, *A Woman Making History: Mary Ritter Beard Through Her Letters* (New Haven, Yale University Press, 1991) and Mary Beard's own works including *Women's Work in Municipalities* (1915), *On Understanding Women* (1931) and *Women as Force in History* (1946). Ellen Swallow is the subject of Robert Clarke's biography: *Ellen Swallow: The Woman who Founded Ecology* (Chicago, Follett Publishing, 1973). Margaret Mead tells her story in *Blackberry Winter: My Earlier Years* (New York, Simon and Schuster, 1972). *Male and Female: A Study of the Sexes in a Changing World* (New York, William Morrow, 1949) contains her gender research.

Dorothy M. Brown, *Setting a Course: American Women in the 1920s* (Boston, Twayne, 1986) gives an overview of this period's literature. Laura Hapke, *Daughters of the Great Depression, Women, Work and Fiction in the American 1930s* (Athens, University of Georgia Press, 1995) analyzes the literature in its economic and political contexts, as do Paula Rabinowitz, *Labor and Desire: Women's Revolutionary Fiction in Depression America* (Chapel Hill, University of North Carolina Press, 1991) and Barbara Foley, *Radical Representations: Politics and Form in US Proletarian Fiction, 1929–1941* (Durham, NC, Duke University Press, 1993).

Zora Neale Hurston's *Their Eyes Were Watching God* (New York, Buccaneer Books, 1995) first appeared in 1937. Her autobiography *Dust Tracks on a Road: An Autobiography* (New York, Lippincott, 1942) probes the racial and gender issues bound up in social and geographical mobility. Robert E. Hemenway, *Zora Neale Hurston: A Literary Biography* (Urbana, University of Illinois Press, 1977), comments on Hurston's life and work as does Lillie P. Howard, *Zora Neale Hurston* (Boston, Twayne, 1980). Marcy Knopf, *The Sleeper Wakes; Harlem Renaissance Stories by Women* (New Brunswick, NJ, Rutgers University Press, 1993), and Cherry A. Wall, *Women of the Harlem Renaissance* (Bloomington, Indiana University Press, 1995) contain useful background information on this literary movement. For an overview see Hazel Carby, *Reconstructing Womanhood: The Emergence of the Afro-American Woman Novelist* (New York, Oxford University Press, 1987).

Anzia Yezierska, *Hungry Hearts* (1920), *Salome of the Tenements* (1923), *Bread Givers* (1925), and *Children of Loneliness: Stories of Immigrant Life* (New York, Funk & Wagnalls, 1923) are among her best works. For her own story see *Red Ribbon on a White Horse* (1950). Alice Kessler-Harris, *The Open Cage: An Anzia Yezierska Collection* (New York, Persea, 1979) is an excellent starting place. *How I Found America: Collected Stories of Anzia Yezierska*, introduction by Vivian Gornick (New York, Persea Books, 1991) also provides an appraisal of her work. *Anzia Yezierska: A Writer's Life* (New Brunswick, NJ Rutgers University Press, 1988) was written by her daughter Louise Levitas Henriksen with Jo Ann Boydson.

Proletarian novels have been listed in the text including Myra Page, *Daughter of the Hills: A Woman's Part in the Coal Miners' Struggle* (1932); *The Gathering Storm: A Story of the Black Belt;* Mary Heaton Vorse, *Strike* (1930); Grace Lumpkin, *To Make My Bread* (1932); Alice Smedley, *Daughter of Earth* (1929); and Meridel LeSueur, *The Girl* and *Ripening: Selected Work, 1927–1980*, edited with an introduction by Elaine Hedges. Janice R. MacKinnon and Stephen R. MacKinnon, *Agnes Smedley: The Life and Times of an American Radical* (Berkeley, University of California Press, 1988) gives a contextual analysis of her writing. John Steinbeck's *Grapes of Wrath* (1939) has been the subject of many literary histories. See for example, Nellie Y. McKay "Happy [?] Wife and Motherdom: The Portrayal of Ma Joad in John Steinbeck's *The Grapes of Wrath,*" in David Wyatt (ed.), *New Essays on the Grapes of Wrath* (Cambridge, Cambridge University Press, 1990).

Barbara Melosh, *Engendering Culture: Manhood and Womanhood in New Deal Public Art and Theater* (Washington, DC, Smithsonian Institution Press, 1991) furnishes an excellent overview of the gender issues in the New Deal arts programs. Ellen Wiley Todd, *The New Woman Revised: Painting and Gender Politics on Fourteenth Street* (Berkeley, University of California Press, 1993) looks at female artists. Elizabeth Faue, *Community of Suffering and Struggle: Women, Men, and the Labor Movement in Minneapolis, 1915–1945* (Chapel Hill, University of North Carolina Press, 1991) considers the iconography of the labor movement and the representation of women workers. Anne Tucker (ed.), *The Woman's Eye: Selections from the Work of Gertrude Kasebier, Frances Benjamin Johnston, Margaret Bourke-White, Dorothea Lange, Berenice Abbott, Barbara Morgan, Diane Arbus, Alia Wells, Judy Date, Bea Nettles* (New York, Alfred A. Knopf, 1973) contains a good range of photographs from this period. On nurses' stories see Deborah Philips, "Sue Barton, Lavinia Lloyd Dock, Lilian Wald, and the Henry Street Clinic," *Journal of American Studies*, 33 (1999).

The literature on women in cinema includes: Molly Haskell, *From Reverence to Rape: The Treatment of Women in the Movies* (New York, Penguin Books, 1974); Robert Sklar, *Movie-Made America: A Social History of American Movies* (New York, Random House, 1975); Marjorie Rosen, *Popcorn Venus: Women, Movies and the American Dream* (New York, Coward, McCann and Geoghegan, 1973); Elizabeth Bell, Lynda Haas, and Laura Sells (eds), *From Mouse to Mermaid: The Politics of Film, Gender, and Culture* (Bloomington, University of Indiana Press, 1995); Teresa de Lauretis, *Technologies of Gender: Essays on Theory, Film, and Fiction* (Bloomington, Indiana University Press, 1987); Patricia Erens (ed.), *Issues in Feminist Film Criticism* (Bloomington, Indiana University Press, 1990); Donald Bogle, *Toms, Coons, Mulattoes, Mammies, and Bucks: An Interpretive History of Blacks in American Film* (New York, Continuum, 1990); Tania Modelski, *Feminism without Women* (New York, Routledge, 1991). Christopher Finch, *The Art of Walt Disney: From Mickey Mouse to the Magic Kingdom* (New York, Harry N. Abrams, 1983) contains splendid illustrations from Disney cartoons and a clear explanation of the animators' art as practiced in the 1920s–1940s.

Apart from reading scholarly commentaries, the best way to understand the popular culture of this period is to view the films, literature, and cartoons produced. Periodicals from these years contain a wealth of visual images which trace the shift from flappers, to Depression, and thence to Rosie the Riveter. *The Saturday Evening Post, Life, Look, McCall's,* and *Ladies' Home Journal* give fascinating insights into the rapid shifts in attitudes towards women in the home, labor force, and as citizens. Melissa Dabakis, "Gendered Labor: Norman Rockwell's Rosie the Riveter and the Discourses of Wartime Womanhood," in Barbara Melosh (ed.), *Gender and American History since 1890* (London, Routledge, 1993), argues for a complex analysis of wartime iconography. Maureen Honey, "Images of Women in the *Saturday Evening Post*, 1931–1936," *Journal of Popular Culture* (Fall 1976), analyzes the content of this popular journal.

On radio see Margaret T. McFadden, "American's Boy Friend Who Can't Get a Date," Gender, Race, and the Cultural Work of the Jack Benny Program, 1932–1946," *Journal of American History,* 80 (June, 1993), 113–34. Lizabeth Cohen, *Making a New Deal: Industrial Workers in Chicago, 1919–1939* (Cambridge, Cambridge University Press, 1990) explores the role of radio in working-class culture. Jeanne Westin, in *Making Do. How Women Survived the '30s* (Chicago, Follet Publishing, 1976) interviewed Virginia Payne whose long-time portrayal of Ma Perkins gave her insights into the minds of Depression era radio listeners.

Chapter 12

The wealth of scholarship on suffrage and its aftermath is reviewed by Gayle Veronica Fischer, "The Seventy-Fifth Anniversary of Woman Suffrage in the United States: A Bibliographic Essay," *Journal of Women's History,* 7 (1995), 172–99. Anne Firor Scott, "After Suffrage: Southern Women in the 1920s," *Journal of Southern History,* 30 (1963), 298–318 pioneered the study of southern women after the Nineteenth Amendment. J. Stanley Lemons, *The Woman Citizen: Social Feminism in the 1920s* (Urbana, University of Illinois Press, 1975) looks at how women continued to be active after suffrage. William O'Neill in *Everyone Was Brave: The Rise and Fall of Feminism in the United States* (Chicago, Quadrangle, 1970) explores the presumed failure of suffrage to galvanize a permanent revolution for women in the United States.

William H. Chafe, *The American Woman: Her Changing Economic, Social, and Political Role, 1920–1970* (New York, Oxford University Press, 1972) in a sweeping study of women in the post-suffrage period concludes that suffrage was a failure because it failed to change women's situation. He examines World War II as a turning point in American women's history and discusses the seeming paradox that the aftermath of a war which seemed to change so much for women resulted in their reimmersion in domesticity. Detailed studies of female voting patterns are contained in Sara Alpern and Dale Baum, "Female Ballots: The Impact of the Nineteenth Amendment," *Journal of Interdisciplinary History,* 16 (1985), 43–67, and Paul Kleppner,

"Were Women to Blame? Female Suffrage and Voter Turnout," *Journal of Interdisciplinary History*, 12 (1982), 621–43. Elizabeth Israels Perry, *Belle Moskowitz: Feminine Politics and the Exercise of Power in the Age of Alfred E. Smith* (New York, Oxford University Press, 1987) probes the life of a fascinating woman who carved a route for herself in the boss-ridden world of New York State Democratic politics.

Nancy Cott, *The Grounding of Modern Feminism* (New Haven, Yale University Press, 1987) analyzes not only the roots of feminism as a term and a movement, but also the continued political activity of women in the second quarter of the twentieth century. Felice Dosik Gordon, *After Winning: The Legacy of the New Jersey Suffragists, 1920–1947* (New Brunswick, NJ, Rutgers University Press, 1986) takes a close look at women's politics after the vote. Carole Nichols, *Votes and More for Women: Suffrage and After in Connecticut* (New York, Haworth Press, 1983) does the same for Connecticut. Kathryn Anderson, "Practicing Feminist Politics: Emily Newell Blair and US Women's Political Choices in the Early Twentieth Century," *Journal of Women's History*, 9 (Autumn 1997), 50–72, discusses how one woman resolved the dilemmas between party politics and women's place. Kristi Andersen, *After Suffrage: Women in Partisan and Electoral Politics before the New Deal* (Chicago, University of Chicago Press, 1996) views these dilemmas in the national perspective. Leo Kanowitz, *Women and the Law: The Unfinished Revolution* (Albuquerque, University of New Mexico Press, 1967) supplies detailed case histories of women's fight for legal equity.

Contemporary analyses of women's political activity include Sophonisba Breckinridge, *Women in the Twentieth Century: A Study of Their Political, Social and Economic Activities* (1933) and Florence E. Allen, "Participation of Women in Government," *Annals of the American Academy of Political and Social Science*, 251 (May 1947). Not all politics were based around election campaigns. See Kathleen M. Blee, *Women of the Ku Klux Klan: Racism and Gendering the 1920s* (Berkeley: University of California Press, 1991); Jacquelyn Dowd Hall, *The Revolt against Chivalry: Jessie Daniel Ames and the Women's Campaign Against Lynching* (New York, Columbia University Press, 1979).

Robyn L. Muncy, *Creating a Female Dominion in American Reform, 1890–1935* (New York, Oxford University Press, 1990); Gwendolyn Mink, *The Wages of Motherhood;* and Molly Ladd-Taylor, *Mother Work: Women, Child Welfare and the State, 1890–1930* (Urbana, University of Illinois Press, 1994) focus on the politicization of motherhood and the growing resistance to female social reform in the 1920s and 1930s. Richard A. Meckel, *Save the Babies: American Public Health Reform and the Prevention of Infant Mortality, 1850–1929* (Baltimore, Johns Hopkins University Press, 1990) examines the successes and failures of health reform. S.J. Kleinberg, "The Economic Origins of the Welfare State, 1870–1939," in Hans Bak, Frits van Holthooon and Hans Krabbendam (eds), *Social and Secure? Politics and Culture of the Welfare State: A Comparative Inquiry* (Amsterdam, V.U. Press, 1996), pp. 94–116 traces the economic and demographic background to social welfare policies.

There is a growing literature on women's politics in the Great Depression and New Deal. See Susan Ware, *Beyond Suffrage: Women in the New Deal* (Cambridge, Mass., Harvard University Press, 1981); Joan Jensen, "Pink Sisters", Susan Becker, "International Feminism between the Wars"; Lois Scharf, "The Forgotten Woman"; Rosalyn Terborg-Penn, "Discontented Black Feminists" and Sherna Gluck, "Socialist Feminism between the Two World Wars" in Scharf and Jensen, *Decades of Discontent*; Joan Jensen, "Disfranchisement is a Disgrace: Women and Politics in New Mexico, 1900–1940," *New Mexico Historical Review,* 56 (January 1981); Susan D. Becker, *The Origins of the Equal Rights Amendment: American Feminism between the Wars* (Westport, Conn., Greenwood Press, 1981).

There is a wealth of material on Eleanor Roosevelt. Her own writings *(The Autobiography of Eleanor Roosevelt; This I Remember; It's Up to the Women)* cover this period. Blanche Wiesen Cook, *Eleanor Roosevelt, 1884–1933* (New York, Viking, 1992), is a penetrating analysis of ER's personal and political actions. Eleanor Roosevelt, *It's Up to the Women* (1933) reveals her sense of difference. Joan Hoff Wilson and Marjorie Lightman (eds), *Without Precedent: The Life and Career of Eleanor Roosevelt* (Bloomington, Indiana University Press, 1984); Joseph P. Lash, *Love, Eleanor Roosevelt and Her Friends* (Garden City, NY, Doubleday, 1982), Lash, *A World of Love: Eleanor Roosevelt and Her Friends, 1943–1962* (Garden City, NY, Doubleday, 1984) and Tamara Hareven, *Eleanor Roosevelt: An American Conscience* (Chicago, Quadrangle, 1968) contain insights into the personal world of ER. William H. Chafe, "The Personal and the Political: Two Case Studies" in Kerber, Kessler-Harris and Sklar, *US History as Women's History,* pp. 189–213 discusses the ramifications of Franklin Roosevelt's affair with Lucy Mercer.

In *One Third of a Nation: Lorena Hickok Reports on the Great Depression,* ed. Richard Lowitt and Maurine Beasley (Urbana, University of Illinois Press, 1981) one of the key female New Dealers reports on her encounters with the Depression. Susan Ware writes on *Partner and I: Molly Dewson, Feminism, and New Deal Politics* (New Haven, Yale University Press, 1987). Elaine M. Smith, "Mary McLeod Bethune and the National Youth Administration," in Mabel Deutrich and Virginia Purdy, *Clio Was a Woman* (Washington, DC, Howard University Press, 1980) illuminates the career of a remarkable woman. Frances Perkins, *The Roosevelt I Knew* (New York, Viking Press, 1946) ponders her involvement in the New Deal.

Alice Kessler-Harris, "Designing Women and Old Fools: The Construction of the Social Security Amendments of 1939," in Kerber, Kessler-Harris and Sklar, *US History as Women's History*, pp. 87–108 gives an insightful reading into the gendered politics of the Social Security Act and its amendments. Roy Lubove, *The Struggle for Social Security* (Cambridge, Mass., Harvard University Press, 1965) is a more traditional reading. Walter Graebner*, A History of Retirement* (New Haven, Conn., Yale University Press, 1980) and Edwin Amenta and Bruce G. Carruthers, "The Formative Years of U.S. Social Spending Policies: Theories of the Welfare State and the American States During the Great Depression," *American Sociological Review,* 53 (1988), 661–78, set the Social Security Act in historical perspective. Frances Fox Piven and Richard Cloward, *Regulating the*

Poor, The Functions of Public Welfare (New York, 1971) and Gunnar Myrdal, *An American Dilemma: The Negro Problem and Modern Democracy* (New York, Harper & Row, 1944), show how the Social Security Act disadvantaged African Americans.

On women in World War II see Susan M. Hartmann, "Women's Organizations During World War II: The Interaction of Class, Race, and Feminism," in Mary Kelley (ed.), *Woman's Being, Woman's Place: Female Identity and Vocation in American History* (Boston, G.K. Hall, 1979) and her overview of women in the 1940s, *The Home Front and Beyond: American Women in the 1940s* (Boston, Twayne, 1982). Eleanor Straube, "United States Government Policy toward Civilian Women during World War II," *Prologue*, 5 (Winter 1973), 240–54, highlights the inadequacies in planning. Karen Anderson, *Wartime Women: Sex Roles, Family Relations, and the Status of Women during World War II* (Westport, Conn., Greenwood Press, 1981); D'Ann Campbell, *Women at War with America: Private Lives in a Patriotic Era* (Cambridge, Mass., Harvard University Press, 1984); Leila Rupp, *Mobilizing Women for War: German and American propaganda, 1939–1945* (Princeton, NJ, Princeton University Press, 1978) are general studies which stress continuity. On women in the army also see, Mattie E. Treadwell, *The United States Army in World War II*, Vol. VIII, *The Women's Army Corps* (Washington DC, Department of the Army, 1954). As an official history of the WAC this presents a fairly sanguine picture of their treatment.

The treatment of the Japanese is examined in Bill Hosokawa, *Nisei, The Quiet Americans, The Story of a People* (New York, Morrow, 1969) and Mine Okubo, *Citizen 13660* (New York, Columbia University Press, 1946). Also see Roger Daniels, *Concentration Camps, USA: Japanese Americans and World War II* (New York, Holt, Rinehart, Winston, 1972).

On the post-war period see, crucially, Betty Friedan, *Feminine Mystique* (New York, Norton, 1963) who more than any single author established the issues which documented the reasons for the emergence of women's liberation. It is also worth reading Ferdinand Lundberg and Marynia F. Farnham, *Modern Woman: The Lost Sex* (New York, Harper and Brothers, 1947); Philip Wylie, *Generation of Vipers* (New York, Rinehart & Co., 1942) and Lynn White, Jr, *Educating Our Daughters* (New York, Harper & Co, 1950) to see the obstacles women confronted in the late 1940s and 1950s. Eugenia Kaledin, *Mothers and More: American Women in the 1950s* (Boston, Twayne, 1984) contains an inclusive overview of this period. Cynthia Harrison, *On Account of Sex: The Politics of Women's Issues, 1945–1968* (Berkeley, University of California Press, 1988) follows the political issues regarding the Equal Rights Amendment, the New Frontier, and the Civil Rights acts. Leila J. Rupp and Verta Taylor, *Survival in the Doldrums: The American Women's Rights Movement, 1945 to the 1960s* (Columbus, Ohio State University Press, 1990) covers much of the same ground, but also considers the interaction of the women's rights movement with other social movements. Susan Lynn, *Progressive Women in Conservative Times: Racial Justice, Peace, and Feminism, 1945 to the 1960s* (New Brunswick, Rutgers University Press, 1992) explicitly considers the Civil Rights, anti-war, and feminist movements.

Index

Abbott, Berenice, 269
Abbott, Edith, 27
Abbott, Grace, 291, 299
abolitionism, 2, 7, 35, 62, 69, 77,
    88–92
  and education, 65–6
  and politicization of women, 41,
    88–97, 100–1, 177, 191
  and religion, 66, 73, 80, 86, 92
  and women's rights, 76, 89,
    192–3, 199
abortion, 37, 140
activism,
  domesticity, 147, 196–7
  framework for women's history, 1,
    2, 7
  literacy, 6, 79
  post-World War II, 316
  rural, 181–4
  Second Great Awakening, 81–5
  Thirteenth Amendment, 101
  urban, 92, 184–91
  see also clubs, suffrage, reform,
    labor unrest, women's rights
    movement
actresses, 113, 173–4
Adams, Abigail, 60
Adams, Harriet Stratemeyer, 263
Addams, Jane, 114, 188, 196, 198,
    202, 283, 286
adolescence, 172, 209, 238, 242–3,
    244, 238–46
adoption, 250
advertising, 113, 171–2, 241, 274,
    310
African Americans, 70, 73, 75–7,
    102, 134, 180, 190–2, 238,
    267–8, 271

abolitionists, 91, 94–9
agriculture, 3, 12, 14, 17, 19
  child welfare, 146–7, 164, 186,
    249
  clubs, 177, 201
  economic activity, 3, 17–18, 26,
    33, 100, 105–10, 112–18,
    121, 124, 137–9, 150, 154–5,
    189, 207–8, 212–14, 216,
    218, 224, 229, 231, 254, 305
  education, 65–7, 73–4, 98, 154–5,
    162, 164–5, 239, 256,
    259–60, 271, 305, 315
  families, 22–4, 138, 239, 249
  fertility, 127, 140, 234
  Great Depression, 127, 249
  literature, 75–7, 146, 168–9, 265
  migration, 137–9
  politics, 65–7, 75, 89, 191–3,
    199–203, 299
  radio, 275
  slavery, 6, 8, 19, 21–6, 31, 32, 34,
    43–9, 51, 66, 75, 90–1, 96–8
  Social Security, 300–2
  widowhood, 138
  women's clubs, 146–7, 150,
    164–5, 201
  World War II, 305
  see also Great Migration, racism,
    segregation, slavery
agriculture, 11–14, 17, 19, 134–89,
    213
  commercial, 4, 5, 13, 17, 19–21,
    213–14, 216
  Native American, 12–13, 19, 49,
    183–4
  sharecropping, 137–8, 208, 269
  slave, 12, 14, 21–6, 32

agriculture (*continued*)
  Social Security Act, 300
  subsistence, 4, 11–15, 19, 134
Aid to Dependent Children, 248,
  250, 301–2
Akron Women's Rights Convention,
  96
Albany Women's Rights
  Convention, 97
Alcott, Bronson, 67
Alcott, Louisa May, 63, 67, 166–7,
  263
Alien Land Law, 131
All-American Girls' Baseball
  League, 274
Allen, Gracie, 275
American Anti-slavery Society, 91,
  97
American Association of University
  Women, 163, 260, 286, 305
American College of Medicine, 261
American Equal Rights Association,
  191–2
American Federation of Labor,
  121–2, 214–15
American Home Economics
  Association, 162
American Legion Women's
  Auxiliary, 286–7
American Library Association, 161
American Medical Association, 261
American Revolution, 3, 26, 35, 60
American Woman Suffrage
  Association, 193, 195
American Women's Medical
  Association, 261
Americanization, 135–7, 150
Ames, Jessie Daniel, 285–6
Andersen, Kristi, 294
Anderson, Karen, 253
Anderson, Marian, 271–2
Anderson, Mary, 216, 246, 291, 304
Anthony, Daniel, 289
Anthony, Susan B., 70, 73, 84,
  100–1, 121, 192–3, 195, 268,
  289
anti-communism, 292, 309, 314
anti-suffrage, 196–8, 283

Anti-Saloon League, 180
Arizona, 298
Armed Forces, 112, 226–8, 250–2,
  262, 305–6
Armitage, Susan, 133
art, 7, 69–70, 174, 223, 268–80
Arzner, Dorothy, 276–7
assimilation, 136–7, 152, 178
Association of American Women
  Composers, 271
Association of Southern Women for
  the Prevention of Lynching,
  285–6
Association of Women Lawyers, 287
Association Opposed to the Further
  Extension of Suffrage to
  Women, 197
athletics, 172, 273–4
Atlanta Neighborhood Union, 189
automobile industry, 209–10, 220,
  224–5, 230, 252
Ayer, Harriet Hubbard, 113

baby boom, 309–11
Bagley, Sarah, 30–1, 78
Baker, Josephine, 273
Baker, Paula, 283
Ball, Lucille, 279, 312
Baltimore, 63, 66, 141, 149
banking, 5, 113
Baptists, 81
Bara, Theda, 174
Barry, Leonora, 125
Barrymore, Ethel, 270
Beach, Amy Marcy, 271
Beard, Mary Ritter, 260
beauty products, 112–13
Beecher, Catharine, 39–41, 61, 64,
  77, 90, 146, 178, 188
Benedict, Ruth, 260
benevolent societies, 82–3, 92–3,
  101, 184–7
Benny, Jack, 276
Berkeley, Busby, 278–9
Bethune, Mary McLeod, 190, 259,
  298–9, 305
Betty Boop, 226
Bickerdyke, Mary Ann, 100

Birney, Alice McLellan, 146
birth control, 36–7, 87, 140–1, 173, 234
birth rate, *see* fertility
Blackwell, Elizabeth, 68, 98–9
Blackwell, Henry, 193, 200
Blatch, Harriot Stanton, 201, 258
Blewett, Mary, 32
Bloomer, Amelia, 53, 85, 87
boardinghouse keeping, 16, 27, 128, 133, 207, 231
boarders, 29–30, 144–5, 147, 207
Bogan, Louise, 264
Bok, Edward, 171
boll weevil, 214
Bolton Act, 262
Bonney, Mary Lucinda, 183
Borden, Hannah, 27
Boston, 59, 64, 67, 82, 91, 161, 168
Boston Marriage, 297
Bourke-White, Margaret, 269
Bow, Clara, 277
Boydston, Jeanne, 21
Boylston, Helen Dore, 263
Bradwell, Myra, 160
Breckinridge, Sophonisba, 160
Brent, Mistress Margaret, 93
Brice, Fanny, 270
Bright, Julia, 194
Broken Blossoms, 144
Brown, Charlotte Hawkins, 285
Brown, Dee, 51
Brown, Dorothy M., 212, 263
Bryn Mawr, 224, 264
Buck, Pearl, 264
Bureau of Home Economics, 238
Bureau of Indian Affairs, 136
Burns, George, 275
Burns, Lucy, 201
Burroughs, Nannie, 190, 294
Burstall, Sara, 154
businesswomen, 15–16, 111–14, 210–12, 217, 223, 232
butter and butter making, 14, 20–1, 135, 181

Caledonian Ladies' Aid Society, 165
Calhoun, Arthur C., 62

California, 116, 125, 130–1, 141, 247, 269, 314
Campbell, D'Ann, 255, 304
Campbell, Helen, 149
Carey, Mathew, 18
Carlisle Indian Boarding School, 155–6
Carpenter, Helen, 53
cartoons, 279–81
Cassatt, Mary, 174
Cather, Willa, 135, 166, 168, 263–4
Catt, Carrie Chapman, 94, 199, 201–2, 282, 284
census, *see* US Census
Chafe, William, 4, 234, 304, 310
Chaplin, Charlie, 174, 277
Chapman, Maria Weston, 91
Charity Organization Society, 185–7
Chesnut, Mary Boykin, 24, 99
Chicago, 149, 161
Child, Lydia Maria, 41–2, 62–3, 93, 96
childbirth, 36, 42, 128
children, 17, 37–9, 146–7, 159, 164, 183, 234–8, 240–1, 288
  abuse, 142–3
  custody, 88, 95, 141, 195
  during World War II, 250–53
  employment, 2, 108, 115, 122–5, 134, 147, 187, 190, 198–200, 208–9, 214, 247, 291
  mortality, 159, 235–6, 292
  slavery, 45–7
  welfare, 176, 186, 198, 248–50
Children's Bureau, 147, 144, 159, 190, 203, 235, 291–9, 303, 305
Chinese Exclusion Act, 130–1
Chinese immigration, 7, 55, 117, 130, 138, 298
Chopin, Kate, 166, 168–9
Church of Jesus Christ of Latter Day Saints, 53–4, 56, 85–6, 194
Cigar Makers' International Union, 121
Cincinnati, 65–6
cinema, 173–4, 210, 242–4, 267–8, 276–81

citizenship, 4, 7, 62, 88, 96, 131,
    191–203, 282, 287–9, 305–7
Civil Rights Act of 1964, 313
civil rights movement, 305, 307,
    309, 311, 315
Civil Service Commission, 298
Civil War, 3, 97–102, 152–3, 176–8
Civil Works Administration, 220
Civilian Conservation Corps, 221,
    298
Clay, Anne, 81
Clay, Laura, 199–200
clerical work, *see* white-collar work
Cleveland, Grover, 198
clubs,
    literary, 151, 166
    reform, 151
    women's, 162–5, 175, 177, 201,
        285–6, 314
Coit, Stanton, 188
Colbert, Claudette, 279
Collar Laundry Union, 120
Colorado, 54, 134, 195, 223
Columbia Exposition, 164
communism, 271, 292
Confederacy, 97–100, 177
Congress, 194, 202
Congress of Industrial
    Organizations, 217, 225
Congressional Union, 201
Connecticut, 234, 288, 290
consumerism, 14, 128, 170–1, 208,
    231, 241, 253–4, 282
contracts, 19, 21, 195, 282
cooking, 238–9, 247, 274–5
Coolidge, Calvin, 258
Cooper, Anna Julia, 156, 168
Cott, Nancy, 4, 285
Country Life Commission, 183
courts of law, 125–6, 138, 141–3,
    159, 169, 181, 195, 202, 247,
    290, 291
    Supreme Court, 126–7, 160, 202,
        247, 288
Cousins, Norman, 219
Cowan, Ruth Schwartz, 238
Crandall, Prudence, 66–7
Crawford, Joan, 279

Croly, Jane, 163
cult of true womanhood, 6, 38, 41,
    56, 62
    and race, 55, 75, 76
    during Great Depression, 218–19,
        246–8
    rejection of, 64, 73–4, 79, 168–70
    see also domesticity

dairy industry, 14, 17, 20
Daughters of St. Crispin, 120
Daughters of Temperance, 84
Daughters of the American
    Revolution, 235, 272, 286, 292,
    307
Davis, Allen F., 160
Davis, Jefferson, 99
Davis, Pauline Wright, 88
Davis, Rebecca Harding, 79
Dawes Act, 136, 184
Declaration of Independence, 94–5
Declaration of Sentiments, Seneca
    Falls, 74, 94–5
Del Mar, Peterson, 243
Democratic Party, 192, 194, 197,
    222, 226, 294–8, 290, 303,
    314–15
demography, 5–6, 11, 36–8, 128,
    138–40, 164, 234–7
    sex ratios, 51, 129–30, 134, 139
    western, 55, 134
    see also fertility, family structure
department stores, 171–2, 212
depression, post–partum, 148, 170
Deutsch, Helene, 312
Dewson, Molly, 295, 297, 303
Dickinson, Emily, 166–7
Didrickson, Babe, 273–4
Dietrich, Marlene, 277–8
Dilling, Elizabeth, 286
Dimock, Susan, 158
Disney, Walt, 280–1
divorce, 86, 95, 108, 141–2, 195,
    243–4, 289, 301
Dix, Dorothea, 82, 99
Dix, Dorothy, 246, 237
Dock, Lavinia Lloyd, 263
doctors, 68, 114, 261, 292

Dollard, John, 198, 249
domestic advisers, 171, 236–7, 241
domestic service, 7, 16–18, 23, 36,
    40, 109, 124, 126, 131, 144,
    147, 210, 213, 219, 233–4, 237,
    311
    Great Depression, 218–19, 225
    Social Security Act, 7, 225–6
domestic technology, 137, 144,
    149–50, 171–2, 237–42, 247,
    310
domestic violence, 97, 141–4, 243–4
domesticity, 11, 28, 33–9, 41–4,
    54–7, 71, 92, 127–8, 166–9,
    185, 232, 309, 311–12
    and race, 42–51, 55–6
    and suffrage, 197
    education, 260
    family wage ideology, 122
    post-World War II, 311
    western, 54–6
Dorchester, Merial A., 135
Douglas, Ann, 69
Douglas, Helen Gahagan, 314
Douglass, Frederick, 95–6, 192–3
dress reform, 87, 172, 193
DuBois Ellen C., 192
Du Bois, W. E. B., 190
Duffy, Mary, 199

Earhart, Amelia, 273
Eastman, Crystal, 160, 233
Eastman, Linda, 161
Edmunds–Tucker Act, 195
✗ education, 2, 5–6, 58–79, 146–7,
    152–62, 165, 175, 209, 210,
    230–2, 257–62, 313
    African-American, 65–7, 73–4,
      98, 154–5, 162, 164–5, 239,
      256, 259, 271, 305, 315
    citizenship, 60, 62, 154–5
    employment, 111–12, 209, 281
    high school, 153–5, 257–8
    Native American, 135–6, 155–6
    religious, 62, 67, 153–4
    segregation, 65, 155, 156
Edwards, India, 314
Eisenhower, Dwight D., 306

Elder, Glen, 247
elderly, 186, 248–50, 299
emancipation, 100–1, 191
Emerson, Ralph Waldo, 74
employment, 11–19, 26–34, 150,
    207–9, 217–26, 306, 309
    age, 107–8, 111, 209–10, 251–2
    ethnicity and race, 105–9,
      212–14, 216–18, 254
    location, 106–7
    manual labor, 114–18
    marital status, 107–10, 207–9,
      246–50
    wartime, 118–19, 228–32, 309–11
Engerman, Stanley, 23, 47
Equal Rights Amendment, 284,
    289–91, 315
Exodusters, 137

Fair Employment Practices
    Commission, 305
Fair Labor Standards Act, 303
family economy, 15, 57, 110–11,
    124, 128–9, 219, 230–3,
    246–8, 250–60, 299–301, 307,
    309–10
family structure, 35–7, 128, 144–6,
    177, 234–7
family wage ideology, 122, 220,
    249–56, 300, 303
Faragher, John Mack, 52
Farley, Harriet, 78
Farm Security Administration, 269
Farmer, Fannie, 238
Farmers' Alliance, 181–3
Farnham, Marynia, 256, 312
Farrar, Eliza, 71
fatherhood, 39, 147, 247–8, 302
Fauset, Jessie Redmond, 265
Faust, Drew Gilpin, 178
Federal Arts Project, 223, 269
Federal Emergency Relief
    Administration, 220–1, 299
Federal Theater Project, 223, 271
Federal Works Administration, 252,
    305
Federal Writers' Project, 223, 266
Female Anti-slavery Society, 91

feminine mystique, 309–16
feminism, 92–7, 162, 217, 283, 287,
    289–91, 307–8, 314, 316
Ferguson, Catherine, 65
Ferguson, Marian, 'Ma', 296
fertility, 36, 139–40, 150, 234–5,
    256, 311
    domesticity, 36–8, 234–5
    slave women, 26, 45
Fifteenth Amendment, 191, 195
Fitzgerald, F. Scott, 263
Flanagan, Hallie, 270
flappers, 242, 277
Fleischer, Max and David, 280
Flexner, Abraham, 161
Flynn, Elizabeth Gurley, 197, 202
Fogel, Robert, 23, 47
Forten, Charlotte, 89, 91, 98
Forten, Margaretta, 65, 89, 91
Forten, Sarah, 65, 89, 91
Fourteenth Amendment, 191, 195
Frederick, Christine, 148–9, 171,
    237, 240
French–Canadian immigrants,
    109–10, 130–1, 186
Friedan, Betty, 240, 312
Froumountaine, Julian, 66
Fuller, Margaret, 72–5, 101

Gabin, Nancy, 230
Galbraith, John Kenneth, 233
Garbo, Greta, 277
Garden, Mary, 271
garment industry, 108, 122–4, 132,
    215
Garrison, William Lloyd, 66, 94
Gellhorn, Martha, 264
gender, 1–8, 100–1, 128, 210,
    260–1, 279–81, 287–9, 299,
    303–4, 308, 316
gender roles, 1–8, 11–12, 80, 92,
    178, 219–26, 231, 242–4
    and race, 48–9, 21–6, 183–4
General Federation of Women's
    Clubs, 163–4, 179, 201, 286–7,
    290, 315
Gentleman's Agreement, 131
Georgia, 25, 66, 189

German immigrants, 35–6, 178, 186
Gilman, Charlotte Perkins, 148, 166,
    169–70, 183, 201
Gish, Lillian, 277
Glasgow, Ellen, 264
Godey's Lady's Book, 39, 71–2
Gold Diggers, 277–9
Goldin, Claudia, 209
Goldman, Emma, 197, 202
Gone with the Wind, 267–8
Gordon, Linda, 143, 162, 250
Grange (Patrons of Husbandry),
    181–3
Grapes of Wrath, 245
Great Depression, 4, 8, 208–12,
    216–26, 243–50, 265–6, 283,
    292
Great Migration, 137–9, 244
Greeley, Horace, 191–2
Greenhow, Rose O'Neal, 99
Griffith, D. W., 144
Grimké, Sarah, 41, 62, 88–90
Grimké, Angelina, 88–90, 100
Griswald vs. Connecticut, 234
Gutiérrez, Ramon, 49
Gutman, Herbert, 47

Hadassah, 165
Hagood, Margaret, 236
Haines Institute, 155
Hale, Sarah Josepha, 39, 71–2
Hamilton, Dr. Alice, 289
Hammett, Dashiel, 270
Hampton Institute, 155
Hapke, Laura, 267
Harlem, 244–5, 269
    Renaissance, 265
Harlow, Jean, 278
Harper, Frances Ellen Watkins, 166,
    168–9, 180
Harrison, Cynthia, 307
Harrison, Hazel, 271
Hartman, Susan, 304
Haskell, Molly, 244, 277
Hawthorne, Nathaniel, 74
Hayes, Helen, 270
Hedges, Elaine, 170
Held, John, 242

Hellman, Lillian, 270
Henie, Sonja, 273
Henry Street Settlement, 189, 263
Hepburn, Katherine, 279
Hickey, Margaret, 304–5, 307
Hickok, Lorena, 298
higher education, 67–9, 152–3,
    155–8, 160–2, 174, 258–60,
    262, 313
Holiday, Billie, 272
Hollywood Production Code, 276,
    278
home economics, 146, 148–50, 156,
    162, 170, 172, 238, 260
Homestead Act, 134–5
homework, 116, 123, 222, 231
hooks, bell, 48
Hoover, Herbert, 294–5
Hope, Lugenia Burns, 189
Hopkins, Harry, 223
Hopkins, Miriam, 278
Hopkins, Pauline, 168–9
Hopkins, Sarah Winnemucca, 50,
    183
hospitals, 98–100, 112, 235, 261
housewifery, 40–1, 48, 54–5, 58–9,
    70, 135, 146–51, 170, 172, 232,
    237–42, 247, 260, 309–10
Howe, Julia Ward, 193
Hull House, 160, 188–90
Hunt, Harriot, 68
Hurston, Zora Neale, 243–4, 265

Idaho, 195
Illinois, 52, 117, 129, 160, 190, 200
immigrants, immigration, 5, 6, 17,
    19, 29, 31, 34–6, 100, 107,
    128–9, 145, 152–3, 159, 165,
    178–9, 187, 209, 258, 287
  charity, 131–2, 186, 189
  citizenship, 287
  demography, 129, 140
  employment, 33, 109–11, 114,
      117, 123
  see also specific ethnic groups
Incidents in the Life of a Slave Girl,
    31, 75–6
Indian Reorganization Act, 298

Indian School Service, 135–6
individualism, 132–3
Industrial Workers of the World,
    123–4
industrialization, 1, 4–5, 6–8, 11, 16,
    26–32, 34, 41, 115, 185, 218
  family wage ideology, 32
  homework, 116, 123, 222, 231
  impact on family, 101, 128, 147
  labor unrest, 28–33
  literary protests, 77–9
Ingalls, Caroline Lake Quiner, 110
insane asylums, 82–3
International Ladies' Garment
    Workers' Union, 123, 130,
    214–15, 225, 303
International Molders' Union,
    214–15
Iowa, 53, 55, 67
Irish immigrants, 17–18, 35–6, 100,
    114, 130, 140, 178, 197
Italian immigrants, 109–10, 114,
    116, 129, 131–2, 140, 197

Jacobs, Harriet, 23, 31, 75–7
Jameson, Elizabeth, 133
Japanese immigrants, 7, 116–17,
    131, 138, 298, 305–6
Jefferson, Thomas, 26
Jeffrey, Julie Roy, 52, 56
Jensen, Joan, 14, 133, 181, 294
Jewett, Sarah Orne, 166, 168
Jewish immigrants, 88, 116, 123,
    129, 131–3, 165, 189, 197, 258,
    261, 266, 271, 275, 286
Johnson, Adelaide, 268
Johnson, Amelia, 146
Johnson, Hugh, 222
Johnson, Kathryn, 190
Jones, Jacqueline, 46
Jones, Mary Harris, 197
Joyner, Charles, 48
Judaism, 189
jury service, 285–6

Kansas, 137, 182, 192–4
Kelley, Florence, 123, 160, 189–90,
    198, 235, 290

Kellie, Luna, 182, 196–7
Kelly, Joan, 3
Kemble, Frances, 46
Kennicott, Carol, 150–1, 241–42
Kentucky, 65, 67, 116, 160, 199, 218
Kenyon, Dorothy, 314
Kerber, Linda, 3, 35
Kerr, Florence, 298
Kessler-Harris, Alice, 303
Knights of Labor, 120–1
Knights of St. Crispin, 120
Krantz, Frances, 252, 261–2

labor unions, 119–25, 198–9,
    214–17, 224–5, 230–1, 303, 311
Ladd-Taylor, Molly, 235, 292
Ladies' Catholic Benevolent
    Association, 165
Ladies' Cigar Maker's Union, 120
Ladies' Home Journal, 171–2
Lane, Rose Wilder, 110
Laney, Lucy Craft, 155
Lange, Dorothea, 269
Larcom, Lucy, 27, 29, 63
Lathrop, Julia, 190, 235, 291
lawyers, 114, 159–60, 287
laundry industry, 119–20
League of Women Voters, 7, 222,
    283–5, 289, 297, 315
Lease, Mary, 182
Leginska, Ethel, 271
Legion of Decency, 276, 278
legislation, 7, 96, 114, 152, 155–60,
    194–5, 235–6, 248–50, 262,
    283, 313–14
  protective, 123, 125–7, 190, 198,
    210, 224–6, 290
  suffrage, 194–5, 198–9, 202
  welfare, 187–8
Leigh, Vivien, 267
leisure activities, 172–3, 189, 273–4
Lemlich, Clara, 122
Lemons, Stanley J., 285
Lenroot, Katharine, 303
Lerner, Gerda, 1
lesbianism, 228, 270, 296
LeSueur, Meridel, 218, 266
Lewis, Annie K., 201

Lewis, Edmondia, 174
Lewis, John L., 225
Lewis, Sinclair, 150–1, 241
librarians, 161–2
Life in the Iron Mills, 79
literacy, 6, 58, 60, 70–5, 79, 91,
    152–3
literature, 69–79, 146, 151, 163,
    166–70, 263–8
  magazines, 34, 38–9, 71–2,
    170–2, 276–82
Little Mothers' League, 235
Little Women, 63, 166–7
Livermore, Mary Ashton, 98
Lockwood, Belva, 160
Loos, Anita, 277
Loray Mill, 267
Lowell Female Labor Reform
    Association, 30–1
Lowell, Francis Cabot, 27
Lowell, Josephine Shaw, 186
Lowell Offering, 77–8
Loy, Myrna, 270
Lundberg, Ferdinand, 256, 312
lynching, 169, 285–6
Lynd, Helen Merrell, 208, 236, 247,
    260, 273
Lyon, Mary, 64

Ma Perkins, 275
Malkiel, Theresa, 168
Marion, Frances, 173, 277
marriage, age at, 139
  economic activity, 19–20, 41, 106,
    108–111, 208–9, 214,
    219–20, 233–4, 309
  expectations of, 150, 233, 243–4
  Native American, 49–50
  picture brides, 131
  plural, 85
  slave, 47
  utopian, 86–7
  see also domesticity, divorce
Martha Washington Society, 84–5
Martinez, Maria Montoya, 174
Maryland, 63, 66, 91, 210
masculinity, 41–2, 225, 240, 243–4,
    247–8, 292

Massachusetts, 26, 82–3, 90, 120, 142–3, 287–8
  education, 59–60, 63–5
  immigration, 129, 132, 286
  suffrage, 197, 201
Maternity and Infancy Protection Act, *see* Sheppard–Towner Act
May, Elaine Tyler, 315
Mayo, Sara Tew, 158
McCarthy, Joseph, 314
McCarthy, Kathleen D., 69
McCarthy, Mary, 267
McCullers, Carson, 267
McDaniel, Hattie, 267, 275
Mead, Margaret, 260–1, 281, 309
medical schools, 158–9, 260–1
medicine, 36–7, 68–9, 114, 152, 155, 157–8, 210, 252, 292
Mergler, Marie, 158
Metcalf, Betsey, 15
Methodists, 81, 189
Mexican immigrants, 7, 42, 130, 134–8, 187, 249
  employment, 107, 116, 214, 216, 218
  politics, 294
Michigan, 125, 202, 295
Middlebury Female Seminary, 63
midwifery, 24, 37, 159
migration, 6, 9, 17, 35, 50–4, 133–9, 244–6, 252, 311
Millay, Edna St. Vincent, 264
mining industry, 55, 122
Minor, Lucy Carter, 25
Minor, Virginia, 195
missions, missionaries, 68, 136, 155–6, 163, 183–4
Mississippi, 88, 124, 137, 153, 225
  State Industrial Institute and College, 153
Missouri, 195
Mitchell, Margaret, 267
Mohr, James, 37
momism, 255–6
Montagu, Ashley, 312
Moravians, 82
Moreno, Luisa, 216

Mormons, *see* Church of Jesus Christ of Latter Day Saints
Morris, Ester McQuigg, 194
Moskowitz, Belle, 295
Moten, Lucy Ella, 157
Mothers' pensions, *see* widows' pensions
motherhood, 35, 67, 146–50, 152, 166, 175, 234–8, 247, 255–6
  employment, 15, 22, 26, 108–11, 123–7, 208–9, 215–16, 222, 231, 310
  public policy, 176–8, 185, 196, 235–7, 288–92, 301–2
  social, 177–8, 190
  and suffrage, 195–8
Motion Picture Producers and Distributors Association, 278
Mott, Lucretia, 29, 89, 91, 93–5, 100
Mount Holyoke, 64, 297
Muller vs. Oregon, 126
Muncie, Indiana, 223, 236, 247, 260, 273
Murray, Judith Sargent, 58–61, 74
Museum of Modern Art, 268
musicians, 271–3

Nation, Carrie, 180
National American Woman Suffrage Association, 193–4, 199–202
National Association for the Advancement of Colored People, 164, 190, 200, 265, 285, 305, 315
National Association of Business and Professional Women, 219, 290, 305, 307, 315
National Association of Colored Women, 146, 164–5, 171, 200, 294
National Association Opposed to Woman Suffrage, 197
National Association of Women Painters and Sculptors, 269
National Board of Popular Education, 68
National Civic Federation, 284

National Conference on Charities and Correction, 161
National Congress of American Indians, 298
National Congress of Mothers, 146, 150, 163, 187
National Consumers' League, 164, 222, 286–7, 289, 293, 296, 315
National Convention of Colored Freedmen, 96
National Council of Jewish Women, 165, 286
National Council of Negro Women, 299, 305, 314
National Council of Women, 286
National Economy Act, 219
National Industrial Recovery Act, 302–3
National Labor Relations Act, 225, 303
National League of Republican Colored Women, 294
National Recovery Administration, 220, 222–6
National Woman Suffrage Association, 193–5
National Women's Loyal League, 101
National Woman's Party, 201, 219, 222, 284, 289–91, 304, 307, 315
National Youth Administration, 259, 298
Native Americans, 9, 7, 19, 33, 70, 74, 135–6, 138, 174, 187, 298
    agriculture, 12–13, 19, 49, 183–4
    economic activity, 107, 213
    education, 135–6, 155–6
    gender roles, 12, 13, 50, 183–4
nativism, 84
Nebraska, 134–5, 137, 156, 182
Negro Higher Education Fund, 259
Negro Rural School Fund, 162
Neighborhood Union, 189
Neshoba Colony, 86
New Deal, 7, 220–6, 239, 248, 269–70, 293, 296–304
New England, 15, 26–32, 78, 91, 94, 109, 122, 158, 197

New Jersey, 14, 141
New Mexico, 135, 294
New Orleans, 118, 137, 158
    Family Service Society, 249
    Hospital and Dispensary for Women and Children, 158
New Woman, 242
New York, 28, 65, 88, 97–8, 100–1, 108, 116–17, 132, 140, 149, 159, 165, 284, 297–8
    charities, 68, 82–3, 140, 185–6, 188–9
    education, 63–5
    suffrage, 196, 200, 202
Newcomer, Mabel, 258
Nichols, Anne, 270
Nicols, Ruth, 273
Nineteenth Amendment, 4, 202, 282, 288, 293
Nixon, Richard, 314
Nobel Prize, 264, 286
North Carolina, 210, 214–16, 267, 285
northern women, 176–8, 227
    employment, 18–19, 26–8, 213–14
Noyes, John Humphrey, 86–7
nuns, 66–7, 86
nurses, 98–100, 112–14, 227, 263, 313
    training, 158, 261–2

O'Keeffe, Georgia, 174, 268
O'Neill, William, 141
O'Sullivan, Mary Kenney, 121
Oberlin College, 20, 67, 68, 174
Oblate Sisters of Providence, 66
Ohio Woman's Rights Convention, 22
Oklahoma, 202, 295
Okubo, Mine, 306
Old Age Assistance, 249–50, 300
Olsen, Tillie, 266
Oneida Community, 86–7
Oregon, 52–3, 126
orphanages, 55, 109, 147, 164
orphans, 82, 177, 186, 188
Overland Trail, 52–3, 134

Ovington, Mary White, 190

Page, Dorothy Myra, 267
Parent–Teachers Association, 164, 237, 285
Parker, Dorothy, 264
Parker, Theodore, 81
Parks, Rosa L., 315
Parsons, Talcott, 240
Parton, Sara, 39
Patapsco Female Institute, 63
Patrons of Husbandry, *see* Grange
Paul, Alice, 201–2, 290
Paulson, Ross Evans, 180
Payne, Virginia, 275
Pennsylvania, 60, 65, 88, 129, 143
Perkins, Frances, 210, 220, 223, 225–6, 297–8, 300, 303
Pesotta, Rose, 225
Petersburg, Virginia, 15
Phelps, Almira, 63
Philadelphia, 28–9, 40, 91, 141, 143, 190
  education in, 59, 65, 153
Philips, Deborah, 263
Phillips, Wendell, 191
photography, 269
Pickford, Mary, 173–4, 276–7
Pierce, Sarah, 61
Pinkham, Lydia Estes, 112–13
Pittsburgh, 18, 88, 117, 153, 140, 274
Plessy vs. Ferguson, 138
plumbing, 40, 149
Polish immigrants, 123, 132, 140, 165
politics, 7, 92–7, 178, 277, 283–7, 295–6
  see also abolition, feminism, temperance
Pollak, Vivian R., 167
popular culture, 4, 170–4, 272–81, 312–13
Populism, 8, 181–3, 196
Porter, Katherine Anne, 267
Portland Sewing Circle, 94
Powell, William, 270
pregnancy, 23, 45–6, 228

Preiss, Kathy, 173
Presbyterians, 155, 189
professors, 157, 174, 258
privacy, 144
Procter & Gamble, 172, 275
Progressivism, 114, 116–17, 176–7, 184–91, 196–7, 201
Prohibition, 179–80
  see also temperance
property rights, 7, 13, 21, 86, 88, 95, 195, 288–7
prostitution, 55, 69, 83, 117–18, 130, 140, 193, 245
Prout, Mary, 113
psychology, 236, 243–4, 309, 312
public health, 292–3
public speaking, 92–3
Public Works Administration, 221, 270
Pulitzer Prize, 264, 267
Putman-Jacobi, Dr. Mary, 196

Quakers, 79, 89, 95, 162
quilting, 70, 116
Quinton, Amelia Stone, 183

racism, 7, 66–7, 75–7, 100, 126, 137, 140, 148, 169, 180, 187, 189, 198–201, 229, 249, 255–6, 272, 294, 298, 300
radio, 274–6
Rainey, Ma, 272
Rankin, Jeanette, 296
Ransom, Roger L., 106
rape, 44
Ream, Vinnie, 69
Red Cross, 7, 255, 262
Red Heads, 274
reform, 92, 114, 123, 125–6, 143–5, 151, 160–1, 176–203, 285
  see also abolition, clubs, temperance, feminism, welfare
religion, 5, 11, 18, 62, 73, 75, 77, 81–5, 92, 136, 186, 189, 291
  domesticity, 37, 43
  education, 67, 153–5, 165
  immigration, 31, 130
  and politics, 85, 178–9, 197

republican motherhood, 3, 17, 35,
    60, 62
Republican Party, 191–2, 194, 285,
    288, 290, 294, 314–15
Richards, Ellen Swallow, 149, 162
Richmond, Mary, 161
Rochester Ladies' Anti-slavery
    Society, 96
Rockefeller, Abby Aldrich, 268
Rogers, Edith N., 226
Rogers, Elizabeth Flynn, 121
Rogers, Ginger, 279
Roman Catholics, 154, 178, 180,
    186, 189, 197, 234, 258–9
Rombauer, Irma, 238
Roosevelt, Eleanor, 221–3, 246–7,
    255, 272, 284, 291, 294–9
Roosevelt, Franklin D., 210, 222,
    227, 251, 295–7, 300, 306
Roosevelt, Theodore, 183
Rose, Ernestine, 88, 96, 101
Rosen, Marjorie, 173
Rosenberg, Rosalind, 261
Rosie the Riveter, 228, 251, 256,
    270
Ross, Nellie Tayloe, 295–6
Rossiter, Margaret, 257
Roth, Phillip, 265
Rupp, Leila, 306, 315
Rural Electrification Administration,
    239
rural women, 17, 19, 20, 50, 181–4,
    189, 218, 234, 236, 239, 249,
    293
Rush, Benjamin, 60
Russell, Lillian, 173
Russell, Rosalind, 278
Russell Sage Foundation, 186

St. Frances Academy, 66
St. Luke's Penny Savings Bank, 113
St. Vincent de Paul Society, 130
Sanger, Margaret, 140–1
Sanitary Commission, 98–9
Sarah Lawrence, 260
Savage, Augusta, 269
Savannah, 14, 66, 98
Savitt, Todd, 46

Scandinavian immigrants, 35–6, 114
Scharf, Lois, 299
Schneiderman, Rose, 302
seamstresses, 18–19, 28–9, 96
Seaton, Elizabeth Mother, 67
Seattle, Washington, 253
Second Great Awakening, 38, 62,
    75, 81–5
Seeger, Ruth Crawford, 271
segregation, 66–7, 112, 138, 155–6,
    169, 202, 259, 262, 272, 294
sex, 210–12, 220, 227
Seneca Falls Women's Rights
    Convention, 74, 94–6, 314
separate spheres, 33–5, 39–40, 91
    division of labor, 56, 71–2, 100
    politics, 95, 198
    see also domesticity
settlement house movement, 114,
    159–60, 188–91, 263
sexual harassment, 117, 138
sexuality, 23, 25, 43, 45, 179,
    193–4, 242–3, 277–8, 289
Shakers, 86
sharecropping, *see* agriculture
Shaver, Dorothy, 212
Sheppard–Towner Act, 147, 235–6,
    290–2
shoe industry, 32, 36, 108, 115, 219
shopping, 2, 39, 253–4
Showalter, Elaine, 70, 168
Shuler, Nettie Rogers, 94
Shurtz, Carl, 183
Sigourney, Lydia Huntley, 38
Sinclair, Upton, 117
Sisters of Charity, 67
Skocpol, Theda, 291
slavery, 21–6, 32, 34, 43–9, 51, 66,
    75, 91, 97–8
    families, 21–2, 45–7, 140
    narratives, 75–6
    sexual terror, 22–3, 43–4, 90
    work, 3, 21–4, 31, 44, 96
Slavic immigrants, 117, 133, 209
Smedley, Agnes, 266–7
Smith, Al, 295
Smith, Bessie, 272
Smith, Daniel Scott, 92

Smith, Hilda W., 221, 298
Smith, Jessie Wilcox, 171
Smith, Joseph, 85
Smith, Kate, 276
Smith, Margaret Chase, 314
Smith–Hughes Vocational Education
    Act, 238
Smith–Lever Act, 238
soap operas, 275
Social Security Act, 7, 225–6,
    248–50, 297, 299–303
social work, 161, 186–7, 292–3, 296
Societies for the Prevention of the
    Cruelty to Children, 143–4
sororities, 259
Sothern, Ann, 279
South Dakota, 202
southern,
    employment, 213–16, 224
    suffrage, 137–8, 191–3, 197–8,
        199–200, 285, 294, 298
    women, 18, 176–8, 227
Southern Homestead Act, 137
Southern Tenant Farmers' Union,
    225
Spock, Dr. Benjamin, 311
sports, *see* athletics
Stansell, Christine, 42
Stanton, Elizabeth Cady, 73, 87–9,
    94, 100–1, 192, 201
Stanton, Henry, 94, 100
Stanwyck, Barbara, 279
Starr, Ellen Gates, 188
state legislatures, 31, 62, 83, 88, 90,
    96, 123, 131, 142–3, 146–7,
    152, 159, 179, 181
Steinbeck, John, 245, 265
Stevenson, Brenda E., 48
Stewart, Maria W., 89–90
Stirling, Mary, 121
Stone, Lucy, 68, 89, 100, 193
Storer, Maria Longworth Nichols,
    174
Stowe, Harriet Beecher, 39, 40, 61,
    77, 90, 146
Stratemeyer, Edward, 263
strikes, 28–32, 119–24, 215–17, 267
suburbs, 310, 316

suffrage, 3, 4, 7, 70, 80, 93, 96, 102,
    176, 179, 182–3, 191–203, 258,
    282
    anti-suffrage, 197–8
    nativism, 199
    political participation, 4, 96,
        293–4
    racism, 199–200, 298
Sunday Schools, 81
Sutch, Richard, 106
sweatshops, 116
Swisshelm, Jane, 88
Szold, Henrietta, 165

Talbert, Mary B., 190, 285
Talbot, Marion, 162
Tarbell, Ida, 170
Taylor, Susie King, 98
Taylor, Verta, 315
teaching, 64–5, 113, 152, 156–7,
    164–74, 210–17, 219
    see also education
Teapot Dome, 285
Teasdale, Sara, 264
television, 312
temperance, 2, 35, 53, 80, 83–5, 87,
    89, 143–4, 163, 178–81
    politicization of women, 92–5,
        196
Tennessee, 143, 169
Tennessee Valley Authority, 239,
    298
Terrell, Mary Church, 165, 190, 200,
    216
Texas, 116, 124, 135, 218, 296
Texas A & M, 156
textile industry, 14, 16, 18–19, 21,
    25–7, 29, 32, 36, 77–8, 106,
    109, 115, 119–20, 122–3, 131,
    209, 215, 218–19, 222, 224,
    267
theater, 173, 270–2
Their Eyes Were Watching God,
    243–4, 265
Thirteenth Amendment, 101
Thomas, Mary Martha, 199
Thompson, "Box-Car" Bertha, 245
Thompson, Dorothy, 264

tobacco industry, 116, 120–1, 213,
    216, 218, 224
Tompkins, Sally, 99
Trail of Tears, 13
Transcendentalism, 73–4
transport, 19, 26, 53
Travelers' Aid Society, 131
Triangle Shirtwaist Company,
    116–17, 297
Trollope, Frances, 70
Troy Female Seminary, 63
Truman, Harry S., 306, 314
Truth, Sojourner, 22, 89, 96, 191
Tsichtinako, 12
Tubman, Harriet, 91
Turkel, Studs, 245
Turner, Frederick Jackson, 51, 133
Turner, Lana, 279
Tuskegee Institute, 155, 270

US Census, 2, 107–12, 117, 133,
    208, 211, 213, 217
Uncle Tom's Cabin, 77
underground railroad, 91, 169
unemployment, 217–20, 254, 309
unions, *see* labor unions
Unitarians, 73
United Auto Workers, 220, 225, 230,
    253
United Cannery, Agricultural, and
    Allied Workers of America,
    216, 225
United Electrical Workers, 230
United Laundry Workers, 217
United Nations Commission on the
    Status of Women, 314
United Service Organization, 255
United Tailoresses Society, 28
United Textile Workers, 217
universities, 67–8, 156–60, 259–60,
    271
Urban League, 189
urban women, 18, 19, 20, 35, 138–9,
    149–50, 184–91, 213–14, 229,
    235, 239, 248, 255
Utah, 194–5
utopian movements, 72–3, 79, 80,
    85–7

Van Joosen, Bertha, 261
Van Lew, Elizabeth, 99
Vassar, 234, 258
Vaughan, Mary C., 83–4
Veblen, Thorstein, 171
veterans, 167–7, 228, 231, 260,
    309–10, 313
Vorse, Mary Heaton, 267
voting, 285–6, 293–4

Wade, Ernestine, 275
wage differentials, 30, 64, 122, 194,
    214, 216, 221–2, 225, 230,
    306
wages, 32, 117, 120, 195, 210, 218
Wagner Act, see National Labor
    Relations Act
Wald, Lillian, 114, 159, 190
Walker, Alice, 165
Walker, Cornelia, 75
Walker, Madame C. J., 113
Walker, Maggie Lena, 113
Wallace, Lila Acheson, 264
War Manpower Commission,
    229–30, 304–5
War Relocation Authority, 269
Ware, Susan, 221, 247, 314
Washington, DC, 119, 149, 156,
    164–5, 225
Washington Temperance Society,
    84
Weber, Lois, 173
Webster, Daniel, 39
Weinberger vs. Wiesenfeld, 250
Weld, Theodore, 91
welfare, 2, 176–8, 184–91, 248–50,
    291–3
Wells, Emmeline Blanch Woodward,
    194–5
Wells, Helen, 263
Wells-Barnett, Ida B., 169, 190, 200,
    285
Welter, Barbara, 6, 38
West, Mae, 277–8
western,
    domesticity, 54–6
    employment, 19–20
    expansion, 13, 50–4, 133–6

Western Reserve School of Applied
Social Sciences, 161
Wharton, Edith, 166, 170, 264
Whigs, 83, 92, 95
White, Alfred, 136
White, Deborah Gray, 45, 48
White, Kevin, 243
White, Lynn, Jr., 260
White, Walter, 200
white-collar employment, 4, 105–6,
111–14, 118–19, 127, 153,
209–13, 232, 311
race and ethnicity, 112, 209,
212–14, 232
see also businesswomen,
teachers
White House Conference on the
Emergency Needs of Women,
223
white women, 24
agriculture, 13–14, 19–21
and true womanhood, 6, 38, 41
employment, 108–11, 114–16,
207–9, 216–17, 270
marriage, 208–9
middle class, 170–2, 236–7
organizations, 177, 184–8
Whites, LeeAnn, 3, 143, 177
Whitman, Narcissa, 53
Whitney, Anne, 69
Whitney, Gertrude Vanderbilt, 268
Whitney Museum of American Art,
268
Whittlesey, Abigail, 38
widowers, 16, 301
widows, 3, 16, 82, 128, 145–6, 177,
195
economic activity, 3, 108–110
pensions, 147–8, 150, 187–8,
248–50, 301–3
Wiggins, Ella May, 215, 217
Wilder, Laura Ingalls, 52, 110–11,
263
Willard, Emma, 62–4
Willard, Frances, 179
Williams, Fannie Barrier, 203
Wilson, Harriet E., 76
Wilson, Woodrow, 201–2

Winnemucca, Sarah, *see* Hopkins,
Winnemucca Sarah
Wisconsin, 268, 290
Wittenmyer, Annie, 179
Wollstonecraft, Mary, 61
Woman's Medical College of
Pennsylvania, 158
womanist, 165
women writers, *see* literature
Women's Advisory Committee, 230,
304–5
Women's Airforce Service Pilots,
228
Women's Bureau, 215, 216, 246,
291, 304, 307
Women's Christian Temperance
Union, 143, 150, 178–80, 187,
200, 286–90
women's clubs, *see* clubs
Women's Committee for World
Disarmament, 286
Women's International League for
Peace and Freedom, 286
Women's Joint Congressional
Committee, 235, 286–7, 289
women's liberation movement, 1,
310–11, 315–16
Women's National Indian
Association, 156, 183
Women's National Press Club, 163
women's network, 194–6, 304
Women's Peace Party, 202
women's rights movement, 92–7
see also feminism, women's
liberation movement
Women's Trade Union League, 123,
125, 215, 222, 293, 286–7, 289,
293, 297
Women's Typographical Union, 120
Woodhull, Victoria Claflin, 193–5,
286
Woodward, Ellen, 223, 298–9
Worcester Women's Rights
Convention, 96
working-class women, 18–19,
26–32, 113–24, 197–8
working women's clubs, 121, 162,
165

Works Progress Administration,
    223–5, 242–3, 298
World Center for Women's Archives,
    260
World War I, 3, 118–19, 139, 201–2,
    209
World War II, 6, 119, 250–56,
    228–32, 274, 304–7, 293, 309
    childcare, 250–53
    women's employment, 228–32, 283
Wright, Carroll D., 199
Wright, Frances, 86, 93

Wylie, Phillip, 255
Wyoming, 194

Yellin, Jean Fagin, 93
Yezierska, Anzia, 132–3, 265–6
Young Women's Christian
    Association, 7, 235, 273, 286
Young Women's Hebrew
    Association, 7

Zakrzewska, Dr. Marie E., 68
Zionism, 165, 314